ROUTLEDGE LIBRARY EDITIONS: WAR AND SECURITY IN THE MIDDLE EAST

Volume 2

DEFENDING ARABIA

DEFENDING ARABIA

J.E. PETERSON

LONDON AND NEW YORK

First published in 1986 by Croom Helm Ltd

This edition first published in 2017
by Routledge
2 Park Square, Milton Park, Abingdon, Oxon OX14 4RN

and by Routledge
711 Third Avenue, New York, NY 10017

Routledge is an imprint of the Taylor & Francis Group, an informa business

© 1986 J.E. Peterson

All rights reserved. No part of this book may be reprinted or reproduced or utilised in any form or by any electronic, mechanical, or other means, now known or hereafter invented, including photocopying and recording, or in any information storage or retrieval system, without permission in writing from the publishers.

Trademark notice: Product or corporate names may be trademarks or registered trademarks, and are used only for identification and explanation without intent to infringe.

British Library Cataloguing in Publication Data
A catalogue record for this book is available from the British Library

ISBN: 978-1-138-19428-1 (Set)
ISBN: 978-1-315-54183-9 (Set) (ebk)
ISBN: 978-1-138-64751-0 (Volume 2) (hbk)
ISBN: 978-1-138-65296-5 (Volume 2) (pbk)
ISBN: 978-1-315-62477-8 (Volume 2) (ebk)

Publisher's Note
The publisher has gone to great lengths to ensure the quality of this reprint but points out that some imperfections in the original copies may be apparent.

Disclaimer
The publisher has made every effort to trace copyright holders and would welcome correspondence from those they have been unable to trace.

DEFENDING ARABIA

J.E. Peterson

CROOM HELM
London & Sydney

© 1986 J.E. Peterson
Croom Helm Ltd, Provident House, Burrell Row,
Beckenham, Kent BR3 1AT
Croom Helm Australia Pty Ltd, Suite 4, 6th Floor,
64–76 Kippax Street, Surry Hills, NSW 2010, Australia

British Library Cataloguing in Publication Data

Peterson, J.E.
  Defending Arabia.
  1. Persian Gulf — Strategic aspects
  I. Title
  327.1'16   UA853.P46
  ISBN 0-7099-2044-X

Phototypeset by Sunrise Setting, Torquay, Devon
Printed and bound in Great Britain
by Billing & Sons Limited, Worcester.

Contents

Abbreviations	vii
Preface	ix
1. Introduction	1
The Emergence and Evolution of Security Concerns in Arabia	2
Origins of British Involvement in Arabia	9
2. Air Power and Empire in the Arabian Peninsula	18
The First Air Routes: Persian Gulf and Basra–Aden	18
Policing and Air Operations	28
The Growing Strategic Importance of the Gulf	40
The Arabian Peninsula in the Second World War	50
Postwar Reassessments	56
3. Postwar Policy: British Retreat and Imperial Vestiges	75
Air Operations in Aden Protectorate	78
Evolving Commitments and the Oman War	83
The Problem of Deployment and the Defence of Kuwait	88
The Struggle for Aden	92
The Last Outpost: Oman and the Dhufar Rebellion	99
4. The US and Gulf Security	111
The Changing of the Guard	111
US Interests in the Gulf in the 1980s	118
Threats to Gulf Security: The Paradigm	120
Evaluating External Threats	122
Evaluating Regional Threats	127
Evaluating Internal Threats	134
5. US Military Options in the Gulf	145
US Commitment to Defend the Gulf	145
The Rapid Deployment Force: Origins, Evolution and Structure	151
Evaluating RDF Capabilities	155
Assessing RDF Performance	167

6. Gulf Security and Gulf Self-Defence 185
   The Emergence of Arabian Nation States 186
   Saudi Military Capabilities 191
   Other GCC Defence Capabilities 204
   The Iranian Revolution and the Formation of
      the Gulf Cooperation Council 213

7. Defending Arabia in the 1980s 229
   The British Legacy 229
   The American Intent 232
   The GCC and the Future 242

Bibliography 249

Index 267

Abbreviations

AHQ	Air Headquarters
AIR	Air Ministry records in the PRO
ANM	Arab Nationalists' Movement
AOC	Air Officer Commanding
ASW	Antisubmarine Warfare
AWACS	Airborne Warning and Control System
CAB	Cabinet records in the PRO
CID	Committee of Imperial Defence
C-in-C	Commander-in-Chief
CO	Colonial Office records in the PRO
DEFE	Ministry of Defence records in the PRO
FBIS	Foreign Broadcast Information Service (Middle East and South Asia)
FO	Foreign Office records in the PRO
GCC	Gulf Cooperation Council
GOC	General Officer Commanding
HMG	His/Her Majesty's Government
IOLR	India Office Library and Records (London)
IPC	Iraq Petroleum Company
JRCAS	*Journal of the Royal Central Asian Society*
JRUSI	*Journal of the Royal United Service Institution*
L/P&S	Government of India, External Department, records in the IOLR
MAB	Marine Amphibious Brigade
MEED	*Middle East Economic Digest*
NCO	Non-Commissioned Officer
NLF	National Liberation Front (South Yemen)
PDRY	People's Democratic Republic of Yemen
PFLO/AG	Popular Front for the Liberation of Oman; previously Popular Front for the Liberation of Oman and the Arabian Gulf or Popular Front for the Liberation of the Occupied Arabian Gulf
PGSC	Persian Gulf Sub-Committee of the CID
PRO	Public Record Office (London)
PRPG	Political Resident in the Persian Gulf

PSP	People's Socialist Party (South Yemen)
R/15	Political Residency in the Persian Gulf records in the IOLR
R/20	Political Residency, Aden, records in the IOLR
RAF	Royal Air Force
RDF	Rapid Deployment Force
RDJTF	Rapid Deployment Joint Task Force (US)
RNAS	Royal Navy Air Services
RUSI	Royal United Service Institution
SAF	Sultan's Armed Forces (Oman)
SAS	Special Air Service (British)
SNO	Senior Naval Officer
UAE	United Arab Emirates
USAAF	US Army Air Force
USAF	US Air Force
USCENTCOM	US Central Command
USGPO	US Government Printing Office
USMTM	US Military Training Mission
YAR	Yemen Arab Republic

Preface

The topic of Gulf security has received considerable attention in the United States and Western Europe in recent years, in addition to the natural concern expressed in the Gulf itself, and this interest has spawned a virtual flood of literature on the subject. Many of these publications have been annotated in my *Security in the Arabian Peninsula and Gulf States, 1973–84*.[1] Not surprisingly, most of this literature deals only with the period since 1979 or so and is primarily or exclusively concerned with US (and, to a lesser extent, Western European) national interests and political, economic and military policy options. By the time the writing on this book was completed in October 1985, the monographs by James Noyes, Anthony Cordesman, Bruce Kuniholm and Thomas McNaugher could be singled out from among the hundreds of books, articles, Congressional prints, and other publications on Gulf security and recommended as essential reading on the subject.[2]

In the light of this mass of publications on Gulf security, it is logical to ask what original contribution this book may make to a burgeoning field. First, it is a major thesis that the parameters and ramifications of security in the Gulf, as well as the constraints on both outside and indigenous actors, cannot be fully appreciated without an understanding of the historical background to the topic of Gulf security. This has not been comprehensively discussed elsewhere. Second, I have consciously avoided writing another handbook for US policy and have attempted to portray, as accurately and objectively as I can, the concerns and policies of the three principal actors or groups of actors that have sought to exercise responsibility for Gulf security in this century: Britain, the United States and the members of the Gulf Cooperation Council.

No book is ever solely the product of its author, and this one would not have seen the light of day without the assistance I received from a large number of institutions and individuals. The Earhart Foundation generously provided funds for archival research in London during the summer of 1982, and the opportunity to continue this research was provided by invitations to give papers at symposia of the University of Exeter's Centre for Arab Gulf

Studies in 1983 and 1985. Part of this book was written under the auspices of the Foreign Policy Research Institute in Philadelphia, while I served as the 1983–4 Thornton D. Hooper Fellow in International Security Affairs. The maps, which were prepared originally for my article on 'Defending Arabia: Evolution of Responsibility' in *Orbis*, appear here courtesy of the Foreign Policy Research Institute. I am sorry to say that my request to discuss the subject of this book with individuals in the USCENTCOM headquarters while on a visit to Tampa was summarily rejected. I can only hope that this flat refusal to provide any assistance or co-operation is not indicative of the command's attitude towards relations with the governments and people of the Middle East and Gulf.

Among the many people who have helped me, I would like to thank the following individuals who graciously commented on drafts of one or more chapters: Dr Rosemarie Said Zahlan (Chapter 2), Sir John Wilton and Ambassador Edward Henderson (Chapter 3), Dr Thomas L. McNaugher and Lt Col. Maxwell Orme Johnson (Chapters 4 and 5), Dr Edmund Ghareeb and Richard Henninghausen (Chapter 6). Their suggestions and criticisms were invaluable. I am particularly grateful to John H. Maurer, who not only read and commented on the entire manuscript, but directed me to a multitude of sources of which I would have otherwise remained ignorant. Needless to say, complete responsibility for all errors of fact and interpretation is mine alone.

Notes

1. Washington, National Council on US–Arab Relations, 1985.
2. James H. Noyes, *The Clouded Lens: Persian Gulf Security and U.S. Policy*, 2nd edn. (Stanford, Ca, Hoover Institution Press, 1982; Hoover International Studies); Anthony H. Cordesman, *The Gulf and the Search for Strategic Stability: Saudi Arabia, the Military Balance in the Gulf, and Trends in the Arab–Israeli Military Balance* (Boulder, Co, Westview Press; London, Mansell, 1984); Bruce R. Kuniholm, *The Persian Gulf and United States Policy: A Guide to Issues and References* (Claremont, Ca, Regina Books, 1984; Regina Guides to Contemporary Issues); and Thomas L. McNaugher, *Arms and Oil: U.S. Military Strategy and the Persian Gulf* (Washington, Brookings Institution, 1985).

1 Introduction

Concerns over the security and military defence of the Arabian or Persian Gulf and, in particular, the Arabian Peninsula have steadily intensified over the course of the twentieth century. At the same time, the actors assuming (or proclaiming) their responsibility for the security of the Peninsula have also changed. Additionally, as perceived threats to the security of this area have changed, so have the means — and thus, necessarily, the strategies — to defend the Peninsula. Consequently, any contemporary strategy concerned with Peninsula and/or Gulf security (including and especially that of the United States), to be viable, must: (1) not only be concerned with external threats to Gulf security; but also (2) be intimate with the immediate environment and nature of social, economic, and political conditions in the Gulf itself, both past and present.

The three actors or groups concerned with Peninsula security in this century have been Britain, the United States and the six states now comprising the Gulf Cooperation Council (GCC): Saudi Arabia, Kuwait, Bahrain, Qatar, the United Arab Emirates (UAE) and Oman. Britain exercised primary responsibility for the security of this region because of its predominant position in the Gulf from the turn of the century through the Second World War, and it continued to be directly concerned with the area until final withdrawal in 1971. While American military and security interests originated around the time of the Second World War, it was not until after 1971 that the US became increasingly and directly concerned with the defence of the region and Western interests there. The expression of security concerns by the Arab littoral states was also late in emerging, principally due to the nature of British legal responsibility for defence and external affairs in most of these states, as well as predominant British influence over international relations in the Gulf generally.

The year 1971 also marked a watershed in the way many of the littoral states viewed the security of the Gulf. The centuries-old British shield had been removed and new responsibilities for self-defence and regional policing fell by default to newly emerging nation states. While the roots of the contemporary state of Saudi

Arabia are several centuries old, the establishment of the kingdom in its present territory dates back only half a century and concern with affairs beyond the Peninsula has been present only in the last several decades. Oman, while always legally independent, spent the twentieth century within a British sphere of influence until emerging from its isolation with an intra-family *coup d'état* in 1970. The smaller amirates of the Gulf became independent only in 1971, with the exception of Kuwait (1961).

Their increasing concern over external affairs and growing profile in international relations can be traced to a number of factors, including the impact of nationalism, tighter integration into Arab politics, politicisation and nationalisation of oil resources, identification with the Third World on political and North/South issues, emerging suspicions of superpower rivalry in the Gulf and Middle East, and a recent climate of fears of burgeoning threats to these self-perceived fragile and vulnerable states and societies.

Despite their many obvious differences, the two external powers and the Arab Gulf littoral states concerned with Gulf security have exhibited similar strategic interests in the Arabian Peninsula. Essentially, these have been: (1) preservation of global and particularly Western access to Gulf oil; and (2) denial of penetration or intrusion by hostile or rival forces. While the strategic interests have been similar, the means or methods of protecting those interests — i.e. the tactical objectives — differ considerably. This is not only due to differing national interests and perceptions, but also to dramatically changing circumstances and situations over the last three-quarters of a century, both in the Gulf itself and on a much broader level. Consequently, comparison of the perceptions and experience of each of these three actors or groups is not only a useful historical exercise, but provides insights into the constraints, limitations and necessary direction of contemporary US and GCC policy in that region.

The Emergence and Evolution of Security Concerns in Arabia

The British connection with the Gulf originated in the early seventeenth century. Over the next 300 years, British interests multiplied and intensified to the point that British supremacy in the Gulf was clearly recognisable by the early decades of the present century. By the end of the First World War, the Gulf had for all intents and purposes become a British 'lake'. All the external challenges to British supremacy there had been beaten back, and, at the same time, Britain became more closely involved in local politics in order to protect what were increasingly seen as important interests in the Gulf.

During the 1920s and 1930s, it became apparent that several British strategic interests — certainly strategic if not yet 'vital' — were to be found along the shores of the Gulf. The first of these and, in the end, the more permanent and important one, was the growing dependence on Gulf oil. The first oil finds in the region occurred in Persia (later Iran) in 1904 and oil was discovered in Iraq shortly after the First World War. Subsequently, fields were brought into production down the Arab side of the Gulf, including Bahrain, Kuwait, Saudi Arabia, Qatar, the UAE and Oman. Within a relatively short period of time, the presence of this oil was seen as a strategic resource for the British empire, since the Royal Navy heavily depended on Gulf oil for fuel; British commercial interests held the majority of concessions in the region, and Gulf oil played a major part in enabling the steady expansion of oil consumption throughout the empire.[1]

The second factor reviving the strategic importance of the Gulf to Britain resulted from the development of imperial air routes and the emerging doctrine of air power. The Gulf provided one of the earliest links in the London–India route, despite the false start caused by political problems in establishing a route through Persia (Iran) and the subsequent necessity of rerouting along the Arab littoral. The coming of the air age gave the Gulf — and in particular the Arabian Peninsula — a renewed importance as a link in the transcontinental transportation and communication networks. At the same time, the newly emergent key role of the Royal Air Force in the region, particularly in Iraq and Aden, provided another spur to the establishment of air facilities along the Gulf and Arabian Sea periphery of the Peninsula, in order to link RAF commands.

A third reason for the Gulf's emerging importance to London at this time was actually a continuing manifestation of its geopolitical significance. For centuries, Britain had sought to prevent rivals from penetrating its cocoon around the Gulf, and the emphasis on this enduring policy was further confirmed by the emergence of the factors of air and oil. Consequently, by approximately the mid-1930s, the Gulf's peripheral place in the imperial scheme of things had been transformed to an area of increasing strategic importance.

While the era of *pax Britannica* in the Gulf can be said to have existed for a century or more, complete and effective British control over external access to the Gulf and internal politics in most of the littoral states was more ephemeral, lasting only a few short decades. The apogee of British concern over Gulf security and its ability to guarantee that security was reached during the decade of the 1930s. From then on, the notion of the Gulf as a British 'lake' became increasingly dated, and the next quarter-century exhibited a steady British retreat from its predominant position.

In many ways, the Second World War marked a significant turning-point and the beginning of the end of British imperial standing. While the Gulf and Arabian Peninsula were not at the centre of attention during the war, they did play a role in the conflict. Bombing raids were conducted from Aden during the Italian East African campaign early in the war, Aden and other airfields along the southern perimeter of the Peninsula were useful for convoy escorts and anti-submarine patrols, the Gulf and Iranian corridor was used as a key Allied supply route to the Soviet Union, and air routes through the Gulf and along the Southern Arabian rim served as important links in the ferrying of men and material to the Pacific theatre in the latter stages of the war. One lasting effect of even the relatively minor impact of the war on the Peninsula was the first stripping away of the isolation which the British had imposed.

American penetration of this British domain, bitterly resented by the British, had begun in the decade before the war but benefited heavily from the need for co-operation in war efforts and became more pronounced in subsequent years. The process had begun with American minority interest in British oil concessions and then became pronounced with the establishment of the Arabian–American Oil Company (ARAMCO) concession in Saudi Arabia. American armed forces utilised Gulf air facilities during the Second World War. Subsequently, the US built an airfield at Dhahran (Saudi Arabia), established a small naval presence in the Gulf, and initiated a long and close relationship with Iran under the rule of Muhammad Reza Shah. Thus, by the early 1950s, the predominance of British influence in two of the most important countries of the Gulf had been replaced by American influence.

The slowly emerging American penetration of the Peninsula occurred simultaneously with a gradual British retrenchment from the existing position in the Gulf and Middle East. This phenomenon was only the local manifestation of a broader process involving the dismemberment of the British empire and the cumulative abandonment of long-held East-of-Suez responsibilities. The Peninsula and Gulf constituted the tail-end of a retreat punctuated by exits from India (1947), Egypt (1954), Iraq (1958), and finally Aden (1967) and the Gulf (1971).

Withdrawal from Aden — also signifying abandonment of Britain's last major military installation in the Middle East — turned out to be a long, involved and bloody process. In contrast, withdrawal from the Gulf seemed far less painful. The military implications were negligible, and at the time the political impact as seen from London and Washington seemed relatively minimal. The impact on the Gulf was more substantial, especially in the smaller amirates of the Gulf. Britain had served as judge, arbiter, administrator and, of course, protector of this littoral for well over a century. Departure in 1971 was tantamount to removal of the safety-net. Obviously, the currents of nationalist and modernist sentiments and ideas had begun to circulate along the shores of the Gulf even before the influx of oil revenues. Apart from Iraq and perhaps Kuwait and Saudi Arabia, few people in the Arab littoral seemed really prepared for the burden of complete political and international responsibilities.

Nevertheless, the newly independent states of Bahrain, Qatar and the UAE — along with the not so much older nations of Kuwait and Saudi Arabia — adjusted quickly enough. As an indication of the durability of arrangements made at this time, the 16 years between the momentous announcement of withdrawal and 1984 passed without any serious adverse developments occurring in any of the former British-protected areas of the Gulf. More than one prophet of doom in the West has been proved wrong in this regard.

The 'changing of the guard' in the Gulf, from Britain to the US, took place during a long process stretching over several decades and US interests in the Gulf were considerable when Britain withdrew in 1971. Still, even with three years or more advance notice, the US was not fully prepared to accept direct responsibility for the security of the Gulf and Peninsula, let alone take up Britain's shield. Close working relations existed only with Iran and Saudi Arabia, American diplomats had yet to take up residence in the newly independent states, US military capabilities in the Gulf were minuscule, and — apart from the oil companies — there was virtually no cadre of officials who were familiar with the region.

The apparent American inaction concerning the Gulf at this time would not seem to be due to indifference, although the Gulf's role in the looming global oil crisis was not generally appreciated at the outset of the 1970s. Rather, the explanation lay elsewhere. Except for the ties to Iran and, to a lesser extent, Saudi Arabia, the Gulf had always been unfamiliar territory. Even later, Washington's perceptions of events and situations in the region in large part were filtered through Pahlavi Tehran and Riyadh. In addition, the simultaneous American dilemma in Vietnam made direct involvement along the lines of the British experience impossible. The consequence was the 'twin pillar' system.

In addition to a different approach and outlook, the US also faced a radically changed situation from the prewar era of British predominance. While Gulf oil had been important to Britain then, in the 1970s that oil was at the heart of global dependence on an increasingly 'vital' resource. The political environment had changed also: no longer was the Gulf ringed by minor possessions and quasi-dependencies of an empire, but independent states, fully integrated into the international system, had appeared.

Even though the American strategic interest of denying entry to the Gulf to its superpower rival echoed earlier British attempts at quarantine, there were differences even here. The East–West rivalry and the supremacy of the US and the USSR in a bipolar system represented a far more direct challenge than those of previous years, as illustrated in the stubborn Soviet presence in northern Iran after the Second World War and emerging Soviet influence in Iraq after 1958.

Finally, the US came cold to its role as guardian of the Gulf. Britain had had three and a half centuries of experience in that region and had worked up to its position of predominance and security responsibility gradually over the course of at least a century. In 1971, the US found itself thrust into a role not of its choosing. For most of the ensuing decade, Washington looked benignly on the Gulf from a distance, blithely assuming that the status quo would remain undisturbed and that the amount of regulation required could be provided by its two principal clients, Iran and Saudi Arabia. Neither the oil crisis of 1973–4 nor the spillover from continued Arab–Israeli strife shook this complacency, but only the events of 1979. The laissez-faire attitude of the 1970s was replaced by a skittish, hawkish attitude in the 1980s. In many ways, the formulation of an effective yet subtle, permanent and proper, policy for the gulf has yet to emerge out of the first years of the American era in the Gulf.

American policy in the Gulf since 1971 falls into two distinctive, almost schismatic, periods: 1971–9 and 1979 to the present. While the first was characterised by benign inaction, the second has tended towards overreaction. American policy towards the Gulf during the first period was predicated on the Nixon Doctrine, which provided the foundations of the so-called 'twin pillar' policy, by which the US relied upon Iran and, to a lesser extent, Saudi Arabia, as its surrogates in the Gulf. The extension of Iranian assistance in putting down the Marxist-led rebellion in Oman's province of Dhufar in the early 1970s seemed to justify this surrogate policy.

But a series of troubling events in the region around 1979, particularly Soviet inroads in several countries and the fall of the Pahlavi regime in Iran, forced a re-evaluation of this policy. The indirect, even inattentive, American approach of the past decade was reversed in a spasm of concern and rhetorical reaction. The broader Gulf region was characterised as an 'arc of crisis', the Carter Doctrine threatened the Soviet Union with retaliation, simmering plans for a more direct and stronger American role in the region were put on the front burner, and eventually the US Central Command was created to provide the military wherewithal to intervene in the Gulf if deemed necessary. While the immediate reversal of policy occurred during the Carter administration, this policy shift has been made permanent by the actions of the subsequent Reagan administration.

Despite the continuing soft world oil market and declining international oil prices, the Gulf remains a key area of US strategic interest. As Secretary of State George Shultz proclaimed in early 1985,

> Another major U.S. interest in the Middle East is to maintain free world access to the vital oil supplies of the Persian Gulf now and in the future. The Persian Gulf countries produce over 25% of the free world's supply. Through our assistance, we help to improve the security of our friends in this area. Oman is cooperating closely with the United States toward our common goal of maintaining security and stability in that vital area and freedom of navigation through the Strait of Hormuz; Oman's agreement to permit access to its facilities represents a key asset for the U.S. Central Command. Although not recipients of U.S. financial assistance, the other gulf states and Saudi Arabia, as

members with Oman in the Gulf Cooperation Council, have shown the will and the ability to defend themselves against encroachment of the Iran–Iraq war. The Administration is embarking on a comprehensive review of our security interests and strategy in the area, focusing on how our various programs in the security field complement our efforts in the peace process and contribute to the general stability of the region.[2]

American resolve and military preparation constitutes only one aspect of the Gulf security question, and it is vitally dependent on co-operation with and from its friends within the GCC. The principal responsibility or burden of maintaining security in the Gulf necessarily must rest on the shoulders of the littoral states. Furthermore, as long as ultimately there will be divergent perceptions between the US and the Gulf states of potential threats or challenges to Gulf security, policy differences are inevitable. It is undeniable that important — and even vital — national interests of the United States reside in the Gulf. At the same time, however, American preoccupation with access to a single natural resource is only 'temporary' in the broader scheme of things. To Saudi Arabia and its smaller allies, the security of the Gulf will always be of paramount importance, the risks higher, and a misstep catastrophic.

The Arab states of the Gulf have taken a variety of steps to enhance their security. First, they have banded together in the Gulf Cooperation Council, a sensible move that not only provides a little more bulk or manpower or financial resources for defence purposes, but also makes sense in economic and cultural terms. These six states are remarkably similar in many ways and the GCC undoubtedly represents the best chance of any for eventually successful integration within the Arab world.

Led by Saudi Arabia's predominant size and financial resources, the GCC states have embarked on ambitious military modernisation programmes, which cannot overcome obvious constraints of small size and manpower problems but nevertheless will help these countries to meet a myriad of lesser security threats. They have worked towards accommodation with more powerful and radical neighbours, in the Gulf, elsewhere in the Arabian Peninsula, and in the Levant. They have also sought friendship and economic and political co-operation with the United States and the West. But, mindful of the lessons of the past, they have insisted that military co-operation remain limited to an 'over the horizon' role. Admittedly, such a compromise is less than militarily ideal, but it is a political necessity.

Any examination of the proper relationship between the United States and the GCC in the question of Gulf security must begin with a look at how this responsibility was first handled. And this requires a brief overview of the pre-eminent British role in shaping much of the present complexion of Gulf politics.

Origins of British Involvement in Arabia

The paramountcy of British authority in the Gulf during the first half of the twentieth century was the end-result of a steady accumulation of British interests there over the course of the past three centuries and the empire's gradual entanglement in the web of this imperial eddy. Eventually, Britain found itself not only maintaining security for what had come to be regarded as a British 'lake', but also exercising heavy responsibility for the internal affairs of the emerging states of the Arabian littoral as well. The progress of this deepening entanglement can be traced through the development of at least eight significant interests during the period between first British entrance in the region and final achievement, in the post-Second World War era, of unchallenged supremacy there.

British involvement in the beginning was predicated exclusively upon commercial interests.[3] Trade with the Gulf commenced in 1617 and quickly supplanted declining Portuguese commerce while competing favourably with the Dutch and the French. A century later, though, the importance of Gulf trade had diminished considerably and by the end of the eighteenth century it had virtually disappeared. Continued British representation in the Gulf and the occasional patrols there by the Bombay Marine could be reasonably justified only in terms of protection of the minor 'country' trade from India. Nevertheless, new factors appeared to prevent complete British withdrawal from the area.

In 1798, Napoleon Bonaparte landed an army in Egypt and easily overpowered that country's Mamluk rulers. In British eyes, however, the real goal was India and this suspicion was given additional credence with the interception of Napoleon's letters to the rulers of Muscat and Mysore. The destruction of the French fleet at the Battle of Aboukir in 1798 and then Napoleon's ignominious flight to Europe after the unsuccessful siege of Acre in 1799 proved to be only temporary setbacks to French designs.

Instead, France changed tactics and a small fleet was dispatched to the Indian Ocean in 1803, and was followed by the posting of a commercial agent to Muscat in 1807. The Treaty of Finkenstein, signed in the same year, would have obligated Napoleon to restrain Russian expansionism in the direction of Persia in return for the Qajar Shah's declaration of war upon India. This agreement came to naught, however, as France soon reconciled with Russia and Britain subsequently imposed a new treaty on Persia in 1809. The final blow to Napoleonic ambitions came with the British capture of Île de France (thereafter named Mauritius) in 1810, depriving France of its last major base in the Indian Ocean.

The third cause of British involvement provided the spark for a permanent presence in the region and partial supervision of Gulf affairs. Despite the decline in trade, British and British-protected vessels continued to ply Gulf waters and were attacked with increasing frequency in the early years of the nineteenth century. There are various reasons for the emergence of what the British termed 'piracy', including depressed economic conditions along Gulf shores and the decline of existing political authority in the region.

The Portuguese had first applied the term 'pirates' in the seventeenth century to the Ya'ariba rulers of Oman, who were then busily engaged in expelling the Portuguese from their strongholds in the Gulf and East Africa. A century and a half later, the British tended to regard the activities of the Qawasim (sing., Qasimi), who were based along the southern shore of the Arabian littoral, in the same light. The strength of Muscat's rulers was quickly fading at the time and local opposition to their dominance was enflamed by the alliance with the British. In short order, Muscat's possessions on both shores of the Gulf fell to Qasimi control. The anti-Muscat and anti-European inclinations of the Qawasim were further exacerbated by their conversion to Wahhabism, the puritanical strain of Sunni Islam prevailing in central Arabia and being spread by the efforts of the Al Sa'ud. As a consequence, Qasimi attacks on the shipping of various flags were lumped together with the activities of the Gulf's freebooters and labelled piracy.

The efforts of the Government of Bombay to eradicate this piracy eventually culminated in the trucial system operating under British aegis. The idea of a base in the Gulf to protect commercial interests had been broached a century earlier, but the scheme advanced in 1808 derived from political and strategic considerations. A military presence on, say, Kharg Island or Qishm Island, it was argued, would not only offer protection against pirates, but also serve to counter Persian and French designs in the area. While the scheme enjoyed the support of officialdom in India, it was rejected by London, which preferred instead to rely upon diplomacy to advance its strategic interests in the Gulf. Actual occupation of Qishm Island in 1820 proved shortlived as the garrison quickly fell prey to disease and entanglement in local politics and warfare. It was withdrawn in 1823 and the idea of a military base languished, with a few limited exceptions, for nearly another century.

The principal British response to 'piracy' came in the form of punitive expeditions launched against Qasimi ports along the so-called 'Pirate Coast' and elsewhere. The first of these was prompted by the growing seriousness of the situation in 1808, when many of those aboard an East India Company cruiser were massacred and Qasimi vessels began to appear for the first time in Indian waters. Consequently, an eleven-ship armada laid siege in 1809 to the Qasimi capital at Ra's al-Khayma and burned it. Another Qasimi stronghold at Lingeh (on the Persian coast) was stormed next and finally a joint British–Muscati fleet captured Shinas (on Oman's Batina coast) following a fierce battle. Despite these successes, the power of the Qawasim was broken only temporarily.

By 1812, the Qasimi fleet had been restored and soon their dhows reappeared off the coast of India. British resolve to act forcefully against the renewed threat was stiffened by the success of Egypt's Muhammad 'Ali in defeating the Al Sa'ud, presumed to be backing their fellow Wahhabis. After extensive planning and a suitable respite in internal Indian troubles, a second expedition, again relying on Muscat's help, stormed Ra's al-Khayma in 1819–20. The town was captured after considerable loss of Arab life while smaller parties were sent out to gain the surrender of neighbouring ports and towns. The small garrison left behind when the fleet withdrew and then transferred to Qishm Island, was responsible for triggering a third expedition.

Ordered to investigate reports of piracy by the Bani Bu 'Ali tribe (residing at the southeastern corner of the Omani coast), a ship from the Qishm garrison was attacked by the tribe. The attempt of the garrison's commander, Captain T. Perronet Thompson, to punish the Bani Bu 'Ali ended in catastrophe when the tribe counter-attacked and nearly massacred Thompson's forces. A new punitive expedition was sent out from India. In early 1821, in combination with Muscati troops, the Bani Bu 'Ali were defeated in a fierce battle, their main settlements razed and their leaders imprisoned in Muscat. Subsequently, Thompson was court-martialled for unnecessarily involving Britain in a campaign in the interior of Arabia, and publicly reprimanded.

The inconclusive result of these expeditions eventually led the Government of Bombay to the realisation that a *modus vivendi* with the 'pirates' was necessary. The first step in the erection of a productive and durable trucial system appeared in the aftermath of the 1820 siege of Ra's al-Khayma.[4] The 'General Treaty of Peace with the Arab Tribes', which the area's shaykhs were forced to sign, prohibited piracy and plunder by sea and required their vessels to fly a recognised flag and be registered. In British eyes, the 'Pirate Coast' thereupon became the 'Trucial Coast' (or 'Trucial Oman'), a sobriquet it was to retain until independence in 1971. Enforcement was provided at first by the shortlived base on Qishm Island. Regular Bombay Marine patrols in the Gulf, introduced shortly thereafter, were able to deal effectively with the occasional attacks perpetrated over the next few decades.

One limitation of the 1820 treaty was its failure to regulate the conduct of warfare on sea amongst the Arab tribes, which tended to disrupt the fishing and pearling seasons with some regularity. The British were able finally to arrange a maritime truce in 1835 which forbade all hostilities by sea for a period of six months, with the understanding that Britain would not interfere with wars on land. This proved so successful that it was renewed regularly until 1843 when a ten years' truce was signed. Upon its expiry, Britain induced the shaykhs to accept a 'Treaty of Perpetual Maritime Peace'. By its terms, the British government assumed responsibility for enforcing the treaty; aggression by any signatory upon another was to be met not with retaliation, but instead referred to the British authorities.

The foundation had been laid for Britain's legal and formal predominance in the Gulf. But permanent responsibility entailed permanent *in situ* supervision, and so official representatives gradually were stationed around the Gulf. In final form, British administration there formed one part of the Government of India's far-flung Residency system, with a Political Resident in the Persian Gulf (PRPG) headquartered at Bushire (on the Persian coast) until 1947 and thereafter at Manama, Bahrain. The Resident's subordinates at one time or another included Political Agents, Political Officers, and Native Agents, stationed at Muscat, Bandar 'Abbas, Sharjah, Dubai, Abu Dhabi, Doha, Manama, Kuwait, and Basra (known until 1914 as Turkish Arabia).[5]

In addition to establishing maritime peace, the British pursued two other ancillary interests during the mid-nineteenth century. One involved the restriction and then the elimination of the slave trade. By 1848, Britain had succeeded in pressuring most of the Gulf's rulers to declare illegal the carriage of African slaves in Gulf vessels and later in the century British legations routinely manumitted slaves upon request. Communications constituted the other major interest during this period. The Gulf had served as a principal mail route between London and India until superseded in 1833 by a Red Sea alternative. Direct and reliable postal connections with the Gulf were restored only in 1862 with the introduction of a Bombay–Basra steamer mail service, but the connection to Europe was never renewed. More important for imperial purposes was the laying of a submarine-and-coastal telegraph cable along the Gulf in 1864. This link enabled the Indo-European Telegraph Department (later Cable and Wireless) to provide an essential and profitable service until undercut by wireless competition in the 1920s.[6]

British supervision of Gulf maritime activities and the development of communications lines through the area served to strengthen the British stake in what was seen increasingly as a region of some geopolitical importance. Lord Curzon, the Viceroy of India, categorised British interests in the Gulf as being commercial, political, strategical and telegraphic.[7] As one scholar has put it, the Gulf was not a British 'lake' at this time, but 'an international waterway of steadily increasing importance in an age of imperial rivalries, diplomatic flux, and sizable dangers to international peace of mind in the cycles of decay and revolutionary activity in the Ottoman and Persian states'.[8] Between the middle of the nineteenth century and the First World War, Britain consistently worked to consolidate its position in the Gulf and to deny access to other non-regional powers. Principal threats were seen as emanating from France, Russia, Germany and the Ottoman empire.

There is a long history of French intrigue in Oman, lapsing through much of the nineteenth century but revived with the 1894 appointment of a French consul in Muscat. On various occasions in the next 20 years, France used Oman and its agent there as a springboard for mischief against British interests in Oman, the Gulf and even the North–West Frontier of India. Russia, too, had been a long-time foe in the region, particularly in the competition for influence over Persia. British suspicions were heightened towards the end of the century by tsarist expansionism in Asia and fears that Russia, in competition with Germany, would seek a port in the Gulf to connect with a railway. Both of these rivalries, however, were settled by diplomatic action in the years before the First World War. This was not the case with Britain's other two rivals.

The spearhead of the German assault lay with the establishment of various commercial interests in the Gulf, but the real threat was posed by the squabbling over the location of the eastern terminus of the German-built Ottoman railway. The issue was complicated by questions over the status of Kuwait, the site for the terminus favoured by Berlin and Istanbul. Britain adamantly opposed the unambiguous incorporation of Kuwait into Ottoman territory, as well as the construction of a railhead and port that would threaten British strategic interests. Following years of negotiation, an Anglo-Ottoman understanding to terminate the line in Basra was finally reached in 1913, but the Anglo–German agreement had not been ratified by the time the two European powers found themselves at war.

The railway formed only one aspect of the protracted Anglo-Turkish rivalry. The Ottoman empire, long sovereign in Mesopotamia, had become increasingly expansionist in the mid-nineteenth century. As early as the 1860s, claim was laid to Kuwait, Bahrain, central Arabia, Qatar and even the 'Trucial Coast'. Al-Hasa (now part of Saudi Arabia's Eastern Province) was occupied in 1871 and became a permanent, if unruly, possession until its recapture by the Al Sa'udi in 1911. An attack on Qatar in 1892 ended in disaster and the effort a decade later to introduce Ottoman officials there was aborted by British representations in Istanbul. Ottoman claims to Qatar and parts of Abu Dhabi were eliminated only by the 'Blue Line' agreement of 1913. The status of Kuwait was considerably more ambiguous and was complicated by the railway question. Tentative agreement on recognition of nominal Turkish sovereignty over the shaykhdom in return for its autonomy was mooted by the outbreak of the First World War and Kuwait was subsequently regarded as an independent state under British protection.

The war enabled Britain to take control finally of Mesopotamia.

This region had long been a centre of British interests for such reasons as the heritage of several centuries of British commerce in Mesopotamia, a tradition of political representation there since 1728, the establishment of a postal service in 1862 through the (British) Euphrates and Tigris Steam Navigation Company, the increasing desire to protect the northern reaches of the Gulf from European ambitions and Ottoman expansionism, the perceived need for control over any eventual railhead on the Gulf, and lastly the desire to participate in and control oil exploration. An expeditionary force of the Indian Army landed in Ottoman territory almost immediately upon declaration of war and marched into Basra a few weeks later. But Baghdad was not captured until 1917, after the catastrophic defeat at Kut, and Mosul was not entered until after the armistice had been signed. In the end, though, France, Britain's remaining European rival in the Middle East, bowed to Britain's claims in Mesopotamia and existing control was ratified through the granting of the League of Nations mandate for Iraq to Britain.[9]

By the time hostilities were terminated in 1918, the Gulf had very nearly become a British 'lake' in truth. Through a series of formal agreements in the 1890s, prompted by the 'forward policy' of Lord Curzon (Viceroy of India), Kuwait, Bahrain, Qatar and the 'Trucial Shaykhs' had legally accepted British protection and advice. Similar terms had brought the nominally independent sultanate in Muscat within the British sphere of influence. Iraq had become a British mandate. Only Persia and the Al Sa'ud retained any degree of real independence, yet Britain exercised considerable leverage in Tehran and Sa'udi authority was confined largely to its Najdi base. With British supremacy in the Gulf finally and unquestionably assured, the thrust of British policy increasingly turned towards involvement in local politics to protect the growing list of accrued interests.

Notes

1. For more information on the development of British oil interests, see Stephen Longrigg, *Oil in the Middle East: Its Discovery and Development*, 3rd edn (London, Oxford University Press, for the Royal Institute of International Affairs, 1968); and Benjamin Shwadran, *The Middle East, Oil, and the Great Powers* (New York, John Wiley, 1973). A recent overview of the development of international oil is Steven A.

16   Introduction

Schneider, *The Oil Price Revolution* (Baltimore, Johns Hopkins University Press, 1983).

2. Extract from statement by the Secretary of State before the Committee on Foreign Affairs, US House of Representatives, 19 February 1985. US Department of State, Bureau of Public Affairs, *Current Policy*, no. 656. The perceived importance of Saudi Arabia was echoed in a 1983 public opinion poll, in which 77 per cent of the respondents indicated thát the US had vital interests in Saudi Arabia, a figure topped only by Japan, Canada and Great Britain. Some 25 per cent supported the dispatch of US troops if Iran invaded Saudi Arabia while 39 per cent supported sending troops if Arab oil producers cut off supplies to the US. John E. Reilly (ed.), *American Public Opinion and U.S. Foreign Policy 1983* (Chicago, Chicago Council on Foreign Relations, 1983), pp. 16 and 31.

3. The following discussion of British involvement in the Gulf is largely derived from J. G. Lorimer (comp.), *Gazetteer of the Persian Gulf, Oman, and Central Arabia* (Calcutta, Superintendent, Government Printing, 1908–15; reprinted Farnborough, Hants, Gregg International Publishers, 1970); J. B. Kelly, *Britain and the Persian Gulf, 1795–1880* (Oxford, Clarendon Press, 1968); Briton Cooper Busch, *Britain and the Persian Gulf, 1894–1914* (Berkeley, University of California Press, 1967); and Malcolm Yapp, 'British Policy in the Persian Gulf', in Alvin G. Cottrell (gen. ed.), *The Persian Gulf States: A General Survey* (Baltimore, Johns Hopkins University Press, 1980), pp. 70–100. On the maritime role, see R. St P. Parry, 'The Navy in the Persian Gulf', *Journal of the Royal United Service Institution*, vol. 75 (May 1930), pp. 314–31; and J. F. Standish, 'British Maritime Policy in the Persian Gulf', *Middle Eastern Studies*, vol. 3, no. 4 (1967), pp. 324–54.

4. The texts of the relevant treaties and discussion of their background are to be found in C. U. Aitchison (comp.), *A Collection of Treaties, Engagements and Sanads Relating to India and Neighbouring Countries*, 5th edn (Delhi, Manager of Publications, Government of India, 1933), vol. 11.

5. J. B. Kelly discusses the evolution of this administrative network in 'The Legal and Historical Basis of the British Position in the Persian Gulf', in *St Antony's Papers*, no. 4 (London, Chatto & Windus; New York, Praeger, 1959; Middle Eastern Affairs, no. 1), pp. 119–40.

6. On the slave trade see Lorimer, *Gazetteer*, Appendix L, 'The Slave Trade in the Persian Gulf Region', pp. 2475–516. On communications, see Lorimer, *Gazetteer*, Appendices J, 'The Telegraphs of the Persian Gulf in Their Relation to the Telegraph Systems of Persia and Turkey', pp. 2400–38, and K. 'Mail Communications and the Indian Post Office in the Persian Gulf', pp. 2439–74; and Christina Phelps Harris, 'The Persian Gulf Submarine Telegraph of 1864', *The Geographical Journal*, vol. 134, pt. 2 (June 1969), pp. 169–90.

7. Standish, 'British Maritime Policy', p. 345.

8. Busch, *Britain and the Persian Gulf*, pp. 1–2. Busch quotes Bismark to similar effect: 'In international affairs, there are three wasps' nests besides the Balkans: Morocco and the Mediterranean, the Persian Gulf, and the American Monroe Doctrine; God grant that we may never fall into one of them.' Ibid., p. 1. The growing importance of the Gulf, especially as a back-up to the all-water Suez route, was noted by the geopolitical theorist Captain Alfred Thayer Mahan, in his 'The Persian Gulf and International Relations', *National and English Review*, vol. 40 (September 1902), pp. 27–45. Incidentally, Mahan is given credit for coining the term 'Middle East' on p. 39 of this article.

9. On the establishment of British control over Iraq, see A. J. Barker, *The Neglected War: Mesopotamia, 1914–1918* (London, Faber & Faber, 1967); Edith and E. F. Penrose, *Iraq: International Relations and National Development* (London, Ernest Benn; Boulder, Co, Westview Press, 1978); and V. H. Rothwell, 'Mesopotamia in British War Aims, 1914–18', *The Historical Journal*, vol. 13, no. 2 (1970), pp. 273–94.

2 Air Power and Empire in the Arabian Peninsula

For most of the lifespan of the British empire, the Arabian Peninsula was only of peripheral imperial interest. Despite the steady tightening of British control over the centuries, the Gulf and Peninsula had never been a principal objective but a means to an end, *viz.* securing the approaches to India. But several decades into the present century, this was changing. In the words of Lord Wavell, Viceroy of India, 'There are two main material factors in the revolutionary change that has come over the strategical face of Asia. One is air power, the other is oil.'[1] The discovery and exploitation of oil in the Gulf has been the more important and permanent factor catapulting the region into global attention, but the necessities of air communications and air power were first responsible for British concern with the security of the Arabian Peninsula itself. Not long after the technology of air power had been developed, it was applied to Arabia. It was to remain a principal British tool for providing both internal and external security until final withdrawal in 1971.

The First Air Routes: Persian Gulf and Basra–Aden

Origins of the Use of Airplanes in Arabia

Aircraft made their first appearance in Arabia early on in the air age and were employed during the First World War. RNAS (Royal Navy Air Services) aircraft were used in 1916 to bomb Ottoman forces besieging Aden and, a year later, planes of the Royal Flying Corps were used for artillery spotting along the Tihama coast of the Red Sea.[2] Other RNAS seaplanes and a French squadron were used for reconnaissance at Jidda and German aircraft apparently flew over parts of Arabia as well, providing assistance to their Ottoman allies. In Mesopotamia, British aircraft dropped supplies in early 1916 to forces besieged at al-Kut and later attacked retreating Ottoman troops. In Palestine, British and German planes engaged in aerial warfare in support of their respective allies.

Arabian rulers acquired their first aircraft in the mid-1920s, although the effectiveness of these purchases for military use was extremely limited by the unsuitability of the particular airplanes, the lack of skilled pilots (all of whom were Europeans), inadequate supplies and haphazard maintenance. Britain, the principal European power in and around the Arabian Peninsula at that date, was reluctant to provide air capability to local leaders. Nevertheless, it was prompted to do so on several occasions for fear of being outflanked by European rivals eager to make inroads on the privileged British position.

The willingness of other European states to supply aircraft was demonstrated in Yemen when the Italians landed the first airplane in San'a' to celebrate the signing of the Italo-Yemeni treaty in 1926.[3] Shortly afterwards, Imam Yahya received six airplanes as a gift from the Italian government; fuel and parts for them were landed at al-Hudayda under the supervision of two Italian destroyers.[4] To forestall similar inroads with Ibn Sa'ud, the British provided the Saudi ruler with a pilot and two mechanics for the aircraft he had acquired as a result of his conquest of the Hijaz. They declined, however, his request for additional assistance to repel an expected attack by Imam Yahya.[5]

Four years later, the British sold four de Havilland biplanes, accompanied by British pilots and maintenance crews, to Ibn Sa'ud for use against the rebellious Ikhwan, and a base was established for them at Darin on the shore of the Gulf.[6] These aircraft were a major addition to what was still known as the Hijaz Air Force. Even by 1930, the force was capable only of several long flights and was troubled by lackadaisical attitudes, particularly among the seconded British pilots, and improper maintenance.[7] One outcome of British reluctance to supply Ibn Sa'ud with the aircraft and personnel he desired was the gift of six Italian planes in 1937.[8]

Despite the Hijazi legacy and Ibn Sa'ud's obvious interest in the advantages of air power, his capabilities in this field were sorely constrained by problems in personnel and an empty treasury. An RAF officer visiting Jidda in 1937 reported that he saw three Saudi pilots, one White Russian pilot (who appeared to be the only skilled aviator), and two Russian mechanics. In addition, there was an Italian colonel who was in administrative control of the air force. The aircraft consisted of three 3-engined Capronis for passenger service, two smaller Capronis, a Bellanca formerly owned by an American gold-mining company, a French Caudron Renard passenger craft, and four ancient Wapitis handed over from the

RAF in Iraq — the only planes remotely usable for service purposes.[9] Nevertheless, Ibn Sa'ud was far ahead of his fellow Arabian rulers in utilisation of the skies.

The Persian Gulf Route

A more substantial impact of the air age on Arabia resulted from the establishment of British air routes around the fringes of the Peninsula. The value of air routes linking the various parts of the British empire had been recognised from an early date. The Civil Aerial Transport Committee, established in 1917, urged the setting-up of such routes and emphasised that a strong civil aviation service would provide a basis for rapid military expansion in time of necessity. In 1923, several existing airlines were merged to form Imperial Airways, which was provided with a government subsidy in return for the understanding that its aircraft would be at the disposal of the imperial government in time of war.[10]

Establishment of a London–India air service had been proposed as early as 1912 but rejected as commercially unfeasible. Nevertheless, the cost of subsidising the overland mail route kept interest alive. By the end of the First World War, the route between Cairo and Delhi had been traversed by air for the first time and the Air Ministry put forward a proposal in 1919 for an air service between Cairo and Karachi, noting the benefit it would provide for both military purposes and in carrying mail. The next step was the authorisation given to the RAF at the Cairo Conference of 1921 for opening an air service between Cairo and Baghdad. Inaugurated on 23 June 1921, this service cut the time for mails between London and Baghdad from 28 to nine days. Passenger service between Cairo and Basra, via Gaza, Rutba Wells and Baghdad, was begun by Imperial Airways on 1 January 1927. The remainder of the route to India, however, was to give far more problems, particularly since not all the overflight territory fell within British control, unlike the Cairo–Basra sector.[11]

The Cairo–Karachi route was seen as the most important link in the imperial air network: in Winston Churchill's 1919 observation, it buckled the empire together.[12] In theory, there existed four alternative routes between Cairo and India: (1) along the Red Sea to Aden and then along Southern Arabia to the Makran coast; (2) across the desert to Iraq and then along the Persian coast to Karachi; (3) from Iraq across central Persia to Quetta; and (4) from Iraq along the Arabian coast to Oman and then across to Makran.

The Red Sea–Southern Arabia route suffered from its far greater distance, lack of suitable facilities, and seasonal disruptions by the monsoon. The inland Persian route also contained operational disadvantages as well as political ones.

From an operational or technical point of view, the two coastal alternatives in the Gulf were evenly balanced. The distances were comparable, the climates similar, and they offered equal access to supply by sea. The Persian coast held a slight advantage, however, because of the existence of the Indo-European Telegraph Department's lines along the same stretch and because of presumed political and security obstacles involved in dealing with the various skaykhdoms. The Arabian route suffered from the additional disadvantage of the necessity of bridging the wide gap between a stop on the Trucial Coast and the Makran coast — a new generation of aircraft capable of safely flying this distance came into service only in 1932.

As a consequence, the choice was made to fly along the Persian coast. But serious obstacles surrounded this decision from beginning to end. The prickly question of air rights formed only one aspect of a much larger panoply of Anglo–Persian disputes. British representatives had sounded out Tehran on the possibility of traversing Persia as early as 1924 with little success. Agreement on a fortnightly service was provisionally reached in September 1925 with Reza Khan, then Prime Minister and later Shah, but it became a dead issue after the Majlis (Parliament) refused to ratify it. One difficulty for the British lay with the presence of the German Junkers service, which had begun flying from Berlin to Tehran via Russia in 1924.[13] Another was the ascendancy of Soviet influence at the Persian court and British disfavour because of the use of Persia as a base to back the White Russians. A third area of disagreement concerned the siting of the route, with Tehran insisting on its crossing central Persia and Imperial Airways desiring the more southerly route along the Gulf coast.

Despite a protracted second round of negotiations in 1927, it became clear that the Persian government would never adhere to the original agreement. Finally, compromise was reached in mid-1928 on a limited service along the coast, using only Bushire and Jask as aerodromes, for a period of no more than three years, at the end of which service was to be rerouted through central Persia. The final leg of the Cairo–Karachi service, via Persia, was inaugurated on 5 April 1929 and continued on a regular basis until October 1932, when the route was transferred to the Arab littoral. The fact that Tehran had provided Imperial Airways with details of the central route only months before expiration of the agreement, combined with the company's conclusion that it presented too many natural obstacles, led to a temporary extension of the Persian coast agreement until the Arabian littoral route could be surveyed and developed.[14]

The goal for the Arabian route was to have main refueling stations at 200-mile intervals, and emergency landing grounds laid out every 30 to 50 miles.[15] Service along the route was expected to be provided by flying boats, particularly since the RAF had long used them for operations in the area. The work of surveying the route and making political arrangements for the establishment of facilities went hand-in-hand. The job of surveying fell to the RAF's No. 203 (Flying Boat) Squadron, which had carried out its duties at an earlier date as part of the development of the RAF's Basra–Aden route.[16] No. 203 Squadron began work in April 1929 and had finished its task within a few months, except for the thorny problem of facilities in the vicinity of the Ru'us al-Jibal, the mountainous spine jutting up into the Strait of Hormuz.

Meanwhile, the PRPG was engaged in negotiations with the various rulers from Kuwait to Muscat. The selection of Kuwait and Bahrain was not surprising, since both locations offered excellent facilities, their rulers were co-operative and existing landing grounds already had been used occasionally by the RAF. Muscat was also advantageous from the political point of view but was too far off the direct route from Iraq to India and offered poor conditions for flying boats. Consequently, the search for more suitable facilities moved to the Trucial Coast.

Not unexpectedly, the Trucial Coast posed political problems. Apart from a Native Agent, the British had never permanently stationed a representative there and involvement in internal affairs had been negligible. In addition to forming the most isolated region in the Gulf, its people were seen as the most resistant to outside intrusions. A 1927 RAF expedition from Oman's Batina coast encountered considerable hostility in its survey of the Trucial Coast, a factor that helped shift the balance towards the Persian route.[17]

But when it became necessary to map out the Arab route, the RAF determined that Ra's al-Khayma offered the best facilities, as well as being the closest point to the Makran. But Ra's al-Khayma's ruler, despite the considerable pressure of the Resident, remained unyielding in his refusal to allow use of his creek by a civil air service, let alone the building of a resthouse. Negotiations with Dubai began on a more promising note but eventually the shaykh admitted that he could not get the assent of his relatives.[18] Only in 1937 did the establishment of Imperial Airways' flying-boat route include Dubai as a night-stop (although the passengers had to travel overland to the existing resthouse in Sharjah).[19]

As it gradually became clear that a suitable flying-boat base could not be secured, the decision was made to utilise landplanes. Sharjah, though unsuitable as an anchorage, was perfectly acceptable as the site of a landing ground. While apprehensive, the shaykh of Sharjah was eventually induced to grant his permission, his approval undoubtedly aided by the residence of the Native Agent there, the promise of a subsidy, and the decision to switch the port of call for British India steamships from Dubai to Sharjah.

With Sharjah's selection, the Arabian coastal route was complete. Necessary links for its operation had been set up at Kuwait, Bahrain, Sharjah and then Gwadar on India's Makran coast.[20] There still remained minor problems of acquiring additional landing grounds (especially on the opposite side of the Ru'us al-Jibal from Sharjah, because of the great distance of the Sharjah–Gwadar hop) for emergency use, but these did not present serious obstacles. Despite the haste in which the route was mapped out, it was ready for use by the end of the last extension of permission for the Persian coastal route. Accordingly, service switched to the Arabian littoral in late 1932.[21]

The Basra–Aden Route

The foundations of the Basra–Aden route predate the establishment of the Gulf route in some sectors. Yet the completion of the Basra–Aden route and inauguration of regular service along it occurred later than the Gulf route. The explanation for this seeming anomaly lies in the different purposes for the two routes. The Gulf route arose from the desire to institute civil air service along a key imperial route as soon as possible, while the course from Basra to Aden was important only for occasional RAF use and to provide linkage between several RAF stations. Given the RAF's early presence in the region, it is not surprising that some landing grounds were marked out and some permanent stores established at various points between Iraq and Aden prior to the inauguration of Imperial Airways' service to India.

The Royal Flying Corps made its first appearance in Mesopotamia in 1916 and the RAF assumed administrative control of the Iraq mandate in October 1922. Even before that date, however, British planes had seen service in military operations in southwest Persia and a series of rudimentary landing grounds had been marked out along the northern shore of the Gulf from Baghdad to the Indian frontier. In addition, stores of petrol and oil had been laid down in every place where a political officer was maintained.[22] Thus, occasional flights were made throughout the 1920s to various locations along the Arabian littoral, including Kuwait, Bahrain, Muscat and especially Bushire, seat of the Residency. Furthermore, an RAF flight had been assigned temporarily to Kuwait, to provide protection against an anticipated attack of the Ikhwan.

At the other end of the route, Aden had witnessed an equally long record of British activities in the air. Aircraft from vessels momentarily passing through Aden had been used on various occasions during the war against Ottoman forces besieging Aden. As early as 1919, air sorties were carried out against recalcitrant tribes of the interior, as well as against the Yemen imamate and Somaliland, and a flight was stationed permanently in Aden in 1920. When overall responsibility for the defence of the colony and protectorate was given over to the RAF in 1928, a squadron of bombers from Iraq replaced the existing garrison of British and Indian troops.[23]

The importance of developing air routes along both sides of the Gulf — i.e. the civil route along the Persian shore and the strategic route along the Arabian littoral — was noted in the 1928 Interim Report of the Persian Gulf Sub-Committee of the Committee of Imperial Defence. Given the uncertain diplomatic situation in Persia at the time, the report stressed that every possible effort should be made on the Arabian side to prepare for the air route's development, including securing the necessary aerodromes and other facilities.[24] The increasing importance of Aden to the RAF undoubtedly made the need for a permanent air linkage between the Aden and Iraq commands that much more obvious.

In early 1929, political arrangements and surveying got under way for the facilities along the Arabian littoral as part of the imperial (civil) air route alternative to Persia. At the same time, the Air Ministry directed the Air Officer Commanding (AOC), Aden, to extend the chain of landing grounds eastward to the protectorate border. As British control was relatively secure along the coast of the protectorate, this directive posed few problems of a political or security nature. Consequently, work soon started on facilities at Ahwar, Balhaf, Mukalla and Qishn. The principal problem along the full route came from the expanse of Omani territory between Salala and Muscat. The desert coast was especially wild, even by Arabian standards, and the nominal authority of the sultan could not necessarily be relied upon.[25]

Because of these severe problems, completion of arrangements along the Southern Arabian coast were protracted throughout most of the 1930s. Once surveying had been completed and likely sites identified, an even greater difficulty arose in dealing with the shaykhs of the largely Bedouin tribes, in whose territories the landing grounds were contemplated. An important first step involved convincing the shaykhs of their responsibility for protecting the facilities. A sort of carrot-and-stick approach was employed. On the positive side, the shaykhs were promised payment of a subsidy for guards for the strips and local labour was to be engaged for the construction. On the other hand, the skaykhs were warned of the punishment that would be forthcoming from the sultan and/or the British if the facilities were disturbed. It took several years of semi-annual visits for the Political Agent in Muscat finally to track down the responsible shaykh for just the principal tribe on Masira Island. The later selection of a site at Shuwaymiya (in nearby Sawqara Bay), for use as an emergency landing ground, involved the considerable problem of conclusively determining in which tribe's territory the site was actually situated.[26]

In 1932, the work of actually constructing facilities was kicked off by the meeting of the AOCs of Aden and Iraq at a mid-point of the route in Oman. By the end of the year, a landing ground had been laid out and an oil depot established on Masira. A complete survey of the route was carried out during November 1933 by No. 203 (Flying Boat) Squadron, making intermediate stops at Bahrain, Ra's al-Khayma, Khawr Jarama (Ra's al-Hadd), Mirbat and Mukalla.[27] In 1934, a landing ground was laid out at Khawr Gharim (in Sawqara Bay) and the Sultan of Oman built a petrol store for the RAF at Salala. A second site in Sawqara Bay was reconnoitred several times and a landing ground laid out in 1936 with a petrol dump added in 1938. By 1936, the route was finally complete and the first scheduled flight carried out.[28]

The completion of the two air routes meant that the various stations along the periphery of the Peninsula were no longer so

Map 1: Airfields in the Arabian Peninsula, to the End of the Second World War

physically isolated and dependent on time-consuming travel by sea. As R. J. Gavin has explained,

> This represented a further development in the logic of the new air strategy for now Aden could be rapidly reinforced from the Royal Air Force's principal bases in the Middle East and was linked in with the other recently established imperial air routes

reaching on to India and the East. The whole shape of imperial defence was changing. Air routes were replacing sea routes as defensive arteries, along which military units could be shuttled back and forth, especially in the Middle East where the Air Force was in control, and the security of landing grounds and airfields was coming to equal in importance the protection of naval bases and harbours.[29]

Political Impact of the Routes

The air routes marked a significant change in British policy in the Gulf. Gone were the days when British concern was limited to suppression of maritime warfare. Later had come recognition of rulers and then, at the turn of the century, assumption of formal responsibility for the minor rulers' external affairs. But until the air routes, Britain still maintained a disinterested 'hands-off' attitude towards much of the Arab littoral, except when disruptions spilled across local boundaries. The establishment of the air routes, with their requirements for facilities, resthouses and wireless stations, prompted a deepening, direct, British involvement in internal affairs.

This change affected Kuwait and Bahrain least, where landing grounds and resthouses were readily purchased. Both shaykhdoms were commercial centres, with extensive contacts with the outside. Political Agents had resided there for decades, the ruling families had long co-operated with the British, and there had been previous contact with the RAF, which had stationed officers in the shaykhdoms only a few years before in connection with the Ikhwan threats.

Muscat, as well, was not greatly affected by the new direction in policy. There had been a strong British role in the politics of Muscat since the 1890s. The sultanate's Batina coast (on the Gulf of Oman) was under secure control, as well as the Gulf of Oman coast east from Muscat to Ra's al-Hadd. The quasi-independence of the interior was unimportant, since the air routes followed the coast and the interior could not threaten the sultanate after the early 1920s. The section along the coast of the Arabian Sea, however, was a different matter, and it was a lengthy process to track down the leaders of the Bedouin tribes and extend the effective control of the Muscat government to the desert stretch of coast.

The greatest impact was along the Trucial Coast, and, to a lesser degree, in Qatar. Treaty relations with the Al Thani of Doha were not established until 1916 and the first permanent British representative did not take up residence in Qatar until 1949. In the Trucial Coast, the hostility to British interference present in the late 1920s, largely as a result of Wahhabi influence and the example of Ikhwan activities, lessened somewhat in succeeding years. Nevertheless, considerable pressure was necessary to gain co-operation of the shaykhs in the air routes and, apart from a few aerodromes and ancillary facilities, the coast's isolation remained near complete until well after the Second World War.

The importance of the establishment of air routes in extending British influence and concern over local, domestic, affairs should not be underestimated, particularly given the strategic importance of these routes during the war. Nevertheless, the enduring reason for deepening British involvement was oil, bringing in its wake Political Agents in Doha, Abu Dhabi and Dubai, oil crews, and a myriad of boundary disputes. Along the Arab littoral of the Gulf, the preparations and consequences of the air routes provided an essential bridge.

Policing and Air Operations

Air Control and the RAF

The impact of the air age on Arabia was not limited to the establishment of civil and military routes. The First World War had served as a testing ground for various new applications of military technology, among which was the use of aircraft in warfare. In the immediate postwar period, the manifold advantages of air power were extolled by its proponents in enthusiastic manner. The arguments took many forms, but the rapid mobility of air forces and their capability to strike heavy blows with virtual surprise seemed to give air power a particularly useful role in imperial defence.

The perceived value of aircraft in fighting 'small wars' derived from a number of factors. They exhibited an obvious advantage in reconnaissance, both in the ability quickly and safely to map unknown countryside and in gathering intelligence on enemy movements. Their mobility could be particularly useful in theatres of operation involving relatively small forces spread out over extensive territory. Attack by air was seen as particularly effective where the countryside was rugged and ground movements restricted to a limited number of roads and passes. Aircraft could be used for dropping communications and even some supplies to besieged positions. Finally, artillery spotting could be done more efficiently from the air.[30]

The use of aircraft to support political authorities in maintaining order seemed to be an application of air power that was even more appropriate for 'peacetime' conditions in many areas of the newly expanded empire. In particular, the advantages of air power over ground forces in 'punitive expeditions' were seen to include the ability to: (1) strike a quick blow at a great distance; (2) keep forces concentrated without sacrificing mobility; (3) destroy the morale of tribesmen unable to counter air attacks; and (4) speed up negotiations with rebellious tribes by dropping government terms and landing negotiating officials.[31]

Both Spanish and Italian aircraft had been employed in North Africa before the First World War, but the first British use of air power in colonial policing occurred along the North-West Frontier and in Afghanistan during 1918–20. The attack by one bomber on Kabul in May 1920 was seen as an important factor in the decision to sue for peace.[32] Aircraft were used to even greater effect in Somaliland in early 1920, when the forces of Muhammad bin 'Abdullah (the 'Mad Mullah') were routed by a single bomber squadron in only three weeks. Even more impressive from the British government's point of view was the fact that the total cost of the operation amounted to only £77,000.[33]

The advantages of air policing appealed to a war-weary government strapped for funds. Even as demobilisation of the armed forces proceeded, HMG faced the need for increased expenses and sizable numbers of troops to control new additions to the empire. A rebellion in Iraq during the summer of 1920 clearly illustrated the problem: nearly three divisions of British troops were required to put it down and a large permanent garrison force in Iraq appeared necessary.

The case for utilisation of air power in imperial possessions was forcefully put forward by Air Marshal Sir Hugh Trenchard, the Chief of the Air Staff. Trenchard, the first general officer to command the Royal Flying Corps, had presided over the birth of the RAF, resulting from the merger of the Royal Flying Corps and the Royal Navy Air Services in 1918, and justifiably was regarded as 'the father of the RAF'. Trenchard was kept busy during the first few years of the RAF's existence fighting off the Admiralty and the army, who were determined to reassert their control over the fledgeling air service. He faced particular opposition from Field Marshal Sir Henry Wilson, the Chief of the Imperial General Staff, who had once referred to the RAF as a force 'coming from God knows where, dropping its bombs on God knows what, and going off God knows where'.[34] In his counter-attack, Trenchard extolled air power's advantages in mobility and flexibility, to which could be added significant financial savings. The aerial campaign in Somaliland was brandished like a weapon in Whitehall.

The opportunity to prove the RAF's value in the field came in 1921, when Winston Churchill, Secretary of State for Air and Trenchard's superior, gained the additional portfolio of Colonial Secretary. Churchill immediately sought to transfer administration of British territory in the Middle East from the India and Foreign Offices to the new Middle East Department in the Colonial Office. In March 1921, he summoned and presided over a conference in Cairo, to which the Viceroy of India, the Chief of the Air Staff, and the various Governors and High Commissioners in the region had been invited. Among the decisions taken at Cairo to clarify British policy and administration in the region was the transfer of responsibility for defence of the new state of Iraq from the army to the RAF, over the opposition of Wilson and the civilian and military authorities in Iraq. As a result, 8 RAF squadrons (about one-third of the entire RAF) and a small administrative staff replaced 33 infantry battalions, 6 cavalry regiments, 16 artillery batteries and nearly as many support troops.[35] The RAF acquired more than responsibility for a colony, it had gained a reprieve from the executioner.

The RAF in Iraq

Britain faced two fundamental problems in governing its new mandate of Iraq. The first was political and revolved around the question of how to administer and control a diverse population lacking any sense of national unity. At the same time, Iraq posed economic complications. Colonies (and mandates) were not expected to be a drain on the British Treasury, and the army's bill for Iraq had been more than £32m in 1920–1.[36] In part, the response to the political problem involved the establishment of an Arab, largely Sunni, government, with a large contingent of British advisers. At the apex was King Faysal al-Hashimi, from a prominent family of the Hijaz (his father was Sharif of Mecca and later King of Hijaz) who lately had been driven out of Damascus by the French. 'The Iraq Government was in no sense "popular" or representative: it was almost entirely composed of the Sunni Arab urban communities, who, although more sophisticated and educated than most Shia and Kurds, formed a minority of the total population.'[37] The other aspect of the political problem involved security. here Trenchard pressed his argument that the RAF could maintain just as effective security in Iraq as the army, but at a fraction of the cost, thus potentially solving the economic difficulty.

British airplanes, as noted earlier, had seen action in Mesopotamia during the war, particularly in reconnaissance and artillery spotting but also in punitive actions. Their continued use after the war was viewed favourably by civil and military authorities on the spot, and A. T. Wilson, as Civil Commissioner, advocated increased reliance on the RAF as early as 1919.[38] Since an RAF presence had been maintained in the country since the war, the changeover to RAF control in October 1922 took place smoothly, aided by the fact that the new Air Officer Commanding, Iraq, Air Vice-Marshal Sir John Salmond, had been AOC Iraq during the war and was highly regarded.[39] Headquarters remained in Baghdad, with two main stations near Baghdad, an advanced airfield at Mosul in the north, and emergency landing grounds at appropriate locations. In addition, local ground forces fell to RAF command and became known as the RAF Levies.

The first major test for the RAF's ability to defend the mandate came with the possibility of war with Turkey in 1922; accordingly, five squadrons of aircraft and six battalions of troops were moved north to protect Mosul.[40] Shortly thereafter, a more immediate threat arose from Shaykh Mahmud, the Kurdish governor of Sulaymaniya, who appeared to be working with Turkish forces and Shi'i dissidents to foment a general rebellion against the British. Accordingly, two columns of levies were organised to force Turkish troops out of Iraqi territory and to advance on the Kurdish strongholds. Air support was of inestimable value, given the rugged mountains of Kurdistan and the hit-and-run tactics of the Kurdish rebels.[41] Shortly afterwards, in September 1924, 50 Turkish soldiers were killed when attacked by the RAF after crossing the border into Iraq.

The use of air control for punitive measures was clearly seen as amply justified elsewhere in the mandate. By the time Salmond had vacated his command, 288 air operations had been carried out, not including the 1923-4 action in Kurdistan. One notable instance was the air action taken to bring the shaykhs of al-Rumaytha and al-Samawa (south of Baghdad, along the Euphrates river and astride the Baghdad-Basra railway) under government control. In May 1924, the first ever airlift of British Army personnel was undertaken to prevent sectarian troubles in Kirkuk from spreading. At about the same time, several squadrons from the RAF station at Amman, supported by armoured cars, successfully routed an Ikhwan attack on Amman. While the Ikhwan never again threatened Transjordan to such a degree, the RAF was kept busy in the next few years attempting to thwart attacks on the nomadic tribes of Iraq.

The decision to give control of Iraq to the RAF seemed to be justified by its successful operations and efficiency in the first few years. After reviewing the various successful air actions of a punitive nature undertaken by the RAF in its first six months of control an official report of the mandate administration noted that

> the effectiveness of air control would be only partially considered if mention was omitted of its value as a threat and as a means to close co-ordination and co-operation of administrative effort over an immense area, etc., provided with other means of communication. An aeroplane or formation of aeroplanes either employed for the purpose or on some administrative duty can be seen in the air by a widely spread population and provides a tactful but effective reminder to many of the existence and power of Government.[42]

The air control scheme was also popular from an economic view: the £32m in military expenditure of 1920-1 fell to £4m in 1926-7.[43] Furthermore, as Winston Churchill noted, 'The maintenance of British aircraft in Iraq also enabled any part of the Middle East to be reinforced without trouble or expense, and without any ostentatious movement of force.'[44]

The RAF in Aden

The resounding success of air operations in Iraq had a stimulating effect on the RAF's employment elsewhere. A local uprising on the North-West Frontier was suppressed entirely by air in 1927.[45] Seven instances of air operations took place in Aden between 1919 and 1927, against tribes in the protectorate, tribes in Yemen (to free

Colonel Jacob's mission to the imam in 1919), and the Imam of Yemen's forces. All were judged successful, even though four of the missions consisted only of overhead flights and/or dropping warnings.[46] An even more dramatic example of the RAF's value came in Afghanistan during the winter of 1928-9, when rebel forces besieged King Amanullah in his capital at Kabul. With all contact with the outside world cut off, an RAF airlift racked up 28,160 miles in flights between Peshawar and Kabul and evacuated 586 individuals of various nationalities.[47]

Despite these 'advertisements' for the effectiveness of the RAF in policing and imperial defence, Trenchard still faced considerable opposition from the other services. The Admiralty was particularly hostile to RAF control over all air service, claiming jurisdiction over all forces above the sea, as well as on and under it. The debate over Singapore, which had received increasing attention in the 1920s because of its potential value as a base for naval fleets operating against Japan in the Pacific, was illustrative of this struggle: Trenchard unsuccessfully argued, with some support from Churchill, for reliance on air power to defend Singapore as a far less costly alternative to naval guns.[48]

But even as the Air Ministry lost the fight for Singapore, it was more successful in gaining control of the other major East-of-Suez fortress in Aden. Admiralty opposition was based on Aden's importance as a naval base and its vulnerability to the Japanese navy unless defended by coast-defence guns. The army stressed that troops on the ground were necessary to prevent the forces of the Imam of Yemen from overrunning the protectorate. The possibility of settling the frontier question between Yemen and Aden through diplomacy had grown increasingly remote because of both the imam's inherent obduracy and the support given him by Italy, Britain's increasingly dangerous rival in the Red Sea. The alternative of mounting a ground campaign, involving a full infantry division at a cost of more than £1m, was dismaying.[49] The kidnapping of several protectorate shaykhs by the imam's forces in February 1928 and their capture of al-Dali' a little later provided a golden opportunity for the RAF. A single bomber squadron, which had replaced one of the two battalions of troops at Aden, was able to push the imam's forces back into Yemen within a month, and their success was repeated after a similar incursion a few months later. The total cost of the operation was £8,567 and one British casualty.[50]

As a final clincher, Winston Churchill again saved the day for the RAF. As Chancellor of the Exchequer during this period, he was particularly keen on expanding the economies that the RAF had already produced in Iraq. In a meeting of the Committee of Imperial Defence on Aden, Churchill intervened and disposed of the other services' arguments by pointing out, as the committee's secretary later described it, that

> the distance from Tokyo to Aden was a matter of six or seven thousand miles, and [Churchill] dwelt upon a few of the risks which a Japanese Fleet would run in the course of their long voyage. Did anyone seriously imagine that the attempt would be made? Having demolished the Admiralty case to his own complete satisfaction, he proceeded to deal with the apprehensions of the War Office. 'And now I turn from the Mikado to the Imam,' was his opening gambit. There was no need for further argument.[51]

The projected annual savings of over £100,000 did not hurt his case.[52]

Accordingly, the RAF took over military responsibility for Aden in April 1928.[53] The new garrison was to consist of one RAF squadron, a section of armoured cars, and a small body of local levies. The Indian battalion stationed at Aden had been withdrawn at the beginning of the year but the British battalion remained until 1929 to allow time for the levies to be raised.[54] The transfer of defence responsibilities not only meant that the gradual retreat from a presence in the protectorate (at the time of transfer, the army garrison was able to extend its influence only 25 miles into the hinterland) could be reversed, but that expansion was necessary. The protectorate became the first line of Aden's defence since, for the most effective use of the air weapon, as much prior warning as possible was necessary to maximise the period of air attack.[55]

Given the comparatively short range of aircraft of that time, landing grounds at regular intervals were a necessity, particularly along the coast on the route developed to link Aden with Iraq. In addition, airplanes and landing grounds allowed political officers to visit tribes and settlements in the interior, some of which had not been visited in over 25 years. At the same time, of course, the RAF squadron was periodically engaged in punitive actions against both

Table 2.1: Summary of RAF Air Operations at Aden, 1919–41

Date	Against	Action taken[a]	Casualties[b]
Nov. 1919	al-Zaraniq tribe (of Yemen)[c]	O	None
Jan. 1922	Imam's forces	B	c. 35 killed (opposing)
May 1923	Makhdumi and Mansuri tribes	B	None
Feb. 1925	Hukhais tribe	G	None
July–Oct. 1925	Imam's forces	G	c. 79 killed (opposing)
Aug. 1927	Subayhi tribe	W	None
Sept.–Oct. 1927	Imam's forces	W	None
Feb.–Mar. 1928	Imam's forces	B	40+ killed (opposing)
June–Aug. 1928	Imam's forces	B	25 killed (opposing); 1 RAF pilot
Jan.–Mar. 1929	Subayhi tribe	B	'Not heavy'
May 1931	Ahl Ma'ir tribe	B	None
April 1932	Qutaybi tribe	B	None
Oct. 1933	Imam's forces	O	None
Nov. 1933	Mawsata tribe	B	None
Mar.–May 1934	Qutaybi tribe	B	None
Feb. 1936	Hadrami tribes	B	None
Dec. 1936–Jan. 1937	Mansuri section of Subayhi tribe	O	None
Mar.–Apr. 1937	Shayri tribe	B	None
Sept.–Oct. 1937	Subayhi tribe	B	None
Oct. 1937	Qutaybi tribe	O	None
Dec. 1937	Ahl Haydara and Mansuri section of Subayhi tribe	B	None
Jan. 1938	Sa'ar and Tamini tribes	O	None
Feb. 1938	Hamumi tribe	B	None
April 1938	Subayhi tribe	B	None
July–Sept. 1938	Mansuri section of Subayhi tribe	B	Unknown
Nov. 1938	Lower Yafa'i tribe	O	None
Nov.–Dec. 1938	Imam's forces	O	None
Oct. 1940–Feb. 1941	Qutaybi tribe	B	Unknown

Notes: (a) O = Overflight or no action taken; B = Bombing carried out; G = action taken in support of ground forces; W = warnings dropped only. (b) Only one British air casualty was suffered; most casualties incurred by opposing forces in fighting on the ground. (c) Action taken to free Colonel H. F. Jacob, a British emissary who was taken prisoner by the Zaraniq tribe of Yemen's Tihama region while on his way to see the imam.
Sources: AIR/5/1300, Aden Operations Summary (1919–38); AIR/24/2, Air Staff, AHQ, Aden, Operations Record Book (1940–3).

protectorate tribes and the imam's forces crossing the border (Table 2.1). Not all actions required bombing — in some cases, the dropping of warning leaflets or even mere overflights sufficed to gain the offending parties' compliance. Of the relatively few Arab casualties, most were due to skirmishes with friendly tribes or the levies and not from air action. As of the beginning of the Second World War, only one RAF officer lost his life in these operations. As one officer involved in air control in Aden summarised it:

> It is difficult, perhaps, to find a parallel to this peace time control exercised by the Royal Air Force, but I would suggest that the Royal Air Force has only been continuing in the interior the same civilizing work which the Navy has carried out with such success along the coasts of the Red Sea and Persian Gulf.[56]

The RAF in the Gulf

There were strong similarities in the reasons behind the transfer of military responsibility to the RAF in Iraq and Aden. In both territories, Britain had assumed varying degrees of direct control, while security was threatened internally by rebellious tribes in the hinterland and externally by hostile neighbours. Reliance on air control eliminated the need for large army garrisons. Both were seen as strategically important linkages in the network of imperial defence, especially for the RAF. Most of these factors were far less applicable to the smaller littoral states of the Gulf. Nevertheless, the Air Ministry sought to extend its influence from Iraq and Aden to the entire Arab Gulf littoral, and used several incidents in the late 1920s as ammunition in the bureaucratic battle.

The first of these was the emerging Ikhwan threat to British-controlled territories and subjects. The Ikhwan had been created by Ibn Sa'ud in about 1914 in an effort to channel the martial enthusiasm of newly sedentarised Bedouin into serving Wahhabi and Al Sa'ud expansionism. While the Ikhwan had constituted the principal forces in Ibn Sa'ud's conquest of Jabal Shammar, Hijaz and 'Asir, by the mid-1920s they had grown increasingly uncontrollable by the Saudi ruler. Eventually faced with growing rebelliousness, Ibn Sa'ud was forced to take up arms against his own creation and destroy Ikhwan power through pitched battles.[57]

The effects of the Ikhwan rebellion were not limited to Saudi territory but spilled over into Transjordan and Iraq where the

British had installed kings from the Hashimi family, who had been ousted from their home in the Hijaz and became bitter rivals of the Al Sa'ud. While tribal raiding had long been a fact of life along the Saudi–Iraqi and Saudi–Transjordan desert frontiers, the introduction of the Ikhwan tended to transform camel-raids into massacres. In November 1927, Ikhwan forces raided an Iraqi police post at Busayra, killing several dozen individuals. Similar raids soon followed, with Ibn Sa'ud largely powerless to prevent them. The British sought to extend the air control scheme to counter these new raids and established a system of Special Service Officers (SSO), mainly drawn from the ranks of RAF intelligence, to familiarise themselves with the tribes along the frontier and direct RAF attacks (using both armoured cars and aircraft) against intruders.[58]

As a consequence of the Ikhwan rebellion, Kuwait became of direct interest to the RAF. Ikhwan raiders not only passed through Kuwaiti territory on their way to Iraq but, beginning in December 1927, also attacked Kuwaiti tribes. Furthermore, existing RAF bases in Iraq were too far from the Najdi border for aerial activity to be of much help. It is not surprising, then, that a proposal, strongly supported by the Air Ministry, should be made to use Kuwait as a base for attacking Ikhwan bases in Najd. Additional weight for this course seemed to be provided by the steady deterioration of Kuwaiti–Saudi relations following the death of Shaykh Mubarak of Kuwait.[59]

As the Ikhwan raids intensified, it became obvious that defenceless Kuwait was exceedingly vulnerable to occasional Ikhwan incursions and perhaps even a full invasion. Nevertheless, the Political Resident in the Persian Gulf, backed by the Government of India, resisted proposed RAF operations out of Kuwait. His objection was based in part on a fear of undermining Kuwait's independence *vis-à-vis* Iraq, but it also appeared to reflect bureaucratic rivalries within British officialdom, particularly between the Colonial Office and the Air Ministry, operating in Iraq, and the India Office, hitherto unchallenged along the Gulf littoral. Nevertheless, the increasing seriousness of the situation led, in early 1928, to the dispatch of Captain Gerald de Gaury, the SSO in Basra, to Kuwait for several months.[60] When Ibn Sa'ud's counter-attacks against the Ikhwan in late 1929 forced them northeast towards the Kuwaiti–Iraqi borders, permission was grudgingly given for Glubb, another of the SSOs appointed in response to the 1927 raids, to operate in Kuwait with RAF aircraft and armoured cars and the

Iraqi Desert Police.[61]

Even the temporary stationing of an SSO in Kuwaiti territory in 1928 pointed towards a precedent bitterly opposed by India and its representatives. H. R. P. Dickson, the Political Agent in Kuwait, registered strong opposition to the reposting of an SSO during the height of the Ikhwan crushing in 1929. When the RAF in Iraq suggested in 1932 that the SSO Basra be allowed to make regular visits to Kuwait, Dickson again objected (and was supported by the PRPG), claiming that the SSO in Basra and even Glubb had tried to discredit him during the Ikhwan rebellion.[62] Nevertheless, occasional visits were allowed. At the other end of the Gulf, a temporary SSO was assigned to Sharjah in 1932–3 during the construction of the resthouse there.[63]

The Kuwait precedent led to the posting of an RAF intelligence officer, euphemistically termed an Air Liaison Officer (later redesignated Air Staff Liaison Officer), in Bahrain in early 1937, over the PRPG's objections. The instructions of AHQ Iraq to the Air Staff Liaison Officer in 1946 set out such duties as collecting and transmitting information on tribal matters, following the development of oil resources, keeping tabs on landing grounds and alighting areas, and assisting the RAF station commander in Bahrain in his contacts with local authorities.[64]

RAF action in scouting for and then harrying Ikhwan raiders constituted one argument for the introduction of RAF personnel into the Gulf states, even if temporarily. The incidents in 1928 at Sur, a maritime village at the southeastern tip of Oman, provided somewhat heavier ammunition for the RAF, even though the ramifications of the rebellion there were far less significant than the Ikhwan insurrection. Sur is principally inhabited by two tribes, al-Janaba and Bani Bu 'Ali, with the latter concentrated in the suburb of al-'Ayqa. The history of British dealings with the Bani Bu 'Ali go back to the disastrous expedition to Bilad Bani Bu 'Ali in the early nineteenth century, and the tribe's boats were heavily involved in slave trading and gunrunning in the latter half of the nineteenth and the early twentieth centuries.

As early as 1923, the Bani Bu 'Ali asserted that Sur lay outside the sultan's jurisdiction and refused to acknowledge his customs-post there. Matters came to a head in 1928 when the tribe sought to extend its control over the Janaba quarters of Sur and built its own customs-post at al-'Ayqa.[65] The ability of the sultan to restore his authority in Sur was minimal, since the resources at his disposal amounted to a small patrol steamer and about 70 men of the Muscat infantry, an inadequate number to face the armed tribesmen. He requested British assistance to put down the insurrection.

In analysing the alternative courses of action, the Political Agent in Muscat ventured that naval bombardment would have meagre results. Instead, he suggested that a battalion of Indian infantry be stationed at Sur for a year or two, with the costs being recovered out of increased customs collections and possibly the introduction of Sur as a port of call for British India Company slow mail steamers.[66] The Air Ministry, however, divined another golden opportunity to show the benefits of air power. An internal memorandum suggested that aircraft be used in a demonstration flight over Sur and perhaps to land the sultan's British adviser there and, if necessary, bombard the shaykh's fort by Wapitis. It concludes that

> This case if we bring it off rightly would be of the greatest value for substitution. The navy has bombarded and proved a failure. Military forces cannot be afforded even to occupy Sur. We may bring it off without bombardment; or by a discriminate bombardment destroying only the Shaykh's fort. After all that has been said against air action it would be a great triumph.[67]

The Air Ministry won the day and the customs-post in al-'Ayqa was bombed and levelled in 1930. Even non-RAF officials judged the operation as 'quite a success'.[68]

The Sur operation constituted one of the few instances of air control in the Arab Gulf states. This is not surprising since Britain had no direct presence in any of these states, apart from a few political representatives, and exercised no responsibility for internal affairs. Both Kuwait and Sur represented murky legal territory, and British involvement could be justified legally only on grounds of providing assistance to sovereign rulers who had requested it. Officials negotiating facilities for the air route along the Trucial Coast more than once suggested air action to bring recalcitrant shaykhs around — although their suggestions were quickly scotched. Until well after the Second World War, the only additional instance of the RAF taking action against the local population in these states occurred in Dubai in 1934, when an aerial demonstration was made to show support of the shaykh against his rebellious cousins.[69]

Despite the successes in Iraq and Aden, even the most avid

proponents of 'air control' recognised its inherent limitations. In a final paper written a few weeks before his resignation as Chief of Air Staff in 1929, Trenchard contrasted Transjordan and Palestine. In the former, he maintained, conditions were well suited for air control, particularly because of the low density of population and its tribal organisation. Palestine, however, exhibited a different problem: most if its inhabitants were in urban areas and the threat to order there arose not from tribal truculence, but from deep-seated divisions between Jews and Arabs. 'Insurance against racial or political upheavals in such conditions is to be found neither in aircraft nor artillery, nor in infantry battalions, but in police and gendarmerie forces.'[70] Trenchard's parting shots to the other services also included arguments for replacing naval units in the Red Sea with flying boats, replacing coastal artillery with torpedo bombers and further substituting air power for ground forces in India and Africa.[71]

In the main, conditions favouring the utilisation of air control seemed to hold only for particular times and places. Increasingly few territories completely beyond the pale of central authority remained after the Second World War. In addition, the massive bombardments of that war did much to raise public opinion against any aerial action *vis-à-vis* any civilian population. Air policing continued to be a principal instrument in the Aden protectorate until the early 1960s, but its application in Oman in the 1950s, discussed below, displayed few benefits and provided a potent propaganda tool for anti-British forces.

The Growing Strategic Importance of the Gulf

British involvement with the shaykhdoms in the nineteenth century had been for maritime reasons. By the turn of the century, this process had resulted in a series of treaties in which the shaykhdoms placed themselves under British protection and responsibility for foreign affairs and defence. Later, deepening British involvement was predicated on reasons of air power. While the legal nature of the relationship between Britain and the shaykhdoms remained unchanged, HMG began to exercise more concern over their internal affairs. Furthermore, as oil was discovered along the littoral, British involvement progressively intensified, and increasingly the shaykhdoms were perceived as having an intrinsic importance rather than deriving it solely from their strategic location between London and India.

The Persian Gulf Sub-Committee

The first major review of British policy in the Gulf in nearly 20 years was initiated in the late 1920s when the Committee of Imperial Defence (CID) created a Persian Gulf Sub-Committee (PGSC).[72] The Air Ministry was quick to use this convenient forum to advance its position for a greater say in Gulf policy, basing its arguments on the successes of the RAF in Iraq and later in the Aden protectorate and Sur. The parallel between Iraq and the Arab littoral was not exact since there could be no question of the RAF assuming an air control scheme for the Arab Gulf littoral, as Britain maintained no direct military presence in any of the shaykhdoms. Nevertheless, a heated debate over the means of securing the defence of the Gulf arose between the RAF and the Royal Navy, and involved the Foreign, Colonial, and India Offices as well. In Trenchard's view, RAF control of the British sphere of influence in the Gulf (beyond Iraq) was not simply a matter of status *vis-à-vis* the Admiralty, but a necessary stage in the global expansion of the 'thin red lines' of imperial air routes, which themselves were testimony to the value of the RAF in overseas defence.

Trenchard began the offensive with an Air Staff memorandum in May 1928.[73] Basing his argument on 'certain problems' that arose during recent operations in Iraq and Aden, Trenchard argued that the full value of air power required devolution of greater authority to the RAF and the unification of political control over the Middle East.[74] The battle was escalated with his remarks on the Government of India's response to the rebellion at Sur: 'The view of the Air Staff that the Navy — though it can carry out most efficiently its proper role of controlling sea communications in the Gulf — cannot be expected to extend its influence inland is strikingly borne out by the view of the Commander-in-Chief, East Indies.'[75]

The debate gathered full steam following the CID's creation of the Persian Gulf Sub-Committee to re-examine British interests in the Gulf as a result of the air routes and growing exports of oil.[76] The importance of the topic was confirmed by the sub-committee's endorsement of the opinion of the Chiefs of Staff that 'the maintenance of the British supremacy in the Persian Gulf is even more essential to the security of India and Imperial interests at the present time than it was in the past' and its related conclusion that 'it should be a cardinal feature of our policy to maintain our supremacy in the region'.[77]

At an early meeting of the sub-committee, Trenchard pressed his case by stressing the importance of the imperial air chain through the Gulf, declaring that 'A rupture of the Persian Gulf link would be just as grave a disaster to the Air Force as the closing of the Suez Canal would be to the Navy.'[78] In addition, he raised the possibility of a Russian air threat to the Gulf through Persia, comparing it in naval terms to 'the establishment of a Russian submarine base in the Persian Gulf'. In order to contain the Russian threat, Trenchard placed utmost importance on continuation of the Persian coast civil route, while also recommending the quick development of an alternative route along the Arab coast. There was little argument on this point and the sub-committee directed that the Arabian route 'should be pressed forward with all possible speed'.[79]

Trenchard's attacks on other departments' responsibilities in the Middle East, however, did not go unchallenged. The Colonial Secretary observed that Trenchard's remarks 'are almost exclusively Service considerations', and contended that HMG must often adopt courses of action based on equally compelling considerations that do not allow the adoption of air power to its fullest advantage.[80]

Sir Denys Bray, Foreign Secretary of the Government of India, challenged Trenchard face to face in a meeting of the sub-committee. While acknowledging the usefulness of air power in some situations, as along the North-West Frontier, Bray found fault with Trenchard's demand for greater political control by air officers in air operations. He rejected the suggestion that the Government of India should 'commit harikari' in the Gulf, remarking 'For what is wrong with the Persian Gulf? Nothing on the Arab littoral, for which the Government of India are responsible. What is wrong on the Arab littoral is the backwash of British recession on the Persian littoral, for which the Government of India are not responsible.'[81] Sir Samuel Hoare, the Secretary of State for Air, thereupon cited the RAF's problems in using Kuwait during the Ikhwan operations.

With these opening contentions, a combative discussion commenced:

> BRAY: If the contention is that there is something seriously wrong with the Arabian littoral, I would, of course, pause to develop another line of argument. But I really think the statement that the Arabian littoral is in good case is one which holds water.

HOARE: I should not like to be taken to agree with that.

TRENCHARD: Our reconnaissance party, which you sanctioned to examine the Trucial area, were chased out.

BRAY: You penetrated into the hinterland, which we do not profess to administer.

HOARE: On the Arab littoral you have to look both ways, to Ibn Saud on the one hand, and to Persia on the other.

BRAY: Most certainly.

HOARE: And the most serious trouble in the last two or three years has been that with Ibn Saud. The situation last year was very difficult . . .

BRAY: Koweit has been linked up, rather unfortunately, as we in India think, in its fortunes with Irak. If Ibn Saud has any gratitude in him, while he owes none to Iraq or Feisal, he does owe a good deal to Koweit, as it was in Koweit that he took asylum years ago. Koweit is suffering from the trouble between Ibn Saud and Irak, partly because it has become linked up with Irak, and partly because the Air Force use it as part of the air route for getting at Ibn Saud.

TRENCHARD: After Koweit was attacked and raided.

AMERY: Your argument almost assumes that in any trouble between the British Government and Irak and Ibn Saud, India is a friendly neutral and not equally concerned. I do not want to interrupt, but I do hold the view that Koweit . . . ought to go with Irak.

BRAY: I do not know whether it would be profitable for me to try to enlarge on the assumption; but I do not agree with it for a moment as you put it. I feel myself that the position in what I must now define as the Indian sphere of the Arab littoral is sound and wholesome. Sir Hugh Trenchard's note speaks throughout of 'operations' and 'enemy', and 'offence', and so forth. But the normal state of Bahrein, and of the Trucial Sheikhdoms, and of Muscat, is one of peace — not necessarily, of course, peace amongst themselves on land, not necessarily, of course, peace between the Sultan of Muscat and his unruly tribes in the hinterland, but peace with us and peace on the sea.

TRENCHARD: British forces were in action at Muscat last week. The Navy actually bombarded.

BRAY: How often does the Navy bombard in a year in the Gulf? A few shots? . . .

MADDEN: [Sir Charles Madden, Admiral of the Fleet, First Sea

Lord, and Chief of the Naval Staff]: This particular case happened at Sur. A mud fort, occupied by a man who had stolen and looted a British dhow, was knocked down. It was not political trouble.

BRAY: On average, I should say that we have to use force in the Gulf once a year; and force there is a very small thing. The Gulf, where it is inhabited, consists of petty townships lying on the coast, with the Sheikh's fort as a very pretty target which the Navy have not the slightest trouble in hitting every time. More valuable from the ordinary political control point of view is the relentless patience which the Navy can display. The Navy can take the Resident and lie off some recalcitrant Sheikh for a week or ten days, give the terms, and impose its will without firing a shot. That is the routine when we have trouble with a Sheikh. So that, while I can conceive occasions on which the R.A.F. might with advantage be asked for assistance in dealing with a Sheikh — I can conceive it with difficulty — and while I feel very strongly that the influence of the strategical air route along the Arab littoral is going to be very far-reaching in many ways on the whole position of the Gulf, and on these Arab Sheikhdoms in particular, yet I also feel strongly that it is quite premature to suggest that the Navy should retire.

TRENCHARD: May I interrupt for a moment to say that I have never suggested that. I agree with all that you say about the Navy on the coast. But this Committee have already made recommendations regarding the air route along the Arabian littoral which you yourself have said is vital. That air route cannot possibly be protected by the Navy from Ibn Saud and the interior.

Trenchard continued his offensive at the final meeting of the PGSC a few months later, noting that reliance on naval pressure to support government policy had severe limitations.[82] Naval bombardment, he contended, was not effective beyond the beach — and since the Gulf was so shallow, there was not always a beach. Hoare spoke up in support of Trenchard:

The fact of the matter was that a new situation had arisen with which the old machinery was not fitted to deal. There were two entirely new problems. The first was air defence, the second the air route. [Hoare urged] acceptance of the first proposal of the Chief of the Air Staff, namely, that the broad principles of air control should be widely circulated. This would be an immense help to the Air Staff at home and to Air Officers Commanding abroad, since the problem of air control was so novel that the ordinary civil official, who had never been in contact with it, did not understand how it should be used.[83]

The second problem, Hoare added, should be resolved by an interdepartmental committee, a suggestion accepted by the others.

The end-result of this search for a rationalisation of political control in the Gulf was the decision in 1930 to set up two standing committees to deal with Middle Eastern questions concerning two or more departments. One was to be official, with representatives from the Treasury, Foreign, War and India Offices, the Air Ministry and the Admiralty, to deal with specific problems. The other was conceived as ministerial, composed of the heads of the above-mentioned departments, and would deal with questions that the official committee could not resolve. In addition, the cabinet provided local officials with greater latitude to deal with all problems (except those concerning the air route), close cooperation was urged between the AOC Iraq and the Political Resident in the Persian Gulf (as well as with the Commander-in-Chief, East Indies, and his subordinate, the Senior Naval Representative in the Gulf), and transfer of the Resident's headquarters across the Gulf was urged, 'in view of the growing importance of the Arab littoral'.[84]

Developments in the 1930s

Despite the disbanding of the PGSC and the adoption of these recommendations, the Gulf policy battle was not over. Perceptions of the Gulf's importance continued to grow, while potential threats to the British position were given close attention. Safeguarding the air routes through the Gulf occupied high priority. The difficulties with the Persian government over the air route and treaty left a marked impression in the minds of British officials in the Gulf, some of whom maintained that the affair had lessened British influence on the Arab littoral. The Government of India's proposal drastically to reduce the size of naval operations in the Gulf, in order to save money was seen as a serious mistake, given the Political Resident in the Persian Gulf's reliance on the navy for transportation around the Gulf and the establishment of a Persian navy.[85] Admission of American oil companies to Gulf concessions was viewed with trepidation.

The optimal outlines of British policy in the Gulf were summarised by the PRPG in 1931:

> to maintain the independence of the Arab Shaikhdoms so long as they preserve law and order and maintain a system of administration that will satisfy or at any rate be tolerated by their subjects, to avoid any greater degree of interference in their internal affairs than is forced upon us but at the same time to prevent any other foreign power from dominating them or obtaining any special privileges in the Gulf.[86]

The Resident observed that London had begun to display a much greater concern with Gulf affairs than previously. In part, this was due to the emergence of the Gulf's importance to imperial, rather than Indian, interests, such as the air routes, oil, protection of the Shatt al-'Arab, and relations with Ibn Sa'ud. At the same time, it was noted that the changing political environment in India meant that control of Gulf affairs inevitably would pass at some point from the Government of India to HMG.[87]

The question of changing British policy towards the Gulf states was raised several years later by the next PRPG, T. C. Fowle, who specifically referred to growing British intrusion into the internal affairs of the Trucial Coast. After noting Britain's basic responsibilities there — the protection of British Indian subjects, the prevention of hostilities by sea, and the safety of the air route — he pointed out that the exertion of strong pressure to gain air route facilities had caused the shaykhs of the Trucial Coast to fear future British interference in their politics.[88] While the Resident observed that this fear was unfounded, nevertheless for the first time Britain had a compelling interest in the area's domestic affairs — and this interest quite naturally intensified as oil exploration moved south along the littoral in the coming years.

To the RAF, the establishment of the air routes along the Arab shores, particularly the strategic route, indicated that Britain *ipso facto* had acquired responsibility for internal security in the Trucial states, even to the point of intervening in disputes between rulers.[89] This active position in support of signatory rulers from attack by land did not go unchallenged, particularly by the Admiralty which cited British inability to protect the Shaykh of Muhammara from the Shah. Consequently, a meeting of the CID Official Sub-Committee on the Middle East was convened to sort out the growing policy dispute.[90]

There, the Air Ministry, referring to changed circumstances since Lord Curzon's remarks in 1903 effectively had established policy in the Gulf, pointed out that the advent of air power had both made it possible to prevent hostilities on land and, for strategic reasons, made it necessary. The Foreign Office representative observed that the Gulf had ceased being a British 'lake' since Curzon's day:

> To-day the Persian Gulf was one of the world's highways, bordered by strongly nationalist States, whose interest in the Gulf was real and active, and the discovery of oil had led other foreign Powers to take an increasing interest in Gulf affairs. In his view, the time had come, or was at least rapidly approaching, when His Majesty's Government would no longer be able to maintain their previous policy of merely keeping others out, and living, as it were, from hand to mouth, but would be faced with the necessity of going either forwards or backwards.[91]

In particular, the ambiguous international legal status of these states undoubtedly would begin to raise questions as other countries grew interested in oil, aviation and trade in the Gulf.

While the sub-committee agreed that ultimately international responsibility for the affairs of the Trucial Coast and Qatar must be admitted by the British government, it refrained from adopting a new policy for the area (apart from recommending the posting of an Englishman as agent in Sharjah).[92] A final comment on this unsettled matter was made in an internal Air Ministry note, which pointed out that the other departmental representatives 'came to that meeting with their minds made up that the Air Ministry were going to advocate an entirely new policy — in fact a very forward policy — in the Gulf', and, as a consequence, dug their heels in.[93]

Fowle took advantage of several other opportunities to disseminate his views on Gulf policy. In early 1937, he commented on the strategic importance of the Gulf, pointing out its role as 'the Suez Canal of the air', the naval base and oilfield at Bahrain, the telegraph cables and wireless stations, and the emergence of Iranian and Iraqi armed forces in the Gulf.[94] Two years later, on the eve of his retirement, he ruminated on the subject at greater length, remarking that the British administration along the Arab littoral benefited greatly from possessing the goodwill of the rulers and their people. As a consequence, 'this consideration . . . enables us to "run" the day-to day administration of the Arab side with a handful of officials (one Resident, and three Political Agents), without the payment of a single rupee of subsidy, or the upkeep (on our part) of a single soldier, policeman, or levy'.[95]

Britain had acquired this goodwill, Fowle averred, by allowing the rulers to manage their own affairs, by giving them a 'square deal' on oil and air facilities, and because the rulers and their people realised that only the British protected them from their stronger neighbours. Nevertheless, he recognized that emerging anti-British sentiments in the empire and growing democratic developments in the Gulf would cause increasing difficulties in the future, and this would make Britain's job in protecting its strategic and political interests in the region that much more difficult. Fowle's remarks were remarkably prescient, but the 1930s debate on the merits and dangers of a 'forward policy' in the Gulf was abruptly superseded by wartime exigencies and the Gulf's incorporation into Allied defence schemes.

The Gulf on the Eve of the Second World War

The strategic air routes through the Gulf loomed even more important with the growing prospect of war in the late 1930s. Fowle considered the routes to be a principal reason why the Arab littoral was more important to Britain than the Iranian, in conjunction with the oil supplies there, the naval base at Bahrain, and the borders with Saudi Arabia and Iraq. 'The importance of this route is obvious, as if it is "cut" in time of war, for the period that it remains cut no British civil aircraft, and RAF aircraft only with difficulty (by the Aden Muscat Route) . . . can reach India, Singapore or Australia.'[96] In interdepartmental discussion of defence arrangements in the Gulf, it was agreed that responsibility for defence of the Arab littoral rested with the RAF's Iraq Command, although it was felt that the chief danger of attack would come from neighbouring tribes or sabotage. Since the possibility of attack by air or sea was slight, construction of fixed defences was unnecessary. Instead, local defence forces in Bahrain and Qatar were considered, as was a scheme for expansion of Muscat's forces.[97]

Bahrain was considered to be of particular importance, because of its oilfields and refinery, the naval base at Jufayr, and its selection as the future site of the Residency,[98] and a flight of RAF landplanes was based there beginning in 1938. Indeed, Bahrain's growing production during the late 1930s led to its being regarded as one of

Table 2.2: Air Facilities in the Arabian Peninsula, on Eve of the Second World War

Location	Extent of facilities
Kuwait	Aerodrome and flying-boat alighting area for use of RAF and Imperial Airways; 2 landing grounds for emergency use of RAF; occasional use as halt for Imperial Airways
Bahrain	2 aerodromes and 1 flying-boat alighting area for use of RAF and Imperial Airways; RAF depot with a bomb store; Royal Navy base for Persian Gulf Division, with supply of fuel
Yas Island	Emergency RAF landing ground; seaplane anchorage; fuel and oil depot
Abu Dhabi	RAF landing ground; fuel and oil depot
Dubai	Imperial Airways seaplane anchorage; fuel and oil depot
Sharjah	Imperial Airways landing ground; resthouse; fuel and oil depot; beacon; wireless station
Ra's al-Khayma	Seaplane anchorage; fuel and oil depot
Kalba	Imperial Airways emergency landing ground; fuel and oil depot; beacon; seaplane moorings and shelter for passengers
Shinas	Emergency landing ground with fuel
Suhar	Emergency landing ground
Muscat	RAF depot with wireless station; nearby RAF aerodrome at Bayt al-Falaj and seaplane anchorage at Bandar Jissa
Ra's al-Hadd	RAF landing ground
Khawr Jarama	Seaplane anchorage; fuel and oil depot
Gwadar[a]	Aerodrome 12 miles inland, used by RAF, Imperial Airways, Air France, and KLM
Masira Island	Seaplane anchorage; fuel and oil depot
Umm al-Rasas (Masira Island)	RAF landing ground; fuel and oil depot
Khawr Gharim	RAF landing ground
Shuwaymiya	RAF landing ground
Mirbat	RAF landing ground; seaplane anchorage; fuel and oil depot
Salala	RAF landing ground; fuel and oil depot
Qishn	RAF landing ground
Riyan	RAF landing ground; fuel and oil depot
Aden	Aerodromes at Khormaksar (Khawr Maqsar) in Aden Colony and at al-Shaykh 'Uthman nearby
Perim Island	RAF landing ground; fuel and oil depot; bomb store
Kamaran Island	RAF landing ground; fuel and oil depot

Note: (a) Gwadar is located on the Makran coast of what is now Pakistan and not in the Arabian Peninsula. However, it was a possession of the Sultan of Muscat until 1958.
Sources: L/P&S/12/3727, T. C. Fowle, Political Resident in the Persian Gulf, to J. C. Walton, India Office, 18 January 1938; copy in CAB/104/71; L/P&S/20/C252, India General Staff, *Military Report and Route Book: The Arabian States of the Persian Gulf, 1939* (Simla, Government of India Press, 1940); and AIR/2/2138, 'Middle East Re-inforcement Plan, Aden Detail (1937–9).'

the three major sources in meeting British East-of-Suez oil requirements.[99] A final step in the preparations was the transfer of defence responsibilities from the RAF's Iraq Command to India, since India would be better suited to building up land forces for Gulf defence. This was followed by the appointment by the Chiefs of Staff, India, of a Military Commander for the Persian Gulf, who made an initial reconnaissance of the Gulf in June 1941.[100]

The Arabian Peninsula in the Second World War

For the first time in history, a single war made its effects known on nearly every corner of the earth. Even though the Arabian Peninsula was on the far periphery of the battlefields (to even a greater degree than during the First World War), nevertheless it was touched by the war and made its contribution to the Allied war effort. The Middle East as a whole was an area of geostrategic importance to the combatants, serving as a land-bridge from Europe to Africa and Asia, and was the scene of heavy fighting in North and East Africa.

Hostilities in the Arabian Peninsula and Gulf were rare, but the region also held importance for the Allies. First, the Arabian Peninsula and its surrounding bodies of water — the Gulf and the Red Sea — provided the air and sea gateways to the areas East of Suez: the Indian Ocean, Asia and the Pacific. Second, the Peninsula served as a 'base' or 'staging post' for operations elsewhere: it provided facilities for the air routes and naval convoys to the Far East; played a role in the Italian East Africa campaign; was used for the resupply of the Soviet Union through Iran; and served as a major oil source.

At the same time, the countries of the Peninsula itself were becoming intrinsically more important. The Secretary of State for Foreign Affairs noted in 1943 that 'Friendly relations with Ibn Saud are a matter of particular importance to His Majesty's Government, both because of the former's influence as keeper of the shrine at Mecca, with the large Moslem population in India and in other parts of the British Empire, and because of Saudi Arabia's proximity to the sea route to India.'[101] Furthermore, he added that 'The position of the Yemen on the route to India and on the northern boundary of the Aden Protectorate makes it an interest of His Majesty's Government that no potentially hostile Power should acquire a dominant position in that country.'[102] Finally, he added that 'It is of great importance that no international or inter-Arab rivalries should disturb the existing peaceful conditions [in the Arab Gulf states] and thus impede the development of the oil resources of the area,' or existing air communications.[103]

Far Eastern Reinforcement, ASW and Convoy Escort

Several wartime functions utilised the Arabian Peninsula from the beginning of the war. One of these was reinforcement of the Far Eastern theatre, following the route (in 1941–2) from the UK through Gibraltar, Malta, Egypt, Habbaniya (Baghdad), Basra, Karachi, Allahabad, Calcutta, Mingaladon (Rangoon), Victoria Point and Singapore.[104] A variant route via Wadi Seidna (Sudan), Aden and Karachi, placed in operation slightly later, was of particular use to the US Army Air Force.[105]

Along with aerial reinforcement, the RAF was tasked with convoy escort duties for the duration of the war. At first, the British were concerned with Italian attacks on convoys in the Red Sea, and after the Italian declaration of war and the fall of France in June 1940, naval and aerial convoy escorts were increased throughout the Arabian Sea. Between June and December 1940, the RAF provided air escort to 54 convoys, with only one ship sunk.[106] At the same time, the southern shores of the Peninsula were utilised for overseas reconnaissance and anti-submarine (ASW) operations. From 1939, a GR/FB squadron based at Aden was responsible for ASW in the Red Sea and Gulf of Aden.[107] Regular anti-submarine patrols were carried out by the RAF's Wellingtons from Khormaksar (Aden), Socotra Island and Masira Island, and sometimes from Riyan (Aden Protectorate). Catalina flying boats were employed from bases on Socotra and at Aden, as well as Bandar Qasim, Scuiscuiban (Somalia) and Salala (Dhufar).[108]

Aden's Role in the East African Campaign

Aden Air Command also played an important role in the campaign against the Italians in East Africa, providing patrols over the Red Sea and the Gulf of Aden. Over the course of the campaign, its aircraft successfully attacked Italian supply, fuel and ammunition depots, the airfields at Assab and Dessie, the railway through Diredawa, and then installations in the Addis Ababa area.[109] The Anglo–Italian rivalry in the Red Sea and East Africa had been simmering for several decades and the Red Sea was seen as a potentially major theatre of operations. Fortress Aden was a particularly obvious target, as was Perim, for its value in blocking the Bab al-Mandab Strait and thereby cutting off movement through the Red Sea.[110] The importance of Aden in the early stages of the war was stressed by the Senior Naval Officer in the Red Sea in 1940, who wrote that

> As our forces in the Middle East grow, so does their absolute dependence on our convoys, and those depend absolutely on security and adequacy of Aden as a naval and air base. I submit a little clear thinking on the part of the Axis would show them that Aden is key to Middle East, and once that is realised, Aden will be untenable — unless adequate fighter and bomber forces and anti-aircraft defences are provided covering aerodromes, the port and outer harbour. The AOC agrees that it is only through supineness and false strategy of enemy that Aden is able to fulfil its task.[111]

Nevertheless, Aden's defences at the outbreak of the war were extremely modest. These consisted of three RAF squadrons (one bomber, one fighter, and one reconnaissance), one Indian infantry battalion and approximately 500 Aden levies.[112] Naval facilities at Aden consisted of a cruise and light craft base, with docking, repair and maintenance facilities, an armament depot and important fuel storage. In late 1942, Aden became a fueling base for aircraft carriers and capital ships. Air operations were centred at nearby Khormaksar, although the landing round at al-Shaykh 'Uthman was also pressed into service. Aerodromes for reconnaissance and ferrying operations were also established at Riyan (near Mukalla), Socotra Island and Bandar Qasim (on the British Somaliland coast).[113]

The principal Italian threat to Aden was through bombing raids. Aden Colony was hit on at least twelve occasions between September 1940 and February 1941, Perim three times, and Kamaran Island and al-Shaykh Sa'id (on the North Yemeni mainland) at least once.[114] The Gulf also suffered a raid in October 1940, when three or four Italian bombers took off from Rhodes, dropped their bombs on the Bahrain refinery without causing any damage, and flew on to Eritrea. Another bomber caused slight damage to the oil pipelines near Dhahran.[115]

Italy lost little time after entering the war in June 1940 to mount an offensive in East Africa. In July, the Italians moved from Eritrea into Sudan and soon after occupied British Somaliland. The British counter-attack from Sudan and Kenya had to be delayed until forces had been built up. Nevertheless, the attack mounted from Kenya on Italian Somaliland in February 1941 was surprisingly effective and British troops were able to enter southern Ethiopia only a month later. They were bolstered by other forces moving inland from Berbera, which had been captured in mid-March. Emperor Haile Selassie was able to return to his capital at Addis Ababa in early April. Meanwhile, British forces entering Eritrea from the Sudan in January faced stiffer resistance and it took until early April before Asmar and the port of Massawa were captured. The main body of Italian troops, caught in a pincer between advancing British forces, were forced to surrender in May, although pockets of resistance continued to hold out around Gondar until late November. The Italian defeat in East Africa greatly reduced the threat to Red Sea operations and allowed the transfer of the bulk of British troops to Egypt.[116]

While the RAF in Aden provided air reconnaissance for Red Sea shipping during this campaign, its major contribution was in bombing raids in conjunction with the offensives on Italian-held territory from north and south. Repeated raids were made on Assab, Dessie, Diredawa, Addis Ababa, Alomata and Makalle. In addition, sorties were made against the Diredawa aerodrome in support of the attack on enemy-held Berbera in March. During April, operations were carried out almost entirely in the Dessie area and on the Asab–Dessie road, as well as attacks on the aerodromes at Dessie and Assab. The success of the East African campaign allowed the removal of one of the bomber squadrons to Egypt, leaving a bomber squadron, a reconnaissance squadron and part of a fighter squadron in Aden.[117]

The Gulf Supply Route to the Soviet Union

The threat on the western side of the Peninsula was soon followed by a threat to the north and east. Forces were required in 1941 to put down pro-Axis governments in both Iraq and Persia, and then in 1942 the German advance into the Soviet Union raised the possibility of a Nazi breakthrough to the Middle East and a threat to India. The principal role of the Persia and Iraq Command, established in 1942, however, was to maintain the southern supply route to the Soviet Union.

The development of unexpected threats to this particular region led to a certain amount of command confusion, which lasted throughout much of the war. Although the AOC Iraq reported to the AOC-in-C Middle East during the early stages of the war, there was increasing pressure to transfer jurisdiction to the Senior Air Officer in India, since the command had little connection with the North African campaign, and the troops assigned for the defence of Persia and Iraq came from India.[118] The matter was further confused in November 1941, when the AOC Iraq, under the general direction of the AOC-in-C Middle East, was given responsibility for control of air forces and facilities in Iraq, the Gulf, the Arabian Peninsula (excluding Aden) and part of Persia. In addition, operational control of land forces was transferred from the C-in-C India to the C-in-C Middle East at the beginning of 1942. Soon after, the region was divided into separate commands: Middle East, and Persia and Iraq.[119]

From a small start, British and Indian forces were gradually built up in the area under the jurisdiction of the Persia and Iraq Command. Some of these had been moved into Iraq after the Rashid 'Ali coup in early 1941. The coup had raised the spectre of an Iraqi–Axis alliance and led to direct hostilities, including an attack by the Iraqi army on the RAF station at Habbaniya, its defeat and a subsequent British drive to recapture Baghdad, 30 miles away.[120] Other units were brought in during the latter half of 1942 to meet a potential German advance in Syria and to provide assistance, if necessary, to Soviet forces in the Caucasus. With secure control over the local governments and the disappearance of the German threat to the Soviet Union, many of these troops were moved out to more urgent theatres.

A renewed but unsuccessful effort to place Iraq under India was made in 1943. At that time, the duties of AOC Iraq and Persia were defined as: (1) internal security of Iraq and Persia; (2) administrative duties in connection with the line of communication from the Gulf to Russia; (3) administrative duties in connection with the line of communication from Iraq to India; (4) the defence of the Abadan oilfields; and (5) reconnaissance responsibilities in the Gulf.[121] Due to the reduced threat to Iraq and Persia, RAF installations at Baghdad, Mosul, Kirkuk, Mehrabad and Abadan were disbanded, while Basra was reduced in status, and surplus manpower was sent to Egypt. The stations at Masira and Ra's al-Hadd, which had been under Iraq's control since the establishment of the Basra–Aden air route, were transferred to British forces, Aden, in recognition of their primary role in anti-submarine patrols.[122]

Meanwhile, the decision was made in August 1941 to transfer supplies to the Soviet Union along the difficult route through Iraq and Persia. The task involved the expansion of existing ports, the construction of a new port (located on the Iraqi–Kuwaiti border at Umm Qasr and dismantled for political reasons at the end of the war),[123] building bridges across the region's rivers, and laying railroad tracks north to the Soviet border, as well as the erection of assembly plants for trucks, airplanes and other war material. In addition to supplies, the trans-Persian route was also utilised to repatriate freed Russian prisoners-of-war and — in a reversal of the normal flow — to move exiled Polish soldiers and civilians from Turkistan to Bandar Pahlavi on their way to points west.

By the time, the transport of supplies to the Soviet Union ceased in 1945, over 5m tons had been shipped.[124] The supply effort was not entirely British, of course, and American involvement began in August 1942, with the creation of the Persian Gulf Command within US Armed Forces in the Middle East. Approximately one-quarter of all wartime aid shipped from the Western hemisphere to the Soviet Union passed through the Gulf route, slightly more than the amount sent around the North Cape to Murmansk.[125]

The South Arabian Air Route

The last role played by the Peninsula in the Second World War came with the turnabout of Allied fortunes in Europe and the channelling of increased efforts to the war in the Pacific. In December 1943, the Air Ministry began to develop a chain of airfields from the UK to India to facilitate the transfer of reinforcement aircraft and personnel to the Far Eastern theatre. A number of these airfields lay in the purview of RAF Mediterranean/Middle East (MEDME), including Castel Benito, Marble Arch, El Adem, Cairo West, Almaza, Lydda, HE, Habbaniya, Shaibah, Bahrain and Sharjah. Although these fields had been established some time previously, the majority required major construction work to handle the increased flow of aircraft. This work included the laying of runways, construction of technical facilities and the erection of accommodation for permanent and transit personnel. Trooping began with twin-engined Dakotas with 4-engined aircraft added later, allowing a monthly total of 12,000 troops to be transported by October 1945.[126]

Since the route through the Fertile Crescent was considered vulnerable in the early stages of the war, an alternative route via Sudan and Aden to Karachi was sketched out in mid-1941, with stops at Aden, Riyan, Salala, Masira, Ra's al-Hadd and Jiwani (India). Construction of necessary facilities was carried out at these locations throughout 1942. Nevertheless, at that stage in the war, it was thought that this route would be left for emergency use only.[127] However, the South Arabian air route began to acquire additional importance with the German invasion of North Africa and the American airlifts from the Western hemisphere across West and Central Africa and then along the South Arabian route to India. Extensive use of the South Arabian route was made in the latter stages of the war, for the ferrying of aircraft and troop transport. While the USAAF made the most use of the route, RAF activities (in conjunction with convoy escort and ASW duties) were also prominent, as were BOAC and Pan Am flights.

Postwar Reassessments

The majority of the frenzied military activity in and around the Arabian Peninsula faded away with the end of the war. The bases, airfields and co-operation of the area's governments lost their immediate importance. Nevertheless, the Peninsula did not return to its prewar status of isolation. Postwar political changes in the British empire, oil, the emergence of American interest in the Gulf and the perception of a Soviet threat on the horizon all continued to make Arabia a region of continuing strategic importance.

Wind-down and Peacetime Footing

While the war provided the stimulus for the creation of the South Arabian air route, its use did not end with the Japanese surrender. Troops were ferried back from the Pacific along its points as late as March 1946.[128] British reluctance to quit the route was based principally on its value as part of a worldwide rapid reinforcement network.[129] Nevertheless, the transition from wartime to peacetime use was marked by several complications.

One issue to be settled was future civilian use. Both BOAC and Pan Am, in the service of their respective governments, had made extensive use of the route during the war. BOAC had instituted a weekly service along the route in 1943 when it seemed that the

Middle East was in danger of collapse; the service was retained later primarily because Britain did not wish to leave sole use of the route in American hands. BOAC officials were even posted in several stations during this period.[130] Following the war, BOAC maintained a Cairo–Karachi service until mid-February 1947, dropping it for commercial reasons.[131] With BOAC's withdrawal, use of the route was limited to charter flights by a variety of operators, which continued into the early 1950s.[132] Aden itself was served, from October 1949, by Aden Airways, a BOAC subsidiary which provided service on BOAC's former Red Sea routes.[133]

The lack of sufficient civilian use, particularly after BOAC pulled out, led to a refusal by the new Ministry of Civil Aviation to pay for the continued staffing of the airfields. RAF reluctance to pick up the expenses was outweighted by its desire to keep the airfields ready for future contingency use. As a consequence, nearly all the airfields were reduced to a care-and-maintenance basis or abandoned during the late 1940s.[134]

Socotra was completely shut down. A landing ground had been built on the island early in 1940, abandoned during the Italian threat, and then resurrected in 1942 and used for the rest of the war for anti-submarine patrols and convoy escorts. However, its isolation, long monsoon season and lack of harbour rendered it unsuitable for strategic requirements after the war. Riyan, just outside Mukalla in the Eastern Aden protectorate, had been important for ferrying, ASW and escorting throughout nearly all the war. With the end of hostilities, Riyan was reduced to care-and-maintenance status, and was used by infrequent civil aircraft as an emergency landing ground and also by the RAF, who maintained it for its utility in operations in the protectorate until final withdrawal in the mid-1960s.

The situation regarding Salala and Masira was more complicated, since they were located in the Sultanate of Muscat and Oman. The facilities had expanded from emergency landing grounds in the 1930s to extensive wartime bases — the wartime population of Masira exceeded 700, including British, Americans, Indians, Baluch, Pathans, and Omanis from Muscat; this does not count the tribal population, most of which had departed.[135] This explosion in size and function had been negotiated with the sultan on a wartime basis and the transition to peacetime usage was problematic, apart from the negotiation of a civil air agreement. The proposal had been raised in 1944 for outright purchase of Masira, or its exchange for the nearby Kuriya Muriya Islands (a crown possession since 1854) — but these ideas were eventually rejected. Both RAF stations were put on care-and-maintenance status, along with Riyan, in April 1946. In later years, the importance of Masira increased with its inclusion in East-of-Suez staging schemes, and both it and Salala were instrumental in fighting the Dhufari rebels in the 1960s and 1970s.[136]

Continued utilisation of Khormaksar, on the other hand, was never in doubt, since it was situated within Aden colony and provided a necessary component in the defence of Aden and the protectorate as well as an important link in the strategic route to the Far East. The landing ground at al-Shaykh 'Uthman had been established in 1936 and it was utilised during the war as a staging post for ferrying operations, being used primarily by the USAAF since 1943. After the war, it was reduced to a care-and-maintenance role and then, because of its satellite status to nearby Khormaksar and location in the territory of the Sultan of Lahj, was completely abandoned at the end of 1947.

Similar arrangements had been made with the RAF facilities along the Arab Gulf littoral. Regular use of the aerodrome at Muharraq in Bahrain was retained, partly because the PRPG moved his headquarters to Bahrain in 1947 and partly because of increasing regular civil use. Sharjah was reduced to a care-and-maintenance function after the war, but figured more importantly with the Buraimi crisis of the early 1950s, the rebellion in Oman in the mid-1950s and the British withdrawal from Iraq in 1958.

Emergence of Anglo–American Rivalry

As noted at various places above, Allied military involvement in the Peninsula during the war included American forces as well as British. This was particularly true for the resupply of the Soviet Union through the Gulf, and in ferrying and transport operations to the Far East through the Gulf and South Arabia. The British cocoon around the Peninsula had been pierced earlier by American oil companies, but the war allowed far more significant American penetration, including official representatives in Dhahran. British suspicions were raised that American involvement in the region, once initiated, would be permanent.

In the Gulf, the US held an airfield at Abadan in Iran, in connection with the Persian Gulf Command, and made use of airfields at Habbaniya, Basra and Shaiba in Iraq for reinforcement activities, as well as Bahrain and Sharjah.[137] In return for provision of some rifles, machine guns and lorries to the ruler of Muscat, the US was granted permission to use facilities and erect buildings at Salala, Masira and Ra's al-Hadd, and to station aircraft formations at those places.[138]

Along the South Arabian route, the US Transport Command took over formal control of the RAF station at al-Shaykh 'Uthman in the summer of 1943, and incurred considerable expense in improving the facilities, granted for use as long as the airfield was required as a main staging post for reinforcing. The British, however, were careful to make sure that RAF personnel remained continuously at the station and to reserve the right to take over again in case of military necessity. The United States also established transport and reinforcement facilities at Perim Island, Riyan, Salala and Masira. Minor construction was undertaken at Riyan, but at Salala the US built an administration building, domestic accommodation and a bulk petrol installation.[139]

These facilities were granted with great reluctance by the British, who jealously guarded their exclusive presence in this sphere of influence. Establishment of a Pan Am Airways service between Khartoum and Karachi (under a direct contract with the US War Department for carrying military personnel and cargo), the stationing of Pan Am personnel at Masira and Salala, and Pan Am carriage of US mail instead of BOAC, were all strongly resisted, for fear of granting *de facto* postwar rights along the route.[140]

The British also resisted an American presence along the Arab littoral in the Gulf. While HMG permitted the stationing of an American naval observer in Bahrain briefly in early 1941, a request for a consulate there was turned down by the India Office, fearing the effect it would have on requests by other, particularly Arab, states.[141] The RAF also chafed over USAAF use of the Muharraq aerodrome, declaring that the heavier US aircraft caused considerable damage to the runways, and attempted to ban their use. While the US prevented this, pointing out that Bahrain was the only suitable airport between Karachi and Abadan, it began to search for its own airfields in nearby Saudi Arabia.[142] When in 1944 the US asked for additional facilities in Sharjah, the British agreed to provide the landing grounds and necessary buildings, but decided to construct them to American requirements rather than allow the US to build and thus establish a permanent position there.[143]

One effect of these suspicions of American inroads in a British preserve was the American choice to seek suitable installations in Saudi Arabia, thereby contributing to the undermining of British influence in that country. Faced with the first request in March 1944, Britain initially advised the Saudi king to grant permission only for the duration of the war — and then only for military use. But by the time the US air base was finally completed at Dhahran, the war had ended and US civil carriers began to operate from its runways. The British defeat was not limited to the Dhahran airfield, but also encompassed the Saudi government's rejection of British military equipment and training teams in favour of American ones.[144] The ascendancy of American influence in Riyadh at the expense of the British position prompted the bitter remark of His Majesty's ambassador in 1952 that 'practically the only thing we now have to offer the Saudis is diplomatic advice, and such show of force as we can muster is on the whole antipathetic to them. The Americans on the other hand have luxury, wealth and modernisation to offer and their show of force is in general considered beneficial to Saudi Arabia.'[145]

Strategic Planning for a New Enemy

With the imminent defeat of the Axis powers, British strategic planing turned to postwar responsibilities and interests. The Middle East was seen as a region of continuing importance to the British empire in the postwar era, just as it had been for the previous three decades.

> The Middle East is . . . a region of life-and-death consequences for Britain and the British Empire in four ways: (a) as an indispensable channel of communications between the Empire's Western, Eastern and Southern territories; (b) as a strategic centre, control of which would enable an enemy to disrupt and destroy a considerable part of the British Imperial system and to deprive Britain herself of many supports and resources essential to her status and influence as a major power; (c) as the Empire's main reservoir of mineral oil; (d) as a region in which British political method must make good, if the British way of life is to survive. The vital importance of these four considerations has been established by hard experience in both world wars.[146]

Along with Western Europe, the Iberian Peninsula and India, the Middle East was considered as a strategic area where continued

British influence was necessary in order to defend adequately the four cornerstones of British interests in the UK, the American continent, Southern Africa and Australia.[147]

Major reviews of British defence planning in 1946 revolved around the principal threat of potential war with the Soviet Union. In this scenario, the Middle East's importance increased, both because of the assumption that the Soviet Union continued to desire expansion southward into the region and because the Middle East offered the only base from which to attack vital Soviet industrial and oil-producing areas. In case of war, then, it was deemed to be of great strategic importance to hold the Middle East in order: (1) not to prejudice the security of the UK, the other main support areas of the Commonwealth and the communications between them; (2) to retain the necessary air bases from which to assume the offensive and attack areas vital to the enemy; (3) to secure essential oil supplies; and (4) to deny the Soviet Union the means of securing its most vulnerable flank and also of establishing a formidable base from which to attack the main British support areas.[148]

Wartime requirements to defend the communications routes and the vital oil supplies of the Northern Gulf from a Soviet advance were seen to include operational naval bases at Alexandria and Aden, with advanced bases at Tobruk, Haifa, Port Sudan, Bahrain and Masira Island. Land forces would be concentrated in Palestine, with reserve formations in Egypt. Egypt would be central to air forces, both to defend Egypt and its communications and to provide bases for the strategic bomber force, while air forces in Palestine would support land operations.

In order to fulfil these wartime imperatives, peacetime requirements revolved around maintaining a predominant British political position in the Middle East, to keep the Arab world out of the Soviet orbit, while placing a minimum nucleus of military forces there. Ideally, these would include: naval forces based on Malta, Aden and Ceylon; the use of Palestine as the core of land defences, with a strategic reserve based either in Kenya or Cyrenaica; and fighter forces based in Palestine and Cyrenaica, from where they could be moved forward to Egypt in an emergency; and strategic bomber forces based in Cyrenaica.[149] Iraq, with its RAF bases at Habbaniya and Shaiba, would naturally prove important in defending British oil assets.

The difficulty with Iraq, as it was to prove elsewhere in the Middle East, was that existing arrangements concerning bases were becoming increasingly unpalatable to Arab governments.[150] Already by 1947, Egypt had to be removed from planning for peacetime deployments. As the fighting grew more intense in Palestine, that area's usefulness decreased and, of course, disappeared completely with the independence of Israel in 1948. Aden, long assigned to a marginal role because of its geographic isolation and great distance from the rest of the Middle Eastern theatre, began to assume increasing strategic significance as other locations were denied to the British.

The Middle East continued to be of central importance to the RAF, as it already had been long before the war.[151] In the latter stages of the war, it was considered that

> The Middle East would always be the station for a permanent powerful Air Force, because of the necessity for a secure hold there in the general scheme of Imperial security. This necessity arises not only from the importance of the Imperial lines of communication through, and British interests in, the theatre, but also from the fact that the Middle East is an ideal base for the positioning of strategic air power reserves, which can be moved east or west as required.[152]

At the end of the war, the AHQs in the Middle East were Eastern Mediterranean, British Forces in Aden, East Africa, Iraq and Persia, Levant and Egypt, with an additional RAF station in Khartoum.[153] Yet the RAF was not to escape the same problems of relocation as other British forces in the Middle East faced during the postwar era.

At the same time, it became increasingly clear that anticipated British wartime objectives in the Middle East could not be realised without American assistance. 'Even allowing for the timely arrival of the Americans, it might still not be possible to hold the oil-fields at the head of the Persian Gulf . . . We consider, therefore, that it should be a definite part of our policy to associate the United States in the defence of the Middle East oil-fields.'[154] Co-operation between the UK and the US in the Arabian Peninsula became more evenhanded as Britain was forced to seek American assistance in acquiring permission for contingency use of Saudi facilities. Still, the fear that granting the US military rights in the Gulf and Southern Arabia would lead to a sharing of political control was almost impossible to suppress.[155] The one concession that Britain made was to allow the homeporting of the US Navy's small Middle East Force in Bahrain, beginning in 1949.

The era between the world wars had firmly established the Arabian Peninsula within the orbit of British influence. In three short decades, the Peninsula had acquired central strategic importance to Britain for its communications routes and oil, and had further proved its value during the Second World War. Yet by the end of this short period, British ability to control the Peninsula and the neighbouring region was already waning. The subsequent era, even shorter at two decades, was marked by a steady decline of British influence in the Middle East and, simultaneously, greater reliance on bases in the Peninsula and Gulf and then the abandonment of those facilities. While the interwar period could be termed a time of 'air power and empire' in the Arabian Peninsula, British activities in the postwar years were steadily reduced to tidying up the detritus of imperial entanglements.

Notes

1. Address to the Royal Central Asian Society, June 1949; cited in Olaf Caroe, *The Wells of Power: The Oil-Fields of South-Western Asia* (London, Macmillan, 1951), p. 184.

2. Eric Macro, *Yemen and the Western World Since 1571* (London, C. Hurst, 1968), pp. 43–6. The Royal Air Force was formed in 1918 by the merger of the RNAS with the Royal Flying Corps.

3. Ibid., p. 64.

4. AIR/5/433, 'Note by Mr. Webster on Policy re Native Aviation in Arabia', 24 May 1926.

5. Ibid.

6. David Holden and Richard Johns, *The House of Saud* (New York, Holt, Rinehart & Winston, 1982), p. 104; FO/371/13727, various correspondence.

7. FO/371/14454, E5479/2/91, Air Vice-Marshal R. Brooke-Popham, Air Officer Commanding (AOC), Iraq Command, to the Secretary of State for Air, 23 September 1930.

8. FO/371/20840, various correspondence.

9. FO/371/20841, E4627/244/25, Squadron Leader Jope-Slade, Air Ministry, to George Rendel, Foreign Office, 6 August 1937, enclosing report by Squadron Leader Hindle-James.

10. D. H. Cole, *Imperial Military Geography*, 10th edn (London, Sifton Praed, 1950), pp. 178–9.

11. Discussion of the early stages of the Cairo–Karachi route relies on L/P&S/18/B414, Air Ministry, 'Air Communication in the Persian Gulf', 23 August 1928; H. Burchall, 'The Air Route to India', *The Journal of the Royal Central Asian Society* (*JRCAS*), vol. 14, pt 1 (1927), pp. 3–18; Robin Higham, *Britain's Imperial Air*

Routes, 1918–1939 (London, G. T. Foulis, 1960), pp. 108–33; John Marlowe, *The Persian Gulf in the Twentieth Century* (London, The Cresset Press, 1962), pp. 249–51; and AIR/19/131, R/15/2/263, R/15/6/108.

12. Higham, *Britain's Imperial Air Routes*, p. 111.

13. Marlowe, *Persian Gulf*, p. 249.

14. It seems surprising, given the political difficulties involved in the Persian route, that no consideration was given by either the Air Ministry or Imperial Airways to an Arabian alternative until forced to do so in 1931. A subsequent internal Foreign Office discussion concluded that transfer of the route had been the right decision politically even though the two shores were evenly balanced on technical grounds. As Assistant Under-Secretary of State Sir L. Oliphant put it, 'we moved to the Arab coast of the Persian Gulf, not just because the Persians didn't like our flights, but in order to be independent of Persian goodwill'. FO/371/17894, E5648/139/34, comments of 3 March 1935, on draft memorandum, 'Anglo–Persian Relations'.

15. In addition to Higham, *Britain's Imperial Air Routes*, and Marlowe, *The Persian Gulf in the Twentieth Century*, the following discussion of the Arabian littoral route relies on H. Burchall, 'The Political Aspect of Commercial Air Routes', *JRCAS*, vol. 20, pt 1 (1933), pp. 70–90; G. W. Bentley, 'The Development of the Air Route in the Persian Gulf', *JRCAS*, vol. 20, pt 2 (1933), pp. 173–89; Muhammad Morsy Abdullah, *The United Arab Emirates: A Modern History* (London, Croom Helm; New York, Barnes & Noble, 1978), pp. 48–57; Rosemarie Said Zahlan, *The Origins of the United Arab Emirates* (London, Macmillan, 1978), pp. 92–106; and AIR/5/1216–18.

16. Bentley, 'Development of the Air Route', details the squadron's work as including selecting sites for landing rounds and flying-boat anchorages, marking out landing grounds, laying moorings, installing tanks or other refuelling arrangements, arranging resthouses and erecting W/T stations.

17. Abdullah, *The United Arab Emirates*, pp. 49–51.

18. In early 1932, Yas Island (off the coast of Abu Dhabi) was proposed as an alternative night-stop for flying-boat service, apparently because it was technically suitable and did not seem to raise political questions. Although fuel tanks were installed for emergency use, Yas was never seriously considered as a main stop. AIR/5/1216, 'The Air Route Along the Arabian Shore of the Persian Gulf', 3 August 1930.

19. Zahlan, *Origins of the United Arab Emirates*, pp. 104–5. Other stops on the flying-boat route were Alexandria, Lake Galilee, Baghdad, Basra, Bahrain and Gwadar.

20. Although Gwadar was not a part of British India, it was politically suitable since it was a possession of the Muscat ruler.

21. The usefulness of the new service was extolled in an article in *The Times*, 13 September 1933, entitled 'By Air Mail to India: The Arabian Coast Route'.

22. L/P&S/18/B320, A. T. Wilson, 'The Use of Aeroplanes in Mesopotamia and the Persian Gulf', April 1919.

23. R. J. Gavin, *Aden Under British Rule, 1839–1967* (London, C. Hurst, 1975), pp. 281–2.

24. AIR/8/99, CID, Persian Gulf Sub-Committee, Interim Report, no. 169–D, October 1928.

25. Details of reconnaisance and preliminary arrangements along this section of the route are contained in R/15/6/86.

26. R/15/6/88 and R/15/6/86, various correspondence.
27. AIR/5/1269, 'Report on the Cruise of Two Flying Boats, No. 203 (F.B.) Squadron, Basra to Aden and Return' (1933).
28. Gavin, *Aden Under British Rule*, p. 282. The burst of activity surrounding the decision to establish the route seems to have inspired some Hadrami financiers to contemplate the development of a commercial air route to link Tarim, Mukalla, and Aden. The Sultan of Oman, upon hearing of these plans, suggested the route be extended to Salala. R/15/6/86, Bernard Reilly, Governor of Aden, to G. P. Murphy, Political Agent at Muscat, 5 April 1929. Nothing came of the scheme.
29. Gavin, *Aden Under British Rule*, p. 283.
30. A. E. Borton, 'The Use of Aircraft in Small Wars', *Journal of the Royal United Service Institution (JRUSI)*, vol. 65, no. 458 (May 1920), pp. 310–19.
31. John Bagot Glubb, 'Air and Ground Forces in Punitive Expeditions', *JRUSI*, vol. 71, no. 484 (November 1926), pp. 777–84. The author cautioned that there were certain disadvantages to the air weapon, such as the inability to inflict heavy damages in wooded or mountainous country or against nomadic peoples, the difficulty in identifying the enemy, and the inability of aircraft to force dedicated or disciplined enemies to surrender.
32. Borton, 'Small Wars', p. 314.
33. H. Montgomery Hyde, *British Air Policy Between the Wars, 1918–1939* (London, Heinemann, 1976), pp. 90–1. See also Malcolm Smith, *British Air Strategy Between the Wars* (Oxford, Clarendon Press, 1984).
34. Cited in Andrew Boyle, *Trenchard* (London, Collins, 1962), p. 383. For a personal account of Trenchard and the early years of the Air Ministry and the RAF by the long-serving Secretary of State for Air, see Samuel, Viscount Templewood (Sir Samuel Hoare), *Empire of the Air: The Advent of the Air Age, 1922–1929* (London, Collins, 1957).
35. Hyde, *British Air Policy*, pp. 90–5; Boyle, *Trenchard*, pp. 381–3; and Aaron S. Klieman, *Foundations of British Policy in the Arab World: The Cairo Conference of 1921* (Baltimore, Johns Hopkins University Press, 1970).
36. Peter Sluglett, *Britain in Iraq, 1914–1932* (London, Ithaca Press, for St Antony's College, Oxford, Middle East Centre, 1976), p. 4.
37. Ibid., p. 5.
38. L/P&S/18/B320, Wilson, 'Use of Aeroplanes in Mesopotamia and the Persian Gulf', April 1919. Bringing the three RAF squadrons up to strength at that time, Wilson argued, would allow a reduction of 50 per cent in the number of Indian troops stationed in Mesopotamia. He also advocated the stationing of a flight of airplanes at Bushire in the Gulf, on the same grounds of reducing ground troops. In fact, this step was taken soon after but the planes were returned to Iraq in autumn 1921. L/P&S/18/B414, 'Air Communications in the Persian Gulf'.
39. Salmond left Iraq in 1924 to become the first Air Officer Commanding-in-Chief of the Air Defences of Great Britain.
40. Detail of RAF activities in Iraq in the early 1920s is given in John Salmond, 'The Air Force in Iraq', *JRUSI*. vol. 70, no. 479 (August 1925), pp. 483–98; Hyde, *British Air Policy*, pp. 167–74; Sluglett, *Britain in Iraq*, pp. 259–72; and J. D. Lunt, 'Air Control: Another Myth?' *RUSI — Journal of the Royal United Service Institute for Defence Studies (RUSI)*, vol. 126, no. 4 (December 1981), p. 66–8.
41. 'It came to be almost an annual affair, this chase through the Kurdish mountains, and was therefore never conclusive, but it did keep the Kurds in their

66 Air Power and Empire in the Arabian Peninsula

place at relatively little cost.' Lunt, 'Air Control', p. 67.
  42. AIR/19/131, 'Report on Iraqi Administration, April 1922–Mar. 1923'.
  43. Sluglett, *Britain in Iraq*, p. 259.
  44. Committee of Imperial Defence, Minutes of 25 February 1927, quoted in Martin Gilbert, *Winston S. Churchill*, companion to vol. 5 (1922–39), pt 1 (London, Heinemann, 1980), p. 955.
  45. AIR/19/131, 'Use of the R.A.F. on the N. W. Frontier of India', n.d.
  46. AIR/5/1300, 'Aden Air Operations Summary', 1919–38.
  47. Hyde, *British Air Policy*, pp. 203–8.
  48. James Neidpath, *The Singapore Naval Base and the Defence of Britain's Eastern Empire, 1919–1941* (Oxford, Clarendon Press, 1981), pp. 92–4. On 12 December 1924, Churchill, then Chancellor of the Exchequer, wrote to Sir Samuel Hoare, Secretary of State for Air, arguing that 'There ought to be a large economy in using air power instead of submarines for this purpose,' and suggested that heavy bombing machines might be substituted for the proposed batteries of guns. 'If so, how much better to have this cost represented in mobile air squadrons rather than tied up forever to one spot in two heavy batteries.' See Martin Gilbert, *Winston S. Churchill*, vol. 5 (1922–39) (London, Heinemann, 1976), p. 72. For the text of the letter, see the companion to vol. 5, pt 1 (London, Heinemann, 1980), p. 300.
  49. In connection with the threat from the Imam, the Air Ministry had noted earlier that 'It is apparent that the present military garrison of Aden is entirely inadequate to undertake punitive measures which will restore the situation, and the Resident has stated that the aircraft of his Garrison form the only military weapon which he is able to employ beyond a one day's march from the Aden settlement.' Furthermore, the existing flight of aircraft at Aden was seen as clearly inadequate. AIR/9/55, 'Notes on the Permanent Garrison at Aden', 15 January 1926. RAF aircraft had been permanently stationed at Aden since 1920.
  50. R. A. Cochrane, 'The Work of the Royal Air Force at Aden', *JRUSI*, vol. 76, no. 501 (February 1931), pp. 92–5; Gavin, *Aden Under British Rule*, pp. 281–2; Boyle, *Trenchard*, p. 570; and C. G. Grey, *A History of the Air Ministry* (London, George Allen & Unwin, 1940), p. 204. The bombing of Sanr 'a' from Kamaran Island, then under British control but not sovereignty, was briefly raised and rejected because of expected international complications. AIR/9/55, note on 'Kamaran Island', 29 May 1930; AIR/8/99, CID, Persian Gulf Sub-Committee, meeting of 22 November 1928.
  51. Lord Ismay, *Memoirs* (New York, Viking Press, 1960), p. 60. Trenchard's argument is contained in AIR/9/55, Memorandum by the Chief of the Air Staff, 'The Garrison of Aden', February 1927.
  52. The expenses of forces in Aden totalled £479,000 for maintenance in 1927–8; in 1930, after the RAF had taken control, they were estimated at £340,000. AIR/9/55, unidentified note, 15 March 1930.
  53. The transfer of defence responsibilities followed the transfer of political responsibilities from the Government of India to the Imperial Government, represented by the Secretary of State for Colonies, in December 1926. The subsequent definition of functions is outlined in an India Office note on 'Aden and Its Administration', 1 April 1931, copy in AIR/9/55.
  54. Cochrane, 'Work of the Royal Air Force at Aden', p. 91.
  55. Gavin, *Aden Under British Rule*, p. 282.
  56. Cochrane, 'Work of the Royal Air Force at Aden', p. 98.

57. On the Ikhwan, see John S. Habib, *Ibn Sa'ud's Warriors of Islam: The Ikhwan of Najd and Their Role in the Creation of the Sa'udi Kingdom, 1910–1930* (Leiden, E. J. Brill, 1978); and Christine Moss Helms, *The Cohesion of Saudi Arabia: Evolution of Political Identity* (London, Croom Helm; Baltimore, Johns Hopkins University Press, 1981), pp. 127–50. See also Chapter 6. It should be noted that the question of whether Ibn Sa'ud was responsible for these raids or simply lacked control over the Ikhwan was somewhat confused, partly because of Ibn Sa'ud's employment of Ikhwan raids against British-controlled territory in earlier years.

58. On the RAF role in countering the Ikhwan raiding in Iraq and Transjordan, see Helms, *Cohesion of Saudi Arabia*, pp. 225–49; Clive Leatherdale, *Britain and Saudi Arabia, 1925–1939: The Imperial Oasis* (London, Frank Cass, 1983), pp. 93–135; John Bagot Glubb, *The War in the Desert: An R.A.F. Frontier Campaign* (London, Hodder & Stoughton, 1960); and idem, *Arabian Adventures* (London, Cassell, 1978). Glubb was one of the first SSOs to be appointed, although he was not from the RAF. He later served in the Iraqi civil administration and the Transjordanian armed forces, commanding the Arab Legion from 1939 to 1956. See also the reminiscences of Glubb and Air Chief Marshal Sir Alfred Earle about their experiences in the Middle East, as recorded by the Imperial War Museum, Department of Sound Records, 'Middle East: British Military Personnel 1919–1939'.

59. Much of the dispute had arisen from the 1922 Iraqi–Najdi agreement of 'Uqayr, which resulted in the creation of the Saudi–Iraqi and Saudi–Kuwaiti Neutral Zones and defined certain territory traditionally considered to be Kuwaiti as belonging to the Al Sa'ud. Later, Ibn Sa'ud imposed an economic blockade on Kuwait as a means of gaining a share of Kuwait's prosperity, derived from its role as an *entrepôt* for the surrounding hinterland. Helms, *Cohesion of Saudi Arabia*, pp. 243–4.

60. R/15/5/279, various correspondence.

61. Glubb, *Arabian Adventures*, p. 186. A final complication arose when many of the Ikhwan surrendered to RAF authorities in Kuwait. After considerable internal debate, HMG considered itself bound to turn them over to Ibn Sa'ud, which was done at the end of January 1930. A few weeks later, Ibn Sa'ud and King Faysal of Iraq met for the first time and an initial step was made towards burying the traditional enmity between the two royal houses. Ibid., pp. 186–93.

62. R/15/5/279, Dickson to H. V. Biscoe, PRPG, 18 February 1932.

63. R/15/2/269, various correspondence.

64. R/15/5/279, AHQ Iraq, Air Staff Instruction No. 10/46. The ASLO's area of concern consisted of the Arabian Peninsula coast from the Shatt al-'Arab to the boundary of the RAF's Iraq Command on the coast of Oman.

65. J. E. Peterson, *Oman in the Twentieth Century: Political Foundations of an Emerging State* (London, Croom Helm; New York, Barnes & Noble, 1978), pp. 126–8; and R/15/3/65, G. P. Murphy, 'Report on Sur', 9 October 1928. The Bani Bu 'Ali apparently also raised the Saudi flag over al-'Ayqa, thereby reviving a long-standing connection with the Al Sa'ud which dated to the latter's invasion of that part of Oman in the early nineteenth century and the conversion of the Bani Bu 'Ali to Wahhabism at that time. Peterson, *Oman in the Twentieth Century*, p. 153.

66. R/15/3/65, G. P. Murphy, 'Report on Sur', 9 October 1928.

67. AIR/9/57, 'Note on Possible Operations at Sur', 27 May 1930. The memorandum also suggested that Biscoe, the PRPG, 'has the usual complex about

resentment, bombs, mosques, women and children and if we can show him good photographs we shall have gained a useful friend'. A small naval bombardment had been carried out in November 1928, destroying a small fort behind Sur in order to 'impress tribesmen of intention of British to support Muscat and ability to do so'. Commander-in-Chief East Indies to Admiralty, 14 November 1928 (telegram), copy in AIR/9/57. But even the navy concluded that only occupation by British troops could bring an end to the situation.

68. AIR/9/57, T. C. Fowle, Political Agent in Muscat, to Wing Commander McClaughry, n.d.

69. AIR/2/1612, various correspondence.

70. CAB/24/207, 'The Fuller Employment of Air Power in Imperial Defence', CP 322 (29); cited in Hyde, *British Air Power*, pp. 230–1. Elizabeth Monroe contends that the 1929 rebellion in Palestine reached serious proportions (requiring reinforcements from outside the mandate) because 'too much reliance had been placed on the Trenchard scheme of policing by means of the R.A.F.', thereby resulting in a reduction of the army garrison. *Britain's Moment in the Middle East, 1914–71*, 2nd edn (Baltimore, Johns Hopkins University Press, 1981), p. 81. However, Trenchard pointed out after the rebellion that the army had been responsible for the reduction of the garrison in Palestine, which he had opposed. Hyde, *British Air Policy*, p. 230.

71. Smith, *British Air Strategy*, p. 31.

72. As proposed by the Prime Minister on 25 June 1928, the composition of the sub-committee included Sir Austen Chamberlain, Secretary of State for Foreign Affairs; Lord Hailsham, Lord Chancellor of the Exchequer; L. S. Amery, Secretary of State for Dominion Affairs and Colonies; the Earl of Birkenhead, Secretary of State for India; Sir Samuel Hoare, Secretary of State for Air; W. C. Bridgeman, First Lord of the Admiralty; Sir Philip Cunlifee-Lister, President of the Board of Trade; Viscount Peel, First Commissioner of Works; and Lt Colonel Sir M. P. A. Hankey, Secretary to the CID, and Major H. L. Ismay, the Assistant Secretary. The minutes of the sub-committee are contained in CAB/16/93 and its memoranda in CAB/16/94. An interim report of the sub-committee (No. 169–3, October 1928), incorporating the points made by the Chiefs of Staff, cited below, was approved by the cabinet on 5 November [Cabinet 41 (28)].

73. CAB/16/94, 'The Use of Air Power as Illustrated by the Recent Operations in Arabia', 8 May 1928; printed as Cabinet Paper 160 (28).

74. In addressing the 'problems' Trenchard suggested that their reoccurrence could be prevented by closer co-operation between the AOC and local authorities, improved intelligence for air operations, more latitude given local authorities in initiating air action, and great independence given air authorities in carrying out operations without recourse to the other services. As a final point, he noted the complications of fragmented political control and argued that a single department be given responsibility for the Peninsula, Iraq and Transjordan — and even went so far as to suggest that the India Office and Government of India relieve themselves of their responsibilities in Arabia. Ibid.

75. AIR/9/57, 'Note on the Recent Incident at Sur, as Illustrating the Futility of the Methods of Control of the Arab Littoral as Proposed by Sir Denys Bray and the Government of India and the Political Significance of Incidents of this Nature', 3 December 1928.

76. One enduring result of the sub-committee's work was the publication for

official use of a 'Historical Summary of Events in Territories of the Ottoman Empire, Persia and Arabia Affecting the British Position in the Persian Gulf, 1907-1928' (CID, PGSC, Memorandum PG 13). This comprehensive 170-page document essentially brought up to date the earlier efforts of J. G. Lorimer's *Gazetteer of the Persian Gulf*.

77. CAB/16/93, CID, PGSC, Minutes of the 5th Meeting, 24 October 1928; copy in AIR/8/99. The Chiefs of Staff judged, in addition to the above-quoted conclusion, that 'although the source of the potential dangers to our interests has changed, the dangers remain; and with the advent of air power, they have increased rather than diminished'. In particular, they suggested such measures to maintain supremacy as prevention of the establishment by any foreign power of a naval base in the Gulf, the exclusion — as far as possible — of foreign air undertakings within striking distance of the Gulf, the retention of sufficient harbour facilities for the navy, the securing of strategic and civil air routes along the shores of the Gulf, and maintenance of the political status quo in the Gulf, particularly along the Arabian littoral. CAB/16/94, CID, PGSC, Memorandum P.G. 12, 'The Persian Gulf; Report by the Chiefs of Staff', 11 October 1928.

78. CAB/16/93, CID, PGSC, Minutes of 5th Meeting, 24 October 1928.

79. Ibid.

80. CAB/16/94, CID, PGSC, 'Memorandum by the Secretary of State for the Colonies', P.F. 29, 16 November 1928. While expressing sympathy with Trenchard's desire to reduce the number of departments involved in Middle Eastern consultations, Amery noted that 'Occurrences in Iraq and Arabia, apparently trivial in themselves, frequently have important repercussions in India and in Europe,' thus requiring the interest of the Foreign and India Offices. He also declined to second the recommendation that the Colonial Office take over administration of the Gulf states.

81. CAB/18/93, CID, PGSC, Minutes of 8th Meeting, 22 November 1928.

82. Trenchard had begun with a remark on Bray's observation that India's special position in the Gulf was due to its proximity: 'That was quite true in the past; but the position was now completely reversed. Formerly, the route to the Gulf was via India; whereas at the present time, the quickest route to India was via the Gulf.' CAB/16/93, CID, PGSC, Minutes of 9th Meeting, 18 March 1929.

83. Ibid.

84. CAB/16/93, CID Paper 175-D (August 1930), containing the cabinet conclusions of meetings held on 23 July 1930 [Cabinet 44 (30)] and 30 July 1930 [Cabinet 46 (30)], held to consider the 'Report of the Sub-Committee on Political Control in the Persian Gulf', CID Paper 174-D (December 1929); Copy in AIR/8/99.

85. One incongruous result of this proposal was the opposition of the AOC Iraq, who pointed out the necessity of these ships for the defence of Basra and the south Persian oilfields. L/P&S/12/3727, Air Vice-Marshal E. R. Ludlow-Hewitt to the High Commissioner, Baghdad, 15 January 1932.

86. L/P&S/12/3727, H. V. Biscoe to F. V. Wylie, Deputy Secretary (Foreign) to the Government of India, 24 November 1931. Biscoe's note was generated in response to a note by the Indian Foreign Secretary, E. B. Howell, on the same subject.

87. Ibid. Despite this conclusion, however, Biscoe voiced his opinion that the problem of Gulf policy being controlled from Whitehall but administration from India could be solved by placing all responsibility in the hands of the Secretary of State for India.

88. L/P&S/12/3747, Fowle to Foreign Secretary, Government of India, 16 November 1934; copy in AIR/2/1612. Fowle served as PRPG for an extraordinarily lengthy period, from 1932 to 1939, and exercised perhaps the most influence of any Resident since Sir Percy Cox, who had held the position from 1904 until after the beginning of the First World War. For an assessment of Fowle's impact on British policy in the Gulf, see Zahlan, *The Origins of the United Arab Emirates*, pp. 173–9.

89. AIR/2/1612, Air Headquarters, British Forces in Iraq, to the Secretary of State for Air, 'Policy in the Persian Gulf', 18 December 1934, commenting on Fowle's letter cited in previous note.

90. AIR/2/1612, CID, Standing Official Sub-Committee for Questions Concerning the Middle East, Minutes of the 42nd Meeting, 24 September 1935.

91. Ibid. The remarks belonged to G. W. Rendel, Counsellor, Foreign Office.

92. The first Political Officer was assigned to the Trucial Coast in 1939. Reference was also made to the formal letter of protection provided the ruler of Qatar in 1935, given partly as a means of securing co-operation on the oil concession and partly as a warning to Ibn Sa'ud. See Rosemarie Said Zahlan, *The Creation of Qatar* (London, Croom Helm; New York, Barnes & Noble, 1979), pp. 76–9.

93. AIR/2/1612, Minute from R. Peck to the Deputy Chief of the Air Staff, 25 October 1935.

94. L/P&S/12/3727, Fowle to Sir Aubrey Metcalfe, Foreign Secretary to the Government of India, 18 January 1937.

95. AIR/2/1615, Fowle to Metcalfe, 17 March 1939.

96. L/P&S/12/3727, T. C. Fowle, Political Resident in the Persian Gulf, to J. C. Walton, India Office, 18 January 1938, copy in CAB/104/71.

97. CAB/104/71, Record of an informal discussion held at the India Office on 14 April 1938; L/P&S/12/3727, W. A. Coryton, Air Ministry, to R. T. Peel, India Office, 3 May 1938; and CAB/104/71, CID, Overseas Defence Committee, 'Persian Gulf: Defence Schemes for the Arab Side', ODC Minute 344, 14 June 1939.

98. CAB/104/71, H. Weightman, Office of the PRPG, to Air Vice-Marshal C. L. Courtney, AOC British Forces in Iraq, 4 August 1938.

99. L/P&S/12/3727, CID, Oil Board, Minutes of 36th Meeting, 11 April 1938. The other two sources were Trinidad and Rangoon. It was not surprising, then, that the visit of a Japanese supply ship to Bahrain in February 1938 was regarded as an attempt to gain knowledge of the precise location of the oilfields and refinery for an attack. L/P&S/12/3727, CID, Oil Board, 'The Importance of Oil Supplies from Bahrein', Paper OB 245, March 1938.

100. L/P&S/12/3727, various correspondence.

101. CAB/104/228, War Cabinet, W. P. (43) 301, 'British Policy in the Middle East', Memorandum by the Secretary of State for Foreign Affairs, 12 July 1943.

102. Ibid.

103. Ibid.

104. S. Woodburn Kirby *et al.*, *The War Against Japan*, vol. 1 (*History of the Second World War*, UK Military Series, ed J. R. M. Butler; London, HMSO, 1957), p. 234 n4.

105. The USAAF directed between 10 and 70 aircraft monthly along this route during 1942–3, while RAF usage was significant only between December 1942 and March 1943. AIR/24/2, Air Staff, AHQ, Aden, Operations Record Book (1940–3).

106. Three Italian submarines were captured or sunk, another was grounded, and the remaining four were recalled to Bordeaux in May 1941. All seven Italian

destroyers were put out of action by April 1941. Thereupon, the Red Sea was removed as a 'combat zone' until the arrival of German and Japanese submarines in 1944. See S. W. Roskill, 'Naval Operations in the Red Sea, 1940–41', *JRUSI*, vol. 102, no. 602 (May 1957), pp. 211–15.

107. CAB/80/4, COS (39) Memorandum 95, 'Long Range Reconnaissance in the Indian Ocean, Note by the Chief of the Air Staff', 10 October 1939. The entire Arabian Sea coast, from Perim to Sharjah, was turned over to Aden in November 1943. AIR/24/2, Air Staff, AHQ, Aden, Operations Record Book (1940–43), November 1943.

108. AIR/23/1151, Minutes of Conference held at HQ, RAF, ME, on GR Bases in Aden Command, 25 September 1944; and AIR/24/2, Air Staff, AHQ, Aden, Operations Record Book (1944–5), October 1944.

109. I. S. O. Playfair *et al.*, *The Mediterranean and Middle East* (*History of the Second World War*, UK Military Series, ed J. R. M. Butler; London, HMSO, 1957), vol. 1, p. 420; and CAB/21/1033, 'Despatch of Middle East Air Operations', by Air Chief Marshal Sir A. M. Longmore, C-in-C, RAF Middle East, 1 February 1941.

110. A 1937 evaluation of the Italian threat noted that Perim was vulnerable to shelling from Massawa and attack by either submarines or boats. AIR/2/2138, AOC British Forces in Aden, to the Secretary of State for Air, 8 September 1937.

111. CAB/80/21, COS (40), Memorandum No. 900, 4 November 1940, SNO Red Sea to C-in-C East Indies, 30 October 1940 (telegram). In his covering telegram to C-in-C Middle East, the C-in-C East Indies added that 'The Strength of forces in Egypt and Mediterranean Fleet rests ultimately on flow of supplies through Red Sea. The flow will be most seriously interrupted and reduced if facilities of Aden are denied to use or our shipping collected there suffers much damage.' Ibid.

112. CAB/79/1, War Cabinet, Chiefs of Staff Committee, Minutes of 53rd Meeting, 20 October 1939. RAF capabilities at Aden were later supplemented by units in Sudan and the South African Air Force in Kenya. Roskill, 'Naval Operations in the Red Sea', p. 212.

113. CAB/80/36, War Cabinet, Chiefs of Staff Committee, Memorandum No. 280, 'Defence Plan for the Gulf of Aden', 28 May 1942. The strategic importance of Socotra, despite its lack of a harbour and isolation during monsoons, was stressed as 'it commands the entrance to the Gulf of Aden and is a focal point in the maintenance of our sea communications with the Middle East, Persian Gulf and India.'

114. AIR/24/2, Air Staff, AHQ, Aden, Operations Record Book (1940–3).

115. CAB/21/1033, 'Despatch of Middle East Air Operations', by Air Chief Marshal Sir A. M. Longmore, C-in-C, RAF Middle East, 1 February 1941; and R/15/2/669, Political Agent, Bahrain, to PRPG, 19 October 1940.

116. A summary of the campaign is contained in CAB/106/626, Air Chief Marshal Sir Arthur Longmore, AOC-in-C, RAF Middle East, to the Secretary of State for Air, 24 November 1941. See also B. H. Liddell Hart, *History of the Second World War* (London, Cassell, 1970), pp. 121–7; and MacGregor Knox, *Mussolini Unleashed, 1939–1941: Politics and Strategy in Fascist Italy's Last War* (Cambridge, Cambridge University Press, 1982), pp. 150–7.

117. CAB/106/626, Air Chief Marshal Sir Arthur Longmore, AOC-in-C, RAF Middle East, to the Secretary of State for Air, 24 November 1941. Summaries of these raids and reconnaissance sorties are contained in AIR/24/2, Air Staff, AHQ, Aden, Operations Record Book (1940–3). The total strength of air force personnel in the Aden Command, as noted in the January 1943 report, was 184 officers and

2,308 other ranks.

118. See the deliberations of the War Cabinet's Subcommittee on the Control of Air Forces in Iraq (1941) in CAB/95/6. The Air Ministry resisted the change and the argument that India was not prepared at that time to provide aircraft and supplies for these forces carried the day. While the Chiefs of Staff Committee seconded this decision, General Sir Archibald Wavell, Commander-in-Chief, India, made the point that 'sooner or later the air forces in Iraq must come under the control of India'. CAB/79/14, War Cabinet, Chiefs of Staff Committee, COS (41) 319th Meeting 10 September 1941.

119. WO/106/5824, various correspondence.

120. See Majid Khadduri, *Independent Iraq: A Study in Iraqi Politics Since 1932* (London, Oxford University Press, for the Royal Institute of International Affairs, 1951), pp. 182–205; and Great Britain, Central Office of Information, *PAIFORCE: The Official Story of the Persia and Iraq Command, 1941–46* (London, HMSO, 1948), pp. 14–43.

121. AIR/23/1045, 'Meeting of the Sub-Committee of the Main Organisation Conference held at Air Command Post', n.d. (October 1943). At the same time, a suggestion was made to integrate the Aden and East African Commands but rejected, although the rank of their AOCs was downgraded.

122. AIR/23/1091 and AIR/23/1139, various correspondence.

123. On the Umm Qasr port and its political ramifications for Iraqi-Kuwaiti relations, see J. E. Peterson, 'The Islands of Arabia: Their Recent History and Strategic Importance', *Arabian Studies*, vol. 7 (1985); and Daniel Silverfarb, 'The British Government and the Question of Umm Qasr, 1938–1945', *Asian and African Studies*, vol. 16, no. 2 (July 1982), pp. 215–38.

124. A complete account of the supply route is contained in Great Britain, *PAIFORCE*.

125. T. H. Vail Motter, *The Middle East Theatre: The Persian Corridor and Aid to Russia (United States Army in World War II)* (Washington, Department of the Army, Office of the Chief of Military History, 1952), Appendix A. An anecdotal account by a participant in the US effort in Iraq and Persia is contained in Joel Sayre, *Persian Gulf Command: Some Marvels on the Road to Kazvin* (New York, Random House, 1945).

126. AIR/23/1051, 'Report on the Redeployment and Reorganisation of the Royal Air Force in the Mediterranean and Middle East, 2 May to 16 Oct. 1945'. In another indication of usage, Bahrain recorded 115 landings by RAF reinforcement aircraft and 109 by RAF transport aircraft between 15 November and 30 December 1944. AIR/23/1147, RAF Station Bahrain (1943–6).

127. R/15/6/80–85, various correspondence.

128. The number of troop transports using the route was recorded at 11 eastbound and 2 westbound in January 1946, 37 eastbound and 25 westbound in February and 2 eastbound and 25 westbound in March. None was recorded in April or May. AIR/24/1678, AHQ Aden, Operations Records Books (1946).

129. David Lee, *Flight from the Middle East: A History of the Royal Air Force in the Arabian Peninsula and Adjacent Territories, 1945–1972* (London, HMSO, 1980), p. 15.

130. L/P&S/12/3928, various correspondence. The British Overseas Airways Corporation was established on 24 November 1939, with the board members being appointed by HMG, which held all stock. BOAC operated during the war as a

service of the government, which financed its operations and determined its traffic. R/15/6/85, statement by A. W. Street, Permanent Under-Secretary of State for Air, 23 August 1942.

131. Stages along this route were Cairo, Luxor, Wadi Halfa, Khartoum, Asmara, Aden, Riyan, Salala, Masira and Karachi. R/15/6/85, BOAC timetable for 27 November 1946. A new weekly service was begun in early 1947 through the Gulf, with a stop at Bahrain. R/15/6/109, India Office to PRPG, 22 March 1947.

132. For example, approximately 26 charter flights were recorded during the period between early 1948 and May 1949. Operators included Mistry Airways (later India Overseas), Air Ceylon, Ethiopian Airlines, Chartair, Vickers, Petroleum Concessions Ltd, Indamer, and even Alaska Airlines. R/15/6/92–93, L/P&S/12/2058, and AIR/28/1077, various correspondence.

133. An account of the early years of this operation is contained in 'Aden Airways', *Port of Aden Annual 1952–53* (Letchworth, Herts, 1954).

134. Information on the status of the various airfields is obtainable in a number of Air Ministry files, particularly the Aden Command record books (AIR/24) and the appropriate station record books (AIR/28). See also AIR/20/7140, AIR/23/1120–1121, AIR/23/1147–1148, and AIR/23/1151.

135. Peterson, 'Islands of Arabia'.

136. Ibid.

137. FO/371/42607, Air Ministry, S.4 (C.S.), 'Airfields Conspectus relating to American War-time Occupation (or Use) of Airfields and Bases in British Territory and British Spheres of Influence', 18 August 1944 (draft).

138. FO/371/32385, PRPG to the Secretary of State for India, 17 August 1942.

139. FO/371/42607, Air Ministry, S.4 (C.S.), 'Airfields Conspectus relating to American War-time Occupation (or Use) of Airfields and Bases in British Territory and British Spheres of Influence', 18 August 1944 (draft).

140. FO/371/32385, various correspondence. With perhaps a tinge of irony, the Political Agent's Muscat Intelligence Summary for 16–30 June 1944 noted that the sultan preferred to travel by American aircraft rather than BOAC, perhaps because the Americans carried him for free while BOAC charged him. L/P&S/12/2039.

141. FO/371/34093, E. W. R. Lumby, India Office, to A. A. Dudley, Foreign Office, 10 September 1943.

142. AIR/23/1147, various correspondence.

143. FO/371/42607, Sir James Ross, Air Ministry, to Engineer in Chief, War Office, 8 August 1944.

144. The British side of this topic is covered in CAB/80/93, War Cabinet, Chiefs of Staff Committee, Memorandum 203, 'American Proposal for Building a Military Airfield at Dhahran, Note by the Chief of the Air Staff', 23 March 1945; and in the correspondence in FO/371/75525 and R/15/2/523. On the origins of the US military involvement with Saudi Arabia, see Chapter 6.

145. FO/371/98828, G. C. Pelham, Jidda, to the Secretary of State for Foreign Affairs, 17 December 1952.

146. CAB/104/228, Middle Eastern Defence Committee, 'Imperial Security in the Middle East', undated (c. late May 1945). This opinion seconded the view advanced in 1942 that 'Our particular interests in the Middle East may be defined in general terms as communications and oil, though it is probable that other important economic interests might be brought to light.' CAB/95/1, War Cabinet, Middle East Official Committee, Military Sub-committee, Memorandum M.S.C. (42) 3, 'Post-

War Strategic Requirements — Middle East', undated. For a detailed discussion of British policy in the Middle East following the Second World War, with emphasis on the pivotal role of Ernest Bevin (Foreign Secretary in the Labour government of 1945–51) in determining that policy, see William Roger Louis, *The British Empire in the Middle East, 1945–51: Arab Nationalism, the United States, and Postwar Imperialism* (Oxford, Clarendon Press, 1984).

147. CAB/21/2086, Chiefs of Staff Committee, Joint Planning Staff, J.P. (46) 45 (Revised Final), 'Strategic Position of the British Commonwealth, Report by the J.P.S.', 31 March, 1946. For an analysis of the American view of the new Soviet threat, see Bruce Robellet Kuniholm, *The Origins of the Cold War in the Near East* (Princeton, Princeton University Press, 1980).

148. CAB/21/2086, Cabinet, Defence Committee, D.O. (46) 80, 'British Strategic Requirements in the Middle East, Report by the Chiefs of Staff', 18 June 1946.

149. Ibid.

150. CAB/21/2086, Chiefs of Staff Committee, Joint Planning Staff, J.P. (47) 130. 'Middle East — Brief for Discussion', 26 September 1947.

151. In January 1937, out of the 27 RAF squadrons stationed abroad, 14 were in Egypt, Palestine and Iraq. Cole, *Imperial Military Geography*, p. 187.

152. AIR/23/1051, Air Chief Marshal Sir Guy Garrod, C-in-C RAF, MEDME, 'Report on the Redeployment and Reorganisation of the Royal Air Force in the Mediterranean and Middle East', 15 October 1945.

153. Ibid.

154. CAB/21/2086, Cabinet, Defence Committee, D.O. (46) 80, 'British Strategic Requirements in the Middle East, Report by the Chiefs of Staff', 18 June 1946.

155. Discussion of the American role in defending the Arabian Peninsula after the war is contained in CO/537/4131, various correspondence.

3 Postwar Policy: British Retreat and Imperial Vestiges

Britain's continued military presence East of Suez for nearly a quarter of a century beyond the Second World War in many ways seems to run against the prevailing economic and political logic of Britain's reduced circumstances after the war. While the loss of India logically should have dictated a rundown of the defence establishment in the Indian Ocean in short order, instead the prewar apparatus was resurrected and the region came to be one of the last principal areas where British defence capabilities were extended out of the North Atlantic/European theatre.[1]

There were a number of compelling arguments for retrenchment from overseas obligations, including those East of Suez. Perhaps the most permanent of these was Britain's economic difficulties, particularly acute after the war but more or less continuing up to the present. In his *The Rise and Fall of British Naval Mastery*, Paul M. Kennedy clearly demonstrates the economic underpinnings of the decline of the once-invincible British navy to less than a 'good second-class navy'. His observations are directed at the navy but they are just as applicable to the entire nexus of the British defence dilemma:

> For maritime strength depends, as it always did, upon commercial and industrial strength: if the latter is declining relatively, the former is bound to follow. As Britain's naval rise was rooted in its economic advancement, so too its naval collapse is rooted in its steady loss of economic primacy. We have come full circle.[2]

Concomitantly, as Britain's Gross National Product fell behind that of its wartime adversaries, its defence spending declined steadily in proportion to social expenditures while the cost of military equipment skyrocketed. Nevertheless, for reasons explained below, the costs of an East-of-Suez presence were never thoroughly debated until severe economic straits in the 1960s finally meant that it could not be avoided.

A second argument for retrenchment was a shift in strategic

emphasis following the war. Closer bonds to Western Europe were perceived as necessary and were steadily growing, while the emerging Soviet threat seemed to be poised first at Europe. The Common Market and NATO membership served to reinforce the European emphasis. At the same time, there was widespread belief that any war in which Britain would be involved was likely to be total war and quite possibly nuclear. The latter prospect radically changed the security equation, tending to refocus security attention on Europe and the British homeland. The introduction of the nuclear factor into the East–West confrontation initiated a continuing debate on the proper defence posture. On the one hand, there was the necessity of developing a nuclear deterrent to defend what had become an extremely small and vulnerable island. At the same time, however, there was also the need to maintain conventional forces capable of intervening anywhere in the world where an Eastern bloc threat appeared.

Over the next four decades, the involvement of British forces in such widespread contingencies as Palestine, Korea, Malaya, Kenya, Suez, Oman, Kuwait, Cyprus, Aden, North Borneo, Mauritius, Belize, Anguilla and the Falklands argued persuasively for the continuation of global conventional capabilities, despite economic stringencies. In addition, for reasons of pride and inter-service competition, the continued determination to play a global, as well as European, role provided a counterweight to the strategic de-emphasis of overseas defence commitments. This was particularly true for the navy, which had seen itself in a more imperial and global role than the other services before the war. Afterwards, it never developed an ability to argue for a navy suited to a conflict with the Soviets and consequently stressed a global police role as its *raison d'être*.[3] Revision of the strategic thinking on the role of warfare outside the resort to nuclear weapons, boosted greatly by the experience of a conventional war in Korea, contributed to this.

A third argument came to the fore early with Indian independence in 1947. The principal rationale for an imperial defence apparatus and an Indian Ocean presence disappeared although India remained a member of the Commonwealth. As Lord Curzon had observed years before,

> When India has gone and the great Colonies have gone, do you suppose that we can stop there? Your ports and coaling stations, your fortresses and dockyards, your Crown Colonies and protec-

torates will go too. For either they will be unnecessary as the tollgates and barbicans of an empire that has vanished, or they will be taken by an enemy more powerful than yourselves.[4]

The remaining British strongholds in the region had been acquired and then the effort made to defend them because of their strategic importance to India. The removal of India from the equation required a shift in security emphasis from defending India to fulfilling obligations to remaining colonial possessions, superseded by post-independence obligations. These commitments were costly, since Britain no longer received the income from the empire to cover the expenses of defending large parts of the globe.[5] Furthermore, the loss of India meant conscription was continued in Britain to cover the loss of Indian Army manpower and a new network of bases had to be found in the Middle East — even though these proved to be only temporary.

The principal reason for the continuing presence East of Suez, however, seemed to be inertia, a habit of thinking in terms of imperial and global responsibilities. Rather than relating defence arrangements to the process of decolonisation and scaling down, planning went forward on the basis that the British presence in the region naturally would be permanent. As Phillip Darby notes,

> Thus the defence system originally designed to safeguard the Indian empire was maintained through the fifties to secure what were thought to be Britain's interests and responsibilities in the Middle East, the Far East, and in Africa. And in the early sixties, when Britain's colonial empire had gone the way of the Indian empire, it was refashioned, and in some ways strengthened, to meet the requirements of the post-imperial order.[6]

In addition, three specific factors encouraging a continuing presence may be cited: (1) the difficulty of considering withdrawal when British forces were almost continually engaged in East-of-Suez contingencies; (2) the commitment of the three services to a world role, partly because of their imperial tradition and partly because of inter-service politics in an era of declining defence expenditures; and (3) the inability of British governments during this era to consider long-term implications of commitment in this region and make decisions accordingly.[7] The consequence was a continuing tension between the inevitable conclusion that Britain must leave and the compelling reasons to stay. The unsteady balance between these opposing forces and their respective proponents was periodically adjusted by crises of a political nature in London or of a military nature in the region.

Air Operations in Aden Protectorate

Aden quintessentially fits the description of one of those British strongholds originally acquired to protect the approaches and lines of communications to India. Yet Aden's importance remained and even increased after India's independence, particularly as the search intensified for new and replacement military bases in the Middle East and a suitable location from which to command the forces in the region. The consolidation of Britain's regional military forces in Aden at the end of the 1950s was shortlived, however, as financial stringencies at home and a guerrilla campaign in South Arabia combined to force evacuation from Aden in late 1967.

In the years before the Suez débâcle, British commitment in the Indian Ocean was a given assumption and not subjected to close analysis. Although it was undeniable that its overseas role had changed, the British military presence East of Suez was simply accepted and unquestioned. Three implicit considerations underpinned this presence. First, if Britain was in these places diplomatically, then it was felt that it had to be there militarily, despite the diminishing utility of military power to support diplomatic goals. Second, Britain's economic requirements made it seem logical that there should be military capabilities in proximity to the Gulf's oil-producing areas. A third consideration involved Britain's security interests. Communist ambitions were seen to be not only of local importance, but also affected the overall balance; thus in the Middle East, the potential Soviet threat was seen in terms of a conventional move south towards the Red Sea and the Gulf.[8]

British effectiveness in the Indian Ocean in the early postwar era was hampered by the lack of co-ordination between the separate service commands in the region and the need to find new bases. The regional headquarters of the army and the air force, covering both the Eastern Mediterranean and the Western Indian Ocean, were located in the Canal Zone, although their areas of responsibility were not the same. The navy, however, was divided for obvious reasons between a Mediterranean Command, based in Malta, and the East Indies station, based in Ceylon. The proposal in the late

1940s to consolidate regional operations in Kenya was opposed by the navy, as Mediterranean operations could not be controlled from there, and coolly received by the RAF. An interim regional headquarters was established in the Canal Zone in 1948, while plans called for its eventual relocation to Cyrenaica. The navy required the greatest adjustment, as the new Middle East Command incorporated the Mediterranean Fleet, remaining in Malta (along with the C-in-C Middle East), and a truncated East Indies station.[9]

The rise of nationalism in the Middle East meant that the withdrawal of the British military presence from such countries as Egypt and Iraq was inevitable. But there was no immediately satisfactory replacement for the extensive facilities in the Canal Zone. As Emmanuel Shinwell, the Secretary of State for War, expressed the problem in December 1949, 'The Canal Zone of Egypt remains our main base in the Middle East. There is no other suitable location for that base . . . if we have to abandon Egypt we must abandon our status in the Middle East altogether.'[10] Cyprus was suitable for the air force but the army required a mainland location. Kenya was too far away, particularly from the RAF's point of view, and later troubled by the Mau Mau rebellion. Cyrenaica lacked adequate port, water, industrial and manpower facilities. Transjordan (later Jordan) was strongly resisted by all the services, although the RAF later utilised airfields at 'Amman and Mafraq. That left Palestine: the advantages of the mandate included the air base at Lydda, the naval installations at Haifa, and the oil pipeline terminus and refinery also at Haifa, as well as the convenient location close to the Suez Canal and in the centre of the region. But Palestine also displayed insurmountable disadvantages. Arab–Jewish strife was emerging even before the war ended, and Jewish extremists blew up British military headquarters in Jerusalem's King David Hotel in 1946. Still, efforts to utilise Palestine ceased only with the announcement in 1947 that the Palestine Mandate would be abandoned.[11] As a consequence, Britain remained dependent on the Canal Zone base until Egyptian hostility after the 1952 revolution forced the decision to abandon it in 1954; withdrawal was completed early in 1956.[12]

Since developments in the Middle East, even before the Suez débâcle, were fast depriving Britain of potential bases, new emphasis was placed on the concepts of strategic reserve and air mobility. Ideally, such a policy would permit substantial savings in manpower and basing costs and would reduce political entanglements. This approach seemed particularly suited to the Middle East because of the diminishing British position there and the historical pre-eminence of the RAF in the region. Nevertheless, this strategy still required a chain of military bases and airfields, for deploying bomber forces and air trooping, and involved a commitment in ground forces to defend the bases.

In addition, the loss of facilities in Palestine, Egypt and Iraq, and then worsening political relations with many Arab states after Suez served to create an air barrier to the movement of equipment and personnel between the Mediterranean and the Indian Ocean. Thus, the perception deepened that the Mediterranean and the Indian Ocean constituted two separate theatres — and incidentally contributed to a coherence and integration in East-of-Suez strategic thinking, which finally could be divorced from other regional considerations. Aden, hitherto on the periphery of the regional security arrangements, began to move to centre stage in British military planning. Its strategic value had also been enhanced in 1951 when a large oil refinery was built in Aden to replace the huge complex at Abadan, under international boycott as a response to the Iranian government's nationalisation of the Anglo–Iranian Oil Company.

The closure of the Suez Canal after the Anglo–French–Israeli invasion (temporarily) added a sea aspect to the Middle Eastern strategic barrier and thus accelerated the expansion of East-of-Suez capabilities in Aden. The RAF presence in Aden had been strengthened at the end of 1956 and further expansion occurred in 1957 and 1958, prompted in part by increased dissident activities in the Aden protectorate and the rebellion in Oman. 'In the space of three years between 1956 and 1959, the strength of the RAF under the Commander, BFAP, had grown from one fighter squadron at Khormaksar and a handful of communications aircraft divided between Aden, Nairobi and Bahrein, into a force of some nine squadrons.'[13] A unified command — British Forces, Arabian Peninsula (BFAP) — was established in Aden in April 1958 and was upgraded in 1959 to conform with the growing strategic importance of the Arabian Peninsula and the western half of the Indian Ocean. For the first time, British forces in Aden reported directly to the Chiefs of Staff and not through the Mediterranean.[14]

The first decade following the Second World War had seen few changes in Aden. The protectorate still slumbered in near-total isolation, in increasing contrast to the bustling, modernising colony.

Neither the war nor the immediate postwar years had had any effect on the nature of Aden's local security problem. Security in the protectorate depended as always on the RAF, with assistance on the ground provided by either the Aden Protectorate Levies or the Government Guards. Just as before the war, extensive reliance was placed on the utility of air control in enforcing government sanctions, keeping peace between the tribes, and countering incursions from the imamate in the north. The regularity of occasions on which the RAF was called to perform is shown in Table 3.1.

However, both the effectiveness and the 'humaneness' of air control were being called into question. The Middle East, as well as the North-West Frontier, had long been the proving ground for the theory and practice of air control (as shown in the previous chapter) and its open terrain and the peripatetic nature of tribal relations with the authorities made it an ideal environment for air policing. With Iraqi independence in the 1930s and Indian independence in 1947, however, Aden was left as one of the last places where the policy was applied routinely. Aden's isolation before the war, and the presumed exigencies of wartime conditions, had precluded debate over the use of air policing in the protectorate.[15] After the war ended, however, the Colonial Office found itself repeatedly compelled to defend the practice.[16] The RAF not only maintained that air control was still a viable policy, but argued that rocket projectiles and aircraft cannon made it a more precise instrument.[17] A forward policy of stationing political officers in more remote areas of the protectorate and the need to protect them provided another argument for continued air action.[18]

The deterioration of security conditions in the Aden protectorate and a fresh round of RAF activities in the mid-1950s received considerable attention in London. Attacks on government forts by the Rabizi tribe in late 1953 and early 1954 displayed serious implications because of growing anti-British sentiment, backing from Yemen's imam, and the tenacity of the rebels in the face of repeated RAF attacks. The following year saw political disaffection spread to other areas of the protectorate and mutiny and desertion among the Aden Protectorate Levies. The result was a retreat from the forward policy of the previous years and the strengthening of efforts to counter the imam's activities.[19] Further air operations in 1955 were criticised in the House of Commons and a recrudescence of dissident activity supported from Yemen forced the introduction of an army battalion at Aden, where the only ground forces hitherto

Table 3.1: Summary of RAF Air Operations at Aden, 1940–9

Date	Against	Action taken[a]	Casualties
Jan. 1940	Bayhan and Wadi Markha district	O	None
April 1940	Qutaybi tribe	O	None
May 1940	Bin Abdat of al-Ghurfa	G	Unknown
May 1940	Irqa district	W	None
Mar. 1941	Depose and replace sultan at Shuqra	G	Unknown
June 1941	Shooting incident at Say'un	O	Unknown[b]
July 1941	Imam's forces occupying Dar al-Bayda	B	None
Nov. 1941	Bayhan tribe	W[c]	None
Mar. 1942	Abyan district	O	None
Mar. 1945	Surrender of Bin Abdat	B	Unknown
Jan. 1946	Western Subayhi tribe	W	None
Feb.–Mar. 1946	Fadli tribe	G	None
May–Sept. 1946	Amiri–Shayri dispute	O	None
Oct. 1946	Hawshabi–Dhambari dispute	W	None
Nov. 1946	Amiri–Shayri dispute	O	None
April 1947	Ahmadi tribe	B	None[d]
July 1947	Bal Harith tribe	B	1 RAF pilot; opposing casualties unknown
Nov. 1947	Qutaybi tribe	B	None
Feb. 1948	Bal Harith tribe	B	None
June 1948	Hujayli tribe	B	None
Aug. 1948	Saqladi tribe	B	1 RAF pilot killed and 1 navigator wounded; number of opposing casualties unknown
Oct. 1948	Mansuri tribe	B	None
Aug.–Sept. 1949	Imam's forces	B	None

Notes: (a) O = Overflight or no action taken; B = bombing carried out; G = action taken in support of ground forces; W = warnings dropped only. (b) Only casualties incurred as result of fighting between local parties. (c) After delivery of ultimatum by air, tribe agreed to demolition of 2 forts by RAF landing party. (d) Actions taken after British Political Officer was killed by tribesmen and his escort in turn killed several Ahmadis; apparently only material damage done to village when it was destroyed by aerial bombing.

Sources: AIR/24/2, Air Staff, AHQ, Aden, Operations Record Book (1940–3). AIR/2/4, Air Staff, AHQ, Aden, Operations Record Book (1944–5). AIR/2/10483, Aden Protectorate, Punitive Bombing Against Recalcitrant Tribes (1942–9).

had come from the RAF regiment and the Aden Protectorate Levies. The permanent presence of the battalion at Aden also meant that it was available for use elsewhere in the Arabian Peninsula and the Horn of Africa, without having to call upon the strategic reserve from Britain. The army assumed responsibility for protectorate security in 1957, although air policing activities continued into the early 1960s.[20]

Changing strategic requirements were fast creating overcrowded facilities in Aden, followed by a massive construction boom. But even as expansion was occurring in Aden, however, the seeds for eventual withdrawal were sprouting. A revolution in North Yemen in 1962 established the Yemen Arab Republic and introduced Egyptian troops to the Arabian Peninsula. Nasir provided considerable stimulus and support to dissidents in Aden Colony and Protectorate, where nationalist parties opposed to the British presence had already begun to appear.

Evolving Commitments and the Oman War

British participation in the 1956 invasion of the Suez Canal was unquestionably a tremendous débâcle, particularly as it affected Britain's relations with the Arab world — and thus its military presence in many Arab states. Its effect on strategic thinking was somewhat paradoxical. On the one hand, there was an instinctive feeling that all Britain's spending on conventional forces had gone for nought — they might as well be got rid of and the money could be spent more wisely on nuclear defence. This seemed to be the message of the 1957 Sandys White Paper, which stressed a nuclear priority, smaller but more mobile conventional forces, an eventual end to conscription and cuts in defence expenditure.[21]

At the same time, however, it was held by others that the poor showing in military terms at Suez was due to the starving of conventional forces. By this view, the lesson of Suez was that Britain needed to upgrade its forces and mobile capability, since its overseas commitments would require British assistance for some time to come. This opinion not only tied in with government statements since 1954, but was reinforced by service lobbying. In addition to the army and air force, the navy began for the first time to show interest in the concept of limited war and the utility of light carriers; after the 1957 White Paper it became a leading advocate of a continued East-of-Suez role for Britain.[22]

The government sought to balance the opposing views by placing more emphasis on a nuclear umbrella, even for the Far East, and at the same time relying heavily on the potential of an airlifted strategic reserve. As a consequence, strategic mobility became an integral part of British defence policy from the late 1950s through the economic collapse of 1967, and the concept was put to the test in the Arabian Peninsula during the Oman and Kuwait crises.[23] Despite the considerable logic of strategic mobility, the concept also contained real limitations which were largely overlooked. Manned and protected bases around the world were required as much as ever, in addition to considerable investment in strategic lift capability. In addition, the emergence of an air barrier across the Middle East as a result of growing nationalism and especially the Suez débâcle presented problems. Alternative routes had the disadvantage of additional length and both political and technical drawbacks, and the barrier meant that at least part of the strategic reserve had to be physically located East of Suez.[24] To some extent, a sea barrier came into existence as well when control of the Suez Canal passed to Egypt.

A key effect of Suez and the emerging air barrier was to stimulate consideration of the East-of-Suez arena as an independent theatre of operations on its own merits and to open up British strategic debate from sole concentration on a potential total war to fighting limited wars (half-wars). The weakness of the newly independent states of the Indian Ocean basin virtually guaranteed British involvement in local insurgencies, as happened in Malaya and Kenya in the 1950s. Effective response to such low-level conflicts required the development of appropriate force structures and strategies.

The appearance of a rebellion in Oman in the late 1950s very effectively illustrated the problems Britain would face in fulfilling its regional obligations. First the Oman campaign demonstrated the limitations of air power and the need to use ground forces to concentrate insurgents before air operations could be of use. The experience in Oman also strengthened the case for expanding airlift capacity, as well as for the commando carrier project, and it emphasised the need for stationing acclimatised troops in Aden and Kenya. Finally, it drove the lesson home that policing operations must be carried out quickly to avoid awkward political repercussions and hostile opinion from other countries.[25]

Since the early years of the twentieth century, Oman had been politically fragmented between the British-backed sultanate of the coast and a tribally dominated imamate in the interior. The dynasty of Al Bu Sa'id sultans in Muscat had originated in the eighteenth century as imams, quasi-national leaders of the Ibadi sect of Islam who embodied religious as well as secular functions. Gradually, the Al Bu Sa'id rulers had shifted their attention from the isolated interior and its balance-of-power tribal politics to the coast with its opportunities for maritime trade and overseas expansion. By the end of the nineteenth century, the Muscat sultanate had come on hard times and survived only because of the protection and financial assistance of the Government of India. The tribes of the interior united behind a newly elected imam and attacked the capital in 1915; Muscat's fall was prevented by the dispatch of Indian Army troops to defend it. The country's effective division was formalised by the Agreement of al-Sib (1920) which recognised the autonomy of the interior.[26]

While the strong-willed Sultan Sa'id b. Taymur (r. 1932–70) especially chafed at this division, there was little he could do until the highly respected old imam died in 1954. The struggle for succession was dominated by an ambitious trio, composed of Sulayman b. Himyar al-Nabhani, paramount shaykh of the powerful Bani Riyam tribe, and his confederates Talib and Ghalib b. 'Ali al-Hinawi, both of whom had been minor officials in the imamate. Ghalib b. 'Ali was successful in pressing his claims to the office of imam but his election was disputed by many Omanis, thus weakening his claims to legitimacy and eroding tribal support for his leadership.

As divisions were appearing in the interior, Sultan Sa'id b. Taymur revived his efforts to reincorporate the interior into the sultanate. The largely British-owned Petroleum Development (Oman) (PDO) backed the sultan because of the prospect of discovering oil in Oman's interior, while official British assistance was forthcoming because of Saudi involvement. In 1952, a Saudi military party occupied Hamasa in the al-Buraymi oasis on the border between Abu Dhabi and Oman. In addition to potentially pushing Saudi borders far to the east, into territory where oil deposits were thought to be, the Buraymi occupation also enabled Riyadh to expand ties to such figures of the Omani interior as Sulayman b. Himyar and Imam Ghalib, who were willing to accept Saudi money and arms to further their ambitions.

As a consequence, the Muscat and Oman Field Force (MOFF) was formed with PDO funds to escort an oil company exploration team. The joint column assembled on Oman's southern shore in early 1954 and moved inland along the edge of the great Rub' al-Khali desert eventually to the oil-bearing strata at Fahud. The MOFF occupied the town of 'Ibri which sat on the route between al-Buraymi and the heart of inner Oman, and the British-officered Trucial Oman Scouts drove the Saudis out of Hamasa. With the severing of the Saudi connection, the way was open to reoccupation of all the Omani interior. In December 1955, the MOFF moved into Nizwa, the imamate's capital, and soon after Sultan Sa'id made a tour of the interior. Imam Ghalib had made a public abdication and Sulayman b. Himyar offered his submission to the sultan.

Talib b. 'Ali, the erstwhile imam's brother, however, had escaped to Saudi Arabia where he began to gather forces. In mid-1957, Talib secretly made his way back into Oman, accompanied by trained men and Saudi-supplied arms and ammunition. He joined forces with his brother Ghalib, who reasserted his claim to the imamate, and Sulayman b. Himyar, and together the rebels routed the sultan's forces in the interior and raised the flag of the imamate over Nizwa again.

Sultan Sa'id was left with no choice but to call for British assistance.[27] His request, coming in the aftermath of Suez, met with heated parliamentary debate and fears that Britain would become embroiled in a 'second Suez'. British involvement also provoked outside protests. In an unlikely combination, Saudi Arabia and Egypt led vocal opposition within the Arab League to 'British colonialism' in Oman and the outcry was taken up by Third World forces at the United Nations, where it regularly surfaced on the General Assembly's agenda until the early 1970s.[28] The situation was further complicated by the Anglo-American rivalry in the Peninsula; the US had quietly supported Saudi Arabia in its occupation of Hamasa, since the Saudi oil concession was held by American firms, and the Omani rebels utilised American arms and equipment.

In mid-July, the RAF began to launch strikes against key Omani forts by Venom fighters based at Sharjah. It was obvious, however, that these attacks had little effect on the dissidents and that ground forces would be required. Indeed, a principal outcome of the Oman war was to sound the death-knell for the RAF's traditional reliance on air control when dealing with Arab tribes. While Trenchard's policy had been effective in earlier decades in forcing recalcitrant and disorganised tribes to accept the authority of a central government, it was incapable by itself of bringing organised, determined dissidents to submission. Even the heavier firepower of the 1950s-vintage rockets and cannon had little effect on such rebel strongholds as the rock-and-cement fortress at Nizwa or Oman's high-mountain caves to which the rebels eventually retreated.

As a consequence of the limited utility of air strikes, a two-pronged ground attack was mounted. A combined force of sultanate troops, Trucial Oman Scouts (TOS), Cameronians and Ferret armoured cars moved south from al-Buraymi towards Nizwa while another sultanate column left Muscat for the interior via the principal mountain pass. Within a week, Nizwa and the other major settlements of inner Oman had been captured with only a few small skirmishes; casualties amounted to one dead and four wounded among the Anglo-sultanate forces and about 30 deaths among the dissidents. The rebel hard core, however, escaped to the safety of the high plateau of al-Jabal al-Akhdar. Stalemate ensued for the next year and a half. The British troops were withdrawn from Oman but the sultan's forces could only cordon off the Jabal al-Akhdar massif and try to put an end to the rebels' minelaying activities along major roads. In 1958, the small Omani military units were reorganised into the Sultan's Armed Forces (SAF), with a seconded British commander, and attempts were intensified to create a modern, professional military force capable of dealing with the rebels, as well as garrisoning the interior. Meanwhile, Britain's role in Oman continued to be attacked in international fora.

It soon became clear that putting an end to hostile international opinion would require removal of the rebel stronghold in the Omani mountains. Accomplishment of the latter, however, depended on the reintroduction of British forces. Several squadrons of a Special Air Service (SAS) regiment, on their way home from fighting communist insurgents in Malaya, were rerouted to Oman. In January 1959, these squadrons — backed up by SAF units, a TOS squadron, some Life Guards and tribal levies — stormed the Jabal al-Akhdar stronghold in a co-ordinated surprise attack. The majority of the rebels on the high plateau quickly surrendered and gave information identifying rebel sympathisers within the country, who were later captured. This well-planned and virtually bloodless operation essentially put an end to organised resistance in Oman.[29] The three dissident leaders — Sulayman, Ghalib and Talib —

however, managed to escape and set up camp in Saudi Arabia and revolutionary Iraq, where they maintained the 'Oman Liberation Army' for a renewed attack that never came.[30]

The Oman episode went against the general tide of diminishing British military involvement in East-of-Suez obligations. Unlike the case elsewhere, British military — as well as political — ties to the sultanate were actually strengthened. London undertook primary responsibility for the creation of a professional army, air force and putative navy in Oman, and continued to staff the country's principal military positions through the 1980s, by secondment from British forces and private contract of British officers. At the same time, Sultan Sa'id was pressured to open his country up to development; the lack of headway in this regard appears to have prompted British encouragement of the 1970 coup whereby Sa'id was replaced by his modernist-oriented son, Qabus.

From a strategic point of view, the Oman war illustrated the necessity of maintaining appropriate British forces capable of moving quickly to global hotspots and dealing effectively with local insurgencies around the world. Colonel David Stirling, the founder of the SAS, asserted that the SAS by this operation had achieved its 'truce peace-time role'.[31] British concern with the security of the sultanate undoubtedly was influenced by Oman's strategic location at the entrance to the oil-rich Gulf as much as by a sense of obligation to a long-time ally. This concern was to prompt British involvement in Oman's defence against the rebels in Dhufar a few years later, even after Britain had withdrawn officially from the Gulf and the last of its major East-of-Suez commitments.

The Problem of Deployment and the Defence of Kuwait

At the beginning of the 1960s, Britain's role East of Suez not only had not declined but, almost paradoxically, had been strengthened in some respects. Whitehall felt obliged to honour residual colonial commitments throughout the region, and these commitments involved assistance in fairly frequent crises. Furthermore, new multilateral commitments were added, such as SEATO and CENTO obligations. There was also the matter of a largely unstated but nevertheless heartfelt belief that Britain must defend its economic interests; this was especially true for the Gulf due to the heavy capital investment in oil companies and British dependence on Gulf oil supplies. Finally, the ingrained sense that Britain was still a world power with a natural role around the globe underpinned specific commitments. The British presence East of Suez rested on long-standing historical foundations and HMG simply could not pull out of the area without having a very good reason. If the empire had to be dismantled, many felt that the process of withdrawal should be carried out in an orderly fashion and not until viable and durable structures had been left behind.[32]

All of these considerations were particularly applicable to the Gulf. This was recognised in the 1962 Defence White Paper, which emphasised the British role in the Arabian Peninsula, the Gulf and Southeast Asia, and stressed that forces there would have to be maintained, even if this caused a retraction of forces in Europe and the Mediterranean.[33] This renewed mood in favour of a continuing role in the Indian Ocean and in upholding obligations there was put to the test by the Kuwait crisis of 1961. In many ways, the Kuwait operation provides valuable lessons for US planning in the 1980s.

The shaykhdom of Kuwait had come under British protection by the treaty of 1899 and thus was comparable to Bahrain and the Trucial states in its relations with Britain. However, oil production on a large scale began at an earlier date in Kuwait than in any other Peninsula state and so the shaykhdoms was fully prepared for independence earlier than its neighbours. On 19 June 1961, Britain recognised Kuwait's complete independence, promising to provide assistance in defence if required, and Kuwait applied for membership in the Arab League. Less than a week later, Iraq's revolutionary government laid claim to the entirety of Kuwait.[34]

The claim was followed by indications that Iraqi reinforcements and armour were moving south to al-Basra, only a few hours from the Kuwaiti border, although it was unclear whether this was a prelude to invasion or simply part of preparations for a national day parade. As a result, the Kuwaiti amir formally requested British and Saudi Arabian assistance on 30 June.[35] Because of Kuwait's extreme vulnerability, plans for rapid military intervention in the amirate had been drawn up previously under the codename 'Vantage'. One contingency anticipated a need for British assistance in maintaining internal security, while the other was formulated to meet an Iraqi armoured threat, and thus called for deployment in some force. As the Iraqi threat was being evaluated, British authorities in Aden and the Gulf undertook preliminary steps to move forces into position. Consequently, when the formal call for help came, British forces were able to react quickly and some units arrived within 24 hours.

In part, the quick response was due to the pre-positioning of units and supplies in that region. Eight Centurion tanks and ammunition had been stored in Kuwait and a large cache of armoured cars, other vehicles, ammunition and miscellaneous equipment was being held in nearby Bahrain. The navy had an Amphibious Warfare Squadron based at Bahrain, including half a squadron of Centurion tanks on board an LST and another shipfull already in the vicinity preparing to relieve the first. One of the three frigates assigned to the Gulf was in Bahrain at the time and the other two soon returned from Karachi and Mombasa. A carrier group was dispatched from Hong Kong, and arrived on 9 July. Various army and air force units were standing by in Sharjah, Aden and Kenya, and tank crews and fighter aircraft were transferred to Bahrain. Fortuitously, a commando ship of Royal Marines was already on its way to the Gulf for training exercises.

On the morning of 1 July, the Royal Marine commandos were landed at Kuwait airport by helicopter and were joined by two squadrons of Hunter fighters and the first elements of a contingent of Saudi paratroopers. The commandos were soon moved up to join Kuwait army units on a ridge north of Kuwait City. Getting the tanks on land proved to be a problem, due to lack of a landing ramp for the LST, and they had to be ferried ashore. The introduction of men and equipment was hampered also by the temporary and partial ban by Turkey and Sudan of overflight rights and severe dust storms in Kuwait. Many of the aircraft used in the operation had to be based in Bahrain, due to the congestion and lack of ground-control facilities at the Kuwait New airfield. As planned, command arrangements were also concentrated in Bahrain, as the C-in-C Middle East Command temporarily moved his headquarters there, and was joined by his GOC and AOC (all three normally headquartered in Aden), as well as by the Flag Officer, Middle East (permanently based in Bahrain); the Political Resident in the Persian Gulf also resided in Bahrain.

By 9 July, the maximum extent of British forces were in place; British personnel in Kuwait totalled nearly 6,000. They were supported by 1,600 Kuwaiti troops organised into a tank squadron, a field battery, and several mobile groups in jeeps and armoured cars. To meet the Iraqi threat, two battalions were deployed along Mutla Ridge just north of Kuwait Bay, supported by British and

Kuwaiti tanks and artillery and with an advance force of armoured cars between the ridge and the border. A third battalion, with a squadron of Centurions, was kept in reserve as a counter-attack force, a fourth was held in reserve in Kuwait City and a fifth was standing by in Bahrain. The operation was afflicted by problems in communications overloading and the absence of adequate radar capability. Fortunately, the real potential for Iraq to exploit air defence weaknesses was offset by poor visibility and flying conditions caused by the dust storms.

It is probable that an Iraqi attack, if it had been forthcoming, would have been aimed at a largely symbolic seizure of Kuwait's northern oilfields, rather than an all-out assault on Kuwait City, which would have been politically devastating to Iraq's pan-Arab position. If Iraq had carried out such a strategy, the forces defending Kuwait would have been forced on to the tactical offensive and it is questionable whether the British–Kuwaiti forces were adequate to recover a sliver of occupied territory.

However, an Iraqi attack never materialised and it is uncertain whether one was actually intended. In any case, British forces in Kuwait were kept there until after the Iraqi national day (14 July) and then gradually withdrawn. Shortly after Kuwait's admission to the Arab league in August, a small Arab league force replaced remaining British troops and these troops soon numbered between 2,000 and 3,000. In addition, the British army and RAF garrisons at Bahrain were maintained at a higher level than before the crisis.

Despite the fact that the capability of the forces assembled in Kuwait was not tested, the affair had a demonstrable effect in boosting British confidence in both the ability to carry out the strategic mobility doctrine and in the idea that there was still a positive role to be played in far-flung parts of the world. Nevertheless, there were serious lessons to be learned from the Kuwait crisis. British action was generally considered to have prevented or deterred an Iraqi attack, but the greatly superior Iraqi ratio in aircraft and tanks rendered the adequacy of the defending forces questionable if hostilities had occurred.[36] Furthermore, the lack of airspace depth and dependence on shipborne radar severely limited the possibility of early warning. While Britain clearly had demonstrated its determination to defend Kuwait's sovereignty, it had done so at a cost of £1m. Subsequent Iraqi verbal provocations produced a far smaller British response, indicating the futility of mounting a large-scale operation every time the remote possibility of a threat to Kuwait was sensed.

The operation was useful as a 'training exercise' to point up unanticipated problems. For example, the restrictions on overflight made by Turkey and Sudan caused some flights from the UK to proceed via Central Africa and thus taxed British lift capacity to a greater degree than expected. Kuwait quickly became one of the most difficult locations to reach by air. Thus, delays in moving men and equipment into the area combined with inadequate cover for ships on their way to or standing off the amirate and poor flying conditions to point out the need for continued emphasis on the role of sealift and sea power in such operations.

The value of pre-positioning men, arms and equipment in the region was thoroughly demonstrated by the rapidity with which the Centurions were operational. It was of considerable advantage to have Bahrain as a forward command centre — and for use as a reserve location for storing supplies and protecting aircraft. Similarly, the location of regional service commands, equipment and personnel at nearby Aden or even in Cyprus and Kenya greatly simplified the problem of rapid deployment. Furthermore, the value of having troops already stationed in the area was proven by the high incidence of heat casualties among troops flown in from Kenya, Cyprus and the UK (a problem that had also afflicted the Oman operations a few years earlier). Finally, it is questionable whether British ability to move enough force into Kuwait in a matter of days would have been possible without thorough planning for just such a contingency and the full co-operation of the Kuwaiti government.

The Struggle for Aden

During the 1960s, it became increasingly apparent that Britain's overseas commitments, particularly in the Indian Ocean, were becoming increasingly burdensome and expensive — both financially and politically. The United States, with its emerging involvement in Vietnam, encouraged Britain to share Western security burdens in Africa and especially Asia. A plethora of crises around the world in the early to mid-1960s severely strained the capability of British forces to attend to them all, especially as the opposing forces improved.

In many ways, dealing with these isolated hotspots was more

burdensome than defence of the entire empire had been in years past. 'The deterrent force of a British gunboat in the Persian Gulf in the nineteenth century or British aircraft in Iraq in the twenties and thirties had little relevance in the fifties and sixties against well-armed and organized enemies, very often trained and supplied from the outside.'[37] At the same time, British bases were fast disappearing and relocation to more secure locations was not only expensive, but recognised as only a temporary palliative. Apart from Britain, only two main overseas bases remained: Aden and Singapore.

Service rivalry emerged in attempts to get around the dilemma of basing on foreign soil: the RAF promoted an island-staging scheme across the Indian Ocean, while the navy pressed for new aircraft carriers. In many ways, the rivalry in the 1960s amounted to a reprise of the inter-service debate of four decades earlier. During the 1920s, the imperial policing role might well have saved the independent existence of the RAF from the attempts by the army and the navy to partition it. The RAF played a similar card in the mid-1960s when it felt its existence threatened by the gains made by the Royal Navy in providing the strategic nuclear deterrent with nuclear-powered ballistic-missile submarines, rather than bombers.

Thus, the RAF placed considerable emphasis on the East-of-Suez policing role, stressing the strategic and financial advantages of the island-basing scheme over the navy's traditional carrier role. At the heart of the debate was the necessity, for budgetary reasons, of making a choice between development of the RAF's F-111 long-range reconnaissance and bombing aircraft and the navy's CVA-01 class of fleet carriers. Victory went to the RAF in the 1966 Defence White Paper which accepted the RAF argument on East-of-Suez air power and authorised development of the F-111 while scuttling the CVA-01 carrier.[38]

By the late 1950s, Aden had emerged as one of the last secure British footholds in the Middle East, and the development of the air and sea barriers across the Middle East increased the colony's military importance even more. Even Kenya, perceived as another option during the shift away from the Mediterranean in the 1950s, was no longer viable at the beginning of the 1960s. In the three years following the Suez crisis and establishment of a separate Middle East Command, Aden's service population quadrupled and the hitherto isolated colony witnessed the largest military construction programme in British history.[39] By 1964, Aden held over 8,000

British troops, not including dependants.[40]

But even as Fortress Aden was being built up, internal pressures against British ownership were emerging. The consequence of this clash of goals was a full-scale guerrilla war that Britain was unable to win without investing far more political and military capital than it was willing to risk. While eventual withdrawal from Aden was widely accepted, the ferocity of the anti-British struggle certainly accelerated the British retreat.

The net effect of the long British control over Aden was to fossilise the archaic political structure of the protectorate while developing Aden Colony as a 'modernised' enclave populated by a diverse range of ethnic groups and cultural influences. As traditional goals and institutions persisted in the hinterland, the burgeoning city of Aden exhibited strong, centralised control, an effective administration, a professional army and civil service, and a strengthening union movement. Significantly, the Aden Trades Union Congress (ATUC) was in the forefront of the first stirrings of opposition to British rule. When the militant demands of Adeni nationalists were not met, they turned increasingly to campaigns of political violence and by the mid-1960s the British were confronted with a full-scale guerrilla war in both Aden Colony and Protectorate.

Essentially, four different groups had sought to lead the organised opposition to British rule.[41] The first of these was the South Arabian League (SAL), founded in 1950 by young men of the protectorate. Ultimately, the SAL failed to have much impact and was bypassed by more radical organisations, largely because it drew its membership from the protectorate's elite, was dominated by the interests of Lahj (the sultanate just outside Aden), and the ATUC was seen as a more effective vehicle for political protest. The second group, the People's Socialist Party (PSP), formed as the political wing of the ATUC, was dominated by 'Abdullah al-Asnaj, and operated exclusively within the colony. Although, like the SAL, it originally opposed armed struggle, eventually it turned to acts of violence, the most spectacular of which was the assassination attempt on the British High Commissioner's life in December 1963. In 1965, the SAL and the PSP joined together in the Organization for the Liberation of the Occupied South (OLOS) as a result of formidable competition from the newer National Liberation Front and Egyptian pressure for unity among the groups.

The National Liberation Front (NLF) first appeared in the late

1950s as a coalition between the local branch of the Arab Nationalists' Movement (ANM) and several other small groups.[42] While relatively moderate at first, the NLF gradually turned more radical and carried out guerrilla and terrorist operations against the British from an early date. The organisation's uncompromising anti-British stance and its strong ties to the protectorate helped it to dominate the political scene in the mid-1960s and to outmanoeuvre the Front for the Liberation of Occupied South Yemen (FLOSY), its principal rival. FLOSY had grown out of the attempt of President Gamal 'Abd al-Nasir of Egypt to unite the NLF with OLOS in 1966. However, Nasir's domination of the fledgeling Yemen Arab Republic in North Yemen at that time turned the more militant members of the NLF against Nasirism and only a few pro-Nasir NLF leaders remained in FLOSY. The NLF used its strength in the hinterland to take over most of the protectorate in the closing days of the independence struggle and it was to the NLF that Britain left Aden at the end of 1967.[43]

The first major uprising against the British in Aden began in 1963 in the Radfan, an isolated region directly north of Aden itself and not far from the North Yemen border. While the tribes of Radfan were officially under the amirate of al-Dali', in effect they were independent. They had given the British trouble for many years, particularly the Qutaybis, and British air operations had been necessary into the early 1960s. But the revolution in North Yemen and introduction of Egyptian troops and other officials there, coupled with NLF recruiting in the protectorate, added a more serious element of politicisation to traditional tribal truculence.[44]

In early 1964, it became clear that the situation in Radfan was no longer a matter of punishing the Radfani tribes for interrupting road traffic, but the beginning of a guerrilla war. The tribes had become better organised and were armed with modern weapons. British apprehensions had been heightened by the narrowly unsuccessful attempt on the life of Sir Kennedy Trevaskis, the High Commissioner, at Aden airport in December 1963. Consequently, 'Operation Nutcracker' was devised as a full-scale effort to nip the burgeoning rebellion in the bud. In addition to the difficulty of coping with hit-and-run guerrilla tactics by skilled fighters, the operation faced the problems of particularly rugged topography and extreme heat.

In January 1964, a large force consisting of infantry troops from the army of the newly created Federation of South Arabia, one of their armoured car squadrons, and British tanks, artillery and engineers, was assembled at the entrance pass to Radfan, where a light airfield was suitable for RAF use in helicopter support of the operation. The absence of suitable maps and adequate intelligence on insurgent movements made the going difficult but eventually the two main valleys were secured at a cost of less than two dozen casualties. However, it was decided that the risks of maintaining a garrison in Radfan were too great and the force was withdrawn. This development was followed by incursions across the border by Yemeni aircraft and then retaliation by an air attack on a Yemeni fort in March.

A second assault on Radfan strongholds was ordered in April, after it appeared that as many as 200 Egyptian-trained guerrillas had infiltrated into the region. In April, the base at Thumayr was reoccupied and the units of Radforce (short for Radfan Force) were assembled there. This force totalled approximately 3,000 men and included Royal Marine commandoes, paratroopers, two federal army battalions, armoured cars, an artillery battery and a troop of engineers. The lack of sufficient numbers of helicopters ruled out a heliborne assault on the mountains surrounding the main valleys and a longer, more difficult campaign had to be based on a combination of paratroop drops by night and arduous hikes up to the peaks from the valley floor. Control of the region was made all the more difficult by far stronger resistance than expected. It was not until early June that the attacking forces were in position to capture Jabal Hurriya, which dominated all Radfan. The rebels stood their ground on the slopes of the mountain and fought a pitched battle, melting away after dark. The peak was then reached without incident.

The Radfan had been pacified, apart from a dwindling number of attacks over the next few months. A campaign expected to last only three weeks had taken over three months and required far larger forces than anticipated. This was partly because of the lengthy period required to build up adequate forces, but also was due to the skilful tactics, determination and entrenchment of the defending guerrillas. Adequate air forces proved to be absolutely vital in the operation, whether it was helicopters providing necessary mobility in such a forbidding environment and resupplying troops in advanced positions or strike aircraft providing close air support. In the final analysis, however, this forcible occupation of Radfan was only the first step in a long and involved anti-guerrilla campaign.

After Radfan, the focus turned back to Aden.

There, the guerrilla campaign relied on attacks on military installations and assassination attempts on British and Adeni officials, beginning with the PSP's attack on Trevaskis in December 1963.[45] It had been clear for some time that Britain eventually would have to go and in mid-1964 the date of departure was set for 1968. It remained necessary to create a viable structure for afterwards. The preferred solution was the Federation of South Arabia, a cumbersome federal union between centralised and modernised Aden and the tiny, disparate states of the protectorate; this arrangement presumably would allow Britain to retain its military base at Aden. Nevertheless, as the anti-British opposition began to intensify, the federal experiment looked more and more fragile and the British dominant influence more apparent.

The new Labour government of 1964 sought to downplay the federation in favour of conciliation with the nationalists and 'Abd al-Qawi Makkawi, a more moderate PSP leader, was appointed Chief Minister. But even Makkawi proved less than malleable and a year later the British resumed direct control of the Aden government. Clearly, even at this date, hopes for a peaceful transition were fast fading. Consequently, the February 1966 Defence White Paper announced that the Aden base would be abandoned in 1968. At that point, British policy was reduced to finding a graceful way to withdraw its troops and to decide to whom the government should be handed over. It was clear that there would be no place for the protectorate's rulers in an independent state.

None of this was an easy task. The level of fighting between the NLF and FLOSY rivalled that of the nationalists with the British. Terrorist attacks steadily increased and the trustworthiness of the Arab administration, police and federal armed forces increasingly became suspect. Terrorist incidents had increased from 35 in 1964 to nearly 3,000 in 1967.[46] The increase prompted a belated decision to remove British dependants (even as late as January 1967, there were over 9,000 dependants in Aden) and the task was completed in July.[47] At the same time, another irritating security problem arose from the relatively regular border penetration by Egyptian MiGs and the consequent necessity to institute air patrols.

As 1967 began, the more radical NLF gathered strong support in the hinterland and easily outduelled FLOSY. The final nail in FLOSY's coffin was Egypt's defeat in the June 1967 war, which destroyed 'Abd al-Nasir's capacity to help FLOSY and exposed the organisation's complete dependence on a foreign power. At the same time, the NLF stepped up its pressure and attacks on beleaguered British forces, as well as against Adeni leaders and institutions deemed to be tainted with collaboration. The role of the British forces was reduced to steady retreat and in March the date of withdrawal was pushed up to November 1967. There would be no time to build up viable pro-British institutions to leave behind, and any such effort was bound to be futile. By June, the NLF had begun to take control over the protectorate as the British retreated into Aden. Even the important Crater section of Aden was briefly occupied by the NLF that summer. Several months later, FLOSY was decisively driven from the battlefield and the federal army (which had been renamed the South Arabian Army upon the collapse of the federal government) declared for the NLF.

The evacuation of British troops from their newly constructed quarters began in June 1967 and the perimeters around Aden gradually shrank throughout the remainder of the year to the immediate vicinity of Khormaksar airfield. Belated arrangements for the transfer of power from the British to the NLF took place in Geneva in mid-November 1967, and on 28 and 29 November the last 2,000 remaining men were transferred by helicopter to ships waiting offshore. The following day, the People's Republic of Southern Yemen (later renamed the People's Democratic Republic of Yemen) officially declared its independence. British military forces had lost 57 lives and suffered another 651 casualties during the war for Aden, while 18 British civilians were killed and 58 wounded. Total casualties were reckoned at more than 2,000.[48]

With departure from Aden, the British military presence in the Middle East was reduced to installations in Bahrain, Sharjah and Oman, where the mission was to protect Kuwait from external aggression, along with the Gulf states still under British protection. In Bahrain and Sharjah, new arrangements were reached to permit increases in the sizes and manpower strength of the British facilities there. With the imminent closure of Middle East Command, a Commander British Forces Gulf (CBFG) took charge in Bahrain in September 1967 and units of equipment from all three services were systematically transferred to Gulf facilities. Before long, British personnel in the Gulf had grown to between 7,000 and 8,000.[49] There they remained for only four short years until the decision was made to withdraw from the Gulf. That left the two RAF bases in Oman as the only British military installations in the Middle East.

The Last Outpost: Oman and the Dhufar Rebellion

British influence has been strong in Oman for nearly a century, even though the sultanate has always been an independent state. Despite British withdrawal from the Gulf in 1971, the influence in Oman continued at very nearly the same level. A principal reason for this was the rebellion in Oman's southern province of Dhufar. Although the rebellion began as a tribal insurrection against a reactionary and paternalistic sultan, it soon developed nationalist overtones and eventually the rebel leadership fell to committed Marxists supported by newly independent South Yemen.[50]

Oman's sultan, Sa'id b. Taymur, who had united the country with British help in the 1950s, was still on the throne in the late 1960s, when Oman's first oil revenues began. Nevertheless, his reluctance to develop the country and his continued heavyhanded rule provoked increasing discontent. This was particularly the case in Dhufar. In many ways, Dhufar resembles part of Yemen rather than Oman and in fact it was politically annexed to the sultanate only in the latter part of the nineteenth century. For the next century, succeeding sultans used the province's seaside capital at Salala for holidays and as a private estate. But the winds of change and prosperity elsewhere in the Peninsula were wafting across even the isolated Dhufari mountains as Sa'id b. Taymur refused to countenance any change.

In 1962, a group of disgruntled *jibalis* — mountain tribesmen speaking a South Arabic language — made their way to Saudi Arabia where they met the leaders of the old imamate and then to Iraq where a training base for Dhufari rebels was established and sporadic raids were carried out in Dhufar during 1963 and 1964. A more organised approach to dissidence began in 1964 when the Dhufar Liberation Front (DLF) was formed out of a merger between the Dhufar branch of the Arab Nationalists' Movement (ANM), the Dhufar Benevolent Society (DBS) and the Dhufari Soldiers' Organization (many of whom had served in the Trucial Oman Scouts). The newly created DLF held its first conference in June 1965 and soon after attacked a government patrol, thus officially launching the revolution. The rebels were occupied in the next few years by small-scale ambushes on the government's Dhufar Force, attempts to gain footholds in the small coastal towns and in the near-successful assassination attempt on Sultan Sa'id in April 1966.

At the movement's second congress in September 1968, the Marxists displaced the more moderate nationalists in the DLF's leadership and changed its name to the Popular Front for the Liberation of the Occupied Arabian Gulf (PFLOAG; later slightly changed to the Popular Front for the Liberation of Oman and the Arabian Gulf). The establishment of an office in Aden signalled the strong ties between the PFLOAG and the NLF regime in South Yemen. With new sources of support assured, the guerrilla campaign was stepped up and gradually PFLOAG control was extended throughout the western part of the province. Positions along the road from Salala to Thamarit (in the desert behind the mountains) were attacked in early May 1969 and finally Rakhyut, the major town in the west, was overrun in August 1969.

The rest of 1969 and early 1970 saw the extension of the fighting to Thamarit road and Salala Plain, including mortar attacks on the RAF's base at Salala. The Jabal Samhan region of eastern Dhufar gradually slipped under guerrilla control and effective government authority was reduced to Salala Plain, where barbed-wire perimeter fences were built around the few remaining coastal towns under sultanate authority, and the desert behind the mountains.

The PFLOAG's success encouraged similar groups elsewhere in Oman. In June 1970, an offshoot named the National Democratic Front for the Liberation of Oman and the Arabian Gulf launched mortar attacks on army camps in central Oman and prompted the various groups plotting the overthrow of Sultan Sa'id to push their timetable forward. After a brief gunbattle in Sa'id's Salala palace in July 1970, the sultan was persuaded to abdicate in favour of his son Qabus and leave the country. The new sultan's concern for Dhufar ran deep: his mother was of *jibali* origin and he himself was born and raised in Dhufar. Consequently, one of his first acts was to pardon surrendering rebels, which attracted many of the 'tribal' or nationalist dissidents, but was spurned by the ideologues. A comprehensive 'hearts and minds' campaign was launched to build roads, schools, health facilities and wells, under the administration of new Civil Action Teams.

At the same time, the sultanate made use of its financial reserves, which had been steadily accumulating since oil exports began in 1968, to launch a sustained military offensive. Defence expenditure quickly rose to nearly 50 per cent of the national budget as investments were made in British fighters, transport planes, naval patrol craft and American helicopters. The Sultan's Armed Forces (SAF) was overhauled and enlarged, and the heavy ratio of Baluch over Arab ranks was reversed. After years of defensive action, the SAF finally moved forward in early 1971, bombing rebel positions in the west and taking over parts of Jabal Samhan. Still, the SAF offensive was forced to retreat before the annual monsoon and it was not until October 1971 that the Leopard Line was built along the perimeters of Jabal Samhan to cut off supply routes.

This constituted the first phase in a policy of containment, whereby the SAF constructed a number of 'lines', consisting of a series of fortified positions linked by barbed-wire fences and frequent patrols. The intention was to divide the province into isolated sectors: when one area was cleared of rebel activity, the sector to its west would then be isolated and cleared. A similar tactic, 'Operation Simba', undertaken in May 1972, was an attempt to seal off the border with the PDRY; the effort proved premature, however.

With the SAF closedown during the 1972 monsoon season, PFLOAG forces moved back into the mountains, including Jabal Samhan. At this time, the guerrillas launched what was to be their last forward thrust: a rocket attack on Salala which produced a direct hit on the officers' mess at the air base. The rebel drive was thwarted, however, by the failure of twin assaults on the coastal towns of Mirbat and Taqa in July. The PFLOAG's failure to capture the eastern coastal strip marked the military turning-point of the war. From then on, the rebels were steadily pushed back. Operations in the east were reduced to hit-and-run tactics, and the rocket barrages of Salala Plain had ceased by October 1973.

Attempts to extend the scope of the revolt by opening a second front in the north were failures. Some 80 dissidents were rounded up in Muscat in December 1973 and an attempt to disrupt national day celebrations in November 1974 was foiled when a Land-Rover was stopped near Muscat after a brief shoot-out and interrogation led to other conspirators. Meanwhile, the fighting in Dhufar was characterised by rebel setbacks. Even though 'Operation Simba' was not as successful as had been hoped, it resulted in the establishment of the Mainbrace Line, a set of fortified mountaintop positions centred on the border post at Sarfayt and overlooking the strip of wooded hills between the sea coast and the desert. The SAF's success in maintaining Mainbrace during the 1972 monsoon season, despite constant siege by the rebels, meant that valuable time was not lost in the autumn by recapturing positions abandoned the previous spring.

By early spring 1973, government troops had begun to capture key points in the western Jabal Qamar and naval craft stepped up surveillance of the rebel-held coastline. It was clear by this time that the sultanate had gained the upper hand in the rebellion. Not only was SAF able to mobilise 3,500 troops and some 45 aircraft against a rebel total of approximately 2,000 hardcore insurgents but Sultan Qabus had been notably successful in mobilising outside support, including combat troops from Iran. Iranian paratroopers were key elements in 'Operation Thimble' of December 1973, when the Thamarit road was recovered and permanently held open, providing the first ground link between Muscat and Salala in several years.

Subsequent SAF activity was directed towards clearing central Dhufar from enemy control. In early 1974, the Hornbeam Line was built as a major part of this strategy. Stretching inland for nearly 50 miles from Mughsayl on the coast and roughly 20 miles west of the Thamarit road, the Hornbeam Line was the most ambitious of the government lines. Its purpose was to restrict severely supply convoys, including camel trains, from reaching the area to its east. Thus the line divided Dhufar into a largely government-controlled area to the east and a smaller no-man's land to the west, while government forces used the remainder of the spring to attack guerrilla positions in Jabal Qamar. The rapidly crumbling position of the rebels resulted in an inconclusive overture to the Arab League for mediation and then a split between the Dhufari members of the front and the Gulf members — the truncation of the movement's name to the Popular Front for the Liberation of Oman (PFLO) reflected the decision to concentrate military activity on Oman alone.

Following the 1974 monsoon season, the sultanate accelerated its military offensive by engaging in heavy fighting around Sarfayt. By December, the Hammer Line had been built to the west of Hornbeam. Iranian participation in this offensive was complemented by the combined Omani–Iranian assault on Rakhyut in January 1975, and the town was captured at a heavy cost in Iranian lives. Following this success, the Damavand Line was built from Rakhyut northward, bisecting the strip between the Hornbeam Line and the border and thus forcing the rebels into an even smaller operating area.

The government's final push began at the close of the 1975 monsoon season when SAF and Iranian troops moved into areas north of Rahkyut. Other Iranian contingents moved south from Sarfayt towards the sea while the PFLO base at Hawf in South Yemen was attacked by sultanate aircraft. The offensive became a rout by late November as Omani troops occupied the final villages in western Dhufar, unopposed by the rebels who had slipped back into the PDRY. On 11 December 1975, Sultan Qabus officially declared that the Dhufar war was over.

Despite scattered shelling from across the border, the downing of a helicopter carrying the commander of the SAF's Dhufar Brigade and the PFLO's insistence that the rebellion would be carried on, the end apparently had come to over a decade of fighting. Increasing numbers of rebels turned themselves in to the government, with the total number of surrendered reaching 275 in February 1976. Yet, despite all this, the PFLO refused to fold completely, its leaders defiant and its propaganda outlets in South Yemen claiming continued fighting. Relations between conservative Oman and Marxist South Yemen remained hostile until an agreement on exchanging diplomats and demarcating their common border was reached in 1983, with the help of Kuwait and the UAE.

Much of the sultanate's success in the rebellion was the result of assistance marshalled from the outside, and chief among the external supporters was Britain. Although the British had been largely excluded from activity or movement in Dhufar by the cautiousness of Sa'id b. Taymur, the sultan eventually had been forced to call on the British-officered SAF for help there. British casualties were reported in the fighting as early as 1966. By April 1971, there were 49 seconded British officers serving with the SAF, along with another 71 on private contract and 60 pilots.[51] By the end of the rebellion in 1975, the British presence had grown to 700, including 220 officers on private contract, 60 Special Air Service (SAS) members, 75 men from the Royal Engineers, and 147 RAF personnel at Salala air base.[52] Officially, casualties were stated to be 11 killed in action and 18 wounded, but it was rumoured that the SAS toll alone had included 73 deaths.[53]

The role of SAS in Dhufar was long denied, even though the regiment's ties with Oman stretched back to the successful Anglo–Omani assault on al-Jabal al-Akhdar in January 1959 and had been kept current by several training exercises during the following decade. In fact, an SAS squadron had been posted to Dhufar in 1970 under the cover of British Army Training Team (BATT), although this was not officially acknowledged until much later. Continuing reports of SAS casualties in 1972 and afterwards failed to draw Whitehall's confession of combat roles even through early 1974. Nevertheless, these elite troops contributed significantly to eventual victory.

In addition to personnel, the sultanate relied heavily on British equipment and weapons. An order was placed in April 1968 for Jet Provost trainer aircraft, in September 1970 for five Skyvan transport planes, with more ordered in September 1971, followed by an order for a dozen Strikemaster fighters and various naval patrol craft. The culmination of these purchases came in late 1974 when the sultanate contracted for 12 Anglo–French Jaguar fighters and 28 Rapier missiles, at a cost of between £71m and £83m. British interests were also present in commercial activities in Dhufar, such as port construction at Raysut, roadbuilding, banking and communications.

There were also important contributions from Oman's neighbours. The Shah of Iran was more than willing to assist in putting down a Marxist uprising — particularly one that had received considerable support from China and the Soviet Union — and he was encouraged in this move by Washington under the Nixon Doctrine. Dhufar also presented the Shah with a rare opportunity to provide combat training for his troops, and the rapid rotation of Iranians fighting in Dhufar was alleged to have resulted in nearly 200 deaths. Iranian helicopters and paratroopers were sent to Dhufar in early 1973 and by the end of 1974 Iranian troops totalled over 2,000, growing to over 5,000 in 1975. A local headquarters was established at the sprawling air base at Thamarit and Iranian F-5 Phantoms patrolled the PDRY border, while Iranian destroyers shelled the rebel-held Dhufari coast. The Iranians were at the centre of Rakhyut's capture in January 1975 and they played a prominent role in the 'big push' in December.[54]

The termination of the Dhufar rebellion allowed Britain in 1976 to abandon its final military installations in the Middle East, the RAF bases at Salala and on Masira Island. Nevertheless, the British influence in Oman remained strong, particularly in the military where British officers outnumbered Omani officers as late as 1982. It was not until 1985 that Omanis began to replace the seconded British commanders of the sultanate's land forces, air force and navy. US attempts to gain the military co-operation of the Gulf states in its RDF planning were best received in Oman, where, ironically, the British presence remained the strongest and at times British advisers appeared to resent the growing ties between Oman and the US.

Notes

1. The unfolding of British strategic policy regarding the East-of-Suez theatre has been covered in Phillip Darby, *British Defence Policy East of Suez, 1947–1968* (London, Oxford University Press, for the Royal Institute of International Affairs, 1973); C. J. Bartlett, *The Long Retreat: A Short History of British Defence Policy, 1945–70* (London, Macmillan; New York, St Martin's Press, 1972); L. W. Martin, *British Defence Policy: The Long Recessional* (London, Institute for Strategic Studies, November 1969; Adelphi Papers, no. 61); and Jacob Abadi, *Britain's Withdrawal from the Middle East, 1947–1971: The Economic and Strategic Imperatives* (Princeton, NJ, Kingston Press, 1982). Also relevant for the early period is William Roger Louis, *The British Empire in the Middle East, 1945–1951: Arab Nationalism, the United States, and Postwar Imperialism* (Oxford, Clarendon Press, 1984). The 1968 decision to quit the Gulf is discussed more thoroughly in Chapter 4.

2. *The Rise and Fall of British Naval Mastery* (London, Allen Lane, 1976; paperback edn, London, Macmillan, 1983), p. 337.

3. See Kennedy, *British Naval Mastery*.

4. From Lord Curzon's presidential address to the Birmingham and Midland Institute, 1907, cited in Darby, *British Defence Policy*, p. 1.

5. On the other hand, the need to protect investments (reckoned in the 1960s to include £700–800m in Malaysia and Singapore and £1–2b in the Gulf) and trade (almost half of total British trade took place in the East-of-Suez area) was cited as a necessary reason for continuing the British military presence East of Suez. Martin, *British Defence Policy*, p. 5.

6. *British Defence Policy*, p. 327.

7. Ibid., p. 331.

8. Ibid., pp. 59–60. This factor provided part of the reason for British participation in the Baghdad Pact.

9. AIR/20/6610, COS (48), 59th Meeting, 28 April 1948, and various other correspondence; AIR/20/6611, various correspondence. A new Far East Command was created for the navy with the dividing line at Sumatra. For practical reasons, the C-in-C Middle East was to remain at Malta while a liaison office was established at the new regional headquarters.

10. Cited in Louis, *British Empire in the Middle East*, p. 17. Louis's description gives an idea of the size of the base: 'The Suez enclave stretched not only from the Mediterranean to the Red Sea but also westwards three-quarters of the way to Cairo ... The enclave's physical structure consisted of a network of roads, railways, harbours, ports, military garrisons, airfields, and a flying-boat station. There were ammunition dumps and extensive repair facilities that were irreplaceable. In short it was a vast arsenal. The region of hills and scrub in the south as well as the barren desert areas provided splendid grounds for manoeuvres and training. The canal from Cairo provided fresh water ... Before 1947 Suez was the largest reservoir of British military strength outside India.' Ibid., p. 9.

11. Elizabeth Monroe, *Britain's Moment in the Middle East, 1914-71*, 2nd edn (Baltimore, Johns Hopkins University Press, 1981), pp. 156-8.

12. Despite the political problems with Palestine/Israel, the overwhelming advantages of a base in the vicinity of the Canal had led British military planners as late as 1951 to conclude that the only practicable solution to the loss of Suez would be an interim base in Israel. DEFE/7/25, Chiefs of Staff Committee, Joint Planning Staff, J.P. (50) 141(S) and J.A.P. (50) Final, 'Location of Forces and Administrative Installations in the Middle East, Report by the Joint Planning and the Joint Administrative Planning Staff', 17 January 1951.

13. David Lee, *Flight From the Middle East: A History of the Royal Air Force in the Arabian Peninsula and Adjacent Territories, 1945-1972* (London, HMSO, 1980), p. 155.

14. Ibid., pp. 29-34. See also the descriptive surveys of BFAP's responsibilities by its former commander in M. L. Heath, 'Arabian Extremities', *JRCAS*, vol. 47, pt 3 and 4 (July-October 1960), pp. 260-9; and idem, 'Stability in the Arabian Peninsula', *JRUSI*, vol. 105, no. 618 (May 1960), pp. 174-85. The Aden Command was renamed Middle East Command in 1961 while Cyprus became the Near East Command.

15. RAF forces based in Aden were also used for operations against tribes in Somalia and Eritrea in the postwar period. Ibid., p. 42.

16. See, for example, AIR/2/10483, Trafford Smith (Colonial Office) to C. W. Baxter (Foreign Office), February 1947: 'The practice of punitive air action against recalcitrant tribes is, in the case of the Aden Protectorate, well established and understood by those against whom it is likely to be used. It is, of course, liable to uninformed criticism. Nevertheless, our feeling here is that in suitable circumstances punitive air action as hitherto carried out remains the method of maintaining order most effective and least costly in human life . . . In actual fact, casualties, on such occasions, are usually negligible if not nonexistent, and as time goes on the occasions regarding the use of this weapon become progressively rarer. My Secretary of State is in agreement with the view expressed above and endorses the principles hitherto accepted. The question of the use of air action against hostile Yemeni forces is of course an international matter which presents greater difficulty and requires careful examination.'

17. In an RAF note on the Qutaybi operations of 1947, it was pointed out that 'in 1934 and 1940/1941 air operations against the Quteibis lasted 61 and 127 days respectively. In 1947 the RAF obtained the submission of Quteibis in the equivalent of three days operations without the loss of a single life and without injury to any individuals on either side.' AIR/2/10483, C-in-C RAF Middle East to the Undersecretary of State for Air, 22 December 1947.

18. AIR/2/10483, 'The Aden Command, 1945-1947'.

19. R. J. Gavin, *Aden Under British Rule, 1839-1967* (London, C. Hurst, 1975), pp. 336-8; and Lee, *Flight From the Middle East*, pp. 142-8.

20. Darby, *British Defence Policy*, pp. 90-1; and Lee, *Flight From the Middle East*, pp. 148-55.

21. The background on British strategy for this section is drawn largely from Darby, *British Defence Policy*, pp. 84-133.

22. DeWitt, C. Armstrong, 'The British Re-Value Their Strategic Bases', *JRUSI*, vol. 104, no. 616 (November 1959), pp. 423-32. The loss of Trincomalee in 1958 was a serious blow to the navy. The East Indies Command was abolished and its respon-

sibilities divided between a Far East Command and a new Arabian Sea and Persian Gulf station — the rank of Senior Naval Officer, Persian Gulf, was upgraded to Commodore to take charge of the new command and he was named Naval Deputy to the Commander of British Forces, Arabian Peninsula. Darby, *British Defence Policy*, p. 128.

23. A guiding formulation of this policy was Neville Brown's *Strategic Mobility* (London, Chatto & Windus, for the Institute for Strategic Studies, 1963; New York, Frederick A. Praeger, 1964). See also A. D. R. G. Wilson, 'The Relevance of Air Mobility to the Middle East', *Army Quarterly*, vol. 69, no. 2 (January 1955), pp. 161–84; Robert Saundby, 'Air Power in Limited Wars', *JRUSI* vol. 103, no. 611 (August 1958), pp. 378–83; and Anthony Verrier, 'Strategically Mobile Forces — U.S. Theory and British Practice', *JRUSI*, vol. 106, no. 624 (November 1961), pp. 479–85.

24. By 1960, the British air traffic was rerouted from Malta to Kano, Nigeria, and then across central Africa to Nairobi. The potential of similar problems with nationalist opposition to British bases in South and Southeast Asia was sidestepped with the building of the base on Gan, in the Maldives. Armstrong, 'The British Re-Value Their Strategic Bases', pp. 423–32.

25. Darby, *British Defence Policy*, pp. 128–33.

26. For more information, see J. E. Peterson, *Oman in the Twentieth Century: Political Foundations of an Emerging State* (London, Croom Helm; New York: Barnes & Noble, 1978).

27. The following discussion of this insurgency is drawn principally from J. E. Peterson, 'Britain and "the Oman War": An Arabian Entanglement', *Asian Affairs* (London), vol. 63, pt 3 (October 1976), pp. 285–98. Other important sources include David de C. Smiley, 'Muscat and Oman', *JRUSI*, vol. 105, no. 617 (February 1960), pp. 29–47; Phillip Warner, *The Special Air Service* (London, William Kimber, 1971), pp. 209–21; Colin Maxwell, *Short History of the Sultan's Armed Forces* (Bayt al-Falaj, Oman, mimeographed, November 1969); and Lee, *Flight from the Middle East*, pp. 122–37. For autobiographical accounts, see Anthony Shepherd, *Arabian Adventure* (London, Collins, 1961); P. S. Allfree, *Warlords of Oman* (London, Robert Hale, 1967); David de C. Smiley, with Peter Kemp, *Arabian Assignment* (London, Leo Cooper, 1975); and Frank Kitson, *Bunch of Five* (London, Faber & Faber, 1977).

28. Two UN fact-finding missions were sent to the region, although the sultan allowed only the first to enter the country. Their reports are contained in United Nations General Assembly, 18th Session, 8 October 1963, *Report of the Special Representative of the Secretary-General on His Visit to Oman*, A/5562 ('The de Ribbing Report'); and UN General Assembly, 19th Session, 22 January 1965, *Question of Oman; Report of the Ad Hoc Committee on Oman*, A/5846 ('The Jiménez Report'). The Arab Information Center in New York published several pro-imamate pamphlets during this period.

29. Despite the decisive role of ground forces in this campaign, David Lee points out the value of air power operating in tandem with the ground forces, particularly in reconnaissance, softening up rebel positions and resupplying British troops. In addition, he mentions the advantage of mounting sizable air operations without generating the kind of publicity that the sending of large numbers of British troops would have attracted. Lee, *Flight from the Middle East*, p. 137.

30. The erstwhile imamate leaders continued to enjoy the rhetorical support of radical Arab and Third World states for years to come but were never able to return

to Oman. During the 1960s, the rebels were only a minor nuisance to British interests in the Gulf, capable only of setting off an occasional bomb, bungling an assassination attempt on an Omani official, and sinking a British India passenger ship. After the palace *coup d'état* in Oman in 1970, brief reconciliation talks were held without any positive results and the rebel leaders remained in exile in Saudi Arabia.

31. Letter to the editor, *The Times*, 10 April 1959.
32. Darby, *British Defence Policy*, pp. 147–56.
33. Ibid., pp. 223–4.
34. The legal basis of the Iraqi claim rested on Kuwait's previous ambiguous status within the Ottoman empire. While the shaykhs of Kuwait had been forced to cooperate with Ottoman authorities in al-Basra during the nineteenth century, they had not considered themselves Ottoman subjects nor was Ottoman sovereignty over Kuwait ever recognised by Britain. Furthermore, the newly independent Iraqi monarchy had recognised Kuwait's sovereignty in the Iraq–Kuwait treaty of 1932. Further evidence that the 1961 Iraqi claim was advanced for political purposes rather than being legal in character came in 1963, when the Qasim government was overthrown and the new regime officially recognised the sovereign status of Kuwait in October of that year. For a discussion of the merits of the Iraqi claim, see Husain M. Albaharna, *The Arabian Gulf States: Their Legal and Political Status and Their International Problems*, 2nd rev. edn (Beirut, Librairie du Liban, 1975), pp. 250–8.
35. The following discussion is drawn principally from Lee, *Flight from the Middle East*, pp. 165–88; Darby, *British Defence Policy*, pp. 219–23 and 244–9; Brown, *Strategic Mobility*, pp. 88–96; and Verrier, 'Strategically Mobile Forces'. See also Majid Khadduri, *Republican Iraq* (London, Oxford University Press, 1969), pp. 166–73.
36. Neville Brown notes that out of a total Iraqi army strength of four or five infantry divisions and several armoured brigades, the Baghdad government would have had to keep one in the centre of the country to support the government against political and tribal intrigues while Kurdish insurgency in the north would have required one or two divisions, leaving a small margin of troops available for offensive operations outside of Iraq. On the other hand, the increase in the firepower and mobility from the influx of first British and then Soviet equipment in the 1950s undoubtedly raised the confidence of the Iraqi armed forces and by 1961 their pilots had become familiarised with their new Soviet planes and had the advantage of first strike. *Strategic Mobility*, pp. 91–2.
37. Darby, *British Defence Policy*, pp. 329–30.
38. On reaction to the loss of base facilities, see Armstrong, 'The British Re-Value Their Strategic Bases', pp. 423–32; for a discussion of the merits of the island-staging scheme, see Neville Brown, *Arms Without Empire: British Defence Role in the Modern World* (Baltimore, Penguin, 1967), pp. 51–7; on the F-111/CVA-01 battle, see Desmond Wettern, *The Decline of British Seapower* (London, Jane's, 1982), pp. 263–76.
39. Darby, *British Defence Policy*, pp. 209–10.
40. Gavin, *Aden Under British Rule*, p. 344.
41. Background on the political factions in Aden can be found in a variety of sources, especially Abdallah S. Bujra, 'Urban Elites and Colonialism: The Nationalist Elites of Aden and South Arabia', *Middle Eastern Studies*, vol. 6, no. 2 (1970), pp. 189–211; Jean-Pierre Viennot, 'L'Experience révolutionnaire du Sud-Yemen', *Maghreb-Machrek*, no. 59 (September–October 1973), pp. 73–80; Gavin,

Aden Under British Rule; Fred Halliday, *Arabia Without Sultans* (Harmondsworth, Penguin, 1974; New York, Vintage, 1975); Robert W., Stookey, *South Yemen: A Marxist Republic in Arabia* (Boulder, Co, Westview Press; London, Croom Helm, 1982); and Joseph Kostiner, *The Struggle for South Yemen* (London, Croom Helm; New York, St Martin's Press, 1984).

42. The ANM played a very strong role in the ideological evolution of many Arab intellectuals, including Lebanese, Palestinian, Jordanian, Kuwaiti and other groups. For a comprehensive study of the ANM, see Walid W. Kazziha, *Revolutionary Transformation in the Arab World: Habash and His Comrades from Nationalism to Marxism* (London, Charles Knight, 1975).

43. This brief survey cannot do justice to the myriad of factions and ideological tendencies contained within the NLF during the 1960s and 1970s. After independence, the hardcore Marxist wing of the party was able to strengthen its stranglehold on power as the result of actions in 1969, 1971 and 1978 — before a relatively more moderate leadership assumed charge in 1980. In addition to the above sources, see Fred Halliday, 'Yemen's Unfinished Revolution: Socialism in the South', *MERIP Reports*, no. 81 (October 1979), pp. 3–20; and J. E. Peterson, *Conflict in the Yemens and Superpower Involvement* (Washington, Georgetown University, Centre for Contemporary Arab Studies, 1981; Occasional Paper).

44. The Radfan campaign is covered by T. M. P. Stevens, 'Operations in the Radfan, 1964', *JRUSI*, vol. 110, no. 640 (November 1965), pp. 335–46; Julian Paget, *Last Post: Aden 1964–67* (London, Faber & Faber, 1969), pp. 23–110; and Lee, *Flight From the Middle East*, pp. 203–19. For a critical view, see Halliday, *Arabia Without Sultans*, pp. 195–9.

45. On the struggle for Aden see Paget, *Last Post: Aden*, pp. 113–260; Halliday, *Arabia Without Sultans*, pp. 199–222; Gavin, *Aden Under British Rule*, pp. 318–51; Lee, *Flight From the Middle East*, pp. 220–56; Kostiner, *The Struggle for South Yemen*; and David Ledger, *Shifting Sands: The British in South Arabia* (London, Peninsular Publishing, 1983). In addition, see the accounts by two British High Commissioners during this period, in Sir Charles Johnston, *The View from Steamer Point* (London, Collins, 1964); and Sir Kennedy Trevaskis, *Shades of Amber* (London, Hutchinson, 1968).

46. Paget, *Last Post: Aden*, p. 264.
47. Lee, *Flight From the Middle East*, pp. 238–9.
48. Paget, *Last Post: Aden*, p. 264.
49. Sir William Luce, 'Britain's Withdrawal from the Middle East and Persian Gulf', *JRUSI*, vol. 114, no. 653 (March 1969), p. 7.
50. This section is drawn largely from J. E. Peterson, 'Guerrilla Warfare and Ideological Confrontation in the Arabian Peninsula: The Rebellion in Dhufar', *World Affairs*, vol. 139, no. 4 (Spring 1977), pp. 278–95. Other key sources include Fred Halliday, *Arabia Without Sultans*, pp. 304–60; D. L. Price, 'Oman: Insurgency and Development', *Conflict Studies*, no. 53 (January 1975); and John Townsend, *Oman: The Making of a Modern State* (London, Croom Helm, 1977), pp. 95–112. See also the reminiscences by British officers involved in the fighting: Ranulph Fiennes, *Where Soldiers Fear to Tread* (London, Hodder & Stoughton, 1975); K. Perkins, 'Oman 1975: The Year of Decision', *JRUSI*, vol. 124, no. 1 (March 1979), pp. 38–45; Tony Jeapes, *SAS: Operation Oman* (London, William Kimber, 1980); and John Akehurst, *We Won a War: The Campaign in Oman, 1965–1975* (London, Michael Russell, 1983).

51. *The Economist*, 3 April 1971.
52. *The Times*, 9 December 1975.
53. *The Observer*, 11 January 1976.
54. Iranian involvement in Dhufar was viewed with suspicion by most other Arab states, including Oman's neighbours in the Gulf. Nevertheless, Saudi Arabia and the UAE provided the sultanate with welcome financial assistance while Jordan contributed staff officers and NCOs, intelligence officers, engineer units and a combat battalion briefly in 1975.

4 The US and Gulf Security

The Changing of the Guard

British Withdrawal from the Gulf

The year 1971 is often used as a convenient date for determining when responsibility for Gulf security shifted from British to the US. But in many ways, this is an artificial threshold, since the process of 'changing the guard' occurred gradually over the course of several decades. British withdrawal from the Gulf was completed, not initiated, in 1971. The process of withdrawal from the Gulf was but one small part of a much more drawn-out withdrawal from the long-standing British position 'East of Suez'. The Second World War marks the beginning of the decline of British interests in the larger region, with the gradual and cumulative divestiture of interests in India, East Africa and the Middle East. In the Arabian Peninsula, this process had involved the granting of independence to Kuwait under peaceful conditions in 1961 and the more violent departure from Aden in late 1967.

Even as the postwar years witnessed a gradual decline in the British position, the roots of American involvement in the region were being established. Among the early reasons for American concern were the acquisition of oil concessions in the Gulf (of which ARAMCO proved to be the most important), military use of the Peninsula and surrounding areas for the war effort (as described in Chapter 2), and the steady proliferation and deepening of the American position in Iran.[1]

Consequently, the late 1940s, the 1950s and the 1960s represent a long period of transition and overlapping of interests, goals and responsibilities in the region on the part of the two Western powers. Rather than co-operation, this overlapping more often resulted in serious competition and even open hostility. The first section of this chapter, then, is concerned with these two simultaneous processes at work: the gradual British relinquishment of its position in the Gulf, and the intensification of US interests there.

It was abundantly clear at the end of the Second World War that Britain's imperial role was greatly diminished. Indeed, the entry of the US into the war had saved not only Britain from invasion, but also its colonial possessions. But in the eyes of many British, the US, through its global participation in the war, had gained a toehold in areas from which it previously had been successfully excluded. One of these areas was the Gulf. Not only had the Gulf been held as an exclusively British 'lake' since the early years of the century, but British oil firms controlled the lion's share of the Gulf's oil, long seen as vital not only for use at home, but also for supplying the Royal Navy. Consequently, even as it became apparent that Britain must downgrade its East-of-Suez capabilities, attempts continued to try and fend off American penetration of the Gulf.

The first of the American intrusions revolved around oil and penetration of the Gulf fields. By the beginning of the war, American oil interests were represented in Kuwait, Saudi Arabia, Iraq and Bahrain. On top of this challenge came American insistence on access to British facilities in the Gulf to prosecute the war effort. One area in which American participation occurred was the Persian Gulf Command, responsible for channelling military assistance to the Soviet Union via the Gulf and Iran. As the focus of the war shifted from the European to the Pacific theatre, US forces made greater use of the Persian Gulf and South Arabian air routes. While London recognised the necessity of USAAF use of these routes and airfields, permission was granted only grudgingly for Pan Am's use of these routes (fearing the establishment of claims to civilian traffic rights after the war).

British suspicions of American intentions were furthered by American plans, from as early as 1944, to build an air force base at Dhahran in eastern Saudi Arabia. This proposal met repeated objections from the British, who regarded it — with considerable justification — as a bare-faced attempt to create a political and strategic presence in Saudi Arabia, as well as facilities that would be translated into civilian air use following the war. Nevertheless, Washington's efforts to gain Saudi approval were redoubled and justified to the British on war grounds. The base was constructed in 1946 and occupied by the USAF until turned over to the Saudi government in 1962. Furthermore, Dhahran airfield constituted only one part of a growing American wedge between British–Saudi ties, as the US provided loans and credits to the kingdom, constructed roads there, and eventually supplanted the British military mission. These actions, when combined with the considerable activities of ARAMCO after the war, worked to transfer predominant outside influence in Saudi Arabia from Britain to the United States, which has held it ever since.[2]

Another instance of American penetration was the establishment of the US Navy's Middle East Force (MIDEASTFOR) in the Gulf. Partly because of growing economic interests there and partly because of the Cold War, the navy decided to deploy two destroyers and a seaplane tender to the Gulf in 1949, acquiring berthing space — later homeporting rights — at the British HMS *Jufair* base on Bahrain. MIDEASTFOR has remained in the Gulf ever since, although after British withdrawal the American use of facilities was downgraded officially at the request of the Bahraini government.[3]

The smouldering Anglo–American postwar rivalry in the region came to a head of sorts with the Buraymi oasis crisis of the 1950s. Sovereignty over the oasis had been shared by the Rulers of Abu Dhabi and Muscat but not recognised by the Al Sa'ud, who had controlled the oasis on several previous occasions over the past century and a half. The dispute took a new turn when an armed Saudi detachment occupied the village of al-Hamasa in the oasis in October 1952. Britain, acting on behalf of both Abu Dhabi and Oman, protested this action to Riyadh. The consequence was an agreement to submit the case to a tribunal, with both sides contributing exhaustive memorials justifying their positions. But the tribunal never rendered judgement, as Britain charged Saudi Arabia with obstruction and withdrew. There the matter lay until October 1955, when a unit of the British-officered Trucial Oman Scouts ejected the Saudi detachment from the oasis and Abu Dhabi and Omani control over their respective villages was restored.

The significance of the dispute went beyond questions of borders, however. At the heart of the Saudi action, and the reason for the spirited British objection, was the possibility of oil in the area. ARAMCO held the concession for Saudi Arabia, while the largely British firm, Iraq Petroleum Company, held the concessions in Abu Dhabi and Oman. Consequently, London and Washington found themselves arrayed on opposing sides and American and British individuals prepared the opposing memorials.[4]

The debate over Britain's continued military presence East of Suez grew more intense during the 1960s, as discussed in Chapter 3. In large part, of course, the East-of-Suez dilemma was only one part of an even wider concern: was Britain to remain in some small way an imperial or global power, or was it to be reduced to simply one more mid-sized European state? Although the psychological dimensions of this debate were enormous, the battle essentially was fought on financial grounds.

The question of the British military role in the Middle East and the Gulf was then only a marginal concern of the Defence White Paper of 1966. The gradual attrition of Middle East military installations was implicitly acknowledged and more were added to the list of closures.[5] After the loss of Egypt, Palestine and Iraq, Whitehall announced its intention to withdraw from Aden in either 1967 or 1968. As a result, the shrunken British presence in the Middle East was to rest upon a small increase in the forces stationed at Bahrain and Sharjah. The Middle East drawdown was reconfirmed in the 1967 Defence White Paper, and the intensification of fighting in Aden caused the withdrawal to be pushed up to November 1967.

The 14 per cent devaluation of the pound sterling in 1967 served to accelerate the impetus for abandonment of military commitments in the Indian Ocean basin. Even though the burden of keeping a presence in the Gulf was minimal compared to other obligations farther east (and since various Gulf rulers reportedly offered to underwrite British expenses), withdrawal from the Gulf was announced in January 1968. This decision, like the decision to withdraw from Aden, was the product of a Labour government. The Conservatives in opposition branded this policy as irresponsible and the decision to vacate the Gulf as particularly shortsighted. Nevertheless, the announcement, once made, acquired the air of finality and, when the Tories came to power in 1970, the decision was allowed to stand.[6]

Since British forces in the Gulf were miniscule, numbering only 9,000 men in 1971, impending withdrawal promised little military change.[7] The political impact was far more important, particularly since the amirates of the Arab littoral were still bound legally to Britain. A viable formula for their future existence had to be devised. The ideal solution seemed to be federation of all nine mini-states, and the subject was first broached at a meeting of the nine rulers in February 1968. Even though the idea was carefully and positively considered by all, it soon became apparent that significant differences in the sizes of the states and the varying degree of their modernisation, as well as outstanding political rivalries, constituted insurmountable obstacles in the path to federation. Bahrain and Qatar, the two largest amirates, chose to go their own ways as separate independent states. The remaining seven (Abu Dhabi, Dubai, Sharjah, 'Ajman, Ra's al-Khayma, Umm al-

Qaywayn, and al-Fujayra), despite considerable outstanding differences, formed the United Arab Emirates (UAE).[8]

Administratively, the British withdrawal in December 1971 resulted in the abolition of the office of Political Resident in the Persian Gulf, while the subordinate Political Agents in each of the amirates were restyled Ambassadors. In Oman, the ambiguous relationship of the Consul-General to the Resident was terminated and the post upgraded to an embassy. Among the last loose threads to tie up were new treaties: the defence treaty with Kuwait (signed upon that state's independence in 1961) was converted to a treaty of friendship and similar treaties were signed with Bahrain, Qatar and the UAE. Finally, the RAF bases in Bahrain and Sharjah were closed, leaving only the ones in Oman (at Masira and Salala) to uphold the long British military legacy in the Middle East.

America (Re)Discovers Arabia

The gradual British removal from East of Suez paralleled the diminution of European control and influence throughout the Middle East in the decades following the Second World War. Gradually, the British and French hold on their mandates, colonies, and technically independent but tightly supervised states in the region withered away, in conjunction with the worldwide process of decolonisation. Simultaneously, the emergence of the East–West Cold War as a global rivalry and the inability of Washington's European allies, due to their weakened state after the war, to contain the Soviet Union in their former imperial dominions meant that the US took a stronger and more direct interest in Middle Eastern affairs.

Certainly, it is true that the US government and various American individuals and groups had played a role in the Middle East prior to the war and wartime exigencies had produced a temporary American concern with and presence in a number of countries in the region. But the period of the late 1940s and early 1950s was far more central in laying the foundations for a permanent American concern. Among the milestones in this process can be counted the following factors: (1) American concern with Soviet expansion into the area after the Second World War, particularly evident in the sustained effort to remove Soviet troops from Iran in 1946 and in the promulgation of the Truman Doctrine in 1947; (2) the recognition of Israel in 1948, followed by the first of many attempts to ameliorate the Arab–Israeli conflict through the

Tripartite Declaration of 1950; (3) the deterioration of relations during the 1950s with the emerging radical Arab states, in particular Nasir's Egypt, caused in part by the superimposition of a Cold War perspective on Arab politics and resulting in the ineffectual Baghdad Pact of 1955 (strongly supported by the US, even though it was not a member) and the dispatch of Marines to Lebanon in 1958; and (4) the tremendous postwar growth in Middle Eastern oil production, the majority of which was by then under the control of American corporations.

Underlying this quickening of interest was a long history of connections between the United States and the Arabian Peninsula. Merchant vessels had begun to make frequent calls at such ports as Mocha and Muscat since the end of the eighteenth century.[9] The first Arab emissary to the US was sent from the ruler of Muscat (and Zanzibar) in 1840. In the 1890s, the Arabian Mission of the Reformed Church of America began its work in the Gulf, eventually establishing missions and hospitals in Matrah (Oman), Manama (Bahrain), Kuwait, and Basra and al-'Amara (Iraq). In the twentieth century, the spur to the broadening of American interests was the intrusion of American oil companies into what had been a solely British preserve.

The pressure exerted by Washington (at the behest of the American majors) on London for an 'open-door' policy in the Gulf produced the Red Line Agreement of 1928, the first step in the American penetration. By the agreement's terms, a 'red line' was drawn around Turkey, the Levant and the Arabian Peninsula except for Kuwait, within which it was agreed that only the Iraq Petroleum Company (IPC) would have the right to exploit oilfields. In return, the American companies Standard Oil of New Jersey and Mobil received a share in IPC. Subsequently, Standard Oil of California (SOCAL) and Texaco, operating as CALTEX, acquired the concession for Bahrain, and then SOCAL, later joined by Texaco, Standard of New Jersey and Mobil, acquired the concession for Saudi Arabia and formed ARAMCO. Finally, Gulf Oil took 50 per cent ownership of Kuwait Oil Company. These prewar gains were supplemented after the war by the gradual penetration of the Gulf by American independents, particularly through successful acquisition of new offshore concessions and rebidding on territory relinquished from existing concessions.

The postwar expansion of oil production was accompanied by a corresponding rise in official US establishments in the region. While

The US and Gulf Security 117

consular posts had been established in Muscat and Aden quite early, they had been forgotten outposts (and Muscat was even abandoned in 1915). The 'real' permanent presence in the Peninsula appeared only after the Second World War. Emerging US-Saudi relations, initiated by ARAMCO's presence, prompted the establishment of an embassy in Jidda in 1942 and, later, a consulate in Dhahran, the centre of ARAMCO operations. Since then, the most significant aspects of American involvement in the Peninsula have revolved around Saudi Arabia. The complete absence of any connection less than half a century ago has been completely transformed, building on a combination of the special role played by ARAMCO in Saudi development, the erstwhile American military presence in Dhahran and the burgeoning US arms sales and training teams.[10]

The American connection to the smaller states of the Gulf was far later in arriving and has remained in the shadow of US-Saudi relations. A consulate was opened in Kuwait in 1951 and subsequently upgraded to an embassy upon Kuwaiti independence. The American Ambassador to Kuwait also served as non-resident ambassador to the other amirates after 1971, until other ambassadors took up positions in Bahrain, Qatar, the UAE and Oman during 1974. The central facet of these relations has been trade, greatly increased after the 1973–4 oil price revolution, yet ties between the amirates and Britain remain far stronger even today.

Nevertheless, there are other facets to American involvement with the smaller states of the Gulf. MIDEASTFOR still makes extensive use of Bahraini facilities, American banks are prominent among Bahrain's offshore banking units, and a large proportion of the oil refined in Bahrain (but actually produced in Saudi Arabia) is purchased for use by the US Seventh Fleet. The US–Omani relationship — oldest among the states in the Arabian Peninsula and yet one of the newest — still has not supplanted the older Anglo–Omani connection. Yet Oman's strategic location on the Strait of Hormuz and its willingness to allow American use of its military facilities in emergency situations has made it of key concern to US policy-makers and has prompted attendant military and economic aid and commercial involvement.[11]

The record of the past three decades has seen a steady shift in the balance of British and American influence and power in the Gulf. Britain still remains an important commercial and cultural force in the region, but the torch of military and political power on which the

Gulf states uncertainly depend for certain aspects of their defence has passed to the United States.

US Interests in the Gulf in the 1980s[12]

The United States has two central or strategic interests in the Gulf, preserving access to oil supplies and preventing Soviet expansion there, as shown in Table 4.1.[13] Underlying these twin interests are a number of tactical objectives, i.e. the means by which the US seeks

Table 4.1: US Interests in the Gulf in the 1980s

Strategic interests
 I. Guarantee continued access to Gulf oil
 II. Resist Soviet expansionism in the Gulf

Tactical objectives
 1. Develop the capability for military intervention in the Gulf, through:
    a. Creating a viable military force for use in the Gulf
    b. Continuing naval deployments in the Gulf and northern Arabian Sea
    c. Continuing efforts to gain contingency access to regional military facilities
 2. Deter Soviet military attack and contain Soviet political influence in the Gulf, through:
    a. Stressing US resolve to defend region through use of military force, if necessary
    b. Preventing Soviet penetration of Iran
    c. Limiting Soviet influence in region to existing clients in the PDRY, Ethiopia and Afghanistan
    d. Encouraging Iraqi and North Yemeni movement towards the West
 3. Support the status quo in friendly states of the region, through:
    a. Continuing supportive relationship with Saudi Arabia, including:
       i. Strong economic ties
       ii. US participation in Saudi development efforts
       iii. Enhanced US military presence in and ties to Saudi Arabia
       iv. Continued co-operation on policies regarding the Middle East, particularly the Arab–Israeli conflict
    b. Continuing supportive relationship with the other GCC states, especially in economic field and continued minor arms sales
 4. Promote stability in the region through:
    a. Continuing efforts for a peaceful solution to the Arab–Israeli conflict
    b. Supporting peaceful resolution of the Iran–Iraq war while providing low-profile security assistance to GCC states

to preserve or achieve its strategic interests. It is hardly necessary to emphasise the role of Gulf oil in American interests. Even though American dependence on oil imports from the Gulf has declined markedly in the last few years, Western Europe, Japan and Korea remain heavily dependent on that source (as shown in Chapter 7). Furthermore, it should be remembered that nearly 60 per cent of all world oil reserves are contained in the Middle East, with approximately 25 per cent of the global total in Saudi Arabia alone. Despite the present oil glut and the travails of OPEC, the world's reliance upon Gulf oil is likely to continue for decades to come.

But even if the Gulf held no oil, it is possible that its position as a superpower would require the US to seek to prevent Soviet acquisition of such a geopolitically important asset. The Gulf can serve as a key 'land-bridge' between the Soviet Union and the Middle East, South Asia and East Africa, as well as a window on the Indian Ocean. Add to this the presence of oil in the region, and it is possible — if not probable under peacetime conditions — that Soviet regional goals include denial of Gulf oil to the West and/or the control of the Gulf's oil for Soviet consumption. The first is an unambiguous threat requiring an American counter. The second assumption may not occur if, as is likely, Soviet import needs in the future can be met by the cheaper and more practical means of simply purchasing Gulf oil or acquiring it by barter.

It should be stressed that securing the two central strategic US interests requires employment of a complex, multi-layered strategy, involving all the tactical objectives listed in Table 4.1. This is partly true because threats to these interests may arise from an unknown number of sources, either individually or in combination, and also because a single tool cannot achieve both strategic objectives (or perhaps even one of them alone). Furthermore, while there is a considerable degree of overlap between tactical objectives, some may be contradictory, thus requiring a subtle, multi-faceted policy mix. As will be emphasised again, US military activities form only one part of US tactical objectives in the Gulf. Indeed, military force can be of only limited utility to the US, and is almost entirely restricted to the context of a direct Soviet assault (a relatively unlikely contingency). Most of the other objectives listed are far more important and occur in many more likely circumstances.

Threats to Gulf Security: The Paradigm

A composite paradigm of threats to Gulf security is presented in Table 4.2. It should be noted that this paradigm represents the perceptions of the United States (and its Western allies) and the six GCC states. Naturally, it does not consider the interests of the Soviet Union or Iran. Iraq's inclusion is somewhat problematic, but its interests increasingly parallel those of the GCC states, particularly since the outbreak of the Iran–Iraq war, and thus its perceptions are uncertainly represented in the paradigm as well. As a composite, the paradigm obviously cannot fairly represent the views of each actor. Not all the categories of threats presented in the paradigm are perceived as such by all the actors, nor are all mutually perceived threats seen with the same degree of potentiality or danger. Furthermore, the efforts of one actor to preserve its conception of Gulf security may be directly regarded as a threat by another.[14]

As an example of the last point, 'United States policies' (category I.D in the table) of course do not constitute a threat in American perception, but may constitute one in the opinion of the GCC states under certain circumstances. Category III.C ('Policy changes in existing governments') may be regarded in the same manner. Likewise, the inclusion of I.C ('Israel') reflects a difference of opinion. Certainly, some Israeli policies are regarded as definite threats by the GCC states, but are not likely to be seen as such by US administrations. Furthermore, GCC attempts to enhance their defences against this particular 'threat' will receive little help from Washington.

It may be difficult in practice to distinguish between a regional threat of subversion (II.B) and internally generated dissidence (III.B). While dissidence may be generated solely by internal causes, the dissidents may soon appeal for or rely upon outside support. Similarly, a state may attempt to sow opposition within its neighbour solely for its own purposes and create dissident groups out of nothing. The difference between categories III.A ('Replacement of existing governments') and III.B ('Opposition to existing governments') is simply one of degree of success: in the case of A, there is a change of government and/or leaders, while B represents the existence of attempts to carry out this change without success.

As a final note on the paradigm, these categories represent types

Table 4.2: Threats to Gulf Security

I. External threats (arising from factors external to the immediate Gulf littoral)
   A. Direct Soviet assault on the Gulf and approaches:
      1. Invasion through Iran to Khuzestan
      2. Aerial attack on oil installations (fields, pipelines, terminals)
      3. Air and/or sea attack on sea lines of communication (e.g. on Strait of Hormuz, Bab al-Mandab, or Cape Route)
   B. Indirect Soviet attack on Gulf through manipulation of regional clients:
      1. Pressure from Afghanistan on Iran and/or Pakistan
      2. PDRY attack on Oman, YAR, or Saudi Arabia
      3. Ethiopian attack on Somalia, Djibouti, or Sudan
   C. Israel:
      1. New Arab–Israeli war
      2. Israeli moves perceived as 'provocations' (e.g. action on West Bank, new offensive in Lebanon, aerial raids on Arab territory, aerial or naval confrontation with Saudi Arabia)
   D. United States policies:
      1. Unilateral military deployment to secure oilfields (direct invasion)
      2. Unilateral military action against a Gulf state or states (similar to Iranian hostage rescue attempt)
      3. Collaborative relationship with Israel (perception of US approval of and even participation in Israeli actions)
      4. Economic actions (e.g. import/export or investment restrictions)
II. Regional threats (arising from the interaction of two or more Gulf states)
   A. Armed conflict:
      1. Border tension and clashes
      2. Full-scale war
   B. Subversion directed by one state against another or others:
      1. Radical Islamic movements
      2. Marxist–Leninist movements
      3. Pan–Arab socialist movements
      4. Conservative/tribal opposition
   C. Exacerbation of existing ethnic, religious, and/or social divisions:
      1. Arab–Iranian
      2. Sunni–Shi'i
      3. Ethnic irredentist/separatist movements (e.g. Kurds or Baluch)
      4. Yemeni–Saudi tensions
III. Internal threats (arising from factors within a single Gulf state)
   A. Replacement of existing governments:
      1. Change of government within existing ruling family or power-holding elite
      2. Coup by secular left
      3. Coup by Islamic radicals
   B. Opposition to existing governments (deterioration of authority):
      1. Tensions due to political repression
      2. Isolated attacks on government (sabotage or terrorism)
      3. Insurrection (due to ethnic, sectarian, or ideological divisions)
      4. Civil War or other absence of effective state authority or control
   C. Policy changes in existing governments (conflicting with US policy or interests):
      1. Economic issues of oil pricing and production levels
      2. 'Oil weapon' (the political use of oil supplies to influence or change US policy)

of potential threats, not actual ones. In any neutral assessment of this paradigm (i.e. not from the point of view of any specific actor), some potential threats must be seen as far more likely than others. In addition, the resolution of contradictory 'threats' can be accomplished only by the growth of converging national interests on the part of the West and the GCC states. This said, an evaluation of the relative imminence of the threat categories listed here constitutes a necessary first step before considering the manner and means by which the threats can be countered.

Evaluating External Threats

Of the four categories of external threats described in the paradigm, only two (the direct and indirect Soviet threats) will be discussed here. Discussion of how US policies may contribute to a threat scenario is better left to the next chapter. While the connection of Israel to Gulf security is very real and cannot be ignored, its removal as a 'threat' to Gulf security can be accomplished only by a permanent resolution of the Arab–Israeli dispute, a complex subject which cannot be treated adequately here.

To a far greater degree than is the case with the US and other Western countries, the intentions and motivations of the Soviet Union can only be guessed at. Even the extent of deliberate Soviet activities in various areas of the world is a matter of serious contention among Western observers, let alone the causes behind their moves. Nevertheless, it is undeniable that the Soviet Union has long expressed a close interest in Gulf affairs, if only as a mirror of Western concern with that area.

Western observers have postulated a number of possible Soviet goals in Southwest Asia and the Gulf.[15] At least six discrete goals have been advanced in recent years.

(1) To protect its vulnerable southern borders.

1.1. Southwest Asia is the only major area (apart from Finland) where the Soviet Union adjoins the non-communist world.
1.2. Unrest in Southwest Asia has the potential to spill over into the Muslim Soviet republics in Central Asia.

(2) The geographic importance of the region provides a geopolitical imperative.

2.1. Control of the Gulf would give direct access to the Indian Ocean.[16]
2.2. Southwest Asia can be seen as a 'land-bridge' to the Middle East, Africa and South Asia, or generally the Indian Ocean basin.

(3) To reduce Western influence in the region (through propaganda and other destabilisation measures), contain Chinese influence and expand Soviet influence (through the cultivation of existing states, acquisition of client states, and general support for revolutionary movements).
(4) To prevent Western access to oil (presumably direct action would be under wartime conditions only).[17]
(5) To acquire Gulf oil for domestic use.[18]
(6) To gain acceptance as an equal, a superpower with legitimate interests in the Gulf and Middle East, as elsewhere in the world.

Most of these goals can be seen as having anti-status-quo implications. This is not surprising since the US, in the Gulf as elsewhere in the world, is generally the defender of the status quo. In any objective assessment of the two superpowers' relative position in the Gulf, the US enjoys a far more secure position at present. In order to redress this imbalance, the Soviet Union needs to encourage and even direct political change, if not actually support military action. But even assuming the above goals are accurate, the question arises of the degree of importance that the Kremlin ascribes to them. In other words, how intently are the Soviets likely to pursue any or all of these goals, and what means are they likely to use to achieve them?

A wide spectrum of opinion exists on Soviet strategy in the Gulf, Southwest Asia and the entire northwestern quadrant of the Indian Ocean. At the one extreme, Soviet behaviour is said to be directed by a 'grand design', with each action constituting a step in a plan aimed at gradually achieving total control of the entire Gulf. The other extreme postulates that all recent changes in the region are the sole consequence of internal developments. Among those writers holding views nearer the first extreme are Robert W. Tucker, Albert Wohlstetter, W. Scott Thompson and George Lenczowski.[19]

In general, the 'grand design' viewpoint and its variants hold that the Soviets have instigated the recent changes in this area and, where they have not been responsible for instigation, they have benefited from these changes. The Soviets have manipulated their forces and clients on the periphery of the Gulf in a predetermined 'pincer movement' on the Gulf itself. In addition, it is frequently alleged that Soviet advances have been made possible by a lack of American will or by its unwillingness to defend its vital national interests, around the world as well as in the Gulf.[20]

On the opposing side, various authors challenge the view of omniscient Soviet calculation and execution. They tend to see the primary causes of change as being internal in origin and hold that the Soviets essentially have reacted to favourable developments in the region. In A. Z. Rubinstein's words, 'Opportunism, not ideology, impels Soviet policy, which has taken advantage of, but not determined, the setbacks to Western interests.'[21] Fred Halliday asserts that, in so far as change in the region has been due to external causes, the US has been more responsible for any adverse shift in the balance of influence than the Soviet Union and cites the nature of the American relationship with Pahlavi Iran among other examples.[22] He also points out that the Soviets have shown no more ability to 'control' their clients in the periphery of the Gulf than they displayed in their previous 30 years of relations with 'client states' in the Arab world.

The above debate has risen to the fore as a result of a series of developments in the region over the last decade or so, and particularly those taking place during the tenure of the Carter administration, which gave rise in the West to an immediate sense of urgency about the future of the Gulf. The first worrying development was the 1974 revolution in Ethiopia, resulting in the replacement of the Haile Selassie monarchy by a Marxist republic. This was followed several years later by, in close order, the Somali invasion of the Ogaden region of Ethiopia, the ousting of the Soviets from Somalia and their entrenchment in Ethiopia, and the subsequent dispatch of Cuban troops to defend the Ogaden and later to fight against the Eritreans. Even though Somalia, pushed back from the Ogaden, turned to the West for assistance and alliance, the net outcome of events in the Horn of Africa appeared to have worked to Soviet advantage.

The next significant change occurred on the other side of the Red Sea. In June 1978, the president of the Yemen Arab Republic

(North Yemen) was assassinated by an agent from South Yemen. Two days later, the president of the People's Democratic Republic of Yemen (South Yemen) was also dead, and his replacement appeared to be considerably more pro-Soviet. Less than a year later, North and South Yemen fought a brief border war, during which the South advanced deep into North Yemeni territory. In reaction to this fighting, the Carter administration agreed to supply a number of arms to the YAR government, with payment provided by Saudi Arabia, and stationed a carrier task force off the South Yemen coast.[23]

A major reason why Washington acted with such alacrity on being faced with what must be seen as a relatively minor disruption seems to have been due to events in Iran immediately previous to this. Midway through 1978, it became obvious that Muhammad Reza Shah's regime was in serious trouble. Despite American efforts to ameliorate the tension, which probably could have had only marginal effect in any case, the Shah left the country in early 1979. Soon after, the monarchy was dissolved and the Islamic Republic of Iran proclaimed. Accusations were freely thrown at that time of who was responsible for 'losing' Iran, and fears were widespread that the upheaval in that country could easily spread to its neighbours. The fall of the Shah's regime, the emergence of a new government deeply hostile to the US, and the episode of the American hostages all contributed in no small way to the declining fortunes of the Carter presidency.

The fourth major development, coming on the heels of the last two, was the Soviet move into Afghanistan at the end of 1979. While the Soviet takeover was far from complete, as widespread and persistent resistance sprang up, and although the action was roundly condemned by most states, it was seen by many in the West as one more successful step in a strategy of encirclement. This Soviet action, coming on top of other disappointing turns in Soviet–American relations, finally drove Carter to charge Moscow with betrayal.

The combination of these developments was interpreted widely as either parts of the 'grand design' or as symptoms of a chronic instability in the region by which the Soviet Union had a means of entry. The area seemed to fit the description of 'arc of crisis', as coined by Zbigniew Brzezinski, or 'crescent of instability'. The administration's growing conviction that, at the very least, the Soviet Union could easily exploit these upheavals, and probably had a hand in their development, led to promulgation of the Carter Doctrine, as announced in Carter's State of the Union Address of 23 January 1980: 'Any attempt by any outside forces to gain control of the Persian Gulf region will be regarded as an assault on the vital interests of the United States of America, and such an assault will be repelled by any means necessary, including military force.'[24] In practical terms, this policy hurried the creation of a Rapid Deployment Force (RDF), as well as emphasised increased reliance on military co-operation with and arms sales to Saudi Arabia. The Reagan administration upheld the thrust of the Carter Doctrine, building up RDF capabilities even as it expanded the American warning to Moscow to expect counter-attack for any Gulf invasion at a time, place and manner of American choosing.

The debate over whether the Soviet role in recent developments around the Gulf's periphery was causal or simply exploitive remains unsettled. But it can be said that even if Moscow has attempted to pursue a 'grand design' aiming at control of Gulf oilfields, it has yet to bear much fruit in the Arabian Peninsula. The Soviet Union maintains diplomatic relations with only three of the eight states of the Peninsula (compared to seven of the eight for the US).[25] Relations with Iraq have cooled considerably in recent years (although the level of arms sales went up as the Iran–Iraq war sputtered on) and the Iranian revolution has not provided Moscow with a secure toehold in that country either. As Karen Dawisha notes, 'The presence of troops in Afghanistan may have put the Soviets so near to the Gulf in geographic terms, yet not for many years had Moscow been so far from influencing events in that region.'[26]

South Yemen is the only Peninsula state clearly falling into a Soviet sphere of influence. Yet, even there, changes since 1980 indicate that the degree of Soviet control remains especially limited.[27] The Soviet Union continues to provide economic and military assistance to North Yemen, but this represents less of a subservience on the part of Sanaa than a continuation of a relationship extending back 30 years and a check on external pressures exerted on North Yemen by its neighbours, Saudi Arabia and South Yemen. The third state with which Moscow enjoyed official relations up to mid-1985 is Kuwait, one of the conservative, Western-oriented amirates of the Gulf. Once again, the existence of diplomatic relations is less an indicator of common outlook than an expression of Kuwait's desire to appear neutral or non-aligned in

East–West matters, and as a possible check on Iraq in earlier years when Soviet–Iraqi relations were better and Iraq still held its claim to sovereignty over Kuwait.

Elsewhere, the Soviet record remains embarrassing. Despite periodic rumours of the possible assumption of official relations with Saudi Arabia, this has yet to come to pass nor is it likely to do so in the foreseeable future. The one surprising breakthrough was the decision in September 1985 by Oman to establish relations with Moscow. The Omani government is, however, only slightly less anti-communist than Saudi Arabia and is the GCC state most militarily co-operative with the US; establishment of official (non-resident) ties may be related to the normalisation of relations with South Yemen. Leftist underground movements in the Peninsula apparently have lost much of what little steam they had and, in any case, were far more amenable to guidance from Baghdad (which periodically has purged its own communists) than from Moscow.

In conclusion, few if any developments in the Arabian Peninsula in recent years which might be interpreted as worrisome for Gulf security appear to have been instigated by the Soviets, nor have they produced any unambiguously advantageous results for Moscow. The record of Soviet involvement in the Arabian Peninsula over the past two decades or more indicates that any possible benefits to the USSR have remained minimal and static. There have been no dramatic breakthroughs in the reduction of American or Western influence since the British departure from Aden (hardly engineered by Moscow). No new Soviet client states have emerged since South Yemen became independent in 1967. Moscow has succeeded in establishing diplomatic relations with few Peninsula states since Aden's independence — and staunchly Western-allied ones at that — thereby belatedly achieving equality with arch-rival China. Finally, for well into the foreseeable future, if the Soviet Union wants Gulf oil, it looks as though it will have to resign itself to buying it just as the rest of the world does.

Evaluating Regional Threats

The outbreak and continuing, seemingly inexhaustible, nature of the Iran–Iraq war illustrates the all-too-present danger of regional threats to Gulf security. As the paradigm demonstrates, there are several different kinds of regional tensions. Conflict over borders has been a recurrent theme in the recent history of the Peninsula, particularly as modern nation states have emerged there and oil deposits have made delineation of precise boundaries crucial. Notable examples of this kind of dispute in recent decades would include: (1) the Saudi incursion into Buraimi oasis in the early 1950s; (2) Iraqi claims on Kuwait; (3) the controversy concerning sovereignty over the Shatt al-'Arab; (4) the Saudi–Kuwaiti dispute over ownership of the tiny islands of Qaru and Umm al-Maradim (an unresolved leftover from the division of their Neutral Zone); (4) the Bahraini–Qatari dispute over ownership of the Hawar Islands; and (6) near-clashes over the Oman–Fujayra boundary (as well as the numerous disputes among the members of the UAE).

The Iran–Iraq war, of course, represents a major step beyond border clashes. A complex mix of factors contributed to the outbreak of full-scale hostilities between Iran and Iraq in September 1980. In part, a contributing climate of antagonism may have stemmed from the long-standing rivalry between the two 'great powers' of the Gulf for dominance in the region. Ancient mutual suspicions between Arabs and Persians (as illustrated in recent years by the bitter contest over whether the Gulf should be known as Persian or Arabian) constitutes an overlay on this geopolitical competition, as does the Sunni–Shi'i schism to some degree (although nationalism appears to engender stronger claims on political loyalties).[28]

The question of rights in the jointly shared Shatt al-'Arab waterway provides one of the more immediate causes of the war. A 1937 treaty giving Iraq (a British client state at the time) control over the entire water channel, except in a few locations, was sorely remembered by Iran. The Shah unilaterally abrogated the treaty in 1969 and asserted Iranian claims to an equal division of the main channel by threats of force. This situation was formally recognised by Baghdad through the 1975 Algiers Accord and a subsequent treaty between the two countries, in return for which Iran ceased its support of Kurdish dissidence within Iraq.

The final and most important factor was the Iranian revolution, which added a new ideological dimension to all the existing forms of competition. In some ways, it resembled the impact of the Iraqi revolution, which first disturbed the quiet, conservative waters of the Gulf in 1958. The revolution had introduced unwelcome pressures and the threat of subversion against the other states of the Gulf with the goal of overthrowing them all. Then, in 1979, a new ideological threat appeared. Its goal was and remains the complete socio-political transformation of all the Gulf states, and the attempted subversion of its neighbours was prominent among its early methods.

The initial Iraqi attack on Iran seems to have been predicated both on defensive grounds and on pure opportunism. Iraq was legitimately provoked by Iran's broadcasts of anti-regime propaganda into Iraq and its considerable support for Iraq dissidents. The two countries had been engaged in an irregular campaign of border skirmishes and cross-frontier shelling for nearly a year. In Iraqi eyes, the surprise and shock of a successful attack would cause the collapse of the fragile revolutionary regime in Tehran and thus topple Khomeini and his supporters. Such a strategy promised to eliminate a serious threat from a hostile neighbour, to cut the ground out from under internal Iraqi dissidents, to enhance Iraqi President Saddam Husayn's standing among the Gulf's rulers and in the Arab world, and to solve the border problem by simply occupying the disputed territory. That the initial drive into Iran failed to accomplish either the political goal of bringing down the Iranian regime or the military objective of crushing the Iranian army was thus both a political miscalculation and a military failure.

Clearly, the Iraqi attack launched on 23 September 1980 was intended to be of a limited military nature. Rather than gathering maximum force in one place and launching a sustained drive across the strategically key province of Khuzestan towards Iran's oilfields, Iraqi forces simultaneously attacked at a variety of points along the length of the border. The Iraqis failed to knock out the principal military installations in Khuzestan, nor was there any serious attempt to take or destroy the oilfields. It was conceived as essentially a land-based campaign and Iraq made little attempt to carry the fighting to the air or sea. As a consequence, once the initial objectives were attained, Iraqi forces lost their momentum and the advance ground to an inconclusive halt.[29]

The key Khuzestani city of Khorramshahr fell only after prolonged hand-to-hand combat in its streets and the oil and industrial centre of Abadan was never captured. The Iraqi failure to interdict Iranian supply lines to Abadan and to knock out the Iranian air force when it had the advantage of surprise proved to be nearly fatal. By mid-November 1980, the war had deteriorated into stalemate, with neither side able to advance its positions. The Iraqis seemed content to dig in where they were and wait out the winter;

the Iranians were still too disorganised to establish an effective counter-offensive.

Eventually, however, the momentum shifted from Iraq to Iran. The first thrusts in the long-awaited Iranian counter-offensive took place in 1981, but the major campaign which drove the Iraqis into retreat did not unfold until early 1982. By its end, the Abadan siege had been lifted, the Iraqis pushed out of their positions in northern Khuzestan, and Khorramshahr recaptured. By the end of May 1982, the Iranian offensive had achieved a clear victory and most of the territory lost to Iraq in the initial attack of 1980 had been regained. The looming question for Iran was whether to pressure Iraq to sue for peace or to invade.

While the Iranian counter-attack had succeeded in liberating most of Khuzestan from Iraqi occupation, it did not bring peace. Partially, this was because enclaves of Iranian territory still remained under Iraq's control. Furthermore, the prewar boundary questions over the Shatt al-'Arab and elsewhere were still unsettled. While the Iraqi leadership, reeling from its reverses on the battlefield, was willing to withdraw from all occupied territory and accept the principle of war reparations (which would have to be paid by the Gulf monarchies in any case), the inflexible Iranian demand for the ousting of Saddam Husayn (and even the entire Ba'thi leadership of Iraq) virtually prevented any negotiations. This hardline stance seemed to be dictated by the prevailing insecurity and competition within Iranian domestic politics, along with Ayatollah Khomeini's strong enmity directed towards Saddam Husayn personally.

At the end of the May 1982 offensive, the position of the Iraqi government was perilous, both economically and militarily. Saddam Husayn had no choice but to withdraw all his troops from Iranian territory, announce a unilateral ceasefire, and hope that Iran would agree to negotiations. Iran, however, was unwilling to negotiate a settlement to the war, particularly after the Israeli invasion of Lebanon in June 1982 raised Iranian revolutionary spirit to a fever pitch. The inflexibility and vindictiveness displayed by the Tehran regime, its pan-Islamic revolutionary ideology, and the belief that it had broken the back of the Iraqi military machine all contributed to the decision to invade Iraq. The result was a miscalculation rivalling Baghdad's earlier decision to launch the war.

In mid-July and early August 1982, Iran launched a number of 'human wave' offensives at Iraqi territory with only minimal success and at a tremendous cost in human life. Instead of a series of quick victories as occurred in the 1982 fighting, Iran found itself bogged down in a static war along the border, short of necessary equipment and trained troops, and reduced to sending thousands of its young men to near-certain death in attacks against well-emplaced Iraqi defences. Some bits of territory had been gained, but the effort to stretch Iraqi forces out along nearly 400 miles of fighting had produced no significant benefits. In addition, attempts to raise a Shi'i fifth column in Iraq were no more successful than Iraq had been in gaining the support of the predominantly Arab population of Khuzestan. After two years of fighting, the war had reached a permanent stage of stalemate. Rough parity emerged between the two combatants, whose capabilities were offset by balancing disadvantages. Iran's so-called 'final offensives' in 1983 further confirmed the inability of either side to gain the upper hand in the war.

The continuing stalemate on the battlefront was repeatedly confirmed through 1984 and 1985. Given the military parity between the two combatants and Iran's intransigence regarding negotiations, except with conditions impossible for Iraq to accept, the war simply lumbered on. The next phase was one of 'trench warfare' along the two countries' borders and successive Iraqi attempts to raise the stakes and thereby force Iran towards the negotiating table. This has been a risky game which has not had the results Iraq intended. Instead, Iraqi actions have prompted Iranian counter-escalation, threatening to expand the area of war to the Arab littoral of the Gulf and possibly to hinder traffic through the Strait of Hormuz. And so the war grinds on, adding to its terrible toll in human life and wasted opportunities.[30]

It may well be that this particular war, with the stubborn refusal of one of the combatants to enter negotiations or even agree to a cease-fire, its trench warfare, and its repeated inconclusive offensives, is very atypical of war scenarios in the Gulf — as well as the Third World in general.[31] The very size of the two warring states and their military establishments indicates that such a war could not occur between other countries of the Gulf littoral (as evidenced by the Yemens' periodic bouts). Nevertheless, this does not mean that this stalemated war is not without wider ramifications. Indeed, periodically it has threatened to expand and draw in other participants. One scenario posits an Iraqi collapse, with the installation of an Iranian puppet regime in Baghdad, followed by a drive on Kuwait and Saudi Arabia, and with Iranian 'volunteers' perhaps marching across the Nafud Desert to Syria and Lebanon.

Considerable excitement was generated in the autumn of 1983 and again in early 1984 by Iraq's acquisition of French-supplied Super Etendard aircraft, equipped with Exocet missiles, and its threat to attack the Iranian oil terminal on Kharg Island. This was matched by Iranian threats, if the former were carried out, to close off the Strait of Hormuz. Such an attempt undoubtedly would cause the US and other Western powers to deploy forces to take other action in the strait to prevent its closure. It does seem, though, that Iran's execution of this threat would be only as a desperate last resort, since it would mean economic suicide for that country as well as for the Arab oil producers in the Gulf.

The 'tanker war' of spring and summer 1984, when Iraq for the first time began to employ the Super Etendards and Exocets against shipping bound to and from Kharg Island, also threatened to entangle the other Gulf states in active hostilities. While the US made a point of warning Iran on several occasions against interference with shipping and publicly sought to persuade Saudi Arabia and the UAE to allow it to station USAF fighters in GCC airfields, the GCC states played it very cautiously, directing tanker traffic to new channels close by the Arab littoral. Predictably, the American actions provoked angry words and additional threats from Tehran, without effecting the dénouement of this twist in the war. By midsummer, it appeared that Saudi cautiousness and minimal response to Iranian provocations had paid off: rather than escalating, attacks on tankers eased off, notwithstanding the downing of an Iranian F-4 Phantom by Saudi fighters.[32]

Over 80 ships were attacked between January 1984 and mid-1985. Nevertheless, the effectiveness of the tanker war was negligible, as it prompted no change in either belligerent's policy and oil importers' attention tended to wander during the continuing oil glut. Similarly, the outbreak of a series of bombing attacks on each side's major cities in early 1985 died out after a few weeks and a new round of escalation in the summer, involving a series of Iraqi attacks on the oil facilities of Kharg Island itself, had little permanent impact. A major Iranian offensive in March 1985, which had temporarily reached the Tigris river and momentarily breached Iraq's strategic Basra–Baghdad highway, failed for lack of logistical support and tactical mistakes. New Iraqi pipelines, scheduled to open in the mid-1980s, threatened to erode Iran's economic advantage and to move

Table 4.3: Shi'a Population in the Gulf (in thousands)

Country	Total population	Citizen population	Number of Shi'a	% of Shi'a citizens
Qatar	255	70	11	16
Oman	950	700	28	4
UAE	1,100	250	45	18
Kuwait	1,370	570	137	24
Bahrain	360	240	168	70
Saudi Arabia	8,500	5,500	440	8
Iraq	14,400	13,500	8,100	60
Iran	42,000	40,000	36,800	92
Totals	68,935	60,830	45,729	75

Source: James A. Bill, 'Resurgent Islam in the Persian Gulf', *Foreign Affairs*, vol. 63, no. 1 (fall 1984), p. 120.

the belligerents closer to parity. The apt comparison has often been made with the First World War, where the fighting settled down into years of bloody trench warfare. In the Iran–Iraq war, however, there seems little likelihood of breaking out of the trenches.

The notion of ideological differences, as raised in inter-Yemeni relations and the Iran–Iraq war, points to the possibility of ideological subversion, sponsored and/or supported by one state against its neighbour(s). There are a number of examples of this sort: (1) the rebellion in Oman's southern province of Dhufar, where logistical assistance and refuge was provided by neighbouring South Yemen; (2) the activities of the National Democratic Front in North Yemen, aided by South Yemen, as well as the opposition groups operating from North Yemen against Aden; (3) the 1981 attempted *coup d'état* in Bahrain, apparently organised and supplied by Iran; (4) Iraqi support in years past of movements seeking to overthrow the governments of various GCC states as well as the PDRY (to which may be added Libyan intrigues against some of these same states); and (5) Saudi intrigue in both Yemens. The first two examples reflect Marxist–Leninist goals, the third a radical Islamic orientation, the fourth pan-Arab socialist outlooks, and the fifth a conservative/traditionalist motivation.

Existing ethnic, sectarian, and other divisions hold the potential for future conflict between states, or may create a temptation to interfere in a state weakened by the ravages of such cleavages. The types of schisms listed in the paradigm seem self-explanatory. Iraqi allusions to the ancient battle of al-Qadisiya provide a clear indication of the continued importance of Arab-Persian hostility, as well as deep socio-religious animosities between Sunnis and Shi'is (see Table 4.3). It should be kept in mind, as well, that the Arab-Persian and Sunni-Shi'i schisms are only the principal ones in the Gulf, and that important disaffected ethnic minorities include the Kurds, Baluch, South Asians, Palestinians and others.

Evaluating Internal Threats

On the surface, at least, an internal threat to Gulf security — i.e. political change within one of the states of the region — may be as likely to appear as a regional threat. Yet it is far more difficult to predict and undoubtedly even more problematic for outsiders to deal with. The development of the revolution in Iran led many observers in the West to voice their fears that Saudi Arabia and the smaller states of the Gulf might be next. In support of this contention, they cited such factors as:

1. the influx of uncontrolled wealth into these countries;
2. the impact of rapid socio-economic change;
3. the existence of fragile, 'anachronistic', monarchical forms of government, based on ruling families and lacking political participation; and
4. growing social and ethnic schisms.

In particular, opponents of the F-15 and AWACS sales to Saudi Arabia brought up these arguments, along with reference to political unrest in that country's Eastern Province and the takeover of the Great Mosque in Mecca. The inherent instability of Saudi Arabia was implicitly confirmed by the Reagan 'codicil' to the Carter Doctrine, which held that the US would never allow Saudi Arabia to become another Iran.

But this pessimism over the future of the Arab states of the Gulf, where not motivated by simple hostility, ignores a number of fundamental differences between Saudi Arabia (and the other GCC states) and Iran. These include:

1. The nature of leadership: Iran demonstrated rigid, one-man rule under the Shah while Saudi Arabia is governed by a large ruling family, which in turn is based on principles of consensual tribal leadership.
2. The manner in which the regimes came to power: Reza Shah originally usurped power through the use of force and both he and his son ultimately retained power through repression, while modern Saudi Arabia was created partly through military unification, but even more by the skilful building of alliances by King 'Abd al-'Aziz.
3. Differences in political participation: Muhammad Reza Shah ruled in an imperially aloof manner and rejected any advice outside his immediate family, while major decisions within the Al Sa'ud must represent consensus on the part of a fairly large inner circle and general approval by the rest of the family and even, to some extent, the general body of Saudi citizens.[33]
4. Different attitudes to religion: the Shah sought to downplay Islam, reaching to Iran's pre-Islamic past for nationalist symbols, and adopted an antagonistic policy towards Iran's religious leaders; on the other hand, the impetus for the creation of the modern Saudi state derives from the eighteenth-century alliance between the Al Sa'ud and the religious reformer Muhammad 'Abd al-Wahhab, and the present state acts as the guardian of Islam.
5. Differences in population size: Saudi Arabia's far smaller population has allowed it to provide for universal employment and equitable distribution of oil income more easily than Iran.
6. Opposite experiences in political attitudes of the population: the Shah's policies eventually resulted in the alienation of nearly every class, which in turn fed growing repression, while Saudi Arabia has been able both to maintain tribal alliances and to co-opt the emerging 'middle classes' into supporting the regime by offering limited direct participation in the formulation of policies from within the government.

This is not to say that significant opposition to the present Saudi regime, or the regimes of the other GCC states, is impossible. Even though it appears that these governments have been very capable in adapting to rapidly changing requirements and expectations in the last several decades, the changes required in the future will be even greater and there is no certainty that present political systems will be able to continue to adapt successfully.

One postulation of the paradigm, 'Threats to Gulf Security', is concerned with the possible replacement of existing governments (Table 4.2, category III.A). At the present time, the likelihood of an extra-constitutional change in a GCC government being initiated by a member of the ruling family seems relatively remote. The last attempts in this manner were made in Qatar and Sharjah in 1972.[34] While a greater possibility of a coup from within the power-holding elite holds true for Iraq, under present circumstances such a co-ordinated effort seems likely only in the event of a military collapse. Even then, a successful coup would very likely involve Ba'thist military officers acting solely to remove Saddam Husayn and probably not in order to change Iraq's basic political orientation.

The Yemens present a different case. The poverty of the YAR, the ruggedness of the countryside and the strength of the tribes all combine to make the authority of the central government particularly tenuous. In addition, historical factors work against the legitimacy of the political system. Military *coups d'états* have been a prominent feature of YAR political life, and the present regime is as vulnerable to being overthrown as its predecessors. Political leadership in the PDRY also has been difficult to maintain for any length of time, with forced changes of the men at the top occurring in 1969, 1971, 1978, 1980 and 1986.[35] All of these changes, however, occurred within the elite framework of the National Liberation Front (the nucleus of the present ruling Yemeni Socialist Party) and have tended to tighten the ideological orientation of the elite and therefore the state.

The possibility of the emergence of opposition to existing governments occurring within the GCC (category III.B of the paradigm) seems remote. As noted earlier, repression is minimal within these political systems, as it is in the YAR (there largely because the state has little capacity to carry out such policies). The YAR until recently has seen widespread dissidence orchestrated by the rebel National Democratic Front, based on such causes as ideological differences with the Sanaa government, more personal opposition to present leaders, and the resentment of the Shafi'i (Sunni) half of the population of Zaydi domination. The longevity of the 'Ali 'Abdullah Salih regime in the YAR speaks for a certain amount of emerging stability. There was some active in-country opposition to the PDRY regime following the execution of the president in 1978, but this appears to have withered away. In many respects, the potential foundations of opposition to the singularly narrow ideological focus of the Aden government were eliminated during the 1963–7 struggle for independence.

In Iraq, however, conditions seem to be much more fertile for organised and troublesome opposition to the Baghdad government. Partly, this is due to the existing sectarian and ethnic divisions within the country. The Shi'a of Iraq comprise approximately 60 per cent of the total population yet receive less than their proportional share of political and economic benefits. Iran has had some success in stirring up Shi'i discontent through the Da'wa Party and its offshoots. The Kurds of the north have long sought the establishment of an independent state and, while quiescent at the present, Kurdish resistance to the Iraqi government may reappear at any time in the near future. Furthermore, strictly ideological opposition, particularly from the Iraqi Communist Party, has been prevalent in the past and eliminated only through draconian measures. It too may resurface.

As already mentioned in the case of Iraq, it should be noted that ethnic and sectarian schisms exist within many of these countries, as well as between them. While Iraq represents the most extreme case of fragmentation among the Arab states of the Gulf, significant divisions are also present in Saudi Arabia (with a sizable Shi'i minority in the Eastern Province, and strong geographical identities present in the Hijaz, Jabal Shammar and 'Asir regions); Kuwait (a sizable Shi'i minority, many of whom are also Persian — which has contributed to recent tensions); Bahrain (70 per cent Shi'a, who are generally poorer than the Sunni population, which also dominates in politics); the UAE (with a large number of minorities, including both Arab and Persian Shi'a, as well as armed forces composed in the majority of Omanis); Oman (with a nearly equal division between adherents of the Sunni and Ibadi sects, a substantial minority of Baluch, and an important split between coast and interior); and the YAR (also with a nearly equal division between Zaydis and Sunnis, which has far more important political implications than the sectarian schism of Oman). So far, none of these schisms has demonstrated any real likelihood of moving beyond simmering grievances to open rebellion. This is true even of the Shi'a of Iraq, despite direct provocation from Iran.[36]

The category of 'Policy changes in existing governments' (III.C) is the obverse of the paradigm's 'US policies' (I.D). That is to say, this category represents a threat to Gulf security according to US perceptions. Such perceptions would derive from an adverse reaction to policy shifts on the part of one or more littoral states because of a threat to Gulf security in the latter's perception. Presumably, such a US-perceived threat would have to be of considerable provocation and duration to force Washington to take hostile action and initiate use of military force to secure control of the oilfields, since both military and political risks undoubtedly will be very high.

It seems unlikely that such a provocation will be presented through issues of oil pricing or production levels. First, the ability to alter radically either price or production has been severely reduced by the circumstances of global 'oil glut', which is likely to continue well into the 1990s. Second, the GCC states are the least likely members of OPEC to act rashly, since they have especially strong ties to the US and the West (and have invested heavily there, which would be put at risk) and because they are mostly capital-surplus states and have less need to act as price hawks.

The 'Oil weapon' category (III.C.2) presumably would be activated only under conditions of a new, full-scale Arab–Israeli war. But even then, a genuine concerted effort at embargo or production cutbacks is not guaranteed. The GCC states were extremely reluctant to take action during the 1973 war (and in fact may have allowed as much oil to be lifted during the embargo as before); in 1986 or in the future, they have even more to lose economically and politically by such an action. In addition, assuming that there would still be an oil glut if and when another Arab–Israeli war occurs, the use of the oil weapon would be far less effective than in 1973–4, whether in practical terms or psychologically.

Still, assuming that the use of the oil weapon is a possibility, an American political or diplomatic response would be far more effective, working to bring an end to Arab–Israeli conflict if it has already broken out or to prevent its occurrence by seeking a permanent peaceful resolution. While the possible American invasion of Arab oilfields excites imaginations in the Arab world and among an American fringe, such an action is considered infeasible under all but the most extreme circumstances because of its exorbitant political costs and considerable military difficulties.

Notes

1. On the early period of Anglo–American confrontation, see Aaron David Miller, *Search for Security: Saudi Arabian Oil and American Foreign Policy, 1939–1949* (Chapel Hill, University of North Carolina Press, 1980); Michael B. Stoff, *Oil, War, and American Security: The Search for a National Policy on Foreign Oil, 1941–1947* (New Haven, Yale University Press, 1980); Irvine H. Anderson, *Aramco, the United States and Saudi Arabia: A Study of the Dynamics of Foreign Oil Policy, 1933–1950* (Princeton, Princeton University Press, 1981); and William Roger Louis, *The British Empire in the Middle East, 1945–1951: Arab Nationalism, the United States, and Postwar Imperialism* (Oxford, Clarendon Press, 1984), pp. 173–204.
2. See James L. Gormly, 'Keeping the Door Open in Saudi Arabia: The United States and the Dhahran Airfield, 1945–46,' *Diplomatic History*, vol. 4, no. 2 (1980), pp. 189–205; Barry Rubin, 'Anglo–American Relations in Saudi Arabia, 1941–1945', *Journal of Contemporary History*, vol. 14 (1979), pp. 253–67; and idem, *The Great Powers of the Middle East, 1941–1947* (London, Frank Cass, 1980), pp. 34–72.
3. See Peter W. DeForth, 'U.S. Naval Presence in the Persian Gulf: The Mideast Force Since World War II', *Naval War College Review*, vol. 28, no. 1 (1975), pp. 28–38; and US Congress, Senate, Committee on Foreign Relations, *United States Foreign Policy Objectives and Overseas Military Installations*, prepared by the Congressional Research Service, Library of Congress (Washington, USGPO, 1979).
4. For detailed accounts of the Buraimi dispute and the historical factors leading up to it, see J. B. Kelly, *Eastern Arabian Frontiers* (London, Faber & Faber, 1964); David Holden, *Farewell to Arabia* (London, Faber & Faber, 1966), pp. 201–13; and Husain Albaharna, *The Arabian Gulf States: Their Legal and Political Status and Their International Problems*, 2nd edn (Beirut, Librairie du Liban, 1975), pp. 196–238.
5. For a contemporary view of the value of British bases in the region, see Elizabeth Monroe, 'British Bases in the Middle East: Assets or Liabilities?', *International Affairs* (London), vol. 42, no. 1 (January 1966), pp. 23–34.
6. On the decision and processes of withdrawal, see D. C. Watt, 'The Decision to Withdraw from the Gulf', *Political Quarterly*, vol. 39, no. 3 (July–September 1968), pp. 310–21; *The Gulf: Implications of British Withdrawal* (Washington, Georgetown University, Center for Strategic and International Studies, February 1969; Special Report Series no. 8); William Luce, 'Britain's Withdrawal from the Middle East and Persian Gulf', *JRUSI*, vol. 114, no. 653 (March 1969), pp. 4–10; *The Economist*, 6 June 1970, survey on the Gulf; David Holden, 'The Persian Gulf: After the British Raj', *Foreign Affairs*, vol. 49, no. 4 (July 1971), pp. 721–35; and Elizabeth Monroe (rapporteuse), *The Changing Balance of Power in the Persian Gulf: The Report of an International Seminar at the Center for Mediterranean Studies, Rome* (New York, American Universities Field Staff, 1972).
7. Of this total, 4,700 belonged to the army. The RAF contingent included two fighter squadrons and 3,400 men, while the Royal Navy maintained three destroyer escorts, with small Royal Marine contingents, and six coastal minesweepers. James H. Noyes, *The Clouded Lens: Persian Gulf Security and U.S. Policy*, 2nd edn (Stanford, Ca, Hoover Institution Press, 1982), p. 27.
8. The formation of the UAE was complicated by serious rivalries between the seven amirates and by problems associated with the weighting of representation in

the Federal Council and apportionment of federal cabinet portfolios. One consequence was that Ra's al-Khayma refused to join upon independence in December 1971, apparently believing that a major oil strike was imminent. Failing to strike oil then, the amirate belatedly joined the federation in February 1972. On the regional impact of British withdrawal, see John Duke Anthony, *The Arab States in the Lower Gulf* (Washington, Middle East Institute, 1975); Rosemarie Said Zahlan, *The Origins of the United Arab Emirates* (London, Macmillan, 1978); and Frauke Heard-Bey, *From Trucial States to United Arab Emirates* (London, Longman, 1982).

9. For an overview of American ties to the Peninsula, see Joseph J. Malone, 'America and the Arabian Peninsula: The First Two Hundred Years', *Middle East Journal*, vol. 30, no. 3 (summer 1976), pp. 406-24.

10. Comprehensive studies of the American–Saudi relationship are contained in William B. Quandt, *Saudi Arabia in the 1980s: Foreign Policy, Security, and Oil* (Washington, Brookings Institution, 1981); US Congress, House of Representatives, Committee on Foreign Affairs, Subcommittee on Europe and the Middle East, *Saudi Arabia and the United States: The New Context in an Evolving 'Special Relationship'*, report prepared by the Foreign Affairs and National Defense Division of the Congressional Research Service (Washington, USGPO, 1981); and David Long, *The United States and Saudi Arabia: Ambivalent Allies* (Boulder, Co, Westview Press, 1985).

11. For more on this connection, see J. E. Peterson, 'American Policy in the Gulf and the Sultanate of Oman', *American–Arab Affairs*, no. 8 (summer 1984), pp. 117-30.

12. The subject of US security interests in the Gulf has been treated by: Harold Brown, *U.S. Security Policy in Southwest Asia: A Case Study in Complexity* (Washington, Johns Hopkins University School of Advanced International Studies, Johns Hopkins Foreign Policy Institute, 1981; Occasional Paper); Shahram Chubin, 'U.S. Security Interests in the Persian Gulf in the 1980s', *Daedalus*, vol. 109, no. 4 (1980), pp. 31–65; Anthony H. Cordesman, *The Gulf and the Search for Strategic Stability: Saudi Arabia, the Military Balance in the Gulf, and Trends in the Arab–Israeli Military Balance* (Boulder, Co, Westview Press, 1984); Geoffrey Kemp, 'Strategic Problems in the Persian Gulf Region', in George S. Wise and Charles Issawi (eds), *Middle East Perspectives: The Next Twenty Years* (Princeton, NJ, Darwin Press, 1981), pp. 71-9; and Emile A. Nakhleh, *The Persian Gulf and American Policy* (New York, Praeger, 1982).

13. In addition to the sources listed in the previous note, Congressional prints on US security interests in the Gulf include the reports done for the House of Representatives, Committee on Foreign Affairs, *The United States and the Persian Gulf* (Washington, USGPO, 1972) and *U.S. Security Interests in the Persian Gulf* (Washington, USGPO, 1981); the hearings before the House Committee on Foreign Affairs, published as *U.S. Interests in, and Policies Toward, the Persian Gulf, 1980* (Washington, USGPO, 1980) and (with the Joint Economic Committee) *U.S. Policy Toward the Persian Gulf* (Washington, USGPO, 1983); and the hearings before the Senate Committee on Foreign Relations, *U.S. Security Interests and Policies in Southwest Asia* (Washington, USGPO, 1980).

14. There is a growing body of literature on the topic of threats to Gulf security. A few of the more pertinent sources are: Hermann F. Eilts, 'Security Conditions in the Persian Gulf', *International Security*, vol. 5, no. 2 (1980), pp. 79–113; Hossein Amirsadeghi (ed.), *The Security of the Persian Gulf* (London, Croom Helm, 1981);

Abdel Majid Farid (ed.), *Oil and Security in the Arabian Gulf* (London, Croom Helm, 1981); J. E. Peterson (ed.), *The Politics of Middle Eastern Oil* (Washington, Middle East Institute, 1983); A. Z. Rubinstein (ed.), *The Great Game: Rivalry in the Persian Gulf and South Asia* (New York, Praeger, 1983); Z. Michael Szaz (ed.), *The Impact of the Iranian Events Upon Persian Gulf and United States Security* (Washington, American Foreign Policy Institute, 1979); and the four-part series on *Security in the Persian Gulf* by the International Institute for Strategic Studies (London, Gower, 1982).

15. Some recent recapitulations include the Carnegie Panel on U.S. Security and the Future of Arms Control, *Challenges for U.S. National Security*, 'The Military Balance in the Persian Gulf', pp. 149–94 (Washington, Carnegie Endowment, 1981); Dennis Ross, 'Considering Soviet Threats to the Persian Gulf', *International Security*, vol. 6, no. 2 (1981), pp. 159–80; idem, 'The Soviet Union and the Persian Gulf', *Political Science Quarterly*, vol. 99, no. 4 (winter 1984–5), pp. 615–35; Keith A. Dunn, 'Constraints on the USSR in Southwest Asia', *Orbis*, vol. 25, no. 3 (fall 1981), pp. 607–29; Shahram Chubin, 'Gains for Soviet Policy in the Middle East', *International Security*, vol. 6, no. 4 (1982), pp. 122–52; George Lenczowski, 'The Soviet Union and the Persian Gulf', *International Journal*, vol. 37, no. 2 (1982), pp. 307–27; and Michael Dixon, 'Soviet Policy in the Persian Gulf', *Journal of Defence and Diplomacy*, vol. 3, no. 2 (February 1985), pp. 23–7.

16. This is often mentioned as a continuation of the drive for a warm water port dating from tsarist times, represented by the long-standing interest and interference in Iran's internal affairs and efforts to penetrate the Gulf.

17. The argument has been made that Soviet influence among the states of the region may lead to Soviet leverage over oil exports, thereby eroding the Western alliance by threatening supplies to highly dependent Western Europe and Japan and making these states more responsive to Soviet interests.

18. The prospect of the Soviet Union becoming a net importer of oil in the near future remains a clouded and controversial subject. While some alarmists suggest that Soviet oil requirements will at some point drive Moscow to seek to control directly oil-producing states in the Gulf, others point out that it is cheaper and far less risky to purchase oil imports than to invade the region. It is more difficult to dismiss the rejoinder that Soviet moves on the periphery of the Gulf in recent years have been directed at the gradual insertion of Moscow as an ally of regional states in a long-term strategy to gain control of oil resources. This point is discussed below.

19. See Albert Wohlstetter, '"Meeting the Threat in the Persian Gulf', *Survey*, vol. 25, no. 2 (spring 1980), pp. 128–88; Robert W. Tucker, *The Purposes of American Power: An Essay on National Security* (New York, Praeger, 1981); W. Scott Thompson, 'The Persian Gulf and the Correlation of Forces', *International Security*, vol. 7, no. 1 (1982), pp. 157–80; and George Lenczowski, 'The Soviet Union and the Persian Gulf'. See also Edward Luttwak, 'Cubans in Arabia? Or, the Meaning of Strategy', *Commentary*, vol. 68, no. 6 (December 1979), pp. 62–6; and David Lynn Price, 'Moscow and the Persian Gulf', *Problems of Communism*, vol. 28, no. 2 (March–April 1979), pp. 1–13. The following discussion of where the opposing camps stand relies heavily on Fred Halliday, *Threat From the East? Soviet Policy From Afghanistan and Iran to the Horn of Africa* (Harmondsworth, Penguin Books, 1982).

20. In his book, J. B. Kelly holds that this lack of resolve, or even 'appeasement' is a legacy of British policy (both Labour and Conservative) in the region since the

Second World War, as well as American 'perfidy'. *Arabia, the Gulf, and the West: A Critical View of the Arabs and Their Oil Policy* (London, Weidenfeld & Nicolson; New York, Basic Books, 1980).

21. 'The Soviet Union and the Arabian Peninsula', *The World Today*, vol. 35, no. 11 (November 1979), p. 442. See also his 'Soviet Persian Gulf Policy', *Middle East Review*, vol. 10, no. 2 (winter 1977–8), pp. 47–55.

22. *Threat From the East?*

23. It is highly dubious that South Yemen deliberately instigated this war; instead, it seems to have been an unintended escalation of recurrent border clashes between the two countries that had occurred at various intervals since the early 1970s. Furthermore, the events of June 1978 have been subject to considerable misinterpretation. While it is undeniable that the YAR president was killed by a faction of South Yemen's political elite, the president in the South was not assassinated in a coup but executed by the state after being tried hurriedly for treason, the outcome of a lengthy power struggle based on many factors besides ideology and personal rivalries. See J. E. Peterson, *Conflict in the Yemens and Superpower Involvement* (Washington, Georgetown University, Center for Contemporary Arab Studies, 1981; Occasional Paper).

24. Gary Sick, a National Security Council staff member at the time, points out that the doctrine's prime drafter, Zbigniew Brzezinski, made a December 1979 speech in Montreal, in which he outlined the framework of the doctrine and described the Gulf as a 'third strategic zone . . . of vital importance to the United States and its allies' (in addition to Western Europe and the Far East). Gary Sick, 'The Evolution of U.S. Strategy Toward the Indian Ocean and Persian Gulf Regions', in A. Z. Rubinstein (ed.), *The Great Game: Rivalry in the Persian Gulf and South Asia* (New York, Praeger, 1983), p. 74.

25. It was announced in September 1985 that the Soviet Union and Oman had agreed to establish diplomatic relations, and in December that Moscow and the UAE would also establish relations. These would be the fourth and fifth Peninsula states to have relations with Moscow.

26. 'Moscow Moves in the Direction of the Gulf — So Near and Yet So Far', *Journal of International Affairs*, vol. 34, no. 2 (1980–1), p. 219. The same or similar points have been raised in her 'Soviet Decision-Making and the Middle East: The 1973 October War and the 1980 Gulf War', *International Affairs*, (London), vol. 57, no. 1 (1980–1), pp. 43–59; Francis Fukuyama, *The Soviet Threat to the Persian Gulf* (Santa Monica, Ca, Rand Corporation, March 1981); Michael Collins Dunn, 'Soviet Interests in the Arabian Peninsula: The Aden Pact and Other Paper Tigers', *American–Arab Affairs*, no. 8 (spring 1984), pp. 92–8; Stephen Page, 'Soviet Policy Toward the Arabian Peninsula', in Philip H. Stoddard (ed.), *The Middle East in the 1980s: Problems and Prospects* (Washington, Middle East Institute, 1983), pp. 88–98; and idem, 'Moscow and the Arabian Peninsula', *American–Arab Affairs*, no. 8 (spring 1984), pp. 83–91.

27. In May 1980, 'Abd al-Fattah Isma'il, the pro-Soviet PDRY president since 1978, was forced to resign and subsequently left for exile in Moscow. His successor, 'Ali Nasir Muhammad, always had been seen as a relative 'moderate' or pragmatist, rather than a rigid ideologue, and has shifted the country's foreign policy towards rapprochement with Saudi Arabia, and its bitter enemy of Oman, as well as ordering the departure of most East German and many Cuban 'advisers'. For a thorough discussion of Moscow's relations with North and South Yemen, see Stephen Page,

The Soviet Union and the Yemens: Influence in Asymmetrical Relationships (New York, Praeger, 1985).

28. The most thorough treatment of the background to Iranian–Iraqi relations is contained in Jasim M. Abdulghani, *Iraq and Iran: The Years of Crisis* (London, Croom Helm; Baltimore, Johns Hopkins University Press, 1984). Other sources discussing the causes of the war include: Stephen R. Grummon, *The Iran–Iraq War: Islam Embattled* (New York, Praeger, 1982; Washington Papers, no. 92); Tareq Y. Ismael (ed.), *Iraq and Iran: Roots of Conflict* (Syracuse, Syracuse University Press, 1982); Shirin Tahir-Kheli and Shaheen Ayubi (eds), *The Iran–Iraq War: New Weapons, Old Conflicts* (New York, Praeger, 1983); and M. S. El Azhary (ed.), *The Iran–Iraq War: An Historical, Economic and Political Analysis* (London, Croom Helm; New York, St Martin's Press, 1984).

29. Principal sources on the military aspects of the war include Grummon, *The Iraq–Iraq War*; William O. Staudenmaier, 'A Strategic Analysis', in Tahir-Kheli and Ayubi, *The Iran–Iraq War*, pp. 27–50; Anthony H. Cordesman, *The Gulf and the Search for Strategic Stability* (Boulder, Co, Westview Press, 1983), esp. Chs. 16 and 17; and the annual *Strategic Surveys* (London, International Institute for Strategic Studies), from 1980–1 through 1984–5. The accounts of Staudenmaier and Cordesman, slightly altered, also appeared in *Parameters* and *Armed Forces Journal* respectively.

30. More recent accounts of the war include: Richard Cottam, 'The Iran–Iraq War', *Current History*, vol. 83, no. 4898 (January 1984), pp. 9–12, 40–1; Edmund Ghareeb, 'The Forgotten War', *American–Arab Affairs*, no. 5 (summer 1983), pp. 59–75; Godfrey Jansen, 'The Gulf War: The Contest Continues', *Third World Quarterly*, vol. 6 (October 1984), pp. 950–62; Thomas McNaugher and William Quandt, *Oil and the Outcome of the Iran–Iraq War* (Cambridge, Ma, Cambridge Energy Research Associates, 1984); and Michael Sterner, 'The Iran–Iraq War', *Foreign Affairs*, vol. 63, no. 1 (fall 1984), pp. 128–43. See also the articles in *MERIP Reports*, no. 125–6 (July–September 1984); *American–Arab Affairs*, no. 9 (summer 1984); and *Orbis*, vol. 28, no. 3 (fall 1984).

31. See Shahram Chubin, 'La Guerre irano–irakienne: Paradoxes et particularités', *Politique Etrangère*, vol. 47, no. 2 (June 1982), pp. 381–94.

32. Both Iraq and Iran apparently saw the tanker war as a way to increase pressure on the other side without risking uncontrollable escalation of hostilities. The GCC states were caught in the middle, undoubtedly as both Baghdad and Tehran wished. It seems safe to assume that the decline in Iraqi attacks on Kharg-bound tankers — and consequently in Iranian counterstrikes on Arab shipping — owed much to GCC self-interested persuasion, as well as to the ineffectiveness of the Iraqi attacks in deterring international shipping to Kharg. On this episode of the war, see US Senate, Committee on Foreign Relations, *War in the Gulf*; Staff Report, August 1984 (Washington, USGPO, 1984); and Frederick W. Axelgard, 'The "Tanker War" in the Gulf: Background and Repercussions', *Middle East Insight*, vol. 3, no. 6 (1984), pp. 26–33.

33. As John A. Shaw and David E. Long have written, 'Saudi decision making in general is based on two traditional concepts: *shura*, or consultation, and *ijma'*, or consensus. The role of the king, in this context, is to guide the consultation to a favourable consensus on which to base decisions.' *Saudi Arabian Modernization: The Impact of Change on Stability* (New York, Praeger, 1982; Washington Papers, no. 89), p. 60. The *majlis* constitutes another traditional form of participation, by

which the Saudi king, crown prince, governors, and other officials hold regular audiences open to all Saudis where opinions and grievances may be expressed freely and petitions presented for direct action.

34. The assassination of King Faysal of Saudi Arabia in 1975 was the act of a single individual who, even though a member of the Al Sa'ud, appeared to be motivated by personal and not political reasons.

35. On 13 January 1986, fighting erupted in Aden between two factions of the ruling party and a number of key figures, including former President 'Abd al-Fattah Isme'il, were among the thousands of casualties. After several weeks of intense battles, President 'Ali Nasir Muhammad was forced to leave the country and Prime Minister Haydir al-'Attas took over.

36. The 1981 coup attempt in Bahrain was thwarted at an early stage, yet there is no evidence to support a contention that the plotters represented the views of a large section of Bahraini Shi'a.

5 US Military Options in the Gulf

US Commitment to Defend the Gulf

The process by which American interests in the Gulf emerged and then quickened has already been discussed, as has the transfer of responsibility for the security of the Gulf from Britain to the US in 1971. Thus it can be seen that the United States' assumption of primary responsibility (at least as self-perceived) for this task has been evidenced for little more than a single decade. The official commitment to defend the Gulf physically if necessary, however, emerged only at the beginning of the 1980s, as did the creation of viable machinery to handle this task.[1]

At the time of British withdrawal, there really did not seem to be much evidence of concern, at least among the American public, for the security of oil supplies from the Gulf, nor was there even much recognition of US and Western dependence on Gulf oil. Briefly, American policy in the Gulf since 1971 falls into two distinct periods: 1971–9 and 1979 to the present. While the first was characterised by benign inaction, the second has tended towards overreaction. The initial American response to British withdrawal involved little more than approval of the strengthening of indigenous military capabilities and leaving the US Navy's MIDEASTFOR at its existing strength. American policy towards the Gulf at this time was predicated on the Nixon Doctrine, first enunciated on Guam in 1969, with its minimisation of the role of the US as a world policeman. In large part, the impetus for the doctrine came from America's disillusionment over the war in Vietnam and was aimed at 'military retrenchment without political disengagement'.[2] It was not long before the search was on for a surrogate or surrogates in the Gulf.

Here was the origin of the so-called 'twin pillars' policy, whereby the US pledged to assist Iran and Saudi Arabia in their military development in order to protect common security interests in the region. But these were not really two interchangeable pillars. Saudi Arabia's importance in this scheme was due to its possession of the world's largest oilfields, its paramount position among the states of the Arabian Peninsula, and its emerging influence in pan-Arab politics and councils. But Iran was the militarily more significant partner in this arrangement, due to its much larger population, relatively more developed economy, and more powerful armed forces. Consequently, the US spared no effort to build up the Shah's arsenal, partly in an effort to enhance its ability to police the Gulf (illustrated particularly well by Iran's involvement in the Dhufar rebellion), and partly to satisfy the insistent demands of the Shah and induce his flexibility on oil pricing issues.[3]

But a series of events in the region around 1979 seemed to mark a watershed in US regional policy. In order, these included: the emergence of a Marxist state in Ethiopia; fighting between the new Ethiopian regime and Somalia in the Ogaden; the downfall of the Shah's regime in Iran and subsequent bloody revolutionary process; the short border war between the Yemens in which South Yemen got the upper hand; the Soviet invasion of Afghanistan; and the outbreak of the long-running Iran–Iraq war. The indirect, even inattentive, American approach of the past decade was reversed in a spasm of concern and rhetorical reaction. The broader Gulf region was characterised as an 'arc' or 'crescent of crisis', and simmering plans for a more direct and stronger American role in the region were put on the front burner. A leaked Pentagon study, 'Capabilities in the Persian Gulf' (the 'Wolfowitz Report'), citing American weaknesses in the region compared to the Soviet Union, even advocated the use of tactical nuclear weapons in a superpower Gulf conflict. While the immediate reversal of policy occurred during the Carter administration, this policy shift has been made permanent by the actions of the subsequent Reagan administration.[4]

Of all these events, the fall of the 'peacock throne' in early 1979 had the greatest effect in forcing a radical alteration of existing American policy. For one thing, the Iranian revolution in itself posed a threat to Gulf security. Second, there could be no surrogate policy without a military linchpin and Saudi Arabia was not able to take over that role, even if it had been willing. Third, the Carter administration became convinced that the entire region was prey to increasing instability (thus the 'arc of crisis' characterisation). Fourth, the negative way the administration came to view the Gulf and its periphery (an exceedingly vulnerable and fragile area upon which vital American interests were dependent) was paralleled in the overall deterioration in Soviet–American relations.

The resultant policy was the Carter Doctrine. Obviously, this shift had several objectives, one of which was to display toughness to the Soviet Union. A second, related goal appears to have been to buck up faltering public opinion polls at home. More directly, the doctrine signalled a new resolve on the part of the US to forsake surrogates to carry out American interests and 'go it alone'. Adoption of such a policy depended on the development of appropriate military forces necessary for direct American action if called upon: thus the birth of the Rapid Deployment Force and its evolution into the US Central Command.[5]

The broad outlines of the new Carter policy were continued by the Reagan administration. Washington remained committed to enhancement of RDF capabilities even as it continued a heavy programme of arms sales to and military co-operation with Saudi Arabia. But where Carter had embraced a symmetrical approach to containment, by limiting US response to a Soviet invasion of the Gulf to counter-attack in the Gulf, the Reagan administration altered the emphasis in favour of an asymmetrical approach. Thus, the stakes implicitly were raised and Washington was relieved of its publicly committed reliance solely on a force that might not be capable of confronting a Soviet attack in the Gulf, let alone deterring it.[6]

Even within the first few years of Reagan's term, this established framework witnessed a shift of policy. With Secretary of State Alexander Haig as the architect, the administration at first embraced the idea of 'strategic consensus' between the US and all its friends in the region as a bulwark against Soviet penetration.[7] Washington's new officialdom seemed to brush aside any consideration that this 'consensus' would not work while deep divisions remained between Israel and the Arab states friendly to the US. Nor did it seem aware of the echoes this idea would inevitably raise of the 1950s when the American-engineered Baghdad Pact (later CENTO) increased polarisation in the region. Fortunately, the idea was soon scrapped and was followed by relatively low-profile emphasis on improvement of the RDF, acceptance and approval of the newly formed GCC, and emerging (although distanced) concern over the direction of the Iran–Iraq war.

There is a vast difference between public declaration of a commitment to defend the Gulf militarily and actual capability to do so. While the emphasis in Washington since the Carter Doctrine has been on planning for the direct projection of US force into the region, it may be impossible to rely solely on unilateral intervention. The alternatives of non-intervention and joint intervention must also be considered, not necessarily as exclusive alternatives but as part of a broader (and thus more successful) policy mix.

Non-intervention, or reliance on regional forces, has received much less attention than US military action, even though it may be far better suited to most types and levels of 'threats'. It is true that the US has continued to support the build-up of indigenous military forces, especially in Saudi Arabia and, to a lesser extent, Oman. But there are other motives present. Assistance to Oman largely is a *quid pro quo* for the sultanate's willingness to provide the RDF with access to Omani military facilities. Saudi acquisition of military equipment and plant far outstrips its ability to use all that it has acquired for long into the future; clearly, the US goal is to 'overbuild' Saudi military capabilities as a means of pre-stocking facilities, equipment, arms, and even personnel for emergency use in the Gulf. Of course, Riyadh is not blind to this motivation and may encourage it as a way of guaranteeing that the US will defend Saudi Arabia when required, unlike the experience of the Shah.

At the same time, it is difficult to ascertain any overt enthusiasm in Washington for GCC activities in the area of military and security co-ordination. This may be because the Pentagon regards GCC capabilities as minimal. Or Washington may feel that Saudi Arabia (and, to a lesser extent, Oman) is the significant military actor within the GCC community and will continue to dominate GCC activities. Thus, there is no reason to complicate matters with a superficial channel of interaction on top of existing US–Saudi ones. Or perhaps the newness of the GCC enterprise simply indicates a temporary lag in bureaucratic response.

Joint intervention, in its various shapes, has been a subject of some discussion in published fora but has received very little serious consideration by the governments concerned. There is widespread recognition that American intervention in the Gulf may not be feasible without the assistance of friendly states. Thus, the US has placed considerable emphasis on securing use rights for facilities located in various countries around the Gulf. By 1985, the only states co-operating in this regard were on the periphery of the Gulf, *viz.* Kenya, Somalia, Oman and possibly Egypt, and, within the context of NATO, Turkey.

Saudi Arabia and its neighbours remain convinced that granting such privileges involves more risk than benefit and continue to hold fast to the notion of an 'over the horizon' American defence umbrella. Another American tack in securing regional co-operation has been the effort to upgrade the capability for rapid deployment in Jordanian army units to the Gulf on behalf of the US. While some planning along these lines has taken place, further US enhancement of Jordanian capabilities is problematic in the face of opposition from Israel and its American supporters. Jordan has long assisted in Peninsular military development, including the dispatch of troops to Oman during the Dhufar rebellion. Seconded Jordanian officers included the UAE Chief of Staff from 1976 to 1980. As of 1980, approximately 1,000 Jordanian military advisers were serving in the Gulf and more than 10,000 soldiers from the Peninsula had received training in Jordan.[8]

Co-operation with the US's Western European and Japanese allies has been minimal, despite their much greater dependence on Gulf oil imports, and they consistently have declined to enter planning for military intervention in the Gulf. Japan, which in 1984 received over 60 per cent of its oil from the Gulf, has sought to promote strong economic and political relations with all Gulf states. Tokyo notes that it is prohibited by its constitution from undertaking any military action in the region as well as from participating in any collective security effort. Certainly, there is growing recognition in Japan of the potential necessity to defend its sea lanes, but the capability extends no farther at present than Japan's traditional 'sphere of influence' in Northeast Asia, and not to the Gulf. In addition, there is a fear that such activity may endanger productive commercial ties in the region: Japanese relations with Iran remain strong, despite the US–Iranian hiatus, as do ties to all the other states of the Gulf. At most, Japan may be willing to contribute financially to an American or multilateral security force.[9]

France, nearly as dependent on Gulf oil as Japan, has been just as reticent. One reason is traditional French suspiciousness of American foreign policy and its vagaries (of which Lebanon has been a recent illustration). Furthermore, Paris points out the inappropriateness of intervening in a superpower conflict confined to the Gulf; if such conflict were not limited geographically, then France would be occupied fully in Europe. In case of a non-Soviet threat, France considers its area of responsibility to lie more in Africa than Asia. Nevertheless, there has been some discreet French involvement in internal security matters, as brought to public attention by the recapture of the Great Mosque in Saudi

Arabia. France has also become highly active in arms sales to most of the GCC states. In addition, France has continued to maintain a naval presence in the Indian Ocean, which is based in Reunion and has been increased to three Exocet-armed frigates and supporting vessels in recent years. It also maintains a squadron of Mirages and several thousand Foreign Legion troops in Djibouti, and could presumably deploy elements of its own RDF, the Forces d'Action Rapide, in an emergency.[10]

Even British involvement is modest, rationalised partly by continuing economic retrenchment and partly by current self-sufficiency in oil. Nevertheless, Britain has demonstrated its willingness to contribute forces for Gulf security in crisis situations, as illustrated by activities during the tanker war of mid-1984. Four frigates were placed on patrol in the Arabian Sea, four minesweepers were sent to the nearby Eastern Mediterranean during the same period in case they were needed at the Strait of Hormuz, and a carrier showed its flag in the region as it transited the Indian Ocean. Continuing British assistance to the Sultanate of Oman is also significant, particularly in the secondment of a large number of British officers to the Omani armed forces. Britain has approximately 400 servicemen stationed in the GCC states, with 200 of them in Oman.[11] Furthermore, like France, Britain has been quite active in arms sales to various Gulf states.

A number of observers have advanced schemes for joint allied planning for defence of the Gulf. Jonathan Alford suggests the creation of an ambitious Allied Deployment Force, primarily for use in the Gulf but also in other areas where intervention might be necessary, such as the Mediterranean basin and Africa.[12] Such an approach, he argues, would force European allies to acknowledge their responsibilities in an enlarged definition of Western security, and would provide greater military flexibility. Others see less sweeping schemes. Dov S. Zakheim suggests that allied contributions might take the form of peacetime contributions of naval forces and perhaps surveillance aircraft in the region, or providing the US with the use of airfield and port facilities to facilitate American deployment to the Gulf, or financial support for military construction programmes there (such as British upgrading of their original facilities in Oman or West German refurbishment of air bases in eastern Turkey).[13] At a minimum, contends USCENTCOM's second commander, Lieutenant General Robert C. Kingston, 'We need assistance from our allies for over-flight and landing rights; for refuelling and bunkering facilities; for the use of staging bases and under certain threats for allied air and naval assistance.'[14] But for reasons outlined above, even minimal co-operation along these lines does not seem imminent.

Another necessary source of co-operation is NATO ally Turkey. As Turkish commentator Ali L. Karaosmanoglu has pointed out, Turkey has a vital interest in Gulf security as well.[15] Albert Wohlstetter underscores Turkey's importance by pointing out the strategic location of the NATO air bases in eastern Turkey, near the Soviet Union and situated in close proximity to the head of the Gulf where a potential Soviet attack might be aimed. Furthermore, he points out that the bases already exist and would not have to be created from scratch as elsewhere in the region.[16]

At the same time, however, Turkey is reluctant to damage its deepening economic relations with the Gulf states, including Iran and Iraq as well as the GCC, by allowing use of its air bases for a unilateral and perhaps highly controversial American intervention in the Gulf. There is a long history of Turkish–American contretemps, due not only to the issue of Greece and Cyprus, but also perceived American callousness in its treatment of Ankara. One consequence has been the provision of a minimal amount of military aid, and the tying of the total provided to the amount of aid given Greece. It is not surprising, then, that Ankara maintains that use of its bases is limited to NATO purposes only. In effect, the initiative has been passed back to the Western Europeans.

Finally, efforts have been made to draw Pakistan into co-operation on Gulf security schemes, although these efforts have been complicated by Indo–Pakistani relations, much as Turkish–Greek relations have been problematic in Turkish co-operation. Not only does American support for Pakistan bolster Western defences against Soviet penetration south from Afghanistan, but it helps solidify the American–Saudi–Pakistani triangular relationship, along with Sino–Pakistani ties, and could possibly lead to co-operation with the Pakistani navy.[17] So far, Pakistani troops apparently have been stationed in Saudi Arabia and there is close co-operation between the UAE and Pakistani air forces.

The Rapid Deployment Force: Origins, Evolution and Structure

The genesis of US 'quick reaction' or 'quick strike' forces dates to long before the creation of the RDF. Some observers would trace it to the Vietnam era or even farther back to the aftermath of the Second World War; others see the Marine Corps essentially as always having played that role.[18] During the Kennedy and Johnson administrations, Secretary of Defense Robert McNamara advanced a plan for pre-positioning troops and supplies in the Western Pacific for use in Southeast Asian contingencies, but the idea foundered on Congressional opposition. During 1967–8, the Pentagon fostered a programme for fast logistic ships (FDL) and the C-5A cargo aircraft to enhance abilities for rapid deployment in non-European overseas emergencies, but only the C-5 was built.[19]

More directly, the beginnings of the present RDF planning derive from the Presidential Review Memorandum No. 10 (PRIM-10) of July 1977, which ordered an interagency study on the use of quick reaction forces other than in Europe and Korea. The effect of this directive was to collect information and present papers on options currently available within the armed forces, not to generate ideas on forces which could and/or should be established.[20]

A little more than a year later, Secretary of Defense Harold Brown ordered a Department of Defense position paper on US military options in Southwest Asia. The paper called for the acquisition of regional military facilities, an expanded naval presence in the Indian Ocean, increased military assistance and, especially, upgrading of US military capabilities to intervene with military force in the region. Superimposed on these preliminary internal attempts to deal with an emerging problem were developments in the region itself. In early 1979, the Iranian revolution came to a head, with the departure of the Shah and the establishment of the Islamic Republic of Iran. At roughly the same time, war broke out between the two Yemens, triggering the American response described earlier.

These developments spurred on Pentagon planning for the RDF and speeded up efforts to acquire regional facilities. An interagency review of US military strategy in the region was instituted in April 1979 under the direction of National Security Adviser Zbigniew Brzezinski. The review confirmed the need for regional facilities and in December 1979, a team composed of State Department, Defense Department and National Security Council representatives was sent out to the Gulf to open negotiations for access to facilities. By mid-1980, agreements had been secured with three countries (Kenya, Somalia and Oman) and a promise for co-operation gained from Egypt. Meanwhile, the infrastructure for the Rapid Deployment Joint Task Force (RDJTF) was being laid, units designated, a headquarters established at MacDill Air Force Base (Tampa, Florida), and a position assumed in the command structure subordinate to the US Army Readiness Command. The RDJTF officially came into being on 1 March 1980.

In October 1981, the link to the Readiness Command was severed and the RDJTF became a separate force with its commander reporting directly to the Secretary of Defense through the Joint Chiefs of Staff. Finally, on 1 January 1983, the RDJTF was redesignated one of the six US unified, multi-service commands. As the new US Central Command (USCENTCOM), its specified theatre of operations included Southwest Asia and Northeast Africa, and its commander enjoyed equal standing with other unified commanders, as in the Pacific (USCINCPAC) or Europe (USCINCEUR). As a result of this change, USCINCCENT was given responsibility for essentially all US military activity within this geographical region, including military planning, exercises involving US and regional forces, administration of security assistance, and other representational activities. USCENTCOM exercises command over the American troops of the Multinational Force and Observers (MFO) on the Sinai Peninsula, the AWACS and tanker aircraft stationed at Riyadh, and the 5-ship MIDEASTFOR. Full deployment could involve as many as 300,000 personnel, drawn from the units listed in Table 5.1. Headquarters for USCENTCOM remained at MacDill AFB.

Under present plans, USCENTCOM claims to be prepared to deploy an air force fighter squadron and a battalion of 800 army paratroopers, along with B-52 bomber support, to the Gulf within 48 hours, provided it has received an invitation from a country in the region and five days' warning. Within a week, it could have 3,000 troops on the ground, including two additional battalions of paratroopers and a brigade headquarters. It is more than likely that a carrier task force would be on station as well, since at least one has been regularly deployed to the Arabian Sea for several years. The timing of arrival for the Marine Amphibious Unit depends on its location when orders to move are received.[21]

Follow-on of additional units assigned to USCENTCOM depends upon availability of air- and sealift, at present generally viewed as inadequate. Consequently, the arrival of additional paratroopers and Marine units may take an additional week or

Table 5.1: United States Central Command

Forces assigned to CENTCOM	Personnel
US Central Command Headquarters (augmented)	1,132
US Army Forces Central Command	130,764
Headquarters, US Army Central Command (Third US Army)	
XVIII Airborne Corps Headquarters	
82nd Airborne Division	
101st Airborne Division (Air Assault)	
24th Infantry Division (mechanised)	
6th Cavalry Brigade (Air Combat)	
1st Corps Support Command	
US Navy Forces Central Command	52,538
Headquarters, US Navy Central Command	
3 Carrier Battle Groups	
1 Surface Action Group	
3 Amphibious Ready Groups	
5 Maritime Patrol Squadrons	
US Middle East Force	
US Marine Corps Forces	69,644
1 Marine Amphibious Force, including:	
1 Marine Division (reinforced)	
1 Marine Aircraft Wing	
1 Force Service Support Group	
1 Marine Amphibious Brigade, including:	
1 Marine Regiment (reinforced)	
1 Marine Air Group (composite)	
1 Brigade Service Support Group	
US Air Force Central Command	32,968
Headquarters, US Air Force Central Command	
7 Tactical Fighter Wings	
4 Tactical Fighter Groups	
1 Tactical Fighter Squadron	
1 Airborne Warning and Control Wing	
1 Tactical Reconnaissance Group	
1 Electronic Combat Group	
1 Special Operations Wing	
Unconventional Warfare and Special Operations Force	3,418
Total	**290,434**

Source: Headquarters, US Central Command, Public Affairs Office, *Fact Sheet* (February 1983).

more, as will the pre-positioned supplies on board ships stationed at Diego Garcia. But full deployment of the entire Marine Amphibious Brigade may take two to three weeks and arrival by sea of the army infantry division more than a month. This all assumes a benign landing and the absence of competing contingencies elsewhere.[22]

Despite its very brief existence, the RDF has been the centre of considerable criticism and controversy.[23] To be sure, much of the criticism revolved around differences over the nature of American policy in the Gulf. However, many observers have focused their critiques on the mission, structure and capabilities of the RDF itself, and some have addressed their remarks specifically to certain components of the RDF. These concerns will be discussed in that order.

The hue and cry of the last few years over the RDF makes it easy to overlook the sound premise that US policy regarding the Gulf should consist of more than simply the capacity to undertake military intervention. Any estimation of the necessary military role in this policy is dependent on how the larger policy is defined, which in turn depends on how important the Gulf is to vital national interests and how far the US is prepared to go to defend those interests.

This involves a calculation not only of military capabilities, but also political costs, financial expenditure and manpower availability within the armed forces. Assuming that development of a viable military intervention force is regarded as necessary, as both the Carter and Reagan administrations have done, the construction of that force and determination of its requirements depend upon definition of its mission. What threats must it be prepared to meet? Should the US totally rely on a 'go it alone' approach or should it encourage the Gulf states' self-defence and intervene only as a last resort? Does creation of the military capability bring with it a propensity to use it? How realistic is current planning in meeting potential threats?

Evaluating RDF Capabilities

In just a few short years, the RDF has evolved from a theoretical conception to a given. A major direction, thrust or intent of American policy has already been decided and put into action. But

Map 2: The Gulf and Surrounding Region

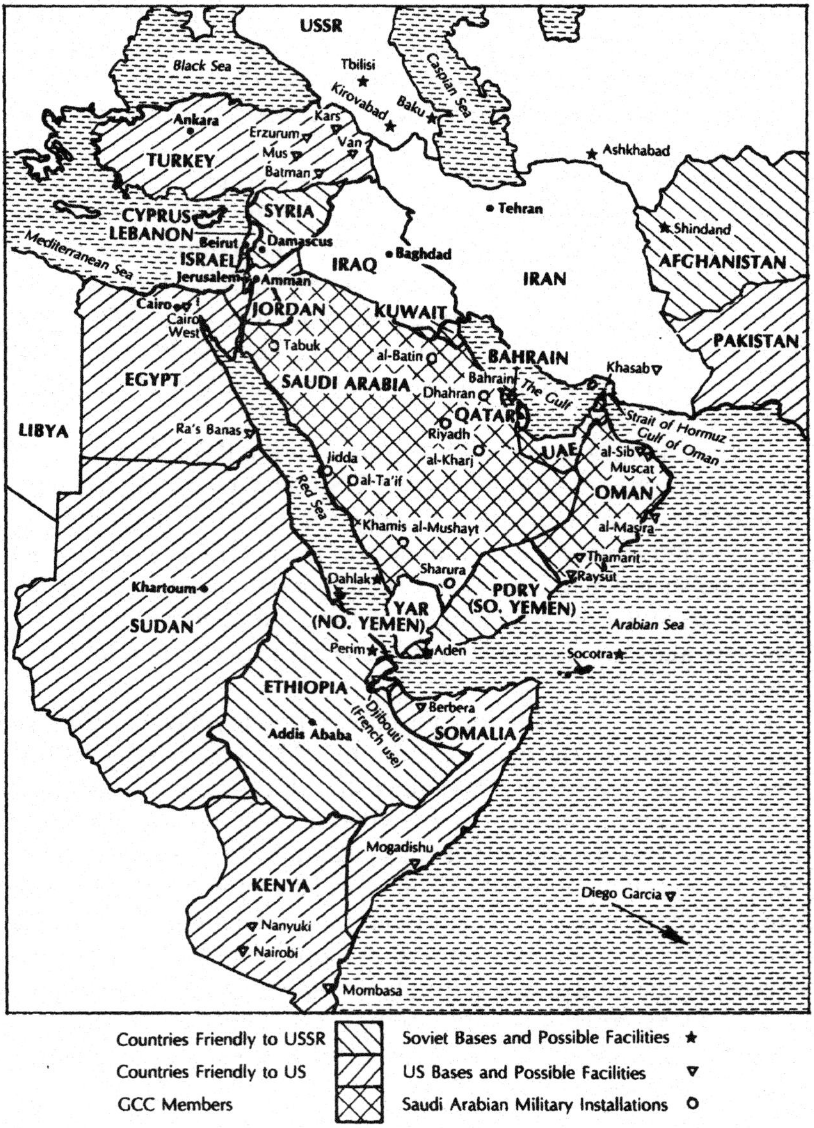

Legend:
- Countries Friendly to USSR
- Countries Friendly to US
- GCC Members
- Soviet Bases and Possible Facilities ★
- US Bases and Possible Facilities ▽
- Saudi Arabian Military Installations ○

it is often charged that the RDF was created haphazardly, that not enough attention has been paid to its conception, to the role it would play in an actual emergency, and to the negative effects that creation of the RDF holds for American defences elsewhere. There are two central questions to the continuing debate over the RDF: what are the goals of the RDF, and how effective is it (or will it be in the future) in meeting those goals and carrying out its mission? With these questions in mind, the following summary of questions regarding RDF can be divided into two categories: conceptual questions and operational questions.

Conceptual Questions

The first conceptual issue concerns the necessity of creating a separate force. Several analysts have suggested that the RDF mission properly belongs to the Marine Corps. Jeffrey Record maintains that turning it over to the Marine Corps, backed up by a new Fifth Fleet, would not only give the job to the service best suited to handling it, but would end inevitable confusion and rivalry inherent in a jerrybuilt, multi-service force.[24] The potential problem in confusion over lines of command has been resolved, at least on paper, by the creation of the independent USCENTCOM structure. A large part of Record's argument rests on his rejection of the assumption that the RDF's introduction into the Gulf would be under friendly conditions, but instead would require the Marine's amphibious, forcible-entry capability. This, however, runs directly counter to USCENTCOM's expectations and its mandate requiring an invitation. The probability of entry under fire depends directly on the type of threat that the RDF is deployed to meet: the initial landing in the Gulf is not likely to occur under hostile conditions in the event of a Soviet attack, or even against various regional threats.

The US government has appeared, publicly at least, to encourage a deliberate ambiguity in delineating the threats that the RDF might be called upon to counter. In part this may reflect a reluctance to be tied down to static declarations in the face of dynamic circumstances, but it may also be meant to obfuscate its response to direct and/or indirect Soviet expansion. It is possible as well that the ambiguity reflects differences of opinion within the government and policy-influencing elite. Which of the three types of threats (external, regional, or internal) should the RDF meet? Is the essential purpose to deter the Soviet Union, to defend the Gulf in the event of a Soviet attack, or to secure control of the oilfields, by invasion if necessary? Can the RDF be designed to serve multiple functions, or is it weakened by not being dedicated to a single purpose?

Kenneth Waltz has argued for the creation of an 'asset-seizing, deterrent force [as] an alternative to a war-fighting defensive force.[25] He goes on to assert that keeping the RDF force structure lean and solely directed at securing oilfields would not only obviate the need for a military base in the Gulf, but would make the Soviet Union less likely to test US defences there. Thomas L. McNaugher, on the other hand, argues that 'The only feasible U.S. military strategy is one of deterrence.'[26] At the extreme, one group places considerable emphasis on a 'show of American power' in the Gulf, viewing the attitude and policies of the Gulf states, especially the Arab ones, as a threat as serious as the Soviet Union. Consequently, the US must not only be prepared to invade in an emergency, but must signal its willingness to do so if these states do not back down from their 'hostile' positions.[27] However, the ability of the US to gain control of the oilfields militarily and to maintain control indefinitely is questionable, as shown at the end of this chapter.

Another central conceptual question arising from planning for intervention in the Gulf concerns the extent of any superpower confrontation in the region. Can fighting between the US and the Soviet Union in the Gulf be confined there, or will it inevitably spread to other arenas and perhaps to full-scale war? The answer to this question may well depend upon whether or not the RDF can provide an effective barrier to a Soviet attack. If so, then can it be considered a credible deterrent force? Or does any deterrence spring from the RDF's role as a tripwire, a mere signal of American resolve to act?

W. Scott Thompson voices the opinion of many in the Reagan administration when he states that the American objective should be to disrupt a Soviet attack and control the battlefield and environs long enough to deploy US reinforcements to the Gulf: 'But most important is the restoration of American *strategic* strength, to which all such events at the theater level are related.'[28] On the other hand, Albert Wohlstetter argues against a tripwire policy and maintains that the US needs to be able to fight a conventional war in the Gulf: 'to declare a bare tripwire policy does not register a determination to use nuclear weapons in a time of crisis; rather it registers a lack of will to prepare before the crisis to meet a non-nuclear threat on its own terms.'[29] Thomas McNaugher concurs: 'Trip-wire strategies are more feasible and less potentially destabilizing than a strategy of outright defense but otherwise make little sense.'[30] He argues for the necessity of conventional deterrence, which has been adopted as a cornerstone of official US policy.

A credible deterrent is dependent upon having a viable RDF; a credible RDF means the US has the ability to engage the Soviet Union in the Gulf and counter a frontal assault — or at least disrupt the attack, thus raising the risks and costs to Moscow. To many, the missing element is feasibility at the present: many of the necessary improvements for the RDF, discussed more fully below, will not be available until the end of the 1980s. Thus, in the interim, the Reagan administration appeared to believe that the only American alternative to deter a Soviet assault (and since such an assault in the early 1980s, in this view, could not be countered effectively by American force projected to the Gulf) was adoption of a threat to deliberately expand the possible arena of conflict, both in geographic terms and in escalation from conventional warfare to nuclear.[31]

The question of current (i.e. as of 1985) US ability to counter a Soviet drive on the Gulf depends on a series of hotly debated factors, including the likelihood and direction of the potential Soviet assault, time available to react, preparedness and mobility of US forces, and extent of assistance from US allies and regional friends.[32] But a number of proposals have been made to improve American prospects, and the effectiveness of the RDF, in the event of a Gulf war.

Some of these concentrate on the limitations of unilateral action and stress the need for allied and regional co-operation. Under peacetime conditions, there has been little evidence of allied assistance. As pointed out above, Europe's involvement has been minimal: France maintains a small naval presence in the Arabian Sea, Britain still provides help for Oman's armed forces, and West Germany and Italy join France and Britain in selling arms to GCC states and Iraq. Japan has declined military participation entirely. Turkey is reluctant to jeopardise its position in the region, and risk Soviet displeasure, except in a joint NATO context. The most that has been offered is assumption of American commitments within NATO in the event of American deployment in the Gulf.

To overcome this perceived lack of reliability on the part of allies, the permanent stationing of American forces in the region has been suggested. The reluctance of the states in the Gulf proper to allow bases has led to a fruitless search for alternatives. Robert W. Tucker proposes bases in the northern Sinai (now restored to Egyptian control) or Israel.[33] Despite his protestations that the Arab–Israeli conflict has no relevance to Gulf security (and his inexplicable statement that Soviet bases in Egypt posed no political problems), such a proposal is likely to encounter complete resistance from all the Arab states. The evidence of its unworkability lies in the failure of Alexander Haig's stillborn 'strategic consensus' idea.

Given these circumstances, an alternative suggestion has been the stationing of a permanent combat presence afloat in the Indian Ocean. James J. Noyes suggests that a major American 'regional military effort should maintain combat forces afloat in the Arabian Sea sufficient for emergency use to support a threatened state in the Gulf'.[34] Wohlstetter supports the idea, noting that the stronger the combat presence in the Gulf, the less rapid and powerful deployment needs to be. Furthermore, the least obtrusive combat presence would be offshore and 'over the horizon'.[35] But he also points out that diverting troops, equipment and naval forces to this purpose means a drawing down of strength in the Mediterranean and Pacific. Essentially, his answer to the dilemma lies within the solution to a larger problem: the ability of the US to fight a 'half-war' (as in the Gulf) as well as a full war (global confrontation with the Soviet Union). This would require a vastly increased commitment to the enlarging and improvement of American armed forces, particularly the navy.

The potential function of the navy in defending Gulf oil lay at the heart of the debate between maritime and coalition strategies. Both sides took as their starting-point the difficulty of unilaterally projecting sufficient US forces into the Gulf to counter a Soviet attack. To overcome this deficiency, the continental/coalition adherents proposed vertical escalation to theatre nuclear weapons. On the other hand, the maritime advocates argued for increased reliance on superior naval power, seen as more flexible since it is not restricted by geography nor dependent on land-based facilities.

Reminiscent of the 1960s British inter-service debate, some naval advocates recommended creation of a number of new carrier battle groups for the US Navy. They held that the intertwining of NATO naval commitments would ensure allied reinforcement of American engagement at sea, unlike a European reluctance to become involved in conflict on distant lands. Other naval proponents argued for a policy that placed less emphasis on (potentially unreliable) NATO support, and rejected the concept of a few super-carriers in favour of a more flexible naval build-up. The Reagan administration, meanwhile, appeared to embrace the attempt to pursue both vertical and horizontal escalation strategies, thus at least partially placating all service lobbies.[36]

A final debate over the conceptualisation of the RDF has been largely superseded by events. Kenneth Waltz, among others, has suggested that creation of the capability to intervene would bring a temptation or even a proclivity to do so: 'An RDF should serve vital interests only and in serving them should be guardedly used... We should avoid the temptation of resorting to force because nothing else will avail. We should use force only if we can see a way of doing so that will enable us to get our way.'[37] The commitment to build a viable force has been made already and RDF enhancement is well under way. Apart from dismantling the present structure, the sole relevance of the above argument lies in the size of the RDF. As it is unlikely that the Pentagon will have an opportunity to build in a comfortable margin above bare requirements, the final size of the RDF inevitably will be a function of its mission. Definition of the mission, in turn, is a function of the threats that the RDF is expected to meet.

Operational Questions

While the above comments have revolved around issues dealing with the formulation of a proper and effective role for the RDF, other critics have focused on perceived problems that the RDF may encounter in carrying out its assigned mission, as presently defined. A number of these operational questions merit discussion here.

Command, Control and Communications. The problem cited earlier of possible confusion over lines of command authority in theory has been resolved by the creation of a command independent of the separate services. But control of nearly all USCENTCOM forces remains outside the jurisdiction of USCINCCENT except in emergency, and even regular joint manoeuvres may not be enough to solve problems of co-ordination inherent in such a large-scale operation as full RDF deployment. Furthermore, USCENTCOM is unique among the US commands in that its headquarters is not physically located in its geographical area of operations. In the event of a contingency in the Gulf, USCENTCOM headquarters and its commander must deploy to the region and rapidly establish effective communications with its subordinate units. In late December 1983, a 'forward headquarters element', comprising less than 20 people, was established aboard the USS *LaSalle*, flagship of the MIDEASTFOR, in an attempt to ameliorate the communications problem.[38]

Assignment of Subordinate Units. Jeffrey Record, writing in late 1980, charged that the RDF consisted of a 'hastily thrown together collection of existing units [most of which were] already earmarked for contingencies outside the Gulf region and improperly equipped or structured for the exacting demands of desert warfare against large and often mechanized potential adversaries in a logistically remote part of the world'.[39] Few of the USCENTCOM forces (with notable exceptions being the headquarters contingent and MIDEASTFOR) are dedicated to the RDF mission. A number of other analysts have pointed out that the units assigned to USCENTCOM must come from forces already earmarked for other contingencies, whether in Europe, Korea, or elsewhere. The only sure way around this problem is a tremendous (and prohibitively expensive) expansion of US armed forces.

It should be remembered, though, that in the event of Soviet–American hostilities in the Gulf, Moscow would find it necessary to draw upon forces earmarked for other contingencies as well. In addition, since the time Record voiced his criticism, considerable effort has been made to improve the ability of assigned forces to fight in Gulf conditions, both by the provision of new equipment and by holding *in situ* exercises. Since its formation, the RDJTF/USCENTCOM has conducted 16 major exercises, five in its area of responsibility.[40]

Force Size. Considerable debate exists over whether the RDF possesses sufficient assets, even if fully deployed, to meet potential threats in the Gulf, particularly a conventional war with the Soviet Union. Undoubtedly, this can be answered fully only by examining the probable extent of Soviet forces committed in such a scenario (addressed below). There is some consensus, however, that the organisation of the RDF, as planned at least on paper, is sufficient for expected purposes. As Thomas McNaugher has put it, further build-up of US forces allocated to the RDF may cause the Soviet Union to give higher priority to its military capability in the Gulf. Furthermore, the size of the force is no more important in providing deterrence than speed, positioning, tactics and support.[41]

Facilities in the Gulf Region. The countries and facilities for which the US has negotiated military use rights in connection with the RDF are listed in Table 5.2. To this list may be added the possible use of the Cairo West and Ra's Banas (on Egypt's Red Sea coast)

Table 5.2: Regional Facilities for RDF Use

Country	Facility	Type
British Indian Ocean Territory	Diego Garcia	Airfield and port
Kenya	Mombasa	Port
	Nairobi	Airfield
	Nanyuki	Airfield
Oman	Khasab	Airfield
	al-Masira	Airfield
	Muscat	Port
	Salala (Raysut)	Port
	al-Sib (Muscat)	Airfield
	Thamarit	Airfield
Somalia	Berbera	Airfield and port
	Mogadishu	Airfield and port

airfields, Djibouti, and Turkish NATO bases at Mus, Batman, Erzurum. In addition, strategic airlift is heavily dependent on Portugal's Lajes airfield in the Azores and Morocco's Sidi Sulaiman air base. While there is no question of the usefulness of these facilities, at least potentially, it should be noted that none of them is located in the Gulf itself.

Kenya and Somalia provide a certain utility for pre-positioning fuel supplies, guarding sea lines of communication, and as places for shore leave. Diego Garcia is important as an anchorage for the fleet of pre-positioned supply ships, a naval port of call, and a potential base for B-52 bombers. Oman's Masira Island has been used for several years for anti-submarine surveillance and for transfer of mail and passengers to US naval forces in the Arabian Sea, and could serve as a principal airfield for the RDF, being conveniently isolated from contact with the indigenous population. The giant air base at Thamarit (far into the desert behind Oman's southern province of Dhufar) is being prepared as a major staging area. On the other side of the Gulf, the Turkish bases are ideally situated to interdict a Soviet drive through Iran.

But the scenario of a Soviet frontal assault through Iran to reach Khuzestan means that an American response must be to assemble troops, equipment and supplies at a point or points near Khuzestan. At present, Washington cannot be assured of access to facilities in the Gulf, although the programme of overbuilding in Saudi Arabia indicates that bases built there and equipment transferred to the

Saudi armed forces would be available for American use in case of these extreme scenarios. In particular, use of the Saudi air base at Dhahran would be of immense value for airstrike operations against invading Soviet columns in Iran; the airfields at the newly completed King Khalid Military City at Hafr al-Batin (near the Iraqi and Kuwaiti borders) are even closer. The other GCC states quite likely also would allow American entry at this time, although the advantages of pre-stocking and familiarisation would be lost.

In addition, the lack of air bases (and the navy's reluctance to send its carriers into the Gulf) creates major difficulties in sustaining an air interdiction campaign against a Soviet attack and in providing air cover for American operations. Basing in eastern Turkey, politically sensitive and vulnerable to attack, is necessary because of the limited range of most strike aircraft, while B-52 bombers could be employed from as far away as Diego Garcia and Australia.[42]

Strategic Airlift. A major bottleneck in quickly inserting RDF forces into action in the Gulf is the lack of sufficient strategic airlift assets. In 1985, the total US inventory consisted of approximately 70 C-5A and 230 C-141 cargo aircraft, as well as aircraft from the civilian reserve. Of these, only the C-5A is capable of handling such outsize cargo as tanks, self-propelled howitzers and air force support equipment. But given the fact that many of the airfields that the RDF aircraft would utilise in the region are relatively small and would be extremely congested during a deployment, the Pentagon has sought to build an alternative to the huge C-5A, as well as to increase inventories of existing craft and enlarge the lift capacity of the C-141. Consequently, the C-17 has been proposed as a purpose-built transport, smaller in size than the C-5A and requiring less runway space yet still able to handle the C-5A's outsize cargoes. The programme, however, has faced political roadblocks in Congress and consequently has been much delayed, with the first C-17s not expected to arrive before the early 1990s.[43] In addition, there is the problem of acquiring sufficient aerial refuelling assets to get both tactical fighters and cargo aircraft to the Gulf.

Strategic Sealift. The inadequacy of airlift requires even more of sealift. There is a trade-off between air- and sealift: the former can move limited numbers of men and equipment quickly, while the latter must bear the burden of transporting the majority of RDF forces into the theatre of combat, particularly the infantry division, most of the heavy equipment and nearly all supplies. Sealift also has the advantage of moving forces into an area without appearing to make a commitment — unlike an airlift, which is inherently high-profile and provocative.

The US faces just as severe a problem in sealift assets as it does in airlift. Two approaches have been taken to overcome the problem. One is the pre-positioning of roll-on/roll-off container ships, filled with equipment and supplies, in the region. A 17-ship NTPS (Near-Term Prepositioned Ship) flotilla anchored at Diego Garcia (with an additional ship in the Mediterranean) carries enough heavy equipment, supplies, ammunition, fuel and water for a single Marine Amphibious Brigade (MAB), as well as supplies for air force and army units. As the name suggests, this is a temporary stop-gap measure intended to fill in until the MPS (Maritime Prepositioned Ship) flotilla, consisting of ships either purpose-built or converted from existing stock, can put into operation. Thirteen MPS vessels, able to support three MABs for 30 days, were expected to be ready in 1986. However, it is not certain that all of the MPS ships are destined for the Gulf, and some have been slated for Pacific and Atlantic bases.[44]

The second approach has been to convert eight SL-7 (Sea–Land Container) ships to RDF configurations. The advantage of these vessels is their speed, nearly twice that of existing conventional cargo ships. It is estimated that the addition of the SL-7s to RDF forces will cut the time necessary to move a mechanised infantry division to the Gulf from 30–35 days to approximately 14 days. Their disadvantage lies in exorbitant fuel consumption, making it likely that they will be used sparingly until called upon.[45]

Tactical Mobility. Once RDF forces arrive in the Gulf, they must be able to move quickly and effectively to the area of combat and be defended. Total reliance on tanks is considered unsuitable, because of their weight and potential difficulty of movement in Gulf terrain. In addition, gunships and assault helicopters may be particularly vulnerable to Soviet tactical air defences. A need was seen for vehicles which are lightweight, easily transportable by air, armoured, and able to manoeuvre and survive in the desert environment of the Gulf. The acquisition of existing armoured wheeled vehicles as a preferable alternative to utilising tanks was widely suggested.[46] As a consequence, the Marine Corps purchased a number of these vehicles.

Forcible-Entry Capability. As pointed out earlier, initiation of RDF deployment is based on invitation from a state in the region. Consequently, planning has been based on a benign entry, with access to necessary airfields and seaports under friendly conditions. Whether or not this will be the case depends upon the scenario envisioned. If the purpose of the RDF is to respond to a Soviet attack, particularly one aimed at Khuzestan, then it may be safely assumed that the initial US landings will be made in GCC countries, with their active co-operation. On the other hand, a response to regional or internal threats may require that US forces fight their way ashore. To meet this contingency, it has been suggested that Marine amphibious capabilities be improved and that additional naval gunfire capability be provided for the RDF.

The following section presents the numerous arguments against the advisability of using US forces in most hostile actions against regional forces. Nevertheless, the issue of naval gunfire support ranges beyond that of simply amphibious assault cover. The potential value in a Gulf conflict (or even deployment for demonstration purposes, as was the case of the *New Jersey* off Lebanon) provides an additional argument for the reactivation of the US Navy's battleships, according to some (this argument ties in with the maritime strategy discussed above).[47]

In addition to the above issues, there exist a number of other operational problems that may seem minor but have serious implications. For one thing, airlift constraints may make it impossible to deploy a general field hospital quickly, yet the US no longer has the hospital ships used during the Vietnam war. Furthermore, the scarcity of fresh water supplies in the Gulf will require US forces to provide their own, requiring the acquisition of additional MPS vessels for this purpose, as well as further development along the lines of ROWPU (Reverse Osmosis Water Processing Units) experiments for field use. Paradoxically, the RDF will also have to provide most of its own fuel, since oil supplies present in the Gulf are limited to crude or refined gasoline. Consequently, a number of NTPS ships have been dedicated to providing stocks of necessary grades of fuel for aircraft, tanks, heavy trucks and other requirements.[48]

Assessing RDF Performance

As previously stressed at various places above, the viability and effectiveness of the RDF depend on the definition of its mission. The greatest utility of US military intervention is likely to be in countering one of the least likely threats. Conversely, the emergence of more probable threats (and which are likely to be perceived as having more apocalyptic effects than they actually are likely to have) will be far less amenable to US military action.

The Soviet Threat

The prospect of Soviet invasion of the Gulf provided the principal impetus for the RDF's creation, particularly because of the heightening of American apprehensions in the late 1970s and the enunciation of the Carter Doctrine. While fears of an imminent Soviet drive on the Gulf seemed to have abated, deterrence of Soviet direct and/or indirect moves in that region remains the key determinant of current American planning. The Department of Defense's 1982 *Defense Guidance* defines the Central Command's mission as follows:

> Our principal objectives are to assure continued access to Persian Gulf oil and to prevent the Soviets from acquiring political-military control of the oil directly or through proxies.
>
> It is essential that the Soviet Union be confronted with the prospect of a major conflict should it seek to reach oil resources of the Gulf. Whatever the circumstances, we should be prepared to introduce American forces directly into the region should it appear that the security of access to Persian Gulf oil is threatened.[49]

For a number of reasons, a direct Soviet attack on the Gulf, independent of general war with the US, appears to be unlikely. As Dennis Ross has observed, 'Soviet use of its indirect means to achieve its goals in the area is far more likely than any direct use of Soviet military force.'[50] Given the assumption that the Soviet Union desires at least the capability of denying Gulf oil to the West if not overt control of that oil, indirect penetration through development aid, arms sales, subversion to acquire clients, and pressure by clients on neighbouring states have all been suggested as less risky options than frontal assault. Thomas L. McNaugher asserts that

The low readiness of ground forces in the Soviet Union's southern military districts and the reactive mode of the Soviet naval buildup in the Indian Ocean suggest that Moscow's interest in its southern flank thus far has not been driven primarily by lust for control of the Gulf's oil. Rather a prudent concern for the area's turbulence and possible U.S. buildup there motivates the Soviets. Nothing in their present force posture suggests that they are poised to impose their will on the area. Rather, the Soviets are best prepared to respond to opportunities, which they have done in the past in other parts of the world, but only when they expected no opposition.[51]

Nevertheless, defence planning must cover all possible contingencies, and not just the likely ones. As Keith A. Dunn has pointed out, evaluation of Moscow's capabilities for a direct attack on the Gulf most frequently has emphasised Soviet advantages (relative to the US) while ignoring various real constraints.[52] Among the Soviet advantages he points out are proximity to the region and, paradoxically, the relative strength of American influence in the Gulf, since political instability and regional military rivalries point to disturbance of the status quo.

At the same time, Dunn notes a number of serious constraints on Soviet military action in the region. One of these involves Soviet ground forces, since most of the approximately 30 divisions along the border and in Afghanistan are unprepared, undermanned, and lack adequate logistical support for a sustained campaign.[53] A second constraint revolves around Soviet tactical air support, as many of the aircraft the Soviets could put into action in Southwest Asia would be less than front-line quality and are limited in their ability to perform close-air-support functions. There are limitations to Soviet naval forces: the USSR only recently has moved from a coastal defence force to a globally deployed navy, and maintains limited (although growing) deployment in the Indian Ocean.

Geography also poses a constraint, as the mountainous and desert terrain of Iran generally does not favour Soviet tank and mechanised divisions with their limited logistical support. Distance also works against Moscow: it may be only a short hop from Soviet territory to Azerbaijan, but it is nearly 1,200 miles to Hormuz and 2,000 miles to Aden. Not all Soviet tactical planes can reach Hormuz, even from Afghanistan, while Soviet naval reinforcements have nearly as far to travel as US naval forces do. The Soviet

Union must also grapple with strategic lift capabilities, just as the US must. Finally, there is the element of risk. The USSR faces the same problem as the US in depending upon regional clients. Dunn concludes that the main constraint is political: 'It involves a lack of friends and allies; a lack of guaranteed access to facilities; and a general dislike and distrust for not only the Soviet Union but also the communist system.'[54]

The invasion of Afghanistan has had some benefit for the Soviet Union, providing a useful test of its strategic reach and its ability to deploy forces into adjoining Southwest Asian territory. It has also given the Soviet armed forces extensive experience in mountain and rough terrain warfare, and a valuable look at the performance of its fighters and helicopters in similar combat conditions. At the same time, however, the strategic value of Afghanistan in an attack on the Gulf itself is marginal. Deployment of ground forces through Afghanistan towards Iran would be more difficult and entail longer time than movement directly across the Soviet border, and to reach the Gulf from Afghanistan by invading Iranian or Pakistani Baluchistan would require an even greater effort — and considerably more costs — than the Afghanistan invasion. The addition of Afghani air bases places tactical fighters only marginally closer to key Iranian targets. At best, Afghanistan allows the Soviets to use tactical air power to harass American forces in the southern Gulf and the Gulf of Oman, and perhaps mount a surprise airborne assault to seize strategic areas until heavier units arrive.[55]

As a consequence of these constraints and American efforts, the widely perceived great military imbalance in Moscow's favour may not actually exist. Joshua M. Epstein, in a step-by-step dissection of the most logical scenario — a Soviet drive through northeastern Iran towards Khuzestan, exiting the mountains at Dezful — discounts an inevitable Soviet victory in head-on confrontation in the Gulf.[56] He argues that the rough terrain and Soviet dependence on a handful of mountain passes would allow the US to delay an overland drive long enough to put four RDF divisions into Khuzestan. This force should prove adequate to meet a probable maximum confronting force of seven Soviet divisions, given US advantages in technology, training, mobility, logistics, co-ordination, and probably even morale after the long, dangerous drive over the mountains.

This 'Zagros Mountains' strategy appears to be at the root of present USCENTCOM planning for a Soviet attack. The 7th

Marine Amphibious Brigade (MAB) would be airlifted to a nearby airfield with a contiguous port (or, if a forcible-entry contingency, would be required to carry out an amphibious operation to secure the port and airfield) where equipment and supplies in the NTPS flotilla could be landed. Army units capable of sustained combat operations ashore are scheduled to follow the Marines and take up defensive positions in the Zagros Mountains, the natural barrier between the northeastern Iranian plateau and the Khuzestan plain. Additional USCENTCOM forces would be deployed as quickly as possible and as required.[57]

The three-pronged attack launched by Iraq against Iran in September 1980 provides an indication of the vulnerability of any American defence of Khuzestan to other routes of egress from the Iranian highlands. While Iraq concentrated the lion's share of its forces on Khuzestan, significant numbers of units were dispatched to northern Iraq, partly to prevent any recrudescence of Iranian-backed Kurdish dissidence but also to seal off the border passes. Capture of the Kurdistan area of Iraq would also provide access to Iraq's northern oilfields and refineries. At the same time, Iraqi forces captured the strategic mountain pass of Sar-e Pol-e Zahab, near the border town of Qasr-e Shirin, and managed to hold it despite repeated Iranian attempts to recapture it. The importance of this pass derives from the road linking the Iranian regional centre of Kermanshah and behind it Tehran to Qasr-e Shirin and Baghdad. Once Qasr-e Shirin is passed, the land becomes flat and easily traversible all the way to Baghdad, less than 100 miles away, or alternatively south all the way to Basra, the Shatt al-'Arab and Khuzestan.

A Soviet airlifted assault, Epstein contends, would be just as vulnerable since the Soviet Union does not possess sufficient fighter escort capability and it would be operating outside its normal range of ground control. Furthermore, even a massed bomber attack on US carriers in the region, in support of a combined overland and airlifted assault, would mean the stripping of Soviet defence elsewhere (after all, Moscow must prepare for even more contingencies than the US) and has no real assurance of success. He concludes that 'The Soviets face the grave threat that the military cost of a move on Iran would vastly outweigh its potential benefits — indeed, the risk that all such benefits would be decisively denied.'[58]

Even if the Soviet Union does not mount a direct assault on the

Gulf, there still remains an indirect Soviet threat through the use of regional clients. Assessment of the likelihood of this scenario evokes a debate over 'grand design' versus 'opportunism'. There are a large number of obvious difficulties in correctly assessing or interpreting such a situation. It may not be always possible to know which side is the instigator in any conflict between US and Soviet clients. The motives of the Soviet client are unknown: there may be no intent to invade. Can the cause of conflict be traced to Soviet machinations or is it just as likely to be due to indigenous factors? Even given Soviet motivations, is Moscow the omnipotent manipulator of its clients or is it often reduced to supporting locally generated policies? An American misreading of an ambiguous situation could result in the initiation of hostilities, instead of reaction to moves already made.

The fighting between the two Yemens in 1979 provides a useful illustration of this problem. The widespread assumption in some quarters that this episode represented Soviet-inspired aggression by South Yemen against North Yemen is not credible for various reasons. There has been a serious rivalry between the two states since the 1960s for the distinction of being the sole legitimate state for all Yemen. To this end, both Sanaa and Aden have supported, in their territories, armed groups opposed to the regime in the other state. This has led to recurrent border tensions that have been prone to escalate into open warfare, as happened in 1972 and as was the case in 1979.

Even the fact that the course of the fighting in 1979 clearly favoured South Yemen, as its troops pushed well into YAR territory in areas, does not prove intention of invasion. Aden's armed forces were better trained, equipped and disciplined than those of Sanaa, and it is not surprising that they were able to move quickly over relatively open terrain (the fighting stopped once the South Yemenis reached the mountains and the North Yemeni troops were reinforced by tribal irregulars). In addition, the speed in reaching a negotiated settlement to the conflict and reaffirmation on both sides of the commitment to unity further disproves the idea of a master Soviet plan.[59] These considerations serve to point out that the emergence of such a conflict scenario is less likely to appear unambiguously as a Soviet threat than as a regional one, and will have to be treated by the US as such. The introduction of RDF forces in such a scenario would be extremely risky — even if they were to be invited, itself rather unlikely.

Regional Threats

Because of their ambiguous nature and unpredictability, either as to imminence or course, regional conflict scenarios pose particular problems for US military policy. With the exception of one or two unique scenarios, it is difficult to see when American intervention definitely would be beneficial and even more difficult to discern when it might be necessary. Indeed, there are many plausible cases in which it may not even be feasible. While in theory it may seem that American intervention to support a Saudi Arabia under attack is unarguable, such a clear-cut situation is only one plausible scenario and perhaps a less likely one at that. It seems more probable that future regional conflict will develop along the lines of the Iran–Iraq war or inter-Yemeni hostilities, where the rationale for intervention (and even on which side) is far less certain. Furthermore, in almost all foreseeable cases, the transfer of equipment and perhaps dispatch of a few advisers will be preferable to the deployment of the RDF for both international and domestic reasons.

The Iran-Iraq war provides a good example of the problem. It is inconceivable that employment of the RDF could have prevented the outbreak of war, even if deployed early enough. Subsequent use of the RDF, as well as the provision of overt political and logistical aid, has been a non-starter because of Washington's official neutrality between the belligerents. Presumably, the RDF could be used to tip the scales of the fighting, but at the cost of permanently alienating the other side and supporters, as well as other countries in the region. In addition, American involvement on one side very likely would provoke Soviet intervention on behalf of the other. Rather than a uniquely complex case, this war would appear to be rather typical of future conflict.[60]

Nevertheless, there may be at least one exception to its lessons. American intervention may be seen as necessary if Iran were to achieve a dramatic breakthrough and its forces advanced on Saudi Arabia. This assumes that Iran would both seek to invade Saudi Arabia and also be prepared to do so — which is by no means given.[61] The necessary preliminary of invitation presumably would be forthcoming, although Riyadh conceivably might wait until the last second to be absolutely certain. If such a chain of circumstances were to occur, it seems unlikely that an Iranian offensive would stand much chance against even limited US force. Iran has virtually no air capability and its apparent inability to launch successful full-scale offensives against Iraq in 1984 and 1985 indicates severe logistical constraints (as well as domestic political differences over the war). Assuming that American military involvement would pass the test of domestic US politics, there remains the problem of extrication. Iran has shown its tenacity in eschewing a negotiated settlement to more than five years of battle with Iraq, and there is little reason to assume that a military defeat in Arabia would cause it to sue for peace, unless the battlefield was widened by carrying the war back to Iran.

It should be stressed that an Iranian attack may be the sole regional threat to Saudi Arabia automatically involving the RDF. Threats from Riyadh's Arab neighbours are far less likely and/or less serious from a military point of view. Even before the war, Iraq was moving closer towards the GCC states and, as a consequence of the war, Baghdad's economic, political and security relations with the GCC states have deepened considerably. Saudi security horizons also involve a potential Israeli threat, but it is inconceivable that the US would become involved in Saudi defence in case of an Israeli strike on Saudi Arabia.

One other regional threat involving possible American military action received prominent attention in late 1983 and early 1984: the possibility of an Iranian attempt to close the Strait of Hormuz. The disruption of Gulf oil supplies through such a scenario would have catastrophic effects on the West. A Congressional Research Service study concluded that a complete cessation of all oil traffic through the strait in 1980 (before the recession took hold) would have caused the major industrialised countries to suffer a shortfall of 20–5 per cent in their oil requirements. Crude oil prices would likely have risen from $30 to between $90 and $300, Gross National Product in these countries would have fallen 12–27 per cent and employment there would have dropped by 15–30 per cent. A projection for a similar disruption in 1982 showed milder but still grave effects.[62] While it is by no means certain that Iran has the capability to close the strait, almost any Iranian action is likely to produce severe psychological effects.

Application of American force to counter such action, if it were to occur, would depend on the type of Iranian measures taken: mining of the strait, aerial or naval attacks on shipping, or shore-based shelling. Naval action would seem to be the most efficient (and least controversial or risky) counter, variously involving minesweepers, escort vessels, or naval gunfire. Such a response would not require RDF mobilisation. Ground-based action, if required and approved, would present considerably more problems. The minimal operation, for example, to take out Iranian gun emplacements along the strait, would be a commando-type raid. Even if successful in its immediate mission, would a single raid be sufficient to prevent future shelling? Fully guaranteeing freedom of passage through the strait might involve occupation of Iranian territory, as well as permanently stationing naval vessels in the immediate vicinity. Such a strategy involves heavy political costs, both internationally and domestically, as well as potential escalation through Soviet assistance to Iran.[63]

Internal Threats

Considerable talk has been generated about the 'instability' of Saudi Arabia and the other GCC states, and President Reagan has indicated that the US would act to prevent a successful *coup d'état* or revolution in Saudi Arabia. It should be noted at the outset that extra-constitutional political change in Saudi Arabia is by no means certain nor inevitable.[64] Nevertheless, the commitment has been made. But is the American commitment to intervene to save the present regime in Saudi Arabia credible?

The emergence of a situation along these lines necessarily raises questions of the political and/or military feasibility of American intervention. The first consideration must be to outline the precise circumstances under which American assistance would be provided. But in the heat and confusion of the first signs of possible problems in Saudi Arabia, it may be extremely difficult — if not impossible — to interpret accurately events and circumstances. What is the source of the threat? If from within the Al Sa'ud, should the US get involved? It is not implausible that a monarch would call upon the US for assistance if faced with opposition from the rest of the Al Sa'ud. But such a development may not constitute a 'threat': the ruling family acted in concert in the 1960s to remove King Sa'ud because of his incompetence. Blanket American interference in inter-familial rivalries may prove counterproductive and conceivably result in propping up an unwanted ruler.

Similar caveats emerge from a challenge to the authority of the Al Sa'ud arising from the military. In the heat of the moment, it may well be impossible to tell who is involved, what their goals are (an attempted overthrow or simply the expression of grievances?), how widespread disaffection is, and how well organised the plotters may be. Even if American forces were to be successful in blocking a military coup, such action could entangle the US in providing troops as a permanent Praetorian Guard for an increasingly unpopular regime. Furthermore, it is not always possible for outsiders to distinguish between dissidence on the part of a minority and the genesis of widespread opposition to an increasingly illegitimate order. It is precisely this distinction that eluded American policy-makers in Iran.

These considerations form only the first part of the equation. Assuming that circumstances actually warrant American intervention, is such action militarily feasible? If US forces are to avoid becoming invaders in a hostile environment, they must act quickly and effectively. Success depends in part on the quality and timeliness of intelligence (in having sufficient warning in advance to move upon command), but also on the speed of deployment. Would the insertion of 800 paratroopers and a USAF fighter squadron within 48 hours, as the Central Command has indicated is possible, be enough to prevent a *coup d'état*? In the case of a military plot, it may be enough only if the rebels were partially thwarted beforehand, if they had failed to seize all the key objectives, if resistance was offered by loyal forces, and if the size of the rebellion was small to begin with. US troops could then tip the balance. In the case of dissidence within the Al Sa'ud, the necessary circumstances for the successful application of US force would seem to be the emergence of two blocs, each with significant support from military or paramilitary units. Otherwise, the US would face the prospect of trying to reverse a *fait accompli*.

All these hypothetical scenarios indicate that successful American intervention to protect an existing Saudi regime (or any other GCC regime) from internal threats is extremely questionable. This, in turn, raises the issue of whether, in the event of a change of regime, American military action is necessary, let alone feasible. As noted earlier, even the emergence of a government in Saudi Arabia hostile to American interests is not a guarantee that American and/or Western access to Saudi oil would be cut off. Despite the reorientation in the political sphere, any Saudi government would still be almost totally dependent on oil income, not to mention having its capital investments in the West held hostage. The necessity for American action would seem dependent on what the long-term changes in the terms for the continued supply of Saudi oil were and, on the other hand, whether there was to be continued provision of Western exports and development assistance. This is to say that even this scenario does not necessarily require American military action. In fact, such action would still remain remote.

American action to take over Saudi oilfields has been actively discussed since the October 1973 war. In the immediate aftermath of the oil price revolution, a small number of 'interventionists' appeared to advocate invasion of Saudi Arabia regardless of whether oil supplies were cut off. One advocate, writing under the pseudonym 'Miles Ignotus', justified invasion on the specious grounds that the OPEC states were 'extortionists', the Arabs 'blackmailers', and 'behind the Arabs stand the Russians'. He called for the US to strike quickly, utilising Israeli bases and assistance, seize the Saudi oilfields and turn them over permanently to compliant (presumably American) oil companies.[65]

Even in the early 1980s, Robert W. Tucker wrote of appeasement of Gulf states 'that have managed to outmaneuver and to intimidate Western powers for over a decade', and argued that American credibility in the Gulf could be restored only by 'a visible demonstration of power and the more impressive the demonstration the better'.[66] In general, the extreme views of these interventionists appear to be coloured not only by their belief in the decline of American 'will' over the last several decades, but also by their views of the Arab oil producers as simply enemies of Israel and therefore of the US. The adoption of their objectives by any US administration would seem particularly unlikely.

At the same time, there are many moderates who, while reluctant to consider the possibility of invasion, maintain that it may be necessary under extreme circumstances — e.g. imposition of another oil embargo, or an oilfield takeover by forces hostile to the US (whether external or internal). RDF action to secure control of the oilfields against active resistance raises similar questions to the hypothetical scenario of the emergence of internal threats.

In a comprehensive study of the viability of using US military force to occupy Saudi Arabia's oilfields, John M. Collins and Clyde R. Mark (both of the Congressional Research Service) conclude that the US could easily defeat defending forces while seizing the oilfields and related facilities.[67] However, they caution that preserving the installations intact would be uncertain even under ideal conditions. It would be nearly impossible to arrive quickly enough to prevent sabotage and a considerable investment in material and works imported from the US, not to mention a lengthy period of time, might be required to repair damages.

Furthermore, several US divisions, complete with adequate air, sea and land support, would be needed on an indefinite basis to maintain security over the installations. This could deplete strategic reserves to the point that little would be left for contingencies elsewhere. Direct Soviet intervention, a distinct possibility, might well make the US mission impossible, particularly in protecting sea lanes. Success, the authors argue, would depend on two prerequisites: slight damage to key intallations and Soviet abstinence from armed intervention.

The above discussion demonstrates the extreme limitations of use of the RDF, apart from one or two slightly possible scenarios. Even though the development of viable US military options is a real and necessary policy, their enactment may never be required, at least not on the scale envisioned in the RDF. Furthermore, American policy in the Gulf is constrained by the problem of ambiguity. The failure to explicitly disavow use of the RDF except in the case of external threats (i.e. external to the Arabian Peninsula) may prove counterproductive in (1) promoting closer co-operation between the US and the GCC states, and (2) acquiring regional facilities for possible use against the Soviet Union.

The RDF may play a useful and even necessary role in the American policy mix for the Gulf, but far more important are other avenues of co-operation and preparation for underpinning Gulf security. In the last analysis, it is the states of the region whose fate is most directly and acutely affected. They must, in many ways, bear the greatest responsibility, and the largest burden, for Gulf security. It is to their options, and the American role therein, that this discussion must now turn.

Notes

1. The development of US policy in regard to the Gulf has been covered by Gary Sick, 'The Evolution of U.S. Strategy Toward the Indian Ocean and Persian Gulf Regions', in A. Z. Rubinstein (ed.), *The Great Game: Rivalry in the Persian Gulf and South Asia* (New York, Praeger, 1983), pp. 49–80; Geoffrey Kemp, 'Military Force and Middle East Oil', in David A. Deese and Joseph S. Nye (eds), *Energy and Security* (Cambridge, Ma, Ballinger, for the Harvard Energy and Security Research Project, 1981), pp. 365–87; and Jacques Vernant, 'L'Occident et la securité du Golfe', *Défense Nationale*, vol. 37 (May 1981), pp. 135–41.

2. Robert E. Osgood, 'The Nixon Doctrine and Strategy', in Osgood (ed.), *Retreat from Empire* (Baltimore, Johns Hopkins University Press, 1973), p. 9.

3. On the American relationship with the late Shah, see Fred Halliday, *Iran: Dictatorship and Development*, 2nd edn (Harmondsworth, Penguin, 1979); R. K. Ramazani, *The United States and Iran: Patterns of Influence* (New York, Praeger, 1982); and Barry Rubin, *Paved with Good Intentions: The American Experience and Iran* (London, Oxford University Press, 1980; Harmondsworth, Penguin, 1981).

4. On the growing climate of alarm, see Zbigniew Brzezinski's comments in *Time*, 15 January 1979, as well as Henry Kissinger's interview in *The Economist*, 3 February 1979, and Robert W. Tucker, 'American Power and the Persian Gulf', *Commentary*, vol. 70, no. 5 (November 1980), pp. 25–41. For a counter-interpretation of the Soviet role, see Fred Halliday, *Threat From the East?: Soviet Policy From Afghanistan and Iran to the Horn of Africa* (Harmondsworth, Penguin, 1982). The Pentagon study was summarised by Richard Burt, *New York Times*, 2 February 1980. Both Paul Wolfowitz and Burt later served in the Reagan administration.

5. As noted at the beginning of this book, the nomenclature for RDF forces has gone through several changes. For simplicity's sake, the term RDF will be used variously to refer to the RDF, the Rapid Deployment Joint Task Force (RDJTF), and the US Central Command (USCENTCOM).

6. See John Lewis Gaddis's assessment of the vacillations by post-Second World War administrations between symmetry and asymmetry in his *Strategies of Containment: A Critical Appraisal of Postwar American National Security Policy* (New York, Oxford University Press, 1982), esp. pp. 352–7. The Reagan administration's response bears a striking resemblance to John Foster Dulles's reaction to Korea: 'the free world [must] develop the will and organize the means to retaliate instantly against open aggression by Red armies, so that, if it occurred anywhere, we could and would strike back where it hurts, by means of our own choosing'. Quoted in ibid., p. 121. For an evaluation of the suitability of an asymmetrical response to Soviet action in the Gulf, see Joshua M. Epstein, 'Horizontal Escalation: Sour Notes on a Recurrent Theme', *International Security*, vol. 8, no. 3 (winter 1983–4), pp. 19–31.

7. Secretary Haig, in Congressional testimony, outlined his conception of strategic consensus as follows: 'the United States regards the peace process and the effort to counter Soviet and regional threats as mutually reinforcing. If our friends are more secure, they will be more able to take risks for peace. If there is progress in the peace process, security co-operation will be facilitated — cooperation is essential to deter intervention by the Soviets and their proxies.' US Congress, Senate, Committee on Foreign Relations, *Persian Gulf Situation; Hearings*, 17 September 1981 (Washington, USGPO, 1981), p. 4.

8. W. Andrew Terrill, 'Jordan and the Defense of the Gulf', *Middle East Insights*, vol. 4, no. 1 (March–April 1985), pp. 34–41.

9. For a study of Japan's response to this situation, see Valerie Yorke, 'Oil, the Middle East and Japan's Search for Security', *International Affairs* (London), vol. 57, no. 3 (1981), pp. 428–48.

10. French interests in the region are analysed in Shahram Chubin, 'La France et le Golfe: opportunisme ou continuité?', *Politique Etrangère*, vol. 48, no. 4 (1983), pp. 879–87. See also Thomas L. McNaugher, *Arms and Oil: U.S. Military Strategy and the Persian Gulf* (Washington, Brookings Institution, 1985), pp. 154–5; and Giovanni de Briganti, 'Forces d'Action Rapide: France's Rapid Deployment Force',

Armed Forces Journal International, vol. 122 (October 1984), pp. 122, 124.

11. T. A. Boam, 'Defending Western Interests Outside NATO: The United Kingdom's Contribution', *Armed Forces Journal International*, vol. 122 (October 1984), p. 116.

12. 'Les Occidentaux et la securité du Golfe', *Politique Etrangère*, vol. 46, no. 3 (September 1981), pp. 667–90.

13. 'Of Allies and Access', *Washington Quarterly*, vol. 4, no. 1 (1981), pp. 87–96. See also Albert Wohlstetter, 'Les Etats-Unis et la securité du Golfe', *Politique Etrangère*, vol. 46, no. 1 (March 1981), pp. 75–88; Christopher Coker and Heinz Schulte, 'A European Option in the Indian Ocean', *International Defense Review*, vol. 13, no. 1 (1982), pp. 27–34; Donald S. Rowe, 'Collective Security and the Rapid Deployment Joint Task Force,' *Joint Perspectives*, vol. 1, no. 3 (winter 1981), pp. 3–17; Rouhollah K. Ramazani, 'Security in the Persian Gulf', *Foreign Affairs*, vol. 57, no. 4 (1979), pp. 821–35; and idem, 'The Strait of Hormuz: The Global Chokepoint', in Larry W. Bowman and Ian Clark (eds), *The Indian Ocean in Global Politics* (Boulder, Co, Westview Press; Nedlands, University of Western Australia, 1981), pp. 7–20.

14. 'From RDF to CENTCOM: New Challenges?', *RUSI — Journal of the Royal United Services Institute for Defence Studies*, vol. 129 (March 1984), p. 17.

15. As evidence, he cites Turkish dependence on Gulf oil, the estimated $10b-worth of contracts held in the Arab world, the 150,000 Turkish workers in the Middle East, and the 44 per cent of total Turkish exports that go to the Middle East. 'Turkey's Security and the Middle East', *Foreign Affairs*, vol. 62, no. 1 (1983), pp. 156–75.

16. 'Meeting the Threat in the Persian Gulf', *Survey*, vol. 25, no. 2 (spring 1980), pp. 175–87. See also Bruce R. Kuniholm, 'Turkey and NATO: Past, Present and Future', *Orbis*, vol. 27, no. 2 (summer 1983), pp. 421–45; and idem, *The Persian Gulf and United States Policy* (Claremont, Ca, Regina Books, 1984), pp. 120–4.

17. See James H. Noyes, *The Clouded Lens: Persian Gulf Security and U.S. Policy*, 2nd edn (Stanford, Ca, Hoover Institution Press, 1982), p. 135; and Kuniholm, *The Persian Gulf and United States Policy*, pp. 129–31. Both the US and France have helped build up the Pakistani navy in recent years, and Pakistan has played a major role in developing the naval establishment of the fledgeling GCC navies. There has been some speculation that the US has sought use of the Pakistani port at Gwadar. See *Middle East International*, no. 224 (4 May 1984).

18. For an overview of this subject, see Robert P. Haffa, Jr, *The Half War: Planning U.S. Rapid Deployment Forces to Meet a Limited Contingency, 1960–1983* (Boulder, Co, Westview Press, 1984).

19. Maxwell Orme Johnson, *The Military as an Instrument of U.S. Policy in Southwest Asia: The Rapid Deployment Joint Task Force, 1979–1982* (Boulder, Co, Westview Press, 1982), pp. 59–60; and Dov S. Zakheim, 'Airlifting the Marine Corps: Mismatch or Wave of the Future?', in Uri Ra'anan, Robert L. Pfaltzgraff, Jr, and Geoffrey Kemp (eds), *Projection of Power: Perspectives, Perceptions and Problems* (Hamden, Ct, Archon Books, 1982), pp. 120–37.

20. Johnson, *Military as an Instrument*, provides a detailed discussion of the evolution of the conception and planning for the RDF, on which much of the following information is based. See also idem, 'Rapid Deployment and the Regional Military Challenge: The Persian Gulf Equation', unpublished paper presented at a US Army War College symposium on 'US Strategic Interests in the Persian Gulf',

27–29 March 1985; and Robert J. Hanks, *The U.S. Military Presence in the Middle East: Problems and Prospects* (Cambridge, Ma, Institute for Foreign Policy Analysis, December 1982).

21. In a 1984 interview, USCENTCOM Commander-in-Chief Robert C. Kingston stated that the Command could get a battalion from the 82nd Airborne Division airlifted to the Iranian side of the Strait of Hormuz within 48 hours and the remainder of the brigade there in less than a week. *Armed Forces Journal International*, vol. 121, no. 12 (July 1984), p. 69. In mid-1985, the Marine Corps' 7th Amphibious Brigade was stated to be in a position to transport 12,500 men to the Gulf within a week, with plans to upgrade that capacity to 16,500 by November 1985, *New York Times*, 10 April 1985.

22. Richard Halloran, 'Poised for the Persian Gulf', *New York Times Magazine*, 1 April 1984, pp. 38–40, 61.

23. David D. Newsom, Undersecretary of State for Political Affairs during 1978–81, voices a number of misgivings, arguing that 'a strategy that places U.S. ground forces in the Persian Gulf should not be undertaken without a thorough national and congressional debate. That debate has yet to begin.' 'America EnGulfed', *Foreign Policy*, no. 43 (summer 1981), p. 32. Newsom also charges that the Carter Doctrine was not properly thought out and 'grew out of last minute pressures for a presidential speech'. Ibid., p. 17. See also Rouhollah K. Ramazani, 'The Genesis of the Carter Doctrine', in George S. Wise and Charles Issawi (eds), *Middle East Perspectives: The Next Twenty Years* (Princeton, NJ, Darwin Press, 1981), pp. 165–80; and Christopher Van Hollen, 'Don't Engulf the Gulf', *Foreign Affairs*, vol. 59, no. 5 (1981), pp. 1064–78.

24. Jeffrey Record, *The Rapid Deployment Force and U.S. Military Intervention in the Persian Gulf* (Cambridge, Ma, Institute for Foreign Policy Analysis, Special Report, February 1981), pp. 70–3. See also his *Revising U.S. Military Strategy: Tailoring Means to Ends* (Washington, Pergamon-Brassey's, 1984), esp. Ch. 4, 'The Carter Doctrine, Rapid Deployment Force, and Worldwide War Strategy, 1979–Present', pp. 36–48. Others arguing that the RDF mission is a Marine Corps job include Martin L. Cover, 'FMF [Fleet Marine Force] for the RDF', *US Naval Institute Proceedings*, vol. 108, no. 6 (June 1982), pp. 51–5; and David A. Quinlan, *The Role of the Marine Corps in Rapid Deployment Forces* (Washington, National Defense University Press, 1983).

25. 'A Strategy for the Rapid Deployment Force', *International Security*, vol. 5, no. 4 (1981), p. 63.

26. 'Balancing Soviet Power in the Persian Gulf', *Brookings Review*, vol. 1, no. 4 (1983), p. 24. See also his *Arms and Oil*.

27. See, *inter alia*, Robert W. Tucker, *The Purposes of American Power: An Essay on National Security* (New York, Praeger, 1981); Miles Ignotus (pseud.), 'Seizing Arab Oil', *Harper's*, vol. 250, no. 1498 (March 1975), pp. 45–62; and Edward Friedland, Paul Seabury and Aaron Wildavsky, *The Great Detente Disaster: Oil and the Decline of American Foreign Policy* (New York, Basic Books, 1975). Tucker equates the Carter Doctrine's failure to address threats other than external ones as 'appeasement' of the Gulf states 'that have managed to outmaneuver and to intimidate Western powers for over a decade'. *Purposes of American Power*, p. 106. See also the observations on this topic of Thomas A. Fabyanic, 'Conceptual Planning and the Rapid Deployment Joint Task Force', *Armed Forces and Society*, vol. 7, no. 3 (1981), pp. 343–65.

28. 'The Persian Gulf and the Correlation of Forces', *International Security*, vol. 7, no. 1 (1982), p. 179.
29. 'Meeting the Threat in the Persian Gulf', pp. 164–5. He has written similarly in 'Half-Wars and Half-Policies in the Persian Gulf', in W. Scott Thompson (ed.), *National Security in the 1980s: From Weakness to Strength* (San Francisco, Institute for Contemporary Studies, 1980), pp. 123–72.
30. *Arms and Oil*, p. 49.
31. To some extent, this view was held also during the Carter administration. See the discussion of the 'Wolfowitz Report' earlier in this chapter. See also the argument against nuclear escalation in favour of horizontal escalation at sea in F. J. West, Jr, 'NATO II: Common Boundaries for Common Interests', *Naval War College Review*, vol. 34, no. 1 (January–February 1981), pp. 59–67.
32. Furthermore, it may be unrealistic to think that a conventional war with the Soviet Union could be limited to the Gulf. If conflict escalates to general war, where will American forces and logistics to fight in the Gulf come from?
33. *Purposes of American Power*, pp. 107–8.
34. *The Clouded Lens*, p. 135.
35. 'Meeting the Threat in the Persian Gulf', p. 167.
36. See West, 'NATO II'; Robert Komer, 'Maritime Strategy vs. Coalition Defense', *Foreign Affairs*, vol. 60, no. 5 (1982), pp. 1124–44; Stansfield Turner and George Thibault, 'Preparing for the Unexpected: The Need for a New Military Strategy', *Foreign Affairs*, vol. 61, no. 2 (1982-3), pp. 64–77; and Keith A. Dunn and William O. Staudenmaier, 'Strategy for Survival', *Foreign Policy*, no. 52 (1983), pp. 22–41. See also the discussion in Bruce R. Kuniholm, *The Persian Gulf and United States Policy*, pp. 49–53.
37. 'Strategy for the RDF', p. 57. See also the comments in John Joseph Stocker, 'Rapid Deployment Force', Issue Brief no. IB 80027, Congressional Research Service, Library of Congress.
38. *Chicago Tribune*, 1 December 1983; Robert C. Kingston, 'US Central Command: Refocusing the Lens of Stability on a Region in Crisis', *Defense '84*, November–December 1984, p. 31. See also Kingston's comments in 'C^{3}I and the U.S. Central Command', *Signal*, November 1983, p. 23–5.
39. *Rapid Deployment Force*, p. vii.
40. Robert C. Kingston interview in *Armed Forces Journal International*, p. 73.
41. 'Balancing Soviet Power in the Persian Gulf'.
42. See the discussion in McNaugher, *Arms and Oil*, pp. 53–64. McNaugher notes that many of the appropriate strike aircraft, such as the B-52, F-111 and A-7 are no longer in production and the A-6 is purchased only in small numbers by the navy. As planning now stands, air cover would have to be provided by carrier-based fighters from the Arabian Sea, or from Masira Island, which is not much better in terms of proximity to the theatre of operations. See also Cordesman, *The Gulf*, pp. 814–17.
43. Johnson, *Military as an Instrument*, pp. 80–7; Zakheim, 'Airlifting the Marine Corps', p. 124; Bruce Schoch, 'Sea Lift for the RDF', *National Defense*, no. 65 (May–June 1981), pp. 71–4; Cordesman, *The Gulf*, pp. 825–9; and Raphael Iungerich, 'US Rapid Deployment Forces — USCENTCOM — What is It? Can It Do the Job?', *Armed Forces Journal International*, vol. 122 (October 1984), p. 97.
44. Iungerich, 'US Rapid Deployment Forces', p. 97. As Iungerich points out, 'Airlift savings associated with the prepositioning concept are enormous. For example, the total ammunition tonnage aboard NTPF ships would require roughly

2,450 C-141 sorties from the East Coast.' Ibid.
45. Johnson, *Military as an Instrument*, pp. 68–80; Zakheim, 'Airlifting the Marine Corps', p. 124.
46. For example, see Richard A. Stewart, 'Tactical Mobility for the Rapid Deployment Forces: The Solution is at Hand', *Armed Forces Journal International*, vol. 117 (March 1980), pp. 70–2, 83; Raymond E. Bell, Jr, 'The Rapid Deployment Force: How Much, How Soon?', *Army*, vol. 30 (July 1980), pp. 18–24; and Record, *Rapid Deployment Force*, pp. 62–3.
47. Johnson, *Military as an Instrument*, pp. 93–5; idem, 'Force Projection in Southwest Asia: The Role of Maritime Based Strategy', *Marine Corps Gazette*, vol. 68 (February 1984), pp. 64–8; and Record, *Rapid Deployment Force*, pp. 65–6. See also William F. Hickman's analysis of the ineffective role of American naval deployment during the Iranian hostage crisis, 'Did It Really Matter?', *Naval War College Review*, vol. 36, no. 2 (March–April 1983), pp. 17–30.
48. Johnson, *Military as an Instrument*, pp. 87–93.
49. Quoted in the *New York Times*, 25 October 1982.
50. 'Considering Soviet Threats to the Persian Gulf', *International Security*, vol. 6, no. 2 (1981), p. 174.
51. *Arms and Oil*, p. 45.
52. 'Constraints on the USSR in Southwest Asia: A Military Analysis', *Orbis*, vol. 25, no. 3 (fall 1981), pp. 607–29.
53. These forces have been improved in recent years, although they are said to be less prepared for a sustained campaign than those in central Europe. The Soviet Southern Theatre of Military Operations also controls 5,200 tanks, 6,600 artillery/mortar pieces and 890 aircraft; the number of Soviet troops in Afghanistan is about 115,000. US Department of Defense, *Soviet Military Power, 1985*, 4th edn (Washington, USGPO, April 1985), pp. 15 and 129. See also Cordesman, *The Gulf*, pp. 818–20.
54. 'Constraints on the USSR', p. 629. In his opinion, the primary response to the Soviet threat 'must continue to be essentially political, bolstered by military capabilities — and not the reverse'. Ibid.
55. Cordesman, *The Gulf*, pp. 843–7.
56. 'Soviet Vulnerabilities in Iran and the RDF Deterrent', *International Security*, vol. 6, no. 2 (1981), pp. 126–59. While Epstein assumes a US entrenchment centred on Abadan, Thomas L. McNaugher suggests that US interdiction of invading Soviet forces should take place farther north, near the point of entry into Iran. 'Deterring Soviet Forces in Southwest Asia', in Stephen J. Cimbala (ed.), *National Security Strategy: Choices and Limits* (New York, Praeger, 1984), pp. 125–54. See also his discussion in *Arms and Oil*, pp. 23–46. Over 25,000 troops took part in Operation Kavkaz-85, held in Soviet Georgia in July–August 1985. The manoeuvres demonstrated Soviet deep penetration ability in the first major Soviet rugged terrain exercise in nine years. *Washington Times*, 5 August 1985. While the setting of the manoeuvres in Georgia rather than Azerbaijan indicated that the adversary was Turkey, the value of this exercise applies equally well to Iran.
57. Johnson, 'Rapid Deployment', p. 4. Cordesman notes that 'the control of Iran is losing some of its strategic importance. The Iran–Iraq War, Iranian revolution, and Iranian civil war have severely cut Iran's near-term oil- and gas-production capabilities and quite probably its ultimate recovery potential. Iran's economy is still weak, and the West has learned to live without a heavy dependence on Iranian gas

and oil. Iran's politics may make any firm Soviet presence untenable for years to come. Accordingly, a Western "defense" of Iran could be limited to de facto partition at the Zagros or Elburz mountains.' *The Gulf*, p. 856.

58. 'Soviet Vulnerabilities in Iran', p. 158. W. Scott Thompson, in his 'The Persian Gulf and the Correlation of Forces', takes issue with some of Epstein's assumptions. Even if the US is able to prevent a Soviet takeover of Khuzestan, Moscow will have occupied northern Iran and thus will be in a far better position to threaten the oilfields and states of the region than it is presently. Furthermore, he contends that an air interdiction campaign against Soviet columns moving into northern Iran is clearly vulnerable to a Soviet pre-emptive strike against American air bases in Turkey.

59. See J. E. Peterson, *Conflict in the Yemens and Superpower Involvement* (Washington, Georgetown University Center for Contemporary Arab Studies, 1981).

60. See the comments of Thomas McNaugher and William Quandt, *Oil and the Outcome of the Iran–Iraq War* (Cambridge, Ma, Cambridge Energy Research Associates, 1984).

61. In fact, this seems unlikely. As James A. Bill points out, while Iran's leaders are keen on exporting their revolution throughout the Gulf, 'force is considered unnecessary, counterproductive, and antithetical to the tenets of Islam'. 'Resurgent Islam in the Persian Gulf', *Foreign Affairs*, vol. 63, no. 1 (fall 1984), p. 118.

62. US Library of Congress, Congressional Research Service, *Western Vulnerability to a Disruption of Persian Gulf Oil Supplies: U.S. Interests and Options* (Washington, 24 March 1983).

63. On this subject, see Thomas M. Johnson and Raymond T. Barrett, 'Mining the Strait of Hormuz', *US Naval Institute Proceedings*, vol. 107, no. 12 (December 1981), pp. 83–5; Rouhollah K. Ramazani, *The Persian Gulf and the Strait of Hormuz* (Alphen aan den Rijn, Sijthoff & Nordhoff, 1979; International Straits of the World, vol. 3); idem, 'The Strait of Hormuz: The Global Chokepoint'; and William L. Dowdy, 'The Strait of Hormuz as a Secure International Waterway', in B. R. Pridham (ed.), *The Arab Gulf and the West* (London, Croom Helm, 1985; for the University of Exeter Centre for Arab Gulf Studies), pp. 162–71.

64. It could be postulated that there is a direct correlation between assertions of Saudi instability and unfamiliarity with that country.

65. 'Seizing Arab Oil', *Harper's*, vol. 250, no. 1498 (March 1975), pp. 45–62. In this vein, see also Edward Friedland, *et al.*, *The Great Detente Disaster*; and the various articles of Robert W. Tucker in *Commentary*. For a response to these views, see I. William Zartman, 'The Power of American Purposes', *Middle East Journal*, vol. 35, no. 2 (spring 1982), pp. 163–77. Leftist assaults on the interventionists — and on US policy in general — are contained in Michael Klare, *Beyond the 'Vietnam Syndrome': U.S. Interventionism in the 1980s* (Washington: Institute for Policy Studies, 1981); and Leila Meo, ed., *U.S. Strategy in the Gulf: Intervention Against Liberation* (Belmont, Ma, Association of Arab–American University Graduates, October 1981).

66. *The Purposes of American Power*, p. 106.

67. US Congress, House of Representatives, Committee on International Relations, *Oil Fields as Military Objectives: A Feasibility Study*, prepared by the Congressional Research Service, Library of Congress (Washington, USGPO, 1975). An updated version of this study was retitled *Petroleum Imports from the Persian*

Gulf: Use of U.S. Armed Force to Ensure Supplies, Congressional Research Service, Issue Brief no. IB 79046 (8 January 1980). See also the discussion in McNaugher, *Arms and Oil*, pp. 183–97.

6 Gulf Security and Gulf Self-Defence

It is frequently overlooked that external concerns over the security of the Arabian Peninsula are matched and even exceeded by the concerns of the governments of that area. When British security responsibility was paramount, only a few short decades ago, the entities of the Peninsula were not in a position to articulate their concern or preferred responses to security problems, let alone assume the military responsibility to defend themselves. But in the 1980s, there has been a far more fundamental change in security responsibility than the mere passing of the torch from London to Washington. In the interim, modern nation states — or, in some cases, city states — have emerged in Arabia. Just as they have taken charge of all domestic matters, they naturally claim responsibility for security affairs that affect their well-being and survival. It is this point that often seems difficult to grasp in Washington. What these states require from Washington is flexible co-operation in military assistance, not a return to a protected status.

There is no doubt that the military defence capabilities of all six GCC states are severely limited, even by comparison to their neighbours in the Middle East. Saudi Arabia and Oman, and the other amirates to a lesser extent, have all engaged in extensive, expensive and sophisticated military modernisation programmes in the last decade or two. Once massive hardware purchases have been delivered and absorbed and indigenous personnel trained to operate sophisticated weaponry and support equipment, the GCC will be in a good position to defend itself against a wide variety of threats. Nevertheless, it is inescapable that the GCC will never have the manpower to allow it to face a frontal assault by Iraq or Iran, nor it is likely to achieve parity with Israel in either arms or skilled personnel. Countering a direct Soviet thrust is even farther beyond the means of these states.

All that this means, however, is that the GCC will always find itself dependent on external defence assistance — the same as every other country or group of countries in the world. At the same time, the threats mentioned above are not the only ones that the GCC faces, nor are they the most likely ones. The GCC also faces potential threats from spillover from the Iran–Iraq war, political pressures and low-level hostilities from regional actors designed to force policy changes, and even internal opposition (perhaps assisted by external actors). The GCC states have made considerable progress in acquiring the capability to deal with these types of potential threats.

Even more importantly, they have pursued a multi-layered strategy for self-defence, of which military strength is only one aspect. They have used oil income and quiet moral suasion to encourage moderation among regional actors and to seek consensus in pan-Arab affairs. They have sought to reconciliate enemies and to contain hostilities, as in GCC peace-making efforts between Oman and South Yemen and between Iran and Iraq. The challenges of oil wealth have been met by extensive policies of income distribution and evolving, albeit often reluctant, adaptation to necessary social and political transformation. The attitude taken by these states to these internal challenges and the progress made in adapting to them form the real security problem. Chances are that preparations made in non-military fields will be more important to the continued survival and security of the Arab Gulf states than the prowess and performance of their armed forces.

The Emergence of Arabian Nation States

In the earlier days of British concern for the security of the Gulf, primary responsibility fell to the British by default. Iraq lay within the outlying provinces of the Ottoman empire. The government in Qajar Iran exercised little control over its hinterland. Sole political authority along the Arabian littoral was embodied in the tribe. As a consequence, there was no alternative for the British but to provide their own security for their own interests and personnel in the area, as well as gradually to establish a *pax Britannica* over the Gulf.

But the increasing importance of the Gulf's security in the last half century has been paralleled by the emergence of national consciousness in the region and the creation of political institutions to represent and safeguard that consciousness. Because of its traditionalism and isolation, this consciousness emerged in the Arabian Peninsula later than elsewhere in the Middle East and the Gulf. At the same time, because of the newness of Arab Gulf nationalism and the very recent development of national political systems there, political change has been most rapid and striking in these states.

Until quite recently the tribe constituted the central political unit in most of the Arabian Peninsula; the traditional states of Yemen and Oman and areas under foreign domination formed notable exceptions. Traditionally, most daily concerns of the individual revolved around the tribe: family relationships, social standing and definition, economic welfare, the regime of daily life, and even physical well-being all were determined within the tribal framework. Islam constituted a broader allegiance, but one that supplemented the corporate identity of the tribe rather than competed with it. Tribal confederations might contain larger political aggregations, but they were far more diffuse and passive, generally serving as temporary instruments for seeking protection from rival tribes or countering serious threats to the confederation as a whole.

Leadership of the tribe was vested in the shaykh. Far from serving as a 'head of state', the shaykh was more of a manager or chairman, whose authority and powers generally were severely restricted. Only in a few tribes did he exercise real daily authority. Furthermore, while tribal territories were relatively clearly defined, the responsibility of the shaykh was limited to people and did not include territory. It can be seen that political power in the tribal system was clearly decentralised. As a consequence, the system proved to be exceedingly vulnerable to both the encroachment of European powers and the emerging ideology of nationalism. By the mid-point of the twentieth century, the supremacy of tribal politics had metamorphosed into states whose tribal origins became increasingly less important.

The most obvious exceptions to this generalisation of a purely tribal political environment were the centuries-old traditional states in Yemen and Oman. In both countries, the presence of smaller Islamic sects had resulted in loosely organised states with elected imams exercising limited authority over the tribes. The physical isolation of the countries, sectarian uniqueness and historical continuity also contributed to the sense of national community. Even though clearly defined 'nations' existed, the traditional form of the state was unable to survive new challenges.

In Oman, the imamate degenerated into dynastic rule in the late eighteenth century and the country's capital relocated to the coast. The oft-repeated pattern of rebirth of a new imamate was interrupted by British support for the coastal rulers, who had been restyled sultans, and repeated attempts in the nineteenth and twentieth centuries to recreate the imamate failed. Nevertheless, the continued survival of the newer sultanate did not seem assured until a palace *coup d'état* in 1970 replaced a traditionalist, reactionary ruler with his modernisation-oriented son. Yemen's transformation has not been so complicated, but perhaps is less complete. By the early twentieth century, the tradition of elected imams had been superseded by the emergence of a dynasty and Yemen's traditionalist rulers also attempted to keep out the modern world. Despite a secular revolution in 1962 led by army officers, the authority of the republican government in Yemen is exceedingly fragile.

The creation of modern Saudi Arabia resulted from a more 'orthodox' expansion of tribal power on to the national level. At various times in the past, energetic shaykhly families were able to establish their control over neighbouring tribes and extensive areas. One such example was that of the Central Arabian family of Al Sa'ud, who in the eighteenth century formed an alliance with an Islamic reformer named Muhammad 'Abd al-Wahhab. As a result of this fusion of political/military strength with moral leadership, Sa'udi power extended far beyond Central Arabia on several occasions.

At the beginning of the twentieth century, 'Abd al-'Aziz Al Sa'ud (better known in the West as Ibn Sa'ud) regained control of the ancestral capital of Riyadh and gradually extended Saudi authority over Central Arabia, east towards the Gulf, north through Jabal Shammar, west across the Hijaz, and south into 'Asir. By the early 1930s, the new state had filled its present boundaries — consisting of all of the Arabian Peninsula except those territories under British domination and the formidable mountains of Yemen — and adopted the name of the Kingdom of Saudi Arabia.

Nevertheless, additional decades passed before a rational administrative structure was implemented and the foundations of a socio-economic infrastructure laid. It took the débâcle of King Sa'ud's reign (1953–64) to reorganise the state and place its finances on a sounder footing. Finally, the permanency of the Saudi state seemed to be assured only with its weathering the challenge posed by the Arab radicals of the 1950s and 1960s: Saudi Arabia emerged after the June 1967 Arab–Israeli war not only intact, but with a growing involvement and weight in inter-Arab affairs.

Elsewhere, the key impetus in state formation was provided by the British. They had encouraged the 'Arab revolt' during the First World War and recognised the Hashimi state in Hijaz. Aden was seized in 1839 and transformed into a crown colony surrounded by a hinterland of British protectorates. The British also established political control over the Arab shores of the Gulf, entering into relations with certain shaykhs whom they endowed with recognition as the rulers of defined territories and populations. The British-created domains of these shaykhs eventually evolved into statehood.

Kuwait and Bahrain were the first of these smaller states to emerge, in large part because they were the first countries in the Peninsula to enjoy substantial oil revenues. The roots of modern Kuwait date back to the consolidation of power by the Al Sabah family in the eighteenth century and the development of Kuwait as a seafaring town and *entrepôt* for its Bedouin hinterland. The creation of an urban centre with a relatively diversified economic base provided the Al Sabah with the nucleus of support necessary to establish a common political consciousness beyond the tribe. The influx of oil revenues after the Second World War dramatically transformed a small, impoverished town into a modern city and welfare state. As a consequence, Kuwait received complete independence in 1961 — the first of the shaykhdoms to acquire this status.

The background of Bahrain is similar to that of Kuwait, with a dominant tribal family — the Al Khalifa — also emerging in the eighteenth century. Agriculture, even more than commerce, was instrumental in creating a sedentary population and feeling of Bahraini identity. Oil production had begun even earlier than in Kuwait. But Bahrain's progress to statehood was hampered by two factors: the meagreness of its oil supplies and its small population size. As a consequence, Bahrain did not receive independence until 1971.

The emergence of states farther down the coast was delayed even more. Here the British influence was far more instrumental in the creation of 'national' identities. Certain shaykhs were recognised as leaders and held responsible for the actions of their tribesmen: if members of a tribe attacked British vessels, then the shaykh and his settlement were open to reprisals. On the other side of the coin, Britain later gave subsidies to compliant shaykhs to ensure their co-operation, providing income which could be utilised to enhance their power. Eventually, this British policy resulted not only in the strengthening of the shaykh's control over his and allied tribes, but also in the association of the shaykh's political authority with a delineated territory as well as people. Thus the basis for a territorial state was established. Beginning in the late nineteenth century, Britain entered into treaty relations with the shaykhs of Qatar, Abu Dhabi, Dubai, Sharjah, 'Ajman, Umm al-Qaywayn, Ra's al-Khayma, al-Fujayra and Kalba (later withdrawn).

The continued existence of separate political entities in these very small settlements was due only to the treaty relationships of their shaykhs with the British. This situation not only protected them from absorption into the emerging Saudi state, but also prevented their amalgamation into one entity under a strong leader. As a consequence, when the time came for Britain to withdraw, there remained the nagging question of what to do with these nine shaykhdoms, barely describable as 'mini-states'. Beginning in 1968, the nine rulers entered into federation talks but these negotiations foundered over the problem of unequal size between Bahrain and Qatar, on the one hand, and the seven tinier Trucial states, on the other. Eventually, Bahrain and Qatar opted to go their separate ways, with the other seven joining in the new United Arab Emirates (UAE).

With independence came full responsibility for both internal and external affairs, including national defence. In the few decades since they began receiving oil income, all of these states have created extensive administrative structures to carry out the vastly expanded functions expected of their governments, including most of the social welfare services found in the West. But the ability of these states to provide properly for their own defence is hampered by their small size and power potential, the short time in which they have begun to develop appropriate and viable military forces, their being surrounded by larger and often hostile neighbours, and the increasingly intense spotlight focused on them due to their abundant supplies of the scarce resource of oil. The development of adequate defence forces provides the Peninsula states with one of their most difficult tasks.

The evolution of Arabian military establishments has been of even more recent vintage than most other economic and political changes evident in the Peninsula. Rulers remained dependent on traditional military forces and organisation until quite recently and the adoption of modern defence structures and equipment is still in a transitional stage. Furthermore, achievement of military potential by these states is restricted by small populations, limited resources and low levels of economic development. The result is pervading weakness, even when compared to nearly all the Peninsula states' neighbours.

Just as central government was hardly a standard feature of the traditional Arabian scene, neither was the standing army. The power of a tribe was determined principally by the combined personal firepower of its tribesmen, who left their herds or crops whenever necessary to provide the defence for tribal territory, property and honour. Major shaykhs employed retainers, drawn from their own and allied tribes, who were responsible for such functions as tax collection and guarding prisoners.

As shaykhs in treaty relationship with the British evolved into rulers, the number of retainers increased while their functions remained essentially the same. The situation was similar for the imams of Yemen and Oman, who relied on larger groups of retainers in the imam's office, as well as in the offices of the imam's representatives and governors in the hinterland, and semi-permanent levies drawn from tribes which were particularly well known as supporters of the imamate and the imam. Only well into the twentieth century did the Yemeni, Omani, Hijazi and Saudi leaders begin to develop small, untrained standing armies. But it took until the 1950s and especially the 1960s for permanent military establishments — reasonably adequately trained and equipped, and dedicated to national defence rather than service as Praetorian Guards and minor functionaries — to take root.

Saudi Military Capabilities

Of all the armed forces of the Arabian Peninsula, that of Saudi Arabia is the most formidable, both in terms of size of personnel and extent and sophistication of its arms and equipment (see Table 6.1). With more than 51,000 men under arms (not including the National Guard) and a defence expenditure of over $22b, the kingdom is easily the dominant force within the GCC. Oman's armed forces, perhaps the most competent and certainly the most battle-hardened, are estimated at only 21,500. While the UAE ranks second in total numbers at 43,000, its armed forces were merged from a number of separate forces only a few years ago and

Table 6.1: Arabian Peninsula States: Military Capabilities

Country	Pop. (millions)	Total no. of armed forces	GDP ($ billions)	Defence expenditure ($ billions)
GCC members				
Bahrain	0.40	2,800	4.617	0.253
Kuwait	1.75	12,500	19.903	1.360
Oman	1.00	21,500	7.600	1.960
Qatar	0.27	6,000	7.903	0.165
Saudi Arabia	8–12	51,500	119.967	22.731
UAE	1.30	43,000	34.978	1.867
The Yemens				
YAR (North)	7.50	36,550	3.208	0.526
PDRY (South)	2.20	27,500	0.923	0.159

Source: *The Military Balance, 1984–1985* (London, international Institute for Strategic Studies, 1984), pp. 59–73.

some, particularly Dubai's, remain relatively autonomous. In addition, while Oman ranks second in defence expenditure at $1.960b, that figure amounts to about 9 per cent of the Saudi total. At the same time, however, it should be kept in mind that the sizes of these armed forces pale beside those of their other Middle Eastern neighbours.[1]

Like the other GCC states (except for Oman), the development of Saudi Arabia's military capability has been quite recent and the enormous defence expenditure over the past decade will require considerable time to digest. Even the organisational structure is relatively new, and there exists wide disparity in the capability of the various components of the armed forces. Furthermore, the kingdom faces serious difficulties in recruiting and retaining competent personnel. For the foreseeable future, the Saudi armed forces will be heavily dependent on foreign assistance in training and the operation of equipment.[2]

Formally, the High Defence Council determines policy, although in practice the king's decisions are final. The council was established in 1961 with membership consisting of the king, the Ministers of Defence and Aviation, Finance and National Economy, Communications, and Foreign Affairs, and the Chief of Staff. The Minister of Defence and Aviation (the office has been occupied by Prince Sultan b. 'Abd al-'Aziz, second in line for the throne, since 1962) controls the army, air force and navy, while the National Guard (commanded by Crown Prince 'Abd Allah b. 'Abd al-'Aziz since 1963) theoretically falls under the control of the Minister of the Interior, along with the Frontier Force, the Coast Guard and internal security forces. In practice, however, the National Guard is answerable only to Prince 'Abd Allah and, through him, the king.

In the early days of his rule, 'Abd al-'Aziz relied on three types of armed forces: regulars, generally drawn from the towns and used to staff garrisons; Bedouin, drawn from tribal allies of the Al Sa'ud; and the Ikhwan.[3] The Ikhwan movement resulted from 'Abd al-'Aziz's encouragement of Islamic revival — with emphasis on Unitarian (Wahhabi) tenets — and settlement among the Bedouin. By 1920, there were an estimated 150,000 fighting men in more than 200 settlements. They provided Al Sa'ud with 'a striking force that could mobilize in hours or days, depending on the size of the raid, a force that could travel great distances on almost uninterrupted marches, endure a battle on the most meager of diets, and plunge into the battle seeking death and paradise. No other ruler could match it!'[4] The military skills of the Ikhwan and the fear they inspired in their opponents were important elements in 'Abd al-'Aziz's capture of 'Asir in 1920, Ha'il in 1921, Jawf in 1922 and Hijaz in 1925. But the same religious fervour responsible for their creation ultimately made them uncontrollable by the ruler of a state. As a consequence, the Ikhwan directly confronted 'Abd al-'Aziz in battle in 1928; their power was permanently broken by their defeat at that time.

'Abd al-'Aziz's instrument for downing the Ikhwan was the new White Army, nucleus of the present National Guard. A lineal descendant of the traditional tribal levies, the Guard's personnel were recruited from the tribes of the Najd. These tribes long had been closely aligned with the Al Sa'ud and have formed the mainstay of Saudi power for several centuries. Consequently, it is not surprising that the National Guard's primary allegiance — as well as that of the smaller but similarly recruited Royal Guard — is to the Al Sa'ud dynasty even more than to the state. Just as it served to protect the position of the Al Sa'ud at the time of the Ikhwan rebellion, the Guard continues to serve as a counterweight to the more recently created army. Only in recent years has the attempt been made to modernise the Guard and expand its role from an essentially tribal levy into a well-equipped and trained fighting force on modern lines.

The kingdom's first attempt at military rationalisation, undertaken after the 1934 Saudi–Yemeni war, resulted in the creation of the Royal Saudi Army. While its mission was defence against external threats, the army remained smaller and less important than the National Guard until well into the 1960s. Although the army has benefited from American training teams and modest arms transfers since the late 1940s, its emergence as the principal military force in the kingdom dates only from the reorganisation under newly crowned King Faysal in the mid-1960s, when the Royal Guards were incorporated into the army and oil income provided the means for major arms purchases and expansion costs.[5] The 1930s were also notable for the purchase of a few British aircraft and the training of some Saudi pilots by Italy, but similarly these putative efforts at an air force capability really had no impact until the massive expansion programmes begun three decades later.

Further efforts at modernisation included the establishment of the Office of the Minister of Defence in 1944, and creation of the Ministry of Defence and Aviation as part of the first Council of Ministers in 1953. Several British training teams worked in the country in the 1930s and US assistance began as a consequence of the emergence of American strategic interest in the Gulf at the time of the Second World War. Nevertheless, the fruits from these efforts were extremely limited and compounded by the accession of Sa'ud b. 'Abd al-'Aziz to the throne in 1953. The overspending, corruption, lack of clear organisation, and flirtation with Egypt's Jamal 'Abd al-Nasir (to the detriment of burgeoning military/security ties with the United States), all hampered efforts at the development of a viable military establishment.

It was not until the return of Sa'ud's brother Faysal as Prime Minister in October 1962, that high priority was given to the reform and modernisation of the Saudi armed forces, as well as to a more efficient bureaucratic structure and development programme in general. The lessening isolation of Saudi Arabia from the outside world, the spreading appeal of radical Arab nationalism, the spectre of revolution and Egyptian aggressiveness in neighbouring Yemen, British retreat from Aden and the emergence of a Marxist republic in South Yemen, the rebellion in Oman's Dhufar province, and then British withdrawal from the Gulf all played their part in provoking greatly increased concern about the defensive capabilities of the kingdom's armed forces during the mid-1960s and early 1970s. Saudi Arabia's massive deposits of oil provided both the income with which to purchase an expensive arsenal and the willingness of the United States to join in partnership with Saudi Arabia in its modernisation schemes. As a consequence, the last two decades have seen dramatic changes in the structure and capabilities of all components of the Saudi armed forces.

The air force has undergone perhaps the most spectacular transformation. The improvement of air defence capability has been given top priority for a variety of reasons. One of these is geography: the fact that the kingdom is bordered by the Gulf, the Red Sea, and wide deserts to the north and south means that attacks on the kingdom would necessarily have to come through the air. This logical assumption is confirmed by the experience of Egyptian air manoeuvres during the Yemen civil war, the separation of Saudi Arabia and South Yemen by the Rub' al-Khali desert, Israeli overflights of Saudi territory, and most recently by an Iranian–Saudi dogfight in June 1984. The sheer size of the country and its long frontiers makes reliance on land-based defence nearly impossible, even if it were not for the severe manpower restrictions faced by the kingdom. The Saudis cannot hope to match the armies of Israel, Jordan, Syria, Egypt, Iraq or Iran in either personnel or firepower. But these disparities can be offset to a large degree by an air force with highly trained personnel and highly sophisticated equipment.

As with the other Saudi services — and to an even greater degree than the army — US guidance and assistance have shaped the development of the Royal Saudi Air Force (RSAF). With the outbreak of the Yemen civil war, a USAF fighter squadron was stationed temporarily along the Yemen border and a comprehensive air defence survey made. The first in a long series of major equipment purchases took place in the mid-1960s, when Britain, at American urging, provided a dozen Lightnings and Hunter fighters and a number of Thunderbird surface-to-air missiles, along with the services of ex-RAF pilots to operate them. The basis for a close working relationship between the US and the RSAF had begun in 1957 with the provision of a dozen F-86 fighters. In 1965, the Saudis purchased four C-130 transports, which provided the RSAF with airlift capability, and the US Corps of Engineers undertook the responsibility of constructing Saudi bases and installations. The next major step involved the acquisition of a basic fighter aircraft. In the early 1970s, the Saudis turned to the US for several variations of the F-5, eventually putting over 100 in operation. This has been followed by the installation of the Hawk

SAM air defence system, under a contract to Raytheon.

But the US-RSAF relationship has been plagued increasingly in the last decade by complications arising from the close ties between the US and Israel, and the latter's ability to influence and even prevent many US arms sales to Arab states. The Saudis had long been interested in the F-4 as a front-line fighter but were discouraged from asking for it because of its offensive potential *vis-à-vis* Israel; later, they were turned away from the F-14, and the F-16 at least partially for the same reason (in addition, the RSAF is wary of single-engined aircraft). Instead, the Saudis purchased 60 F-15 aircraft. While the F-15 is principally an air-superiority fighter and not an attack aircraft, it was deemed suitable for Saudi needs and the sale could not be effectively opposed by Israel which was also receiving it.[6] The US also had a prominent role in the development of Saudi Arabia's Peace Shield programme, a $4b project to create the most technologically advanced integrated air defence system outside of NATO and the Soviet bloc. The first major contract for the Peace Shield system, scheduled to become operational in 1992, was awarded to Boeing in early 1985.[7]

The 1981 request for five E-3A Airborne Warning and Control Systems (AWACS) aircraft was a logical follow-on to the acquisition of the interceptor force. The US had briefly operated an AWACS watch out of Riyadh during the two Yemens' border war in early 1979 and they returned to Saudi Arabia after the Iranian seizure of the US hostages. The permanent stationing of the E-3As over Saudi skies meant that the sale of the new AWACS to Saudi Arabia would have little effect beyond the change in ownership. But the furore and negative publicity over Congressional approval of the AWACS sale, and the close vote, proved to be far more important (as well as troublesome for both parties) for its political ramifications than for its military implications. The Saudi AWACS were scheduled for delivery in 1986. The bruising battle over the AWACS sale contributed strongly to the Reagan administration's reluctance to push further aircraft sales through Congress. The 60 F-15s in the Saudi inventory as a result of the earlier sale were too few to allow the RSAF to maintain a 24-hour combat watch over all vital installations and, as expected, Riyadh formally requested the purchase of an additional 40–48 F-15s at the beginning of 1985. But the US government continued to prevaricate through the first half of the year and in September, Saudi Arabia, apparently with US approval, announced that it would purchase 48 Tornado interdictor/

strike aircraft from the British–German–Italian Panavia consortium instead and finance the sale at least partly through an oil barter arrangement.[8]

Of all the components of the Saudi armed forces, the air force is generally regarded as the most advanced and capable. Service with the RSAF carries more prestige than the other branches, as reflected in the number of Al Sa'ud who have made their careers in the air force. Some have charged that US assistance has been steadier and more professional than elsewhere, and RASF personnel reflect a higher degree of professionalism. In the air force, as throughout the Saudi armed forces, reliance on expatriates for training on equipment and support services is likely to continue indefinitely. Nevertheless, the RSAF undoubtedly is better placed to carry out its assigned mission than the other branches, as well as to provide cover for other GCC states.

While the emphasis, both in Saudi planning and the American military connection, has been on strengthening the air force, considerable effort and expense has been devoted to modernisation of the other Saudi services, particularly the Saudi Arabian Land Forces (SALF). Expansion and modernisation of the army also began in the 1960s, with one of the first steps being the incorporation of the hitherto autonomous Royal Guard battalion into the army in 1964. The modernisation process in the army has been more problematic than in the air force for several reasons. One early problem involved the predominance of Najdis, particularly in the officer corps, at the expense of personnel from other areas of the country, especially Hijaz (this was even more acute for the air force, where technical skills are at a premium). It was not until after a number of military personnel were arrested in 1969 that steps were taken to improve discipline and eliminate corruption and incompetence. A second complicating factor arose out of the decision to divide the army into two parts, one equipped and trained by the US and the other by France. Prominent among French purchases have been 300 AMX-30 light tanks, as well as armoured cars, infantry carriers and anti-aircraft guns.[9]

Since the late 1970s, the US has stepped up its assistance to the SALF, with the provision of 150 M-60 tanks, 16 Improved Hawk SAM batteries, TOW missiles, and various other items. At the same time, the Corps of Engineers has been heavily involved in army construction, particularly in the building of major facilities at Khamis al-Mushayt, Tabuk and Sharura, and the King Khalid and

Asad military cities. These bases have helped to expand SALF strength from its older bases at Jidda, Dammam and al-Ta'if to strategic points closer to potential threats.[10]

The higher priorities given to the air force, its smaller size and prestige status inevitably mean that the army will lag behind the RSAF in modernisation and competence for some time to come. It faces problems in recruitment and training, in co-ordinating brigades that have received either American or French equipment, and an inability to cover all sections of the expansive kingdom. Perhaps most severe in the long run is the small population base of the kingdom and the manpower crunch. Not only will it be impossible for the Saudis to field anywhere the number of men that Iraq or Iran can, employment opportunities elsewhere within the kingdom make recruitment for even a smaller army particularly difficult without turning to expatriates whose loyalty and professionalism may be suspect.[11]

Modernisation of the National Guard has involved even more problems than it has with the army. This has been largely due to the traditional mission of the Guard: internal security as opposed to the army's task of defending the kingdom from external threats. As the security of the state has been inseparable from the security of the royal family, composition of the Guard has always been based on loyalty to the family. Consequently, it has been a tribal force, drawing on the Al Sa'ud's Najdi allies, with some personnel classified as 'regulars' and the other as 'reserves'. The estimated total figure of 25,000 men is misleading, since many guardsmen are either part-time or pensioners from the earlier days of 'Abd al-'Aziz's expansionary moves, and 'phantom Guardsmen' are enrolled by shaykhs in order to receive additional payments.

While the Guard served well as the instrument of the king's power in the first half of this century, it has become increasingly clear that its orientation is unsuitable to such newer tasks as preventing sabotage in the oilfields, countering terrorism, handling civil disturbances, and backing up the army in matters of national defence. In addition, the overall effectiveness of the Guard has been limited in the past by its role as a counterweight to potential opposition within the other military branches and as a power base for Crown Prince 'Abd Allah within the ranks of the Al Sa'ud (and particularly in balancing the power of the so-called 'Sudayri Seven', whose ranks include King Fahd and Prince Sultan, the Minister of Defence and Aviation).[12] Anthony Cordesman contends that the Guard is 'more a means through which the royal family allocates funds to tribal and Bedouin leaders than a modern combat or internal security force . . . The Guard is politically vital but it has not found a clear military mission.'[13] Other assessments note that the National Guard has undergone extensive modernisation and professionalisation in recent years.

While the army and the Guard were roughly co-equal in strength until the early 1960s, the subsequent emphasis on modernisation of the army and the air force weakened the Guard's position. In order to redress the imbalance, a National Guard modernisation programme was initiated in 1972 with the goal of converting the tribal basis of the Guard into a more professional/modern light infantry force with several mechanised battalions. Once again, considerable US input was solicited and provided for the Saudi Arabian National Guard programme (SANG).[14] In true Saudi style, an ambitious armament programme was undertaken, which included the acquisition of over 700 Commando APCs, large numbers of self-propelled Vulcan anti-aircraft guns, M-102 howitzers, TOW anti-tank guided missiles, and possibly several hundred tanks. In addition, the Guard has built its own military cities at al-Hasa in the Eastern Province and at Qasim in the central Najd, along with a new headquarters and academy in Riyadh.

This programme, however, has encountered greater difficulties than its equivalent for the army. On the one hand, the Bedouin background, widespread illiteracy, and lack of discipline and training common to the majority of the Guard's personnel inevitably have meant that training efforts must be more basic and slower. On the other hand, external assistance to the army has been better in terms of quantity and quality, and has had more time in which to show positive results. Other problems have arisen from differences between Prince 'Abd Allah and the contractor, the Vinnell Corporation.[15] Despite a decade of modernisation, questions still remain about the Guard's ability to handle new, sensitive and complicated tasks. The National Guard's effectiveness is of particular concern because it has the assigned role of defending Saudi oilfields, and there have been allegations that the kingdom is quite vulnerable to infiltration and sabotage of its oil installations. Thomas L. McNaugher charges that

> provisions for the protection of oilfields have apparently changed little since 1979. There are no additional barriers, no hardening

of key technologies or port facilities, and no electronic surveillance technologies to scan for intruders. Indeed, U.S. personnel knowledgeable about the oilfields suggest that rigs, pumping stations, and other equipment have deteriorated somewhat since 1973 and that the fields lie fairly open to attack.[16]

On the other hand, a US Senate staff delegation in July 1984 reported that 'ARAMCO has already taken many precautions to stop saboteurs and is currently spending millions more to enhance internal security.'[17] The report went on to note that, because it is impossible to protect all the oil facilities from sabotage, the Saudi government relies on harsh punishment and redundancy within the oil sector to protect the flow of oil.

The Royal Saudi Navy (RSN) is the last of the Saudi armed forces to emerge — and consequently it remains the least developed. Formed as an adjunct of the army in 1957, it received its first naval officer as commander in 1963 and only began functioning as a separate force in 1969. In conjunction with the bold schemes advanced for the other services, the Saudi Naval Expansion Program (SNEP) was launched in 1972, again with American assistance and with overly ambitious plans for a 20–30-ship navy that included major bases at Jubayl on the Gulf and Jidda on the Red Sea, a repair facility at Dammam on the Gulf, and a naval headquarters complex in Riyadh. Even though plans were scaled back several times, serious problems continued to arise due to the lack of Saudi manpower and the US Navy's inability to provide the proper supervision and training personnel. One result was Riyadh's appeal to France for help, thus once again complicating the picture with competing and often incompatible equipment, concepts and training methods. Nevertheless, SNEP's disappointing progress has been ameliorated by the weakness of potential naval threats from Saudi Arabia's neighbours in the Red Sea and Gulf, especially since the Iranian revolution severely crippled the navy built up by the Shah.[18]

The effectiveness of the Saudi armed forces forms the key to the GCC's defensive capabilities. The kingdom is the largest and most powerful of the six GCC states and its oil reserves vastly dwarf those of its neighbours. Its wealth makes it an important actor in Arab, Islamic and Third World arenas. More importantly, its geographic sprawl places it in potential confrontation with many possible enemies.

To the south, Saudi Arabia is the only GCC state that borders both Yemens and a major focus of Saudi security concern has centered on threats from this corner of the Arabian Peninsula since Egypt became involved in the North Yemen civil war of the 1960s. In part, Riyadh has responded to the Yemeni threat by building major bases at Khamis al-Mushayt in 'Asir and at Sharura deep inside the Rub' al-Khali desert, as well as maintaining large numbers of troops there. In terms of total troops, the two Yemens have more military personnel on paper than Saudi Arabia, but the quality of many of their troops, particularly in the YAR, is questionable, and neither North nor South Yemen has been able to acquire weaponry of the level of Saudi Arabia. The ability of both Yemeni states to act in concert against Saudi Arabia is even more doubtful. The long distance between the Yemeni borders and Saudi Arabia's centres of population, capital and oilfields reduces the impact of even a direct, combined Yemeni attack against the kingdom to relatively localised hostilities in the southern province of 'Asir.

Such a direct Yemeni threat is unlikely, and military engagement between Saudi Arabia and its southern neighbours more probably will be limited to the kinds of border skirmishes that have occurred periodically for a number of years. Ever since the 1960s, Saudi Arabia has sought to minimise the Yemeni threat through non-military means. Riyadh has maintained heavy influence, if not control, over the North Yemeni government through such techniques as extensive budget subsidies, heavyhanded pressure on its rulers, intrigues with both military officers and civilian politicians in Sanaa, and subsidies to the northern Yemeni tribes and shaykhs. While the nearly 0.5 million Yemeni workers in Saudi Arabia are often cited as a potential security threat to the kingdom, the loss of their remittances would cripple the YAR's economy.

At the same time, Riyadh generally has sought to isolate the Marxist government in Aden and has in the past supported dissident movements against South Yemen. While the Saudis displayed considerable reluctance to pursue *rapprochement* when favourable occasions presented themselves in 1978 and 1980, they apparently have approved of Kuwaiti and UAE development assistance and reconciliation efforts between South Yemen and its North Yemen and Omani neighbours. From the vantage-point of mid-1985, the surprising stability of the 'Ali 'Abdullah Salih regime in Sanaa has meant that YAR–Saudi relations have remained on an even keel, even if sometimes strained. Furthermore, South Yemen's relations with the GCC and the YAR have steadily improved since 'Ali Nasir Muhammad's consolidation of power in 1980. As a result, the Saudi policy of diplomacy, rather than military confrontation, has paid off in the case of the Yemens.

In the case of potential threats to the kingdom from the northwest (Israel) and the northeast (Iran or Iraq), Saudi Arabia once again must rely basically on non-military means to deter attack. No amount of military build-up would put the Saudis on an equal footing with any of these countries. At the same time, it is unlikely that any of the three would try to invade the kingdom. Despite the protestations of Israel's supporters in the United States, Saudi Arabia is not and never will be a military threat to Israel and confrontation between them will continue to be played out politically through third parties, particularly the United States. At most, Saudi Arabia can hope through its military build-up to deter Israeli aerial and naval violations of Saudi territory without provoking the kind of raids Israel has carried out against Baghdad and Tunis.

As far as the Gulf is concerned, the threat is far greater to Kuwait than to Saudi Arabia, which once again benefits from its strategic depth.[19] Saudi military options are largely limited to its air defence capabilities, as demonstrated in June 1984, although completion of the King Khalid Military City at Hafr al-Batin, near the Iraqi and Kuwaiti borders, will provide a base for modest ground forces capability. Still, a build-up of SALF forces at Hafr al-Batin inevitably will mean starving the other front-line bases at Tabuk and Sharura. As long as the war between Iran and Iraq lasts — and that may be a very long time — a direct Iranian attack on the Arab side will have only nuisance value.

The Iraqi threat continues to recede. Because of the war, the Saddam Husayn regime has become dependent on Saudi and other GCC financial assistance, Saudi willingness to transship Iraqi oil across the kingdom, and, especially at the beginning of the war, the Saudi role as a middleman between Baghdad and Washington. Iraq's oil reserves are second only to those of Saudi Arabia in the Middle East and it has no reason to covet Saudi fields. Rather than military confrontation (or even Ba'thi-sponsored subversion), the potential Iraqi threat to Saudi Arabia in the future would appear to consist of disputes over oil pricing and production quotas due to competition in a stagnant world oil market.

Assuming a worse-case scenario — that Iran emerges victorious against Iraq, rearms and still desires to carry the war forward into the GCC — Saudi Arabia's only option is virtually the same as it would be in the case of a direct Soviet attack. It can use its early-warning system and interceptor aircraft to delay an enemy attack until help arrives from the outside. Militarily, Saudi Arabia is and will remain vitally dependent on outside assistance. In direct terms, Saudi Arabia depends on the approximately 1,700 American military personnel now stationed in the kingdom, as well as the several thousand personnel employed by more than 40 US military contractors.[20] Over 4,000 French and 2,000 British expatriates work in similar capacities and more than 10,000 Pakistanis serve in the Saudi armed forces.[21] Pakistanis are particularly conspicuous in the officer and enlisted ranks of all the GCC naval forces.

While the Saudis have relied heavily on arms purchases from the US, they have also bought from other Western European countries, as well as Brazil and South Korea. The January 1984 agreement with France for the $4b Shahine ground-to-air missile system represented France's biggest arms sale ever. The French have also been highly prominent in the development of the Saudi navy and the Mirage 2000 reportedly was being considered along with the F-15 and the Tornado for the 1985 Saudi interceptor purchase. The Tornado sale announced in September 1985 could not have come at a more propitious time for Britain, given the aircraft's enormous development costs. The purchase may also represent a deepening Saudi desire to diversify arms purchases to lessen dependence on any one country, particularly given the widespread opposition to Saudi Arabia in the US Congress.

On a more indirect but even more important level, the ultimate Saudi defence — and therefore the defence of all the GCC nations — must come from the United States. While the Saudis consistently refuse to allow the stationing of American military forces in the kingdom and do not co-operate with the US in any military exercises, the overstocking built into their weapons and equipment purchases strongly indicates that they recognise that full co-operation with a prompt deployment of USCENTCOM forces is necessary in the case of severe threats, as from the Soviet Union.[22] At the same time, however, it should be remembered that the effectiveness of US military support applies to only a few, relatively unlikely situations. Saudi Arabia's security is most dependent on the skilfulness of its foreign policy and the astuteness of its leaders in adapting to and complying with the demands of its citizenry.

Other GCC Defence Capabilities

Oman

Oman's armed forces have perhaps the longest history of any of the Peninsula states.[23] The Muscat Levy Corps, established in 1921 with a British commander and Indian ranks, served as the nucleus and the sole element of Oman's military establishment until the 1950s. Expansion during that decade was prompted by two factors: the search for oil and tribal rebellion (further complicated by tinges of Arab nationalist sentiment and Saudi intrigues). The Batinah Force was raised in 1952 for the purpose of expelling Saudi troops from Buraimi oasis, although the sultan was dissuaded from taking this action. Several years later, Petroleum Development (Oman) (PDO) sponsored the creation of the Muscat and Oman Field Force (MOFF) which accompanied PDO representatives on a march into the interior and raised the flag of the sultanate over the interior for the first time in half a century.[24]

As a consequence of this modest expansion, the government found itself with three ill-trained, underequipped and separately administered units. As a result of British prodding and assistance (including both financial aid and secondment of personnel), these groups were reorganised into the Sultan's Armed Forces (SAF) in 1958. A headquarters was established, a training camp built, arms purchased, and the lingering al-Jabal al-Akhdar rebellion in the interior put down. Subsequently, the foundations of the Sultan of Oman's Air Force (SOAF) and the Sultan of Oman's Navy (SON) were also laid.

The rebellion in Dhufar provided perhaps the major spur to the extensive build-up and modernisation that Oman's armed forces have undergone since the late 1960s. The ineffectiveness of the ragtag forces formed in Dhufar to fight the rebels in the mid- to late 1960s was in large part due to Sultan Sa'id's insistence that the province be kept as administratively separate from the rest of the country as it was geographically isolated. But the inability of his Dhufar forces to deal with the rebels (as well as the attempt on his life made by his own soldiers in 1966) led to the assumption of SAF responsibility for military affairs in Dhufar following the 1970 *coup d'état*. It was SAF units, combined with considerable external assistance and ex-rebel irregulars, that fought the rebellion and brought it to its end.[25]

The need to deal with a deadly serious threat, the removal of the

British umbrella for regional security, the accession of a Sandhurst-trained sultan, and the opportunity provided by oil income all played parts in the development of the Sultan's Armed Forces into probably the most professional and capable military organisation in the Peninsula. Without doubt, the major factor in the SAF's modernisation was the guidance and manifold assistance provided by Britain. Not only had London prodded Sultan Sa'id into taking the first steps to move his armed forces into the twentieth century, but it also provided financial assistance and arms. Just as importantly, the SAF benefited from a considerable number of seconded officers and even more contract personnel, both civilian and ex-military. The commander of SAF, the commanders of the land forces, air force and navy, remained British through the mid-1980s. In addition to the British, seconded Jordanian and Pakistani administrative personnel, engineers and non-commissioned officers have all been a feature of the SAF's past.

As a result of these efforts, considerable progress was made in the early 1970s to add capability in such specialised areas as training facilities, artillery units, engineering, and air and coastal patrols. In addition, the heavy preponderance of Baluch soldiers in the ranks, many of whom had been recruited from Oman's former possession of Gwadar in Pakistan, was gradually reversed in favour of an Arab majority among the more than 20,000 troops in the military today.[26] Since the great majority of recruits were illiterate, sophisticated training had to await implementation of basic educational programmes. Over the past decade, though, the infusion of more educated Omanis — both male and female — has helped to raise standards and enable Omanis to move into slots as regimental commanders and pilots.[27]

The SOAF has received the lion's share of arms and equipment purchases over the past decade or two, and currently boasts nearly two dozen Jaguars and a dozen ageing Hunters among its combat aircraft, as well as a helicopter squadron equipped mainly with Augusta Bells and a Rapier SAM system. In June 1985, Oman purchased a half-dozen Tornado air defence variant (ADV) aircraft, choosing the West European consortium's aircraft over the US F-20a Tigershark, and it was speculated that it would soon buy another 4–8 planes. In addition to its headquarters, adjacent to al-Sib international airport (outside of Muscat), the SOAF operates out of the former RAF bases on al-Masira Island and at Salala, as well as from a dozen other airstrips.

The Sultanate of Oman Land Forces (SOLF), with approximately 20,000 men (or 80 per cent of the total armed forces), utilises Chieftain tanks, Saladin armoured cars, TOW anti-tank missiles, and Blowpipe SAMs. Considerable progress has been made by the SON, which now has eight fast-attack craft (six equipped with Exocet missiles), a half-dozen smaller patrol boats and various support craft, and has beefed up its presence in the Omani territorial waters around the Strait of Hormuz. Al-Ghanam Island (on the Gulf side of the strait) has been made into a naval base, thus complementing the main base at Muscat, the naval training centre at Sur, and facilities at the Dhufar port of Raysut; a new base is under construction at Wudam 'Alwa along the Batinah coast. In addition, the Royal Oman Police has been built up as a major gendarmerie and frontier force, and several thousand Dhufari irregulars belong to the *firqa* units formed from surrendering rebels. While the *firqa*s have been regrouped into regular army units, they still have not been assigned a mission, presumably because of questions of their loyalty and military suitability.

The traditional lines between the predominantly US tutelage of the Saudi armed forces and British guidance of the Omani military have broken down in recent years, in large part because of British economic decline and military retrenchment. While Oman may still lie within a 'British sphere of influence' through the organisation, armament and expatriate personnel in its armed forces, recent American perceptions of a deteriorating security situation in the Gulf and emphasis on developing a 'go it alone' military capability have led Washington to upgrade its ties to Muscat significantly. The sultanate's apparent willingness to co-operate more fully with the US than its neighbours would like is in part based on its perceptions of vulnerability to external threats and in part on its financial needs. As a consequence, the US has provided development assistance and some military grants in return for the use of Omani military facilities in emergency and some routine situations, and has even undertaken the physical improvement of these facilities. US military spending in Oman has totalled more than $300m, with half of that on the strategic air base on Masira Island.[28] By 1984, however, the Omanis had become noticeably less enthusiastic about the emerging relationship with the US government.[29]

Despite their professionalism and combat experience, the Omani armed forces remain too small and underequipped for the multitude of security tasks they face. While the navy has beefed up its surveillance activities in the Strait of Hormuz (the shipping lanes in the strait run through Omani territorial waters), its ability to handle threats to shipping remains limited to minor hit-and-run attacks using speedboats. Even in the case of mining, Oman would have to call on NATO assistance. The SAF has proven its ability to deal with internal threats of subversion and rebellion on various occasions in the last quarter-century. With considerable outside help, the SAF was successful in putting down the rebellion in Dhufar and it could probably hold its own against a South Yemeni attack, since the PDRY superiority in tanks would be negated by the rugged terrain. Oman is more vulnerable to an Iranian attack, since its air force is very small and its ground forces basically consist of light infantry. It faces the same manpower problems as the other GCC states and is further constrained by the lack of funds for defence expenditure.

Given these limitations and its extreme exposure, it is not unexpected that the Omani government, of all the GCC states, has displayed the most military co-operation with the West. Similarly, it is not surprising that the Omanis have placed considerable emphasis on diplomacy as a tool to enhance their security. Diplomatic relations with the PDRY were established for the first time in 1984, with the help of Kuwaiti and UAE mediation, and ambassadors were exchanged in 1985. Relations with revolutionary Iran have been superficially good, especially in the light of the close ties between the Shah and Sultan Qabus. Despite China's involvement in the early stages of the Dhufar rebellion, Oman recognised the People's Republic in 1975. A similar pragmatic strategy may have been at work when the intention to establish diplomatic relations with the Soviet Union was announced in September 1985.[30] In sum, Oman is capable of providing for its own security in most threat scenarios but must call for outside assistance in case of an all-out Soviet or Iranian attack. Only Oman can join Saudi Arabia in providing out-of-area assistance to the GCC, but its capabilities in this regard are far less than the Saudi armed forces.

The Amirates

The other four GCC members have little of the military potential of Saudi Arabia and Oman, and — for the most part — began to build armed forces at a far later date and for more modest purposes.[31] These smaller states exhibit basically identical problems in self-defence, largely differentiated only by minor details. At the northern end of the Arab littoral, Kuwait is confronted by the inescapable fact that its power inherently is limited by its small population and territorial size, even as its central location and long exploitation of oil makes it a desirable and highly visible target. At the same time, it faces a number of serious threats, externally from its larger neighbours of Iran, Iraq and possibly Saudi Arabia (in the form of pressure rather than aggression), and internally from a population composed in the majority by non-Kuwaitis, as well as from its Shi'a and Persian minorities.

The ruling Al Sabah family has sought to deal with these threats with diplomacy and an even more viable means: money. An extremely large proportion of the oil income has long been distributed as foreign aid, regardless of the recipient's politics. Well before the Iran–Iraq war, Kuwait provided Iraq with generous 'loans' and the Palestinian cause has been the recipient of both financial and verbal support for decades. Internally, oil income has been evenly distributed among the native population, although the country faces a major dilemma regarding expatriates: they are not covered under most benefits of the extensive state welfare system and with few exceptions are not eligible for citizenship, which is particularly rankling to many Palestinians who have spent most or all of their lives in Kuwait.

Kuwait's armed forces have been capable of little more than border protection and internal security. Between independence in 1961 and British withdrawal from the Gulf in 1971, Kuwait could rely on British protection through a treaty negotiated at independence. Since 1971, however, Kuwait has sought to expand its defence capability, increasing the number of men under arms by about 50 per cent. Not surprisingly, the bulk of the armed forces is found in the army, with about 10,000 men, largely drawn from the Bedouin tribes of the area shared by Kuwait, Iraq and Saudi Arabia. In the years since 1971, it has been equipped with Chieftain tanks, Saladin armoured vehicles, Saracen APCs, Ferret scout cars, AMX self-propelled howitzers, and TOW anti-tank missiles. The air force boasts 49 combat aircraft, mostly A-4 Skyhawks but also some Mirage interceptors. In addition, there are three helicopter squadrons equipped with Gazelles and Pumas and several batteries of I-Hawk SAMs. The navy is the least developed of the services, essentially consisting of a coast guard with a few armed patrol craft and some Exocet missiles.

Traditionally, Kuwait has looked to Britain as its principal military supplier; however, the amirate has turned increasingly to the US and France in recent years. For political reasons, Kuwait concluded a highly publicised deal with the Soviet Union in 1977 for SA-7 missiles, purchasing more missiles the following year, and then turned again to Moscow in 1984. It should be emphasised that these token transactions underscore Kuwait's long striving for neutrality, as well as policy differences with the US, rather than any fundamental shift in foreign policy. For example, the 1984 arms deal with the Soviet Union was initiated only after rejection of the Kuwaiti request to the US for Stinger missiles to defend Kuwaiti oil tankers against Iranian air attacks. The amirate continues to rely upon Britain, the US, Pakistan, Jordan and Egypt for military assistance and training, and that orientation is unlikely to change.

Despite its expansion programme, Kuwait's defence situation is not much changed from the 1960s, when British troops and a symbolic Arab League presence was felt necessary to deter Iraqi encroachment. As a small state surrounded by much larger ones, Kuwait's basic strategy necessarily entails keeping on good terms with its neighbours and relying on the collective capabilities of the GCC for protection. The Kuwaiti armed forces suffer from severe manpower problems, both because of the country's population and because of most young Kuwaitis' disdain for a military career; as a consequence, expatriates are ubiquitous in the armed forces and a national draft is less than effective. The quality and professionalism of the Bedouin recruits is suspect and the Shi'a in the armed forces pose a potential problem. The amirate has sought to ameliorate the potentially dangerous effects of this situation by reserving the occupation of pilot for native Kuwaitis and by keeping command positions in the hands of the Al Sabah.

Because of its proximity to Iraq and Iran, Kuwait is the GCC state most vulnerable to attack. It lived under the shadow of Iraqi claims to the entire amirate in the 1960s and, despite its contribution to the Iraqi war effort, still must be on its guard against Iraqi attempts to seize the islands of Warba and Bubiyan, which dominate the approaches to the Iraqi naval base at Umm Qasr. The amirate's hold on the islands was strengthened by the construction of a bridge from the mainland to Bubiyan in the early 1980s. Several Iranian airstrikes on Kuwait installations during the war, Iranian attacks on Kuwaiti shipping, and Iranian support of the terrorist attacks inside the amirate all contribute to Kuwaiti insecurity. Although the prospect of an Iranian breakthrough on the Shatt al-'Arab front seemed to subside after the 1982, 1983, 1984 and February 1985 offensives stalled, it is painfully obvious to the Kuwaitis that a hostile Iranian army is poised less than 30 miles from Kuwaiti borders and that both the Iranian air force and navy are well within striking distance. The smaller GCC states have emphasised their determination to send ground forces to help Kuwait in case of attack, and the Kuwaitis may also call for Jordanian help. However, there is no way around the stark conclusion that both the GCC and the US may have to consider Kuwait expendable in the event of either an Iranian attack or a Soviet assault.

While national defence may be assured only under the GCC umbrella (if then), Kuwait does have a real need for effective internal security forces. In recent years, the amirate has suffered through a number of acts of violence. In the late 1970s, there was a spate of bombings attributed to inter-Palestinian feuding. The Iraqi underground Da'wa movement, apparently with assistance from the Iranian government and Lebanese radical Shi'a, carried out bomb attacks on the US embassy and Kuwaiti installations in December 1983. A Kuwait Airways plane was hijacked to Tehran in December 1984 and two passengers killed and several Kuwaitis wounded. In May 1985, an assassination attempt barely missed killing Kuwait's ruler, and in July 56 people were killed by bombs thrown at seaside cafés. These attacks were also attributed to the radical international Shi'i underground taking credit under the *nom de guerre* of Islamic Jihad. If these attacks by outside forces were not enough, Kuwait has also faced a growing tide of Islamic fundamentalist sentiment and increasingly visible Sunni–Shi'i strife within the amirate. Kuwait's salvation from internal disruption may be the healthiness and vitality of its elected National Assembly, the only one in the GCC.

The United Arab Emirates has generally ranked second in GCC defence spending in recent years. This can be attributed to: the UAE's very late start in all aspects of development; the abundance of oil, particularly in Abu Dhabi, which provides the financial wherewithal; and the long competition — and even strong rivalry — between the UAE's member amirates.[32]

The origins of armed forces in the UAE date back to the early 1950s and the British decision to exercise more influence in internal affairs along the Trucial Coast, a decision motivated by the growing suspicion of oil deposits in the region. The Trucial Oman Levies, later Trucial Oman Scouts (TOS), was formed in 1951 under British supervision and with British officers and Jordanian NCOs. The Scouts soon exhibited their usefulness in keeping the peace between rival shaykhdoms in addition to more fundamental policing functions. They were also instrumental in evicting the Saudi garrison occupying Buraimi oasis in 1955 and then played a supporting role in ending the 1955-9 rebellion in central Oman.

Upon independence, the Scouts were the logical choice for conversion into the armed forces of the new UAE state. They had grown in size from 500 in 1955 to 2,500 in 1971. But the Union Defence Force (UDF), as the Scouts were rechristened, was not the only armed force in the new UAE nor was it even the largest. Over the decade of the 1960s, the continuing competition between the seven shaykhdoms had evolved a new form: the development of competing military units. Thus in 1971, the Abu Dhabi Defence Force (ADDF) far eclipsed the UDF with over 9,500 men, including a small naval force and developing air wing. In addition, there were also the Dubai Defence Force (DDF, with 500 men, a patrol vessel and small air wing), the Ra's al-Khayma Mobile Force, the Sharjah National Guard, and the 'Ajman Defence Force (in the process of formation). Rather than serving as the armed forces for the entire state, the UDF merely existed as a somewhat neutral element among competing forces, which were lineal descendants of the shaykhs' traditional armed retinues.

While logic dictated the merger of all these units, politics militated against it. Abu Dhabi and Dubai had fought a border war as recently as 1948, and all the shaykhdoms — especially the aristocratic and once powerful Qasimi statelets of Ra's al-Khayma and, to a lesser extent, Sharjah — resented Abu Dhabi's newfound wealth and muscle. As modern versions of shaykhly guards, these individual forces not only performed police duties but protected the rulers and their families from attempted coups (more often than not deriving from within the ruler's family), as well as from threats from their neighbours. The infusion of new wealth into traditional rivalries resulted in arms races within the UAE. By 1975, the ADDF had grown to 15,000, equipped with 135 armoured vehicles, two squadrons of Mirage IIIs and Vs, some Hawker Hunters and helicopters, Rapier and Crotale SAMs, Vigilant ATGWs, and Vosper Thornycroft and Fairey Marine Spear class patrol craft. The DDF had also expended to rival the UDF in size, with 3,000 men, Ferret and Saladin armoured cars, several kinds of helicopters and patrol craft. Only the UDF had tanks, however.

Despite the creation of a federal Ministry of Defence and the existence of the UDF, merger of the armed forces lagged behind federal integration in other sectors. It was not until mid-1975 that the first serious discussions on merger took place and formal unification was delayed until the constitutional crisis of 1976. At the end of the year, the UAE Armed Forces formally came into being: the ADDF became the Western Command, the DDF the Central Command, and the Ra's al-Khayma Mobile Force the Northern Command; the UDF was renamed the Yarmuk Brigade, and the Sharjah National Guard was merged with the federal police force. Nevertheless, the merger was still only on paper: the shaykhdoms continued separate arms purchasing policies and each force was commanded by the appropriate ruler's son. The Chief of Staff was able to function effectively only because he was a seconded Jordanian. Efforts were made in subsequent years to strengthen the UAE's military unity by unifying expenditures, upgrading the central headquarters and redirecting lines of command to federal authorities, but with little practical result.

Nevertheless, manifold problems still remain. While the UAE has a modest air defence capability, they lack the early-warning or tactical air capability to defeat an air attack. UAE officials do not consider themselves covered by a GCC or Saudi defence umbrella and therefore argue within the GCC for a conciliatory, rather than a confrontational, attitude to Iran (Iran also remains Dubai's largest trading partner and a number of Iranians reside in the UAE). As in the other GCC states, the UAE armed forces are still heavily dependent on expatriate officers and trainers, and require more time to digest the flood of new arms and equipment. Approximately 85 per cent of the ranks, as well as some officers, are foreign. Finally, the successful integration of the armed forces depends directly on the success of the federation experiment. While a UAE lifespan of well over a decade seemingly augurs well for the future, much depends on the personalities of Abu Dhabi's ruler Zayid and Dubai's Rashid, who has been in poor health in recent years. The newness of the UAE armed forces, their fragmentation and the complicated political situation all work to their disadvantage as a factor in pan-GCC considerations.

The other two GCC states, Bahrain and Qatar, have very modest armed forces, hardly more than internal security units. The Bahrain Defence Force grew out of the Bahrain Levy Corps, established as a model on the Muscat Levies in the 1920s, but it was utilised primarily as a police force until independence. Indeed, the few patrol craft and helicopters possessed by the amirate belong to the police, and are used to control immigration and smuggling. In the last several years, Bahrain has ordered a few F-5 fighters from the US, presumably for reasons of prestige. The 2,300-strong army is equipped with a few armoured cars, TOW anti-tank missiles and the RBS-70 SAM system. Because of the British presence in Bahrain before 1971, the country boasts well-developed military facilities, however, including a large airfield and a naval base, where the US Navy's small Mideastforce was formerly homeported and which it still uses on a regular basis.

Qatar is only slightly better armed. Since Britain was responsible for the amirate's defence before 1971, Qatar's armed forces have emerged out of the small Public Security Department only since independence. In addition to the 5,000-strong army, which operates several dozen AMX-30 tanks and the usual mix of armoured cars, Qatar boasts eight large patrol craft, several equipped with Exocets, and eleven combat aircraft, with more on order. Not surprisingly, both states suffer even more than their neighbours from manpower problems and rely heavily on expatriates. Qatar's situation is complicated further by its close relationship to Saudi Arabia (both ruling families are Wahhabi) and the ruling Al Thani's traditional reliance on Saudi tribes as armed retainers. Neither state provides more than a symbolic contribution to GCC military strength, and both are covered by Saudi combat air patrol and the US AWACS against an Iranian air threat. Indeed, the military capability of all four amirates (Kuwait, Bahrain, Qatar and the UAE) is essentially limited to policing functions and internal security. It falls to Saudi Arabia, and to a far lesser extent Oman and even less to Kuwait, to provide the backbone of GCC defence forces.

The Iranian Revolution and the Formation of the Gulf Cooperation Council

The Iranian revolution posed the most serious security threat to the other states of the Gulf since British withdrawal nearly a decade before. For the Arab states of the Gulf, the 1970s were a turbulent and apprehensive period. The situation prior to 1971 had appeared relatively benign. The British political and military presence provided a regional security umbrella, much as it had for the previous century or more. The smaller states not only benefited from the British umbrella in terms of their external security, but received British supervision and tutelage in such internal matters as dampening endemic quarrels within the ruling families and laying the foundations for modern government and economic infrastructures. Iran, the Gulf state with the greatest power potential, was kept in check first by direct British pressure and then by American influence.

The real threat to the Arab littoral came not from potential invasion, but from the ideology of radical Arab nationalism. The 1950s and 1960s were a period of ideological and nationalist foment in the Arab world, where new military-led revolutionary republics waged aggressive campaigns aimed at the elimination of existing 'reactionary' monarchies. The Arab Cold War spread to the Arabian Peninsula in the 1960s when Yemen became a battlefield by proxy for the two sides. Bahrain, with a head-start in development and education, witnessed demonstrations in its streets during the 1956 and 1967 Arab–Israeli wars, coloured with a strong anti-British and anti-regime character.

But the most serious source of the radical nationalist threat came from Iraq after its revolutions in 1958, 1963 and 1968. The new regime and its like-minded successors were concerned not only with transforming the politics and society of Iraq, but those of their neighbours in the Gulf as well. After 1968, financial assistance, arms and training were provided to underground Ba'thist cells in all these states but particularly in Bahrain. The warriors of the Oman Revolutionary Movement (ORM), once they had been driven from Oman, took up residence in Iraq where they remained until after the 1970 change of government in Muscat. Iraq also provided some assitance to the Dhufar Liberation Front fighting in Oman's southern province, and to the Popular Front for the Liberation of the Occupied Arabian Gulf (PFLOAG), which took control of the Dhufar rebellion in 1968.

As long as the British remained in the Gulf, the Arab monarchies seemed to have little reason to fear external threats. Kuwait provides a good example of the effect of the British presence in deterring Iraq from pressing its claims to the amirate: Baghdad's threatened use of military force to press its claims occurred only after Kuwait received full independence in 1961 and was deterred, at least initially, by the dispatch of British forces to the amirate.[33]

But of course the British umbrella was removed at the end of

1971. Still, the security situation did not seem to deteriorate significantly for a number of reasons. Announcement of withdrawal had occurred three years prior to its implementation, providing time for the development of institutions and frameworks for independent states. The radical Arab threat had seemed to ebb. After the successes of military *coups d'état* in the 1950s and 1960s, only Libya fell in 1969. The monarchies had held their own, aided in part by the desperate straits in which Egypt and Syria found themselves after the 1967 war.

Because of Iraq's growing preoccupation with internal affairs, its emerging conflict with Iran, and then political stabilisation after 1973, Baghdad came to be as interested in bettering relations with the more permanent appearing states in the Gulf as in toppling them. Even the rebellion in Dhufar was blunted and gradually defeated by 1975. Perhaps most importantly, credible internal threats to the states of the Arab littoral never really materialised, partly because of the evolutionary nature of the states (as opposed to the European colonial legacies in Egypt, Syria, Iraq, and elsewhere) and partly because the black gold rush provided financial opportunities and skyrocketing standards of living for nearly every citizen.

Only a few clouds intruded on the bright security horizons of the conservative Peninsula states. Traditional suspicions of Iranian intentions were heightened by the Shah's grandiose plans for economic development and military expansion, and his arrogant attitude towards the other Gulf rulers. Nevertheless, these fears were moderated by their monarchical bond, a shared reliance on the West as the source of technology, education and military assistance, and a common anti-Soviet outlook. Iraq's Ba'thists were still there, but they seemed reasonable: with the termination of the Dhufar rebellion, diplomatic relations were even established between Iraq and Oman — and the last gap between the Arab Gulf states was bridged. Farther afield, there still remained the problem of Israel and radicalised Palestinians. The outbreak of the October 1973 war forced the Gulf states to act against what would otherwise be their principal interests and engage in an oil embargo directed against the United States.

But from a different direction, a gathering storm began to attract worried concern in Riyadh and neighbouring capitals. The Soviet menace seemingly had abated earlier in the decade, with the reverses in Egypt and Sudan and Kissinger's shuttle diplomacy following the 1973 war. Differences had even cropped up between Baghdad and Moscow. But events in Africa, particularly the revolution in Ethiopia and subequent fighting in the Ogaden, and the increasingly radical party core in Aden all increased the wariness of the Gulf rulers. Finally, the downfall of the Shah seemed to remove the most important section of the bulwark between Soviet expansion and the Gulf. The period from 1979 through the mid-1980s was an era of heightened concern for the security of the Arab littoral states from external, regional and internal threats. While the spectre of the Soviet Union has been an Arab concern, though not as looming as in the United States, it has been overshadowed by developments in Iran, which seemed to present a more immediate and insidious danger.

The Iranian revolution has presented the Arab states with three causes for worry. First, it removed one of the Gulf's most stalwart opponents of Moscow, and probably the most formidable regional deterrent to a Soviet advance on the Gulf. The vulnerability of the new and intolerant successor regime, potentially at least, seemed to create fertile ground for Soviet intrigue. Second, the upheavals excited passions on both sides of the Gulf and raised the possibility of political agitation and even revolutionary sentiment among the population — especially the Shi'a elements — of the Arab littoral. Third, it seemed likely that the new Iranian regime would act aggressively against the other states of the Gulf, either in directly engaging in subversive acts, as in fact occurred in Iraq and later in Kuwait, or by supporting indigenous dissidents, as demonstrated in Bahrain in late 1981. There was a parallel to the Russian revolution of 1917 in that the goal of Tehran's new leaders was the overthrow of all governments in Islamic countries and not just Iran.

The outbreak of war between Iran and Iraq seemed to confirm these fears. For the first time in modern history, two of the Gulf's states were engaged in a full-scale war which threatened to involve the remaining littoral governments. The potential Soviet threat from over the horizon had been superseded by a more immediate regional threat, requiring caution and diplomacy as an appropriate response rather than activation of armed forces and reliance on outside military assistance. Somewhat ironically, the war produced the conditions enabling the creation of the long-discussed Gulf Cooperation Council (GCC).[34]

Talk of a Gulf security pact among the Gulf's eight littoral states had been circulating since the early 1970s. Such a pact, it was argued, would provide a joint defence network against external threats, help prevent disputes from flaring into hostilities, and possibly constitute an initial step towards turning the Gulf into a zone of peace. Despite the expressed approval of such a pact by all eight states, putting words into action proved impossible. The attempt to write a security pact at the Gulf Foreign Ministers' meeting in Muscat in December 1976 came to an abrupt end when it was realised that all eight states could not agree on a common formula.

Essentially, the problem was Iraq and Iran: without these two states, the other six formed a very compatible group. Iraq, however, was a source of grave mistrust because of its radical, pan-Arab socialist ideology and history of attempted subversion in the other Gulf states. In addition, it was the only Gulf state armed by the Soviet Union. Iran was suspect because it was non-Arab and suspicions lingered of centuries-old perceived goals of Persian hegemony in the Gulf. Furthermore, the other seven Gulf leaders were particularly wary of the goals and personal ambitions of Muhammad Reza Shah. It was not until the Iran–Iraq war removed these two countries from consideration for participation in a Gulf security pact that the foundations of the GCC could be laid.

The remaining six states formed a cohesive group. Not only did they share a common mistrust of both Iran and Iraq and evidenced close ties to the West, but they exhibited considerable similarities in their political, economic and social systems. It was not unreasonable to assume that any organisation built around these six states conceivably could entail far more co-operation than a security pact to which all eight might adhere. There were, after all, antecedents for co-operation in the political, economic and security spheres.

All six had maintained close ties since the early 1970s — and far earlier in most cases — and a number of the ruling families were interrelated. Federation talks had taken place between the UAE's seven members as well as Bahrain and Qatar in the late 1960s. While an abundance of needless competition seemed to outweigh co-operation in the economic arena, a number of joint projects had been initiated under the aegis of the Organization of Arab Petroleum Exporting Countries (OAPEC; to which all but Oman belonged), not to mention the tradition of bilateral aid provided by the richer (and earlier oil producers) to the poorer states. Saudi Arabia had contributed forces to the defence of Kuwait during the

1961 and 1963 Iraqi threats. The Saudis also provided financial aid and possibly transferred some small arms to Oman during the Dhufar rebellion; the UAE's contribution to that effort included money and border patrols in northern Oman to release SAF forces for duty in Dhufar. In addition, there has long existed an informal intelligence-sharing network among the smaller Gulf states, originally because of ties among the states' British intelligence officers.

It is not surprising, then, that the leaders of the six states should have entertained hopes of building a formal structure on these bases. In May 1976, Shaykh Jabir Al Ahmad Al Sabah (then Prime Minister of Kuwait and the Amir since 1978) formally called for 'the establishment of a Gulf Union with the object of realizing cooperation in all economic, political, educational and informational fields'.[35] This sentiment was stymied by the inconclusive results of the Muscat Conference later that year and the issue remained moot until the war provided a welcome opportunity and galvanised the remaining six into action.

On 4 February 1981, the six Foreign Ministers met in Riyadh to set down the text of the GCC charter and the document was signed by all the heads of state at Abu Dhabi on 25 May 1981, thus bringing the Cooperation Council of the Arab States of the Gulf into formal existence. The stated objectives of the council are:

1. To effect co-ordination, integration and interconnection between member states in all fields in order to achieve unity between them.
2. To deepen and strengthen relations, links and scopes of co-operation now prevailing between their peoples in various fields.
3. To formulate similar regulations in various fields including the following:

   1. economic and financial affairs;
   2. commerce, customs and communications;
   3. education and culture;
   4. social and health affairs;
   5. media and tourism;
   6. legislative and administrative affairs.

4. To stimulate scientific and technological progress in the fields of industry, mineralogy, agriculture, water and animal resources.

5. To further the establishment of scientific research centres, implementation of common projects and encouragement of co-operation by the private sector for the good of their peoples.[36]

The charter also defines the structure of the new organisation. The Supreme Council is the highest authority, and is composed of the six heads of state meeting annually in November or in emergency session at the request of any member; each of the members has one vote and the presidency rotates among them. It appoints the secretary-general, who serves for a term of three years. A Commission for the Settlement of Disputes among the Members is attached to the Supreme Council. The Ministerial Council provides the working basis of co-operation between the member states. It is comprised of the six Foreign Ministers, who rotate as president every three months. The Ministerial Council, which meets every three months or more frequently in extraordinary session, is responsible for hammering out the outlines of proposed GCC policies and making arrangements for the Supreme Council summits.

The Secretariat-General forms the GCC's permanent body and carries out such functions as preparing for council meetings, setting out the budget, and carrying out assigned duties. 'Abdullah Bishara, formerly Kuwait's ambassador to the UN, has been secretary-general since the GCC's inception, and he presides over a staff of about 200. Under him are Assistant Secretaries-General for Political and Economic Affairs and a Chairman of the GCC Military Committee. Recent studies prepared by the Secretariat have focused on a joint agricultural policy, the feasibility of an oil export refinery in Oman, a pipeline network linking member states' gasfields, and a look at economic development in the GCC in the year 2000.[37]

Despite its short history, the GCC has undertaken significant economic, political, and security initiatives. In the economic sphere, a 'Unified Economic Agreement' was drawn up in June 1981 and partly implemented in 1983. The agreement eliminated customs duties between GCC states and established a common external tariff. It also provided for the free movement of labour and capital between member states, for the co-ordination of oil policies, for the standardisation of industrial laws, and for the establishment of a unified investment strategy. The latter was realised in November 1982 when the Gulf Investment Corporation was created with $2.1b capital for investment in regional projects and on the international level.[38]

In political terms (and beyond the intangible benefit of regular meetings and consultation by the leaders and top officials of the member states), the principal effort has been directed towards mediation in the Iran–Iraq war. Beginning with the third GCC summit in November 1982, Kuwaiti and UAE representatives have visited both Tehran and Baghdad, as well as other capitals, in an effort to seek a peaceful solution to the end of the war. While this was not the first mediation effort, it has been the longest serving one and, because of the vital interests of the mediators and their close ties to the combatants, probably stands the best chance of succeeding. GCC efforts have been more successful in prompting the establishment of diplomatic relations between Oman and the PDRY. Efforts have also been made to settle the Hawar Islands dispute between Bahrain and Qatar.[39]

Not surprisingly, collective security efforts, with emphasis on military aspects, have figured high on the GCC's list of priorities. While Oman has urged attention to planning in this area since the GCC was formed, the fear of antagonising Iran and Iraq prevented any serious discussion of security affairs until the November 1982 meeting of the Supreme Council. Bilateral security agreements, a collective air defence system, joint military exercises, a joint strike force, a joint military command and an indigenous arms industry have all been considered.

Not all of these self-defence schemes lend themselves to easy implementation and some should be considered more pipe-dreams. Nevertheless, the council's genuine security accomplishments should not be overlooked. Bilateral security arrangements were signed between Saudi Arabia and all the other states (with the exception of Kuwait) in early 1982, prompted by the scare over the abortive Bahrain coup attempt in December 1981 (not to mention the earlier Mecca incident and Iran's bombing of Kuwait). These agreements called for joint action against security offenders, for the exchange of information, training and equipment, and for the extradition of criminals.[40] Efforts to forge a more comprehensive internal security agreement failed to win approval at the November 1982 summit and have continued to languish. The escalation of Iraqi attacks against Kharg Island in mid-1985 and the attempt to assassinate Kuwait's amir in that same year led to an increased emphasis on security concerns and a reaffirmation of the GCC's readiness to mediate between Iran and Iraq at the November 1985 GCC summit in Muscat.[41]

Establishment of a collective air defence system is more ambitious, but seemingly within the range of GCC capabilities in the near future. Planning for an integrated system began in January 1982 and the go-ahead was received at the November 1982 summit. It is based on Saudi Arabia's AWACS radar and C^3 capabilities, linked to anti-aircraft missiles and interceptor aircraft. Ideally, the UAE's projected Lambda air defence and electronic warfare system and Kuwait's Thomson radars and upgraded Hawk missiles eventually would be plugged into the GCC-*cum*-Saudi system.[42]

Another area in which co-operation has already been evident is joint military exercises, largely bilateral in nature. Saudi F-15s and F-5s were joined by Kuwaiti Skyhawks in eleven-day manoeuvres in November 1983, covering training in air bombardment, air interception operations, fast transfer and takeoff, and other exercises. This followed a Saudi–Bahraini air exercise in land-and-sea search and rescue. Then, in 1984, Oman and the UAE held joint air force exercises in February and April; Saudi, Qatari, Kuwaiti and Bahraini units participated in air mobilisation exercises in Bahrain in April; Thamarit air base in Dhufar was the scene of Saudi–Omani exercises in August; Bahrain and Qatar conducted a naval exercise also in August; and additional manoeuvres were held in Saudi Arabia in October. During 1985, Qatar hosted a joint naval exercise with Kuwait in January; the Kuwaiti and Omani air forces carried out joint manoeuvres near the Strait of Hormuz in March; Abu Dhabi was the site of a UAE–Kuwaiti exercise in March; and the Kuwait navy participated in joint manoeuvres with the Saudi navy in April. Another potential area of co-operation lies in joint naval patrols through the Strait of Hormuz (although only Oman and Saudi Arabia possess the necessary capability at present to contribute to this function).[43]

Ambitious plans for military co-ordination with the GCC framework go far beyond bilateral exercises. A Military Committee was established within the GCC Secretariat, the six Chiefs of Staff first met in September 1981, and regular discussions between ranking military officials from all the member states on the ways and means of developing joint military co-ordination began in mid-1983. As a first step, the GCC has sought to create a joint strike force, and the 'Peninsula Shield' joint exercises held in western Abu Dhabi in October 1983 were meant to demonstrate the feasibility of developing the GCC's own RDF. Infantry, tank and artillery forces from all six states, along with Mirages and Ghazal helicopters from the UAE's air force, participated in a mock attack on an 'enemy-held' hilltop position, with the final assault performed before an audience of the six rulers.[44] 'Peninsula Shield II', held one year later at Hafr al-Batin in northeastern Saudi Arabia, was the second annual exercise of troops earmarked for the GCC RDF. The two weeks of manoeuvres, involving 10,000 men from all six states, included parachute drops of men and equipment, air support and intercept missions, night-time offensives, and anti-aircraft demonstrations.[45]

The council remains far away from realising its RDF objective — not to mention the goal of a unified military command — despite the growing numbers of joint exercises. The difficulties encountered by the UAE in unifying its myriad of armed forces stands as a sobering example of the distance that the GCC has to go. There are more than enough obstacles with the proposed RDF alone:

> Formation of a Gulf strike force, for instance, is certain to face manpower problems and will have to rely mainly on the Saudi army and will most likely have a Saudi commander. Even then, the use of other Arab troops or Pakistani forces will probably have to be considered if the force is to be capable of handling anything other than the most minor local disturbances. There will also be logistical problems arising from the lack of roads suitable for the movement of troops across state borders.[46]

Nevertheless, an announcement was made at the Fifth Supreme Council Meeting, held in Kuwait in November 1984, that it had been decided to create a joint GCC strike force under the command of a Saudi general, even though the GCC's secretary-general was candid enough to say that force would be largely 'symbolic'. Approval for the RDF appeared to be for a limited period, and it was not intended to be a permanent force but would be drawn from units of all six states in an emergency and then disbanded at the end of the crisis. The units participating in the 'Peninsula Shield II' exercises in October 1984 were expected to be earmarked for the RDF.[47]

A final area of proposed co-operation lies in arms acquisition. At present the GCC states are equipped with American, Brazilian, British, Chinese, French, German, Italian, Swiss, and even Soviet arms (in Kuwait), which seriously handicaps joint operations, prevents the transfer of spare parts and ammunition, and hampers effective use of C^3 systems. Given the huge amounts of arms already delivered or on order, full co-ordination of military forces may be unattainable. On the other hand, efforts to implement a unified procurement programme, particularly where relevant to the collective air defence system, cannot help but be beneficial if put into operation immediately. Despite the immense size of their previous purchases, the GCC states' defence spending, at about $40b annually, continues to acount for approximately half of the total amount for the Third World.[48] Even Saudi Arabia, running budget deficits in the order of $1b per month in 1984 and 1985, continued to spend over 25 per cent of its budget on defence; the Omani figure is closer to 40 per cent. One effect of such a unified procurement policy may be a shift away from heavy reliance on purchases from the US (particularly on the part of Saudi Arabia) because of the political difficulties in Arab purchases of sophisticated US arms.

An even more difficult task would be the establishment of an indigenous arms industry, given the level of economic development in these states. Although $1.4b has been allocated for this purpose, co-operation with one or more non-GCC states appears necessary along the lines of the earlier Arab Military Industrialization Organization based in Egypt. Jordan, Egypt, Turkey and Pakistan have all been mentioned as possible partners, although there are drawbacks to consideration of each of these countries.[49] Speculation has also centred on Iraq as a potential partner.

The potential combined military capability of the six GCC states is not entirely negligible, representing 190,000 men, 900 main battle tanks, more than 3,500 other armoured vehicles, over 425 interceptor and ground-attack aircraft, between 500 and 800 helicopters, and 36 fast-attack naval vessels, and of course the highly sophisticated air defence and communications system.[50] GCC ground forces' capability to resist an overland attack rests principally on the Saudi armoured brigades, supported by Kuwait's Chieftain tanks. There is greater variety in strike aircraft, although Saudi Arabia's 100 F-5s form the heart of GCC capabilities, to which the recently purchased Tornado ground-attack fighters can be added, along with Kuwait's A-4 Skyhawks and Oman's Hunters and Jaguars. Most of the GCC states have invested heavily in air defence capabilities, and the Saudi E-3A AWACS will provide the basis for an integrated C^3I

package, to which the Saudi F-15s, the Kuwaiti Mirage 1s, the UAE's Mirage 5s, and Qatar's Mirage 1s and Omani Tornados (both on order) can be linked, along with a wide variety of surface-to-air missile systems.[51]

The absorption of large numbers of highly sophisticated weapons, the complex mix of various types of weapons from a wide variety of suppliers, the small base of indigenous manpower and serious training problems, the intensive competition for skilled manpower, and the lack of combat experience, and, above all, different outlooks and policy goals among the six member states continue to plague GCC attempts at self-defence. One observer notes,

> the GCC can be expected at best to police the Peninsula — to deal with various threats from the Yemens, and hopefully to settle disputes among themselves amicably. But they cannot hope to defend the Peninsula against external attack . . . [where] they can hope at best to deter by promising some damage to the attack, to limit damage initially, and thus to buy time until reinforcements arrive.[52]

But the GCC states have taken significant steps to acquire the ability to buy time until outside help arrives, and they have done very well in protecting themselves from more likely, if more limited, internal and regional threats. As an American military analyst has noted, 'To achieve regional stability [the West] must create strong, stable, and friendly Gulf states that can maintain their own internal security and eventually absorb most of the burden of their local defense.'[53] In the last analysis, it is of course these states who bear the principal burden for their own security. As the secretary-general of the GCC has put it, 'The world may laugh at us when we say that the Gulf countries alone are authorized to defend the region, but whatever our capabilities may be, we insist that this is the basic principle for achieving security and peace for our peoples.'[54]

Notes

1. For example, Iraq has 642,500 men under arms (1 million if the Popular Army is included) while Iran totals 555,000 regular troops and an additional 200–250,000 paramilitary forces. Of course, these figures represent countries at war, but even Israel maintains a standing army of 141,000, with an additional 500,000 reservists.

These figures are from *The Military Balance, 1984–1985* (London, International Institute for Strategic Studies, 1984), pp. 59–73.

2. On the Saudi armed forces, see J. C. Hurewitz, *Middle East Politics: The Military Dimension* (New York, Praeger, for the Council on Foreign Relations, 1969), esp. Ch. 13, 'Saudi Arabia: The Peninsula Under Najdi Rule', pp. 241–52; John Keegan, *World Armies*, 2nd edn (Detroit, Gale Research, 1983), pp. 506–13; Anthony H. Cordesman, *The Gulf and the Search for Strategic Stability* (Boulder, Co, Westview Press, 1984), esp Chs. 3–10; Richard F. Nyrop (ed.), *Saudi Arabia: A Country Study*, 4th edn *(Washington, USGPO, 1984;* American University, Foreign Area Studies); Thomas L. McNaugher, 'Arms and Allies on the Arabian Peninsula', *Orbis*, vol. 28, no. 3 (fall 1984), pp. 489–526; Mordechai Abir, 'Saudi Security and Military Endeavor', *Jerusalem Quarterly*, no. 33 (fall 1984), pp. 79–94; and David E. Long, *The United States and Saudi Arabia: Ambivalent Allies* (Boulder, Co, Westview Press, 1985), esp, Ch. 3, 'U.S.–Saudi Military Relations', pp. 33–72.

3. Christine Moss Helms, *The Cohesion of Saudi Arabia: Evolution of Political Identity* (London, Croom Helm; Baltimore, Johns Hopkins University Press, 1981), p. 143, citing H. R. P. Dickson, the longtime British Political Agent in Kuwait.

4. John S. Habib, *Ibn Sa'ud's Warriors of Islam: The Ikhwan of Najd and Their Role in the Creation of the Sa'udi Kingdom, 1910–1930* (Leiden, E. J. Brill, 1978), p. 67.

5. Between 1950 and 1964, total sales agreements between Saudi Arabia and its principal supplier, the US, totalled $87m. In 1965 alone, they equalled $342m. A decade later, the total was over $2b and by 1980 reached $35b. US Congress, House of Representatives, Committee on Foreign Affairs, Subcommittee on Europe and the Middle East, *Saudi Arabia and the United States: The New Context in an Evolving 'Special Relationship'*; Report (Washington, USGPO, 1981), p. 54.

6. Cordesman, *The Gulf*, pp. 205–17.

7. *New York Times*, 19 May 1985. See also the *Middle East Economic Digest*, 11 May 1984, 14 December 1984 and 1 February 1985.

8. There had long been speculation that the Saudis might purchase either the Tornado or the French Mirage 2000 if it could not get the F-15. The first shipment of 20 Tornados was promised by the beginning of 1987 and the sale also included spare parts, training and 20 Hawk trainer-fighters. There was also speculation that the sale was a setback for the Israeli lobby in the US, since the Europeans were unlikely to impose any restrictions on the basing of the Tornados, unlike US prohibition of F-15 basing at Tabuk air base. It would also mean the loss of a considerable amount of export sales for US manufacturers and could possibly lead to other non-US arms purchases by the Saudis. *Washington Post*, 15 and 17 September 1985; *New York Times*, 16 September 1985; *Jane's Defence Weekly*, 28 September 1985.

9. The government has sought to redress the problem of incompatible equipment and training by concentrating the French-supplied units at Tabuk in the northwest, a move that may also strengthen Saudi request for future arms purchases from the US by reducing the chances for their use against Israel. See Cordesman, *The Gulf*, pp. 170–3. The subsequent purchase of British arms added another layer of complications for the army's effectiveness.

10. Khamis al-Mushayt is located in the southwestern province of 'Asir, just north of Yemen; Tabuk is situated just south of the Jordanian border and near the Gulf of 'Aqaba; Sharura is on the edge of the Rub 'al-Khali desert near the intersection of Saudi borders with both North and South Yemen; King Khalid Military City is

located at Hafr al-Batin, just south of the Iraq–Saudi Arabian Neutral Zone; and Asad Military City is at al-Kharj, south of Riyadh.

11. Mordechai Abir contends that the Saudi 'armed forces have been reduced to recruiting volunteers among the most peripheral and traditional tribes and villages and among elements of questionable nationality', as well as training young teenagers in technical schools. He estimates that thousands of Arab and other Muslim officers, NCOs and technicians now serve in the Saudi armed forces on direct contract, compared to a few hundred in 1970. 'Saudi Security', p. 88.

12. David Long also notes the role played by the National Guard in facing King Sa'ud's supporters in 1964 and helping to ensure a peaceful abdication. *The United States and Saudi Arabia*, p. 52.

13. Cordesman, *The Gulf*, p. 365.

14. A British training team had been brought in to work with the Guard soon after Prince 'Abd Allah took over command in the early 1960s but it operated on a far smaller scale than the SANG programme. Long, *The United States and Saudi Arabia*, p. 52.

15. On problems in the Guard's modernisation, see Abir, 'Saudi Security', pp. 91–3.

16. *Arms and Oil: U.S. Military Strategy and the Persian Gulf* (Washington, Brookings Institution, 1985), p. 131.

17. US Congress, Senate, Committee on Foreign Relations, *War in the Gulf; a Staff Report* (Washington, USGPO, 1984), p. 29.

18. Brief mention may be made of two other auxiliary forces. The Frontier Force and the Coast Guard, with 8,500 men, both fall under the purview of the Ministry of the Interior (as does a helicopter-equipped counter-terrorist unit). Their duties include policing the Bedouin, civil defence duties, and maintaining border and port security.

19. Thomas L. McNaugher acknowledges Saudi Arabia's 'geographic buffers' and postulates that they encourage '"two stage" attacks in which external antagonists acquire a position anywhere on the Peninsula and then seek to exploit it in ways unhampered by geography'. 'Arms and Allies', p. 497. He goes onto point out that Nasir employed such a strategy in the 1960s and speculates that the Soviet foothold in Aden may have a similar effect.

20. *New York Times*, 19 May 1985.

21. Abir, 'Saudi Security', pp. 89–90. Some estimates put the number of Pakistani troops in Saudi Arabia as high as 20,000 and it is conjectured that entire Pakistani units have been loaned to the Saudi armed forces. Some Pakistanis were alleged to have been captured by YAR troops during a 1984 border incident. *Washington Post*, 25 November 1984.

22. In this vein, a secret Reagan administration policy study provided to Congress in mid-1985 announced that 'Although the Saudis have steadfastly resisted formal access agreements, they have stated that access will be forthcoming for the United States forces as necessary to counter Soviet aggression or in regional crises they cannot manage on their own.' Quoted in the *New York Times*, 5 September 1985.

23. For background on the military in Oman, see J. E. Peterson, *Oman in the Twentieth Century: Political Foundations of an Emerging State* (London, Croom Helm; New York, Barnes & Noble, 1978), pp. 90–6; and idem, 'American Policy in the Gulf and the Sultanate of Oman', *American–Arab Affairs*, no. 8 (1984), pp. 117–30.

24. The force was subsequently attacked and routed by tribal dissidents and disbanded; its remaining troops were thereupon incorporated into a new regiment.
25. See Chapter 3 for a discussion of the Dhufar rebellion.
26. Several units in Dhufar are still Baluch-manned and are likely to remain that way.
27. Because of the large numbers of expatriates at all levels of the armed forces, considerable emphasis has been placed on Omanisation. By 1985, the percentage of Omanis in the armed forces had risen to 62 per cent, while the army was 85 percent Omani. Continued progress in this field was hampered by new purchases of high-tech weaponry for the air force and the rapid expansion of the navy. Dale F. Eickelman, oral presentation at the Middle East Institute's annual conference, 28 September 1985.
28. For a recent overview of the Omani armed forces, the extensive Ra'd exercises carried out in early 1985, and the US military role in Oman, see Jean-Loup R. Combemale, 'Oman: Defending the Sultanate', *Journal of Defense and Diplomacy*, vol. 3, no. 6 (June 1985), pp. 42–5.
29. Oman's attitude towards continued US Central Command use of Omani facilities was noticeably tougher during the early 1985 negotiations to renew the 1980 agreement. Omani pique over American demands in these negotiations and US media reports of CIA influence in the sultanate may have contributed to the decision in September 1985 to open talks with the Soviets.
30. In November 1985, a third GCC state, the UAE, announced its intentions of establishing relations with Moscow.
31. On the military background to the four states of Kuwait, UAE, Bahrain and Qatar, see Richard F. Nyrop (ed.), *Area Handbook for the Persian Gulf States* (Washington, USGPO, 1977; American University, Foreign Area Studies); Alvin J. Cottrell, Robert J. Hanks and Frank T. Bray, 'Military Affairs in the Persian Gulf', in Alvin J. Cottrell (gen. ed.), *The Persian Gulf States: A General Survey* (Baltimore, Johns Hopkins University Press, 1980), pp. 140–71; Keegan, *World Armies*; Cordesman, *The Gulf*; US Congress, House of Representatives, Committee on International Relations, *United States Arms Policies in the Persian Gulf and Red Sea Areas: Past, Present and Future*; Report (Washington, USGPO, 197); and US Senate, *War in the Gulf*,. pp. 28–33.
32. In addition to above sources, see Frauke Heard-Bey, *From Trucial States to United Arab Emirates: A Society in Transition* (London, Longman, 1982); and Ali Mohammed Khalifa, *The United Arab Emirates: Unity in Fragmentation* (Boulder, Co, Westview Press, 1979).
33. See chapter 3 for a discussion of the British deployment to Kuwait in 1961.
34. For background on the GCC, see Valerie Yorke, 'Bid for Gulf Unity', *The World Today*, vol. 37, nos 7–8 (July–August 1981), pp. 246–9; Emile A. Nakhleh, *The Persian Gulf and American Policy* (New York, Praeger, 1982), pp. 43–61; 'Abdullah Fahd al-Nafisi, *Majlis al-ta'awun al-Khaliji: al-itar al-siyasi wal-istratiji* (London, Taha Publishers, 1982); Abdulla Yacoub Bishara, 'The GCC: Achievements and Challenges';, *American–Arab Affairs*, no. 7 (winter 1983–4), pp. 40–4; Anthony H. Cordesman, *The Gulf*, pp. 620–36; and John Duke Anthony, 'The Gulf Cooperation Council', in Robert G. Darius, John W. Amos, II, and Ralph H. Magnus (eds), *Gulf Security into the 1980s* (Stanford, Ca, Hoover Institution Press, 1984), pp. 82–92.
35. *Cooperation Council for the Arab States of the Gulf: On the Occasion of the*

Second Anniversary, May 25, 1981–May 25, 1983 (London, Gulf Information and Research Centre, 1983). (Hereafter cited as 'Cooperation Council'.)

36. Charter of the Gulf Cooperation Council, Article 3. The text of the charter is contained in 'Cooperation Council', and *American–Arab Affairs*, no. 7 (winter 1983–4), pp. 157–76.

37. Manama WAKH in Arabic, 8 November 1983 (FBIS, 9 November 1983).

38. The text of the argument is in 'Cooperation Council', and *American–Arab Affairs*, no. 7 (winter 1983–4), pp. 177–97. See also *MEED*, 28 October 1983, pp. 22–3. Not surprisingly, problems remain in the agreement's implementation, notably in the UAE's apparent resistance to unified customs duties and Oman's continuing requirement for non-objection certificates for some GCC nationals. *The Middle East*, no. 110 (December 1983), p. 14. The goals of a Gulf currency and common market clearly remain utopian at this point.

39. In addition to these activities within the Gulf region, the GCC Supreme Council sent Kuwait's Deputy Prime Minister and Qatar's Minister of State for Foreign Affairs to Syria in late 1983 to try to end the infighting within the PLO at that time. Attempts were also made to mediate between Baghdad and Damascus, and Rabat and Algiers.

40. *An-Nahar Arab Report and MEMO*, 1 March 1982. Kuwait's desire to keep a healthy distance from more powerful Saudi Arabia appeared to be at the root of its reticence to sign the bilateral agreement. Similar concerns over Saudi hegemony have delayed, if not prevented, the signing of a GCC collective security agreement.

41. *New York Times*, 7 November 1985; *Washington Post*, 7 November 1985.

42. *The Middle East*, no. 119 (September 1984), pp. 15–18.

43. Riyadh SPA in Arabic, 30 November 1983 (FBIS, 1 December 1983); *MEED*, 20 April 1984; Manama WAKH in Arabic, 12 April 1984 (FBIS, 12 April 1984); Muscat Domestic Service in Arabic, 16 August 1984 (FBIS, 17 August 1984); Manama WAKH in Arabic, 29 August 1984 (FBIS, 30 August 1984)l; *al-Qabas* (Kuwait), 3 September 1984 (FBIS, 5 September 1984); Kuwait KUNA in Arabic, 14 January 1985 (FBIS, 15 January 1985); Manama WAKH in English, 1 March 1985 (FBIS, 5 March 1985); Doha QNA in Arabic, 21 March 1985 (FBIS, 21 March 1985); and Abu Dhabi WAM in Arabic, 27 March 1985 (FBIS, 28 March 1985).

44. Manama WAKH in Arabic, 13 October 1983 (FBIS, 14 October 1983), *New York Times*, 16 October 1983; and *The Middle East*, no. 109 (November 1983), p. 17.

45. Manama WAKH in Arabic, 10 October 1984 (FBIS, 11 October 1984); Riyadh Domestic Service in Arabic, 15 October 1984 (FBIS, 15 October 1984); *Washington Post*, 30 November 1984.

46. *The Middle East*, no. 119 (September 1984), pp. 15–18.

47. *New York Times*, 30 November 1984; *Washington Post*, 30 November 1984; *The Middle East*, no. 123 (January 1985), p. 6.

48. *The Economist*, 21 January 1984, p. 31.

49. *The Middle East*, no. 119 (September 1984), pp. 15–18.

50. *The Economist*, 21 January 1984, p. 31; *Middle East Economic Digest*, 28 October 1983, p. 24.

51. McNaugher, 'Arms and Allies', pp. 505–13.

52. Ibid., p. 517.

53. Cordesman, *The Gulf*, p. 62.

54. 'Abdulla Bishara, quoted in the Kuwaiti newspaper *al-Qabas*, 26 August 1983 (FBIS, 31 August 1983).

7 Defending Arabia in the 1980s

It has been more than half a century since oil was first discovered in the Arabian Peninsula, marking the genesis of Gulf security concerns. It will soon be two decades since Britain announced its withdrawal from the Gulf, amid cries that the fledgeling Gulf states could not long stand on their own and that the Soviet Union would rush in to fill the vacuum. It has been more than a decade since the oil price revolution of 1973–4 first focused widespread international attention on the Gulf, raising fears of the vulnerability of Western oil supplies. Finally, it will shortly be a decade since the Iranian revolution and Soviet gains in various states along the Gulf's periphery have forced the United States to re-evaluate its security policy regarding the Gulf. What conclusions about the future of Gulf security can be drawn from the cumulative impacts of these benchmarks in recent Gulf history?

The British Legacy

The British imperial impulse, as it affected the Arabian Peninsula, was essentially ephemeral. Direct British concern with the security of the Peninsula appeared only during the imperial twilight and therefore remained extremely limited. There was never any desire before the 1920s nor any need subsequently to exercise direct political control over the statelets of the Arab littoral. Indeed, as a British official with long service in the Gulf in the 1930s expressed it, 'the day-to-day administration of the Arab side [was run] with a handful of officials (one Resident, and three Political Agents), without the payment of a single rupee of subsidy, or the upkeep (on our part) of a single soldier, policeman, or levy.'[1]

During the *pax Britannica*, the Gulf was still relatively isolated from the outside world and politically fragmented. The states of the Arab littoral were still in the formative stage and local nationalism had not yet made an effective appearance among the general population, nor was there any great impact of pan-Arab nationalism until well into the 1950s and 1960s. There was no question of any need for Britain to seek military control over the littoral and minuscule armed forces, with British officers but Arab ranks, were necessary only in the limited function of establishing the authority of a central government over the political periphery, as in unruly tribes.

Air control, that effective, cheap and 'high-tech' tool which provided Britain with an attractive means of maintaining a low-cost, low-risk security bubble over the Gulf in the earlier decades of this century, offered limited utility after the Second World War. The particular effectiveness of air control in the Middle East was often explained as deriving from the barren terrain and the undisciplined (or politically unmotivated) response of the Arab tribesmen. As the inhabitants of the region acquired more sophistication in dealing with air power (as well as with other modern forms of warfare) and as their requirements for political organisation moved from the tribe to the state, the capability of air power to carry the day declined dramatically.[2]

The fighting in central Oman in the 1950s provided an unmistakable demonstration of this turning-point. Demonstrations of air power had little effect on the dissidents and it took a carefully thought-out and organised ground campaign to root out a few hundred rebels. Once again, Oman — or, more precisely, Dhufar — in the 1970s provided evidence of another plateau: a plethora of sophisticated hardware, anti-guerrilla techniques, and considerable international assistance was required to enable the 15,000-man Sultan's Armed Forces to defeat a couple of thousand rebels in more than a decade of intense fighting.

If the Gulf had ever been a British 'lake', even during the heyday of the early-to-middle twentieth century, it certainly could not be mistaken as an American 'lake' in the 1970s or 1980s. Much had changed in the Gulf, as well as in the outside world, during the intervening half-century. Obviously, it was no longer possible for the US to emulate the manner in which Britain had been able to exercise direct and efficient responsibility for the security of the Gulf, even if Washington had desired to do so.

In particular, British maintenance of security concerns was handled in a number of ways which are not practical today. First, Britain exercised extensive political (as well as military) supervision over six of the eight littoral states of the Gulf and considerable influence over the remaining two (up until the emergence of a US relationship with Saudi Arabia and Iran). These are all independent states today and naturally they are sensitive to any suggestion of post-colonial vestiges. Control or domination by an outside power is, for all intents and purposes, impossible. But even the exercise of influence requires means of preponderant leverage, and it is not clear that the US (or the Soviet Union, for that matter) has the ability to exercise that leverage. In fact, influence, as the US–Saudi relationship demonstrates, is bidirectional.

Second, Britain exercised a near-monopoly over the oil industry. HMG, either directly or indirectly through private British oil firms, controlled the ownership of oil deposits, exploration, production and distribution. Until relatively recently, the only intrusion on this oil domain came from American major oil corporations whose fundamental interests were basically compatible with those of Britain. Obviously, this situation no longer exists. The old operating companies have been nationalised, new arrangements for exploitation explicitly specify that ownership of oil resources lies with the producing country, and decisions over levels of production and pricing have been shifted from the international oil companies to the producing states.

Third, Britain was able to maintain a presence in the Gulf, with the kind and size of establishment determined solely by British discretion. In the political realm, this was through the institution of the Political Residency in the Persian Gulf. The Resident, responsible to the Government of India (until Indian independence; to the Foreign Office thereafter), was in charge of a network of Political Agents in the various British-protected states of the Gulf, who in turn served not only as the representatives of HMG but essentially as governors-general. Even the location of the Residency, based at the port of Bushire on the Iranian coast until 1947 (and then on Bahrain until 1971), is illustrative of the historic nature of predominant British influence over even the independent states of the Gulf.[3]

The British presence was military as well, through air facilities, naval installations and British-controlled and officered ground forces — the extent and location once again were determined solely by British policy considerations. Contemplation of such a political presence, let alone its military aspects, is clearly out of the question today, for reasons of indigenous nationalist opposition, the emergence of truly independent states in the region, US domestic opposition to such a role, financial considerations and even technological developments.

Fourth, the British were able to regulate the entry into the Gulf of individuals, government representatives and, of course, military forces. The Gulf's isolation that permitted such an exclusionary policy is gone for ever. Since then, the littoral states have become integrated into global, Third World, and Middle Eastern political and economic systems. The Gulf is no longer 'closed' ideologically and subordinate to a Western sphere of influence. The Iraqi revolution of 1958 marked the first intrusion of radical nationalist forces and provided the Soviet Union with a window on the region. The Iranian revolution of 1979 further emphasised that the Gulf, like the rest of the Middle East and the world at large, must contend with sharply divergent ideologies, political systems and foreign policies.

The above points suggest some significant implications for Western policy formulation. It is obvious that many more constraints on the exercise of foreign policy exist today than did even a few decades ago. In some ways, this makes the task of guaranteeing Gulf security far more difficult for the US than it was for the British. But at the same time, the US should not be attempting to administer a region or a situation, even indirectly through the application of influence or pressure on friendly regimes. While British concern eventually extended into nearly all spheres of activity — internal politics, public administration, education, social welfare, economic development — American concern essentially is tangential and should be clearly understood as being as limited to narrowly defined assistance to co-operative actors in the region in a mutually agreed-upon manner.

The American Intent

It is no exaggeration to say that the strategic importance of the Gulf derives from its abundant reservoirs of oil. At the same time, however, it is a dangerous exaggeration to contend that the global reduction of consumption and concomitant increase in non-Gulf and non-OPEC production of recent years eliminates the Gulf's strategic importance. The onset of world recession and enhanced conservation measures resulted in a drop in world oil production of 11 per cent between 1980 and 1985.

Since various non-OPEC producers significantly increased their production during this period, the impact on OPEC and Gulf

Table 7.1: World Crude Oil Production (mbd)

	1980	1981	1982	1983	1984	1985[a]
Middle East						
Algeria	1.0	0.8	0.7	0.7	0.7	0.7
Egypt	0.6	0.6	0.7	0.7	0.8	0.9
Iran	1.6	1.4	2.3	2.5	2.2	2.1
Iraq	2.5	1.0	1.0	0.9	1.2	1.3
Kuwait	1.4	0.9	0.6	0.8	0.9	0.9
Libya	1.8	1.1	1.2	1.1	1.1	1.0
Neutral Zone[b]	0.5	0.4	0.3	0.4	0.4	0.5
Oman	0.3	0.3	0.3	0.4	0.4	0.4
Qatar	0.5	0.4	0.3	0.3	0.4	0.3
Saudi Arabia	9.6	9.6	6.3	4.9	4.4	3.7
UAE	1.7	1.5	1.2	1.1	1.1	1.1
Other non-communist						
Canada	1.4	1.3	1.3	1.4	1.4	1.5
Indonesia	1.6	1.6	1.3	1.4	1.5	1.3
Mexico	1.9	2.3	2.7	2.7	2.7	2.7
Nigeria	2.6	1.4	1.3	1.2	1.4	1.6
United Kingdom	1.6	1.8	2.1	2.3	2.5	2.7
United States	8.6	8.6	8.7	8.7	8.7	8.9
Venezuela	2.1	2.1	1.9	1.8	1.8	1.7
Communist						
USSR	11.7	11.8	11.8	11.8	11.8	11.4
China	2.1	2.0	2.0	2.1	2.3	2.5
World	59.5	55.8	53.0	52.6	53.8	53.2
Total non-communist	45.2	41.6	38.8	38.2	39.2	39.0
Total communist	14.2	14.2	14.2	14.4	14.6	14.3

Notes: (a) First quarter. (b) Production is shared equally between Saudi Arabia and Kuwait.
Source: US Central Intelligence Agency, Directorate of Intelligence, *International Energy Statistical Review* (30 July 1985), p. 1.

producers was far more severe, as Table 7.1 illustrates. For example, Saudi production fell to one-third of its 1980 level in an attempt to keep order within OPEC, and Iraqi production dropped by half because of Iran's destruction of its Gulf terminals. US imports of OPEC oil had been reduced from more than 80 per cent of total net imports in 1960 to 42 per cent in 1970 but then rose to 60 per cent in 1975 (see Table 7.2). By 1983 and 1984, it had finally dropped down to approximately 42 per cent, even though US production had remained the same. The difficulty in reducing US dependence on OPEC oil imports (the percentage of OPEC imports

Table 7.2: US Dependence on OPEC

	Net petroleum imports	Per cent of Petroleum Consumption
1960	81.3	13.4
1965	64.7	12.8
1970	42.5	9.1
1975	61.6	22.0
1977	72.3	33.6
1980	67.4	25.2
1981	61.4	20.6
1982	49.7	14.0
1983	42.7	12.1
1984	43.2	12.8

Source: US Department of Energy, Energy Information Administration, *Annual Energy Review 1984* (April 1985), p. 101.

Table 7.3: Estimated Imports of Crude Oil and Refined Products, 1984 (tbd)

	US	Japan	W. Ger.	France	UK	Italy	Neth.	Other
Algeria	318	7	80	143	33	59	96	71
Bahrain	0	23	0	1	1	0	16	0
Egypt	10	13	27	51	2	136	7	7
Iran	10	272	48	68	56	190	154	210
Iraq	11	14	40	72	8	97	21	203
Kuwait	36	146	25	18	16	109	91	53
Libya	0	0	194	74	23	253	40	194
Qatar	5	236	10	42	2	18	16	0
Saudi A.	322	1,356	93	198	56	204	37	212
UAE	117	630	22	87	3	52	3	15
OPEC	2,022	3,254	795	936	279	1,186	543	1,115
Total	5,381	4,474	1,208	1,892	1,102	1,827	1,530	3,056

Source: US Central Intelligence Agency, Directorate of Intelligence, *International Energy Statistical Review* (30 July 1985), p. 4.

had actually risen throughout the 1970s) seemingly had been overcome in the early 1980s. Imports of Saudi oil, for example, dropped from a high of 21 per cent in 1981 to less than 6 per cent in 1984.

While direct US dependence on OPEC and Gulf oil has dropped considerably in the last few years, American allies remain vitally dependent on these sources, as Table 7.3 shows. In 1984, 73 per cent of Japan's oil imports came from OPEC sources, as did 66 per cent of West Germany's, 50 per cent of France's, and 65 per cent of Italy's. Thus, any disruption in Gulf oil supplies will have severe consequences for the United States, as well as for Japan and Western Europe and nearly every other part of the world. The strategic importance of Gulf oil remains undiminished. Furthermore, this importance is likely to increase in the future. As Table 7.4 shows, nearly 57 per cent of the total world crude oil reserves are to be found in the eight Gulf states, as is 25 per cent of the world's natural gas reserves. While most projections see the world oil glut

Table 7.4: Estimated Crude Oil and Natural Gas Proved Reserves, 1984

Country	Crude oil (billion barrels)	Natural gas (trillion cubic feet)
Middle East		
Algeria	9.0	109
Bahrain	0.2	7
Egypt	3.2	2
Iran	48.5	479
Iraq	44.5	29
Kuwait[a]	92.7	37
Libya	21.1	21
Oman	3.5	7
Qatar	3.4	150
Saudi Arabia[a]	171.7	127
Syria	1.5	1
Tunisia	1.5	2
UAE	32.5	32
Other		
Canada	7.1	92
China	19.1	31
Indonesia	8.7	40
Mexico	48.6	77
Nigeria	16.7	36
Norway	8.3	89
United Kingdom	13.6	28
United States	27.3	198
USSR	63.0	1,450
Venezuela	25.8	55
World Total	698.7	3,402

Note: (a) Includes half of Neutral Zone production.
Source: *Oil and Gas Journal*, 31 December 1984.

continuing until at least 1990, thereafter growing world consumption and declining supplies elsewhere will undoubtedly lead to a substantial increase in demand for OPEC, and particularly Gulf, oil.[4]

As a consequence, while much of the public discussion of the 1970s over the importance of the Gulf to the US and the West, and over US intentions to protect its access to Gulf oil, has died down, the vital, interdependent relationship between the Gulf, particularly the countries of the GCC, and the United States, will continue well into the future. This means that US concerns with the security of the GCC must continue to develop, evolve and mature in order to be effective — but they must not be suffocating or counterproductive. There is much that US policy-makers can learn from British experience in developing security arrangements for Arabia.

First, regardless of whether it emerged unconsciously, or by oversight, British policy in the Gulf was not a haphazard — even if minor — derivation from a grand imperial design. Rather, it had evolved over considerable time and consequently was closely tailored to the local terrain and circumstances. Generally, the British officials directly responsible for administering the region had served there for much of their careers: they knew personally many of the region's people, and they possessed in-depth knowledge of the area's history, languages, societies and religions. Granted, it may have been easier for officials on the spot to devise an appropriate policy for a region that received little routine attention in Delhi, let alone London. Nevertheless, the contrast between a British policy based on familiarity with the region and an American policy basically derived as an offshoot of East–West relations is striking.

Second, the British efforts after the Second World War to exercise and apply force when necessary provide the only directly applicable illustrations for current American planning. In some ways, USCENTCOM can be viewed as a recrudescence of the British strategic mobility argument of the 1960s. But how much more effective can present American preparations be than earlier British ones? Britain was hard-pressed to deploy 6,000 troops to Kuwait in 1961 and equip them with adequate weaponry and supplies, despite having a variety of bases, pre-positioned equipment, naval vessels and troops in the Gulf region. As one observer noted, 'The emergency demonstrates unequivocally that even the most advanced strategic and logistic concepts cannot entirely dispense with theatre and forward bases.'⁵ Detailed plans had been prepared for that very contingency, yet numerous logistical, readiness and operational problems emerged that had not been foreseen.

While the oilfields of the Gulf littoral lie in open, flat terrain, there is no guarantee that any potential fighting will take place in that environment. Oman, the UAE, both Yemens, Saudi Arabia, Iraq and Iran all contain areas of rough, mountainous terrain that is ideally suited for guerrilla warfare. The Radfan campaign of 1963–4 provides another example of the kind of pitfalls that await any external military force. More than three months, 3,000 soldiers and a highly co-ordinated combined arms campaign were required to secure a relatively small valley held by a few guerrillas possessing only small weapons. The enemy stronghold was indeed captured, but the victory was meaningless as the defenders had melted away before the final assault.

In some ways, the British opponents in Radfan represented a transitional stage between more traditional tribal antipathy to central government and an emerging, well-organised and dedicated nationalist movement benefiting from various kinds of external assistance. The subsequent four-year struggle for control of Aden not only illustrates the requirement for an appropriate counter-strategy of force, but the need for the political 'will' in the face of a determined enemy. To be sure, Britain's quitting of Aden was due as much to financial necessities and a psychological retrenchment from colonial obligations as to the effectiveness of the NLF. Nevertheless, the decision to leave Aden ahead of schedule and to turn the entire territory over to an organisation that was anathema to most Britons owed much to the strains that the problem had generated within British politics and in relations with the Arab world. The introduction of USCENTCOM forces in any scenario apart from a solely Soviet attack inevitably carries the risk of a protracted campaign waged against a significant part of the populace (at a minimum) of one or more Gulf countries.

The urban guerrilla warfare in Aden itself during the latter stages of the fighting, and the bloody, protracted street fighting during the Iraqi seizure of Khorramshahr in 1980 and the subsequent Iranian recapture of that city, serve as potent reminders of what would very likely face American forces in any Gulf scenario. The population of much of the Gulf is concentrated in cities and, whether US intervention is against the Soviet Union, in support of a friend against attack by neighbouring countries, or for the purpose of securing oilfields, the seizure and holding of major urban concentrations undoubtedly will be a major priority. Given US experience elsewhere in hostile urban environments, most recently and vividly in Beirut, this potential aspect of military involvement in the Gulf deserves most careful scrutiny.

The Carter Doctrine was promulgated at a time of American insecurity about the Gulf, when the cornerstones of previously adopted US policy seemed to be crumbling and the deterioration of superpower relations appeared to have let loose a nakedly opportunistic grab for a key Western resource. The rhetoric of both the Carter and Reagan administrations, the preparations for a military capability in the Gulf, the public posturings by a few interventionists, the spot shortages of oil products in the US, all played their role in American sabre-rattling. Half a decade later, the Gulf has slipped from the headlines (even new developments in the Iran-Iraq war are buried in obscure sidebars), public concern for Gulf oil supplies has diminished, and foreign-policy attention has shifted to other crisis areas. A variety of observers have even raised the question of whether the Gulf has 'passed its prime'.

At the same time that American perceptions towards the Gulf have been changing, perceptions of the proper role of USCENTCOM have also been evolving. Within USCENTCOM, there is a widespread belief that it has grown more sophisticated in regarding its mission and requirements in just a few years. At the beginning, the Command was only an RDF, an interventionist force. By the middle of the 1980s, its principal mission came to be seen more as deterrence, with a strategy based on helping friendly nations defend themselves. Altered views were reflected in a 1984 Senate committee report which noted that

> Senior U.S. military commanders in the region don't envision any likely contingency in which this full array of U.S. forces might be needed. Whereas 5 years ago the Rapid Deployment Force was created with a Soviet invasion of Iran or other Gulf oil fields in mind, no one now expects this to happen. If the Gulf war should escalate to the point of U.S. military involvement, most military observers believe that a deployment might include several squadrons of U.S. fighter aircraft, additional AWACS and tankers, additional destroyers/frigates for convoy duty, and possibly a second carrier battle group. Senior U.S. military

commanders in the region don't envision the need for U.S. ground troops except for security guard duty.[6]

Such responses as the dispatch of AWACS aircraft to Egypt in February 1983, to Sudan in July 1984, and the deployment of survey and countermeasures teams in the Red Sea during the mining threat of July 1984 (at the request of Egypt and Saudi Arabia) were cited in this regard. Rather than intervention, emphasis was placed on other functions, such as conducting joint manoeuvres, administering security assistance training programmes for the region's armed forces, supervising arms transfers to the region, and promoting military liaison.[7]

The US has registered major accomplishments in a few short years. By 1984, it could be said that the US military presence in the area was considerable but remarkably unobtrusive. There were 11,500 sailors and soldiers in the Gulf and Arabian Sea area, and another 4,000 civilians were working under Defense Department contract in Saudi Arabia. The duties of these Americans included manning TPS-43 radar sites, flying AWACS in support of the Saudi combat air patrol, and flying F-14 patrols in the Arabian Sea. Despite the size of the US presence, it was relatively unobtrusive, with all but about 1,000 military personnel serving at sea. The US Navy presence in particular was considered to be 'out of sight' since it was located outside the Gulf itself. In 1984, the United States deployed about 10 frigate/destroyer class ships in the area, 1 aircraft carrier with over 50 combat aircraft on board, 4 AWACS with 4 tanker aircraft flying out of Riyadh, and 4 support ships, as well as various support aircraft with the carrier.[8]

The arguments of some at the time of British withdrawal, as well as during the crises of 1973-4 and 1979-80, that the US required bases and permanent troops stationed in the Gulf in order to protect US interests have been proven pointless. The inutility, or at least irrelevance, of bases in the Gulf was recognised long ago by the British. As Elizabeth Monroe noted in the 1960s,

> One purely British motive for maintaining the bases springs from a long-standing British conception of world-policemanship. In the Middle East, the British use several courtesy titles for this operation — 'protection of the oil,' 'fulfilment of long-standing obligations to rulers,' 'ability to answer distress calls.' Yet, no matter how useful their presence to themselves and to others, it

presents one major snag from the standpoint of their general Middle Eastern relations.[9]

In part, the renewed concern with overseas bases in the post-colonial era stems from a renaissance of interest in 'geopolitics', or 'an emphasis on a geographic basis of power in international relations involving spatial relations and positioning; strategic access, control, and communications; and the relationship between resources and power'.[10] But, for many of these proponents of forward basing, it is difficult to separate objective arguments from subjective ones. Discussion and analysis of the actual functions and benefits of bases is often buried under the rhetoric and symbolism of moral and ideological struggle between the superpowers, the dictates of national pride, and conceptions of international politics as a zero-sum game.

Similar questions arise with the practical advantages of stationing troops in the Gulf. As former Department of Defense official James H. Noyes points out, the presence of 15,000 combat Marines at a US base in Bahrain, for instance, could have done nothing to alter the course of Iran's revolution, nor would they have deterred the Soviet invasion of Afghanistan or Iraq's attack on Iran. Such a US presence would have threatened the survival of Bahrain's moderate government. Furthermore, 'far larger forces than the British ever maintained in the Gulf could not sustain the British presence in Aden, which finally evacuated under fire and whose legacy disrupts the area today as the only Marxist Arab state.'[11]

Certainly, there may exist a growing realisation that USCENTCOM may never be called upon as a deploying force, partially the consequence of diminishing perceptions of an imminent or even likely Soviet attack on the Gulf and partly due to the lessening of potential threats from either Iran or Iraq as a result of their increasing war-weariness and postwar priorities of reconstruction. The most important effects of the creation of this instrument of American force projection into the Gulf may have little to do with the Gulf at all, but instead lie in the area of more general US defence preparation, such as improving such oft-neglected requirements as strategic lift capabilities.

But this lessening of Western and American concern with Gulf security may be double-edged. On the positive side, the dying down of the frenzy over 'securing the Gulf' is healthy. It may, in part, signal a maturation of the way in which America perceives the Gulf and the constitution and needs of its governments and peoples. The fact that Iran did not become a Soviet satellite and that none of the Arab states of the Gulf has been convulsed in upheaval may have silenced the shrill cries of alarm or hostility. The outbreak of the Iran–Iraq war may have refocused outside attention on far more likely dangers than Soviet adventurism, while the interminable nature of that war has also demonstrated the inability of outsiders to do anything about it.

The decline of overreactions to Western vulnerabilities and dependence on Gulf oil during the past decade provides a welcome breathing space in which to create the very necessary foundations of political co-operation and dialogue, perhaps even a constructive learning process for both Western and Gulf governments. It also means that the US government probably has less opportunity to display its propensity for shooting itself in the foot as far as the Middle East is concerned, for undertaking rash actions and strident rhetoric under the pressure of short-fuse crises, and for disregarding the lessons of past experiences.

On the negative side, the change in American perceptions of the Gulf over the 1980s may represent little more than a limited attention span and a feeling of 'out of sight, out of mind'. During the Reagan administration, the oil glut translated into a deterioration of OPEC and the Arab oil producers' influence in Washington, while Israel's clout increased because of the formation of a coalition government in Israel with a Labour Prime Minister, the Israeli disengagement from Lebanon, and continued strong support for Israel on Capitol Hill. In the atmosphere of a direct danger to Gulf security, the F-15 and AWACS sales cleared Congress despite vehement opposition from Israel's supporters. By 1985, however, plans for additional arms sales to Saudi Arabia were shelved — not over questions concerning Saudi Arabia's security requirements, but simply because the sale would not gain Congressional approval. But no matter what issue crowds the headlines, the Gulf remains a region of strategic importance to the West and the security ramifications regarding that region will not simply go away because they are not addressed. Repeated American policy-makers' responses to Gulf crises by advocating a military solution simply are not healthy, for either American standing in the region or for American friends.

The GCC and the Future

There can no longer be a single dominant power in the Gulf. The devolution of the British presence marked an end to the tradition of external control. Furthermore, no Gulf actor, including Iran and Iraq, possesses overwhelming power. The two great powers of the Gulf — as defined by traditional criteria of geographic size, strategic location, population, industrial might and size of economy — are presently stalemated on the battlefield, neither able to win a clear advantage over the other. Thus, the subsystem of the Gulf is left in a precarious balance of power. The other six Gulf states — small, weak and undeveloped as they may be — still can exercise power through their financial disbursements and can call upon allies in the Arab, Islamic and Western worlds for moral and material assistance. The result is a multipolar system within the Gulf, with Iran, Iraq and Saudi Arabia as the principal poles.

Primary responsibility for defending Arabia necessarily belongs to the GCC, and the US role can be no more than 'back-up'. For the United States, 'reassurance' of its friends in the GCC is just as important as deterrence of the Soviet Union.[12] It is not up to the US to take the initiative, but to provide assistance when asked. The GCC states need and want the assurance that the US will be there when it is required, but they cannot and will not turn over their responsibilities to what often seems like an irresponsible outsider. Furthermore, since divergent perceptions between the US and the Gulf states of potential threats or challenges to Gulf security ultimately are inevitable, policy differences are inescapable. It is undeniable that important — and even vital — national interests of the United States reside in the Gulf. At the same time, however, American preoccupation with access to a single natural resource is only 'temporary' in the broader scheme of things. To Saudi Arabia and its smaller allies, the security of the Gulf will always be of paramount importance, the risks higher, and a misstep catastrophic.

The reluctance of the GCC states to fall in with existing American plans for a build-up of US military capabilities in the region is neither capricious nor temporary. US planning has tended to concentrate on meeting the external threat of the Soviet Union. But to the Gulf states, a direct Soviet assault on the Gulf is one of the least likely threats to occur and co-operating fully with perceived American needs to meet this threat produces considerable negative side-effects and courts both internal and outside opposition. Furthermore, these states see Israel and Israeli policies as posing a far more immediate threat to regional security than Moscow, and in this regard the US is viewed as an uncritical supporter of Israel's actions rather than an ally.[13]

For regional threats, military action — and particularly US direct military intervention — is regarded as the very last resort. In many ways, the Peninsula is naturally shielded from invasion by reason of geography and historical circumstances. Nevertheless, some regional threats do exist, such as attack or subversion emanating from Iran, Iraq, or possibly the Yemens. While the GCC has sought to improve its military preparedness, the small size of its population, limited industrial base, and the lack of available manpower prevent any major military build-up. Logically then, these states must rely on diplomacy, negotiation, financial sweeteners, and other indirect means to resolve disputes, rather than direct confrontation. US rhetorical posturing and high-profile efforts to increase military co-operation and a possible US presence in the region work to inflame delicate situations, rather than diffuse them.

The escalation of the Iran–Iraq conflict in early 1984 into a war on Gulf shipping provides a pertinent illustration. The US made a point of warning Iran on several occasions against interference with oil shipping and publicly sought to persuade Saudi Arabia and the UAE to allow the stationing of USAF fighters in GCC airfields. Predictably, these actions provoked angry words and additional threats from Tehran, without effecting the dénouement of this twist in the war. By mid-summer, it appeared that Saudi cautiousness and minimal response to Iranian provocations had paid off: rather than escalating, attacks on tankers eased off, despite the downing of an Iranian F-4 Phantom by Saudi fighters.

Finally, there is little the US can do to prevent or counter most internal threats to GCC regimes. The closer political and military ties are between the US and any particular GCC state, the more chance there is of a negative impact on domestic politics. Even if this factor is of relatively marginal importance in the states of the Arab littoral (unlike the case with Iran), one must wonder whether it is worth taking the risk in order to improve somewhat the chances of withstanding a relatively unlikely Soviet assault? Not surprisingly, the GCC states think not. Their argument is for an American 'over the horizon' approach. The enormous Saudi military expenditures of recent years, far more than necessary for the use of present or planned Saudi armed forces, provides a clear indication of Saudi thinking in this regard.

Given the delicate, finely tuned balance between their friendship with and dependence on the West and their need to cope with and adjust to far-reaching economic, social and political changes in the region, what can the states of the GCC, individually and collectively, do to assure their future security? First of all, all these states will find it necessary to continue to evolve in political terms to meet constantly changing circumstances and demands. To the outside world, the considerable extent of change made in the last decade or two may not be apparent, but it has been truly far-reaching and even radical. The next several decades, though, will require even greater accommodation on the part of the decision-making establishment.[14]

In addition, logic dictates that the conservative Arab littoral states band together and move towards closer co-operation in economic matters, including development, policy harmonisation, and perhaps eventually integration. The creation of the Gulf Cooperation Council in 1981, while prompted in the immediate sense by the Iran–Iraq war and made possible by the easy exclusion of the two largest Gulf states, built on solid foundations established since 1971 and even before. The record of economic integration around the world, not to mention political integration, is not impressive. Nevertheless, these six states share many fundamental similarities and undoubtedly have as good or better a chance than any group of Third World countries. It is worth noting that one member of the GCC, the United Arab Emirates, is itself a living example of successful integration, or at least confederation, having been formed from the union of seven small shaykhdoms with deep rivalries and even open hostilities for decades prior to independence.

Political co-operation and integration is, of course, most difficult to achieve. The hegemonic role of Saudi Arabia is both an asset and a liability in this regard. There can be no doubt that the Saudis were the driving force behind the creation of the GCC, and the council's headquarters/secretariat is located in Riyadh. On the other hand, the other dynasties of the Gulf have had reason over the past several centuries to regard the Al Sa'ud as foes bent on incorporating the shaykhdoms into their domain. Even today, the sometimes overbearing manner of the Saudis (sometimes referred to as the 'Texans of the Middle East') can raise hackles along the Arab littoral. One recent example of the ambivalent attitude of Saudi

Arabia's neighbours is provided by Kuwait's refusal to sign a bilateral security agreement with Riyadh in the aftermath of the 1981 abortive coup attempt in Bahrain.[15]

The six GCC states have also taken giant steps towards modernisation and improvement of their military establishments. There are serious limitations, of course, on the defence capabilities of these states and, even with all their combined forces, they can be no match for a determined assault from either Iraq or Iran, let alone an external power. Nevertheless, the enhancement of internal security capabilities has proceeded apace and the lion's share of militarisation effort has gone into air defence capabilities. In the last several years, efforts have been made to lay the groundwork for a GCC 'rapid deployment force', to respond to crises within the bounds of the GCC, and for a co-ordinated air defence network, based on the American-supplied AWACS. Saudi Arabia in particular has engaged in overstocking of equipment, supplies and physical assets of military facilities, with the assumption being that these will be available for US military use if and when Riyadh should request it. In this way, the Saudis feel they can minimise the disruptive effects of a foreign military presence while permitting some advantages of a quick US reaction to a sudden threat.

While Saudi Arabia's efforts in this regard are the most extensive, Kuwait, the UAE and Oman have also placed heavy emphasis on the expansion of air, land and sea forces, the purchase of extensive, sophisticated arsenals, and the recruitment and training of military personnel. Naturally; the extent to which these states can provide for their own defence against a serious opponent is severely restricted. While threats deriving from matters of internal security and some, if not all, regional challenges to the GCC, can be countered by GCC military capabilities, it is clear that the survival of these states in an often hostile environment also depends on the utilisation of other methods.

The GCC ultimately must rely on non-confrontational skills and instruments that are presently at their disposal. First, there is effective diplomacy, both directly and publicly as well as behind the scenes. It also means farsightedness in heading off potential confrontation and spillover from other conflicts. The GCC states have acquired a justly deserved reputation as mediators in recent years, as illustrated by the role of Shaykh Zayid, President of the UAE, as the go-between for the Shah of Iran and Iraq's Saddam Husayn in reaching agreement on the Shatt al-'Arab at Algiers in

1975; the effectiveness of Saudi mediation in ending the active phase of the Lebanese civil war in 1976; and the role of Kuwait and the UAE in prodding Oman and South Yemen to establish diplomatic relations for the first time ever in late 1983.

Admittedly, the effectiveness of Saudi Arabia and its neighbours as diplomats and mediators has been enhanced immeasurably by their financial resources. GCC apprehension over Iranian foreign policy in recent years was demonstrated in its provision of some $35b in aid to Iraq for its war effort. While resented by Iran, this largesse was far less provocative than direct military assistance, verbal antipathy or invitations to foreign military forces. As a single instrument of foreign policy, money has its limitations, as recent Saudi efforts to influence Syrian policy have demonstrated. Used skilfully, however, it can serve to substitute for other, more traditional, forms of foreign-policy influence.

As a last resort, there is the 'oil weapon'. But the reluctance of Saudi Arabia to disrupt increasingly profound ties with the United States over a single — if centrally important — issue points to the Saudi influence dilemma, in a mirror-image of US goals regarding Saudi Arabia. Utilisation of this foreign-policy instrument carries the risk of irreparably damaging a complex framework of good relations upon which Riyadh is vitally dependent, without any guarantee of achieving the desired goal — an independent Palestinian state.[16] Just as it is necessary for American policy-makers to be aware of and accommodate the environment and constraints that determine the decisions of Saudi policy-makers, so must the Saudis be sensitive to American political and strategic requirements.

The reverse parallel is not exact, since Saudi leadership is undoubtedly far more knowledgeable about US politics, particularly in the foreign-policy realm, than vice versa, but the principle remains true. The United States and Saudi Arabia — and behind the Saudis, the other five GCC states — will remain mutually dependent far into the next century. Neither can afford to jeopardise the support and co-operation of the other during this period. Consequently, the necessarily close co-ordination of security interests in the Gulf between these states must build on foundations of mutual trust and sensitivity. The consequence of failure for the US and the West is severe economic disruption; for the GCC community, it is complete disaster.

Notes

1. AIR/2/1615, T. C. Fowle, Political Resident in the Persian Gulf, to Sir Aubrey Metcalfe, Foreign Secretary to the Government of India, 17 March 1939.
2. There is considerable difference, not always appreciated, between air policing as practised by the British and air power as a component of national defence. The argument that 'It behooves us in the [US] Air Force to consider seriously the capabilities and doctrine relative to small wars, which the Royal Air Force developed when air power was still very young, to see if we can do it as effectively as the British did so many years ago,' blurs that distinction. The quotation is from David J. Dean, 'Air Power in Small Wars: The British Air Control Experience', *Air University Review*, vol. 34, no. 5 (July–August 1983), p. 31.
3. Another illustration, lying between the legally subordinate status of the amirates and the independent status of Iran, Iraq and Saudi Arabia, is the Omani sultanate. Legally independent for centuries, the rulers of Muscat were subject to British approval and even determination of their foreign and other policies throughout much of the twentieth century.
4. A recent US Geological Survey report estimated that only about half all North American oil has been discovered. Even so, all the undiscovered oil outside the Middle East barely equals the amount in the Middle East's proven reserves. Or, put another way, the Middle East probably has as much undiscovered oil as North America has ever produced. *Washington Post*, 26 September 1985.
5. Anthony Verrier, 'Strategically Mobile Forces — U.S. Theory and British Practice', *JRUSI*, vol. 106, no. 624 (November 1961), p. 484.
6. US Congress, Senate, Committee on Foreign Relations, *War in the Gulf*; a Staff Report, August 1984 (Washington, USGPO, 1984), p. 21.
7. For a recent appraisal of USCENTCOM accomplishments and its role in the region by its commander, see Robert C. Kingston, 'US Central Command: Refocusing the Lens of Stability on a Region in Crisis', *Defence '84*, November–December 1984, pp. 29–34.
8. 'The War in the Gulf', p. 18.
9. 'British Bases in the Middle East: Assets or Liabilities?', *International Affairs* (London), vol. 42, no. 1 (January 1966), pp. 26–7.
10. Robert E. Harkavy, *Great Power Competition for Overseas Bases: The Geopolitics of Access Diplomacy* (New York, Pergamon Press, 1982), p. 9.
11. *The Clouded Lens: Persian Gulf Security and U.S. Policy*, 2nd edn (Stanford, Ca, Hoover Institution Press, 1982),pp. 130–1.
12. 'The object of deterrence is to persuade an adversary that the costs to him of seeking a military solution to his political problems will far outweigh the benefits. The object of reassurance is to persuade one's own people, and those of one's allies, that the benefits of military action, or preparation for it, will outweigh the costs.' Michael Howard, 'Reassurance and Deterrence: Western Defense in the 1980s', *Foreign Affairs*, vol. 61, no. 2 (winter 1982–3), p. 317.
13. In this connection, it might also be noted that the Gulf states still harbour lingering suspicions that the US might be tempted to act rashly and attempt to secure direct control over the oilfields, with or without the pretext of a Gulf crisis. While the fuel for this suspicion was initially provided by the statements of public officials and hostile writers in the year or two following the 1973–4 oil price revolution, advocacy of such an action occasionally still appears.

14. For a representative study of the challenge facing Saudi Arabia in this regard, see John A. Shaw and David E. Long, *Saudi Arabian Modernization: The Impact of Change on Stability* (New York, Praeger, for the Georgetown University Center for Strategic and International Studies, 1982; Washington Papers, no. 89).

15. For a review of the relationship between Saudi Arabia and its smaller neighbours, see Hermann Frederick Eilts, 'Saudi Arabian Foreign Policy Toward the Gulf States and Southwest Asia', in Hafeez Malik (ed.), *International Security in Southwest Asia* (New York, Praeger, 1984), pp. 77–106.

16. For a discussion of the viability of this strategy, see William R. Brown, 'The Oil Weapon', *Middle East Journal*, vol. 36, no. 3 (1982), pp. 301–18; reprinted in J. E. Peterson (ed.), *The Politics of Middle Eastern Oil* (Washington, Middle East Institute, 1983), pp. 126–43.

Bibliography

Primary Materials

India Office Library and Records, London

L/P&S Political and Secret Department, India Office
   L/P&S/10 Departmental Papers: Political and Secret Separate (or Subject) Files (1902–31)
   L/P&S/12 Political (External) Files and Collections (1931–50)
   L/P&S/18 Political and Secret Memoranda
   L/P&S/20 Political and Secret Department Library
R Residency Records
   R/15 Political Residency in the Persian Gulf
      R/15/1 Political Residency, Bushire
      R/15/2 Political Agency, Bahrain
      R/15/4 Political Agency, Trucial Coast
      R/15/5 Political Agency, Kuwait
      R/15/6 Political Agency, Muscat
   R/20 Political Residency, Aden

Public Record Office, London

AIR Air Ministry
   AIR/2 Correspondence of Air Ministry, Code 'B'
   AIR/5 Air Historical Branch Records: Series II
   AIR/8 Chief of Air Staff: Papers
   AIR/9 Directorate of Plans: Papers
   AIR/19 Private Office Papers
   AIR/20 Unregistered Papers
   AIR/23 Overseas Commands
   AIR/24 Operations Records Books: Commands
   AIR/26 Operations Records Books: Operational Groups and Wings
   AIR/27 Operations Records Books: Squadrons
   AIR/28 Operations Records Books: Stations
   AIR/29 Operations Records Books: Miscellaneous Units
   AIR/41 Air Historical Branch: Narratives and Monographs
CAB Cabinet Office
   CAB/2 Committee of Imperial Defence (CID), Minutes of Meetings
   CAB/5 CID, Memoranda: Colonial Defence
   CAB/6 CID, Memoranda: Defence of India
   CAB/16 CID, Ad Hoc Sub-Committees of Enquiry, Proceedings and Memoranda
   CAB/21 Cabinet, Registered Files
   CAB/53 CID, Chiefs of Staff Committee
   CAB/79 War Cabinet, Chiefs of Staff Committee
   CAB/80 War Cabinet, Chiefs of Staff Committee, Memoranda
   CAB/95 War Cabinet, Committee on the Middle East and North Africa

CAB/104 Cabinet, Supplementary Registered Files
CAB/105 War Cabinet, Telegrams
CAB/106 Cabinet Office, Historical Section Files
CO Colonial Office
  CO/537 Supplementary Correspondence
  CO/725 Aden Correspondence
DEFE Ministry of Defence
  DEFE/4 Chiefs of Staff Committee, Minutes
  DEFE/5 Chiefs of Staff Committee, Memoranda
  DEFE/6 Chiefs of Staff Committee, Joint Planning Staff Reports
  DEFE/7 Registered Files: General Series
FO Foreign Office
  FO/371 Political
WO War Office
  WO/106 Directorate of Military Operations and Intelligence: Papers

Published Materials

Abadi, Jacob *Britain's Withdrawal from the Middle East, 1947–1971: The Economic and Strategic Imperatives* (Princeton, NJ, Kingston Press, 1982)

Abdulghani, Jasim M. *Iraq and Iran: The Years of Crisis* (London, Croom Helm; Baltimore, Johns Hopkins University Press, 1984)

Abir, Mordechai *Oil, Power and Politics: Conflict in Arabia, the Red Sea and the Gulf* (London, Frank Cass, 1974)

—— 'Saudi Security and Military Endeavour', *Jerusalem Quarterly*, no. 33 (fall 1984), pp. 79–94

Aburdene, Odeh 'U.S. Economic and Financial Relations with Saudi Arabia, Kuwait, and the United Arab Emirates', *American–Arab Affairs*, no. 7 (winter 1983–4), pp. 76–84

Ahrari, Mohammed E. 'Implications of the Iranian Political Change for the Arab World', *Middle East Review*, vol. 16, no. 3 (spring 1984), pp. 17–29

Akehurst, John *We Won a War: The Campaign in Oman, 1965–1975* (London, Michael Russell, 1983)

Albaharna, Husain M. *The Arabian Gulf States: Their Legal and Political Status and Their International Problems*, 2nd rev. edn (Beirut, Librairie du Liban, 1975)

Alford, Jonathan 'Les Occidentaux et la securité du Golfe', *Politique Etrangère*, vol. 46, no. 3 (September 1981), pp. 667–90

Aliboni, Roberto 'The Strategic and Regional Balance in the Middle East and the Red Sea Region', trans. Richard Walker, *Atlantic Community Quarterly*, vol. 19, no. 4 (1981), pp. 37–49

Amirsadeghi, Hossein (ed.) *The Security of the Persian Gulf* (London, Croom Helm; New York, St Martin's Press, 1981)

Amos, John W. and Ralph H. Magnus 'Regional Perceptions of the American Central Command', *Conflict*, vol. 5, no. 4 (1985), pp. 337–53

Anderson, Irvine H. *Aramco, the United States and Saudi Arabia: A Study of the Dynamics of Foreign Oil Policy, 1933–1950* (Princeton, Princeton University Press, 1981)

Anthony, John Duke *Arab States of the Lower Gulf: People, Politics, Petroleum* (Washington, Middle East Institute, 1975)

—— 'The Gulf Cooperation Council', *Journal of South Asian and Middle Eastern Studies*, vol. 5, no. 4 (summer 1982), pp. 3–18

—— 'The Gulf Cooperation Council', *Orbis*, vol. 28, no. 3 (fall 1984), pp. 447–50

Armitage, M. J. and R. A. Mason *Air Power in the Nuclear Age* (Urbana, University of Illinois Press, 1983)
Armstrong, DeWitt C. 'The British Re-Value Their Strategic Bases', *Journal of the Royal United Service Institution*, vol. 104, no. 616 (November 1959), pp. 423–32
al-Awaji, Ibrahim Mohamed 'U.S.–Saudi Economic and Political Relations', *American–Arab Affairs*, no. 7 (winter 1983–4), pp. 55–9
Axelgard, Frederick W. 'The "Tanker War" in the Gulf: Background and Repercussions', *Middle East Insight*, vol. 3, no. 6 (1984), pp. 26–33
Ayoob, Mohammed 'Blueprint for a Catastrophe: Conducting Oil Diplomacy by "Other Means" in the Middle East and the Persian Gulf', *Australian Outlook*, vol. 33, no. 3 (December 1979), pp. 265–73
El-Azhary, M. S. (ed.) *The Iran–Iraq War: An Historical, Economic and Political Analysis* (London, Croom Helm; New York, St Martin's Press, for the University of Exeter Centre for Arab Gulf Studies and the University of Basra Centre for Arab Gulf Studies, 1984)
Bartlett, C. J. *The Long Retreat: A Short History of British Defence Policy, 1945–70* (London, Macmillan; New York, St Martin's Press, 1972)
Batcheller, G. D. 'Analyzing the RDF', *Marine Corps Gazette*, vol. 64 (June 1980), pp. 16–18
Bates, E. Asa 'The Rapid Deployment Force — Fact or Fiction?', *RUSI — Journal of the Royal United Services Institute for Defence Studies*, vol. 126, no 2 (June 1981), pp. 23–33
Beblawi, Hazem 'Gulf Foreign Investment Co-ordination: Needs and Modalities', *Arab Gulf Journal*, vol. 3, no. 1 (April 1983), pp. 41–59
Bell, Raymond E., Jr 'The Rapid Deployment Force: How Much, How Soon?', *Army*, vol. 30 (July 1980), pp. 18–24
Berner, Wolfgang 'Cuban Intervention in Africa and Arabia', *Aussenpolitik*, vol. 27, no. 3 (1976), pp. 328–35
Beseisu, Fouad Hamdi 'Sub-Regional Economic Cooperation in the Arab Gulf', *Arab Gulf Journal*, vol. 1, no. 1 (October 1981), pp. 45–54
Bidwell, Robin *The Two Yemens* (London, Longman; Boulder, Co, Westview Press, 1983)
Bill, James A. 'The Arab World and the Challenge of Iran', *Journal of Arab Affairs*, vol. 2, no. 2 (spring 1983), pp. 155–71
—— 'Islam, Politics, and Shi'ism in the Gulf', *Middle East Insight*, vol. 3, no. 3 (January–February 1984), pp. 3–12
—— 'Resurgent Islam in the Persian Gulf', *Foreign Affairs*, vol. 63, no. 1 (fall 1984), pp. 108–27
Bishara, Abdulla Yacoub 'The GCC: Achievements and Challenges', *American–Arab Affairs*, no. 7 (winter 1983–4), pp. 40–4
Boam, T. A. 'Defending Western Interests Outside NATO: The United Kingdom's Contribution', *Armed Forces Journal International*, vol. 122 (October 1984), pp. 116, 118, 120
Bonnenfant, Paul (ed.) *La Peninsule arabique d'Aujourd'hui*, 2 vols (Paris, Editions du Centre National de la Recherche Scientifique, for the Centre d'Etudes et de Recherches sur l'Orient arabe contemporain, 1982)
Brown, Harold 'Rapid Deployment Forces', *Asia–Pacific Defense Forum*, vol. 5 (summer 1980), pp. 45–9
—— *U.S. Security Policy in Southwest Asia: A Case Study in Complexity* (Washington, Johns Hopkins University School of Advanced International Studies, Johns Hopkins Foreign Policy Institute, 1981; Occasional Paper)
Brown, Neville *Strategic Mobility* (London, Institute for Strategic Studies, 1963; New York, Frederick A. Praeger, 1964 (Studies in International Security, no. 7))
—— *Arms without Empire: British Defence Role in the Modern World* (Baltimore,

Penguin, 1967)

Brown, William R. 'The Oil Weapon', *Middle East Journal*, vol. 36, no. 3 (1982), pp. 301–18

—— 'Middle East Policy and Gulf Defense', *Middle East Insight*, vol. 2, no. 5 (January–February 1983), pp. 39–44

Buchan, Alastair 'Britain East of Suez: Part One — The Problem of Power', *Journal of the Royal United Service Institution*, vol. 112, no. 647 (August 1967), pp. 209–15

Burrell, R. M. *The Persian Gulf* (New York, Library Press, for the Georgetown University Center for Strategic and International Studies, 1972 (Washington Papers, no. 1))

Carnegie Panel on US Security and the Future of Arms Control *Challenges for U.S. National Security — Assessing the Balance: Defense Spending and Conventional Forces*, A Preliminary Report, Part II: 'The Military Balance in the Persian Gulf', pp. 149–94 (Washington, Carnegie, 1981)

Chubin, Shahram 'U.S. Security Interests in the Persian Gulf in the 1980s', *Daedalus*, vol. 109, no. 4 (1980), pp. 31–65

—— *Soviet Policy Towards Iran and the Gulf* (London, International Institute for Strategic Studies, 1980 (Adelphi Papers, no. 157))

—— (ed.) *Domestic Political Factors* (London, Gower, for the International Institute for Strategic Studies, 1981 (Security in the Persian Gulf, no. 1))

—— *The Role of Outside Powers* (London, Gower, for the International Institute for Strategic Studies, 1982 (Security in the Persian Gulf, no. 4))

—— 'Gains for Soviet Policy in the Middle East', *International Security*, vol. 6, no. 4 (1982), pp. 122–52

—— 'La France et la Golfe: opportunisme ou continuité', *Politique Etrangère*, vol. 48, no. 4 (1983), pp. 879–88

—— 'The Iran–Iraq War and Persian Gulf Security', *International Defense Review*, vol. 17, no. 6 (1984), pp. 705–12

Coker, Christopher and Heinz Schulte 'A European Option in the Indian Ocean', *International Defense Review*, vol. 13, no. 1 (1982), pp. 27–34

Collins, John M. 'Rapid Deployment Forces: Fact Versus Fantasy', *Marine Corps Gazette*, vol. 65 (February 1981), pp. 68–9

—— *U.S.–Soviet Military Balance: Concepts and Capabilities, 1960–1980* (New York, McGraw-Hill, 1980)

Collins, John M., Clyde R. Mark and Elizabeth Ann Severns 'Petroleum Imports from the Persian Gulf: Use of U.S. Armed Force to Ensure Supplies', Library of Congress, Congressional Research Service, Issue Brief No. IB 79046 (1980)

Cordesman, Anthony H. *The Gulf and the Search for Strategic Stability: Saudi Arabia, the Military Balance in the Gulf, and Trends in the Arab–Israeli Military Balance* (Boulder, Co, Westview Press; London, Mansell, 1984)

—— 'The Gulf Crisis and Strategic Interests: A Military Analysis', *American–Arab Affairs*, no. 9 (summer 1984), pp. 8–15

Cordier, Sherwood S. *U.S. Military Power and Rapid Deployment Requirements in the 1980s* (Boulder, Co, Westview Press, 1983 (Westview Replica Edition))

Cottrell, Alvin J. 'The Political–Military Balance in the Persian Gulf Region', in Joseph S. Szyliowicz and Bard E. O'Neill (eds) *The Energy Crisis and U.S. Foreign Policy* (New York, Praeger, 1975), pp. 125–38

Cottrell, Alvin J., Robert J. Hanks and Frank T. Bray 'Military Affairs in the Persian Gulf', in Alvin J. Cottrell (ed.) *The Persian Gulf States: A General Survey* (Baltimore, Johns Hopkins University Press, 1980), pp. 140–71

Cottrell, Alvin J. and Michael L. Moodie *The United States and the Persian Gulf: Past Mistakes, Present Needs* (New York, National Strategy Information Center, 1984 (Agenda Paper no. 13))

Countryman, John R. *Iran in the View of the Persian Gulf Emirates* (Carlisle Barracks, Pa, US Army War College, Military Studies Program Paper, 1976)

Crowe, William J., Jr 'The Persian Gulf: Central or Peripheral to United States Strategy?', *US Naval Institute Proceedings, Naval Review, 1978*, pp. 185–209

Cummings, John Thomas, Hussein G. Askari and Michael Skinner 'Military Expenditures and Manpower Requirements in the Arabian Peninsula', *Arab Studies Quarterly*, vol. 2, no. 1 (1980), pp. 38–49

Dadant, P. M. *Improving U.S. Capability to Deploy Ground Forces to Southwest Asia in the 1990s — A Briefing* (Santa Monica, Ca, Rand Corporation, February 1983 (Rand Note, N-1943-AF, prepared for the US Air Force))

Danziger, Raphael 'The Naval Race in the Persian Gulf', *US Naval Institute Proceedings*, vol. 108, no. 3 (March 1982), pp. 92–8

Darby, Phillip 'Beyond East of Suez', *International Affairs* (London), vol. 46, no. 4 (October 1970), pp. 655–69

—— *British Defence Policy East of Suez, 1947–68* (London, Oxford University Press, for the Royal Institute of International Affairs, 1973)

Darius, Robert G., John W. Amos, II, and Ralph H. Magnus (eds) *Gulf Security into the 1980s* (Stanford, Ca, Hoover Institution Press, 1984)

Davis, Eric 'The Political Economy of the Arab Oil-Producing Nations: Convergence with Western Interests', *Studies in Comparative International Development*, vol. 14, no. 2 (1979), pp. 75–94

Dawisha, Adeed 'Internal Values and External Threats: The Making of Saudi Foreign Policy', *Orbis*, vol. 23, no. 1 (spring 1979), pp. 129–43

—— *Saudi Arabia's Search for Security* (London, International Institute for Strategic Studies, 1979–80 (Adelphi Papers, no. 158))

—— 'Iraq and the Arab World: The Gulf War and After', *The World Today*, vol. 37, no. 5 (May 1981), pp. 188–94

—— 'Iran's Mullahs and the Arab Masses', *Washington Quarterly*, vol. 6, no. 3 (1983), pp. 162–8

Dawisha, Adeed and Karen Dawisha (eds) *The Soviet Union in the Middle East: Policies and Perspectives* (New York, Holmes & Meier, for the Royal Institute of International Affairs, 1982)

Dawisha, Karen 'Moscow's Moves in the Direction of the Gulf — So Near and Yet So Far', *Journal of International Affairs*, vol. 34, no. 2 (1980–1), pp. 219–34

—— 'Moscow and the Gulf', *The World Today*, vol. 37, no. 1 (January 1981), pp. 8–14

Dean, David J. 'Air Power in Small Wars: The British Air Control Experience', *Air University Review*, vol. 34, no. 5 (July–August 1983), pp. 24–31

de Briganti, Giovanni 'Forces d'Action Rapide: France's Rapid Deployment Force', *Armed Forces Journal International*, vol. 122 (October 1984), pp. 122 and 124

'Defending the Gulf: A Survey', *The Economist*, 6 June 1981, pp. 1–38

DeForth, Peter W. 'U.S. Naval Presence in the Persian Gulf: The Mideast Force Since World War II', *Naval War College Review*, vol. 28, no. 1 (1975), pp. 38–38

Dixon, Michael 'Soviet Policy in the Persian Gulf', *Journal of Defense and Diplomacy*, vol. 3, no. 2 (February 1985), pp. 23–7

Dunn, Keith A. 'Constraints on the USSR in Southwest Asia: A Military Analysis', *Orbis*, vol. 25, no. 3 (fall 1981), pp. 607–29

Dunn, Michael Collins 'Soviet Interests in the Arabian Peninsula: The Aden Pact and Other Paper Tigers', *American–Arab Affairs*, no. 8 (spring 1984), pp. 92–8

al-Ebraheem, Hassan Ali *Kuwait and the Gulf: Small States and the International System* (Washington, Georgetown University, Center for Contemporary Arab Studies; London, Croom Helm, 1984)

Eilts, Hermann Frederick 'Security Considerations in the Persian Gulf', *International Security*, vol. 5, no. 2 (1980), pp. 79–113

Epstein, Joshua M. 'Soviet Vulnerabilities in Iran and the RDF Deterrent' *International Security*, vol. 6, no. 2 (fall 1981), pp. 126–58
—— 'Horizontal Escalation: Sour Notes of a Recurrent Theme', *International Security*, vol. 8, no. 3 (winter 1983–4), pp. 19–31
Erb, Richard D. (guest ed.) 'The Arab Oil-Producing States of the Gulf: Political and Economic Developments', *AEI Foreign Policy and Defense Review*, vol. 2, nos 3–4 (1980), pp. 1–88 (entire issue)
Fabyanic, Thomas A. 'Conceptual Planning and the Rapid Deployment Joint Task Force', *Armed Forces and Society*, vol. 7, no. 3 (1981), pp. 343–65
Farid, Abdel Magid (ed.) *Oil and Security in the Arabian Gulf* (London, Croom Helm, for the Arab Research Centre, 1981)
—— (ed.) *The Red Sea: Prospects for Stability* (London, Croom Helm; New York, St Martin's Press, 1984)
Farley, Jonathan 'The Gulf War and the Littoral States', *The World Today*, vol. 40, no. 7 (July 1984), pp. 269–76.
Fiennes, Ranulph *Where Soldiers Fear to Tread* (London, Hodder & Stoughton, 1975)
Friedland, Edward, Paul Seabury and Aaron Wildavsky *The Great Detente Disaster: Oil and the Decline of American Foreign Policy* (New York, Basic Books, 1974)
Fukuyama, Francis *The Soviet Threat to the Persian Gulf* (Santa Monica, Ca, Rand Corporation, March 1981 (Rand Paper, no. P-6596))
Gavin, R. J. *Aden Under British Rule, 1839–1967* (London, C. Hurst, 1975)
Gordon, Michael R. 'The Rapid Deployment Force — Too Large, Too Small or Just Right for Its Task?', *National Journal*, 13 March 1982, pp. 451–5
Gormly, James L. 'Keeping the Door Open in Saudi Arabia: The United States and the Dhahran Airfield, 1945–46', *Diplomatic History*, vol. 4, no. 2 (1980), pp. 189–205
Greig, Ian 'The Security of Persian Gulf Oil', *Atlantic Community Quarterly*, vol. 18, no. 2 (1980), pp. 193–200
Grummon, Stephen R. *The Iran–Iraq War: Islam Embattled* (New York, Praeger, for the Georgetown University Center for Strategic and International Studies, 1982 (Washington Papers, no. 92))
The Gulf: Implications for British Withdrawal (Washington, Georgetown University, Center for Strategic and International Studies, February 1969 (Special Report Series, no. 8))
Haffa, Robert P., Jr *The Half War: Planning U.S. Rapid Deployment Forces to Meet a Limited Contingency, 1960–1983* (Boulder, Co, Westview Press, 1984 (Westview Replica Edition))
Halliday, Fred *Arabia Without Sultans* (Harmondsworth, Penguin, 1974; New York, Vintage, 1975)
—— *Mercenaries: 'Counter-Insurgency' in the Gulf* (Nottingham, Spokesman, 1977)
—— 'The Iranian Revolution in International Affairs: Programme and Practice', *Millennium: Journal of International Studies*, vol. 9, no. 2 (1981), pp. 108–21
—— *Soviet Policy in the Arc of Crisis* (Washington, Institute for Policy Studies, 1981). Revised and retitled *Threat From the East? Soviet Policy from Afghanistan and Iran to the Horn of Africa* (Harmondsworth, Penguin Books, 1982)
—— 'South Yemen: Proxyland for Cold Warriors', *Nation*, vol. 238 (26 May 1984), pp. 638–40
—— 'The Yemens: Conflict and Coexistence', *The World Today*, vol. 40, nos 8–9 (August–September 1984), pp. 355–62
Halloran Richard 'Poised for the Persian Gulf', *New York Times Magazine*, 1 April 1984, pp. 38–40, 61
Hanks, Robert J. 'Rapid Deployment in Perspective', *Strategic Review*, vol. 9, no. 2 (1981), pp. 17–23

—— *The U.S. Military Presence in the Middle East: Problems and Prospects* (Cambridge, Ma, Institute for Foreign Policy Analysis, December 1982 (Foreign Policy Report))

Harkavy, Robert E. *Great Power Competition for Overseas Bases: The Geopolitics of Access Diplomacy* (New York, Pergamon Press, 1982)

Hartley, Keith 'Can the UK Afford a Rapid Deployment Force?' *RUSI — Journal of the Royal United Service Institute for Defence Studies*, vol. 127 (March 1982), pp. 18–21

Heath, M. L. 'Stability in the Arabian Peninsula', *Journal of the Royal United Service Institution*, vol. 105, no. 618 (May 1980), pp. 174–85

—— 'Arabian Extremities', *Journal of the Royal Central Asian Society*, vol. 47, pt 3 and 4 (July–October 1960), pp. 260–9

Helms, Christine Moss *Iraq: Eastern Flank of the Arab World* (Washington, Brookings Institution, 1984)

Hensel, Howard M. 'Soviet Policy Towards the Rebellion in Dhofar', *Asian Affairs* (London), vol. 13 (OS 69), pt 2 (July 1982), pp. 183–207

Hickman, William F. 'Did It Really Matter?', *Naval War College Review*, vol. 36, no. 2 (March–April 1983), pp. 17–30

Hoagland, Jim and J. P. Smith 'Saudi Arabia and the United States: Security and Interdependence', *Survival*, vol. 20, no. 2 (March–April 1978), pp. 80–3

Holden, David 'The Persian Gulf: After the British Raj', *Foreign Affairs*, vol. 49, no. 4 (July 1971), pp. 721–35

Holden, David and Richard Johns, with James Buchan *The House of Saud: The Rise and Rule of the Most Powerful Dynasty in the Arab World* (New York, Holt, Rinehart & Winston, 1982)

Howarth, H. M. F. 'The Impact of the Iraq–Iran War on Military Requirements in the Gulf States', *International Defense Review*, no. 10 (1983), pp. 1405–9

Hunter, Shireen 'Arab–Iranian Relations and Stability in the Persian Gulf' *Washington Quarterly*, vol. 7, no. 3 (summer 1984), pp. 67–76

Hurewitz, J. C. *The Persian Gulf: Prospects for Stability* (New York, Foreign Policy Association, April 1974 (Headline Series, no. 220)). Revised and retitled, *The Persian Gulf: After Iran's Revolution* (New York, Foreign Policy Association, April 1979 (Headline Series, no. 244)).

Ignotus, Miles (pseud.) 'Seizing Arab Oil', *Harper's*, vol. 250, no. 1498 (March 1975), pp. 45–62

Islami, A. Reza S. and Rostam Mehraban Kavoussi *The Political Economy of Saudi Arabia* (Seattle, University of Washington, 1984 (Near Eastern Studies, no. 1))

Ismael, Jacqueline S. *Kuwait: Social Change in Historical Perspective* (Syracuse, Syracuse University Press, 1982)

Ismael, Tareq Y. *Iraq and Iran: Roots of Conflict* (Syracuse, Syracuse University Press, 1982)

Iungerich, Raphael 'US Rapid Deployment Forces — USCENTCOM — What is It? Can It Do the Job?', *Armed Forces Journal International*, vol. 122 (October 1984), pp. 88–111 passim, 134

Jabber, Paul, 'Oil, Arms, and Regional Diplomacy: Strategic Dimensions of the Saudi–Egyptian Relationship', in Malcolm H. Kerr and El Sayed Yassin (eds) *Rich and Poor States in the Middle East: Egypt and the New Arab Order* (Boulder, Co, Westview; Cairo, AUC Press, 1981), pp. 415–47

Jeapes, Tony *SAS: Operation Oman* (London, William Kimber, 1980)

Johnson, Maxwell Orme *The Military as an Instrument of U.S. Policy in Southwest Asia: The Rapid Deployment Joint Task Force, 1979–1982* (Boulder, Co, Westview Press, 1982 (Westview Replica Edition))

—— 'Force Projection in Southwest Asia: The Role of Maritime Based Strategy', *Marine Corps Gazette*, vol. 68 (February 1984), pp. 64–8

—— 'Rapid Deployment and the Regional Military Challenge: The Persian Gulf Equation', unpublished paper presented at a US Army War College symposium on 'US Strategic Interests in the Persian Gulf', 27–9 March 1985

Johnson, Thomas M. and Raymond T. Barrett 'The Rapid Deployment Joint Task Force', *US Naval Institute Proceedings*, vol. 106, no. 11 (November 1980), pp. 95–8

—— 'Mining the Strait of Hormuz', *US Naval Institute Proceedings*, vol. 107, no. 12 (December 1981), pp. 83–5

—— 'Omani Navy: Operating in Troubled Waters', *US Naval Institute Proceedings*, vol. 108, no. 3 (March 1982), pp. 99–103

Jordan, Amos A., Jr 'Saudi Arabia: The Next Iran?', *Parameters: Journal of the US Army War College*, vol. 9, no. 1 (March 1979), pp. 2–8

Karaosmanoglu, Ali L. 'Turkey's Security and the Middle East', *Foreign Affairs*, vol. 62, no. 1 (1983), pp. 156–75

Katz, Mark N. 'Soviet Policy in the Gulf States', *Current History*, vol. 84, no. 498 (January 1985), pp. 25–8, 41

Kelidar, A. R. 'The Problem of Succession in Saudi Arabia', *Asian Affairs* (London), vol. 65 (NS 9), pt 1 (February 1978), pp. 23–30

Kelley, P. X. 'Progress in the RDJTF', *Marine Corps Gazette*, vol. 65 (June 1981), pp. 38–44

—— 'A Discussion of the Rapid Deployment Force With Lieutenant General P. X. Kelley', *AER Special Analysis*, no. 80–4 (Washington, American Enterprise Institute for Public Policy Research, 1980)

—— 'Rapid Deployment: A Vital Trump', *Parameters: Journal of the US Army War College*, vol. 11, no. 1 (March 1981), pp. 50–3

Kelly, J. B. *Arabia, the Gulf and the West: A Critical View of the Arabs and Their Oil Policy* (London, Weidenfeld & Nicolson; New York, Basic Books, 1980)

—— 'Great Game or Grand Illusion?', *Survey*, vol. 25, no. 2 (1980), pp. 109–27

Kemp, Geoffrey 'Scarcity and Strategy', Foreign Affairs, vol. 56, no. 2 (January 1978), pp. 396–414

—— 'Military Force and Middle East Oil', in David A. Deese and Joseph S. Nye (eds) *Energy and Security* (Cambridge, Ma, Ballinger, for the Harvard Energy and Security Research Project, 1981), pp. 365–87

—— 'Strategic Problems in the Persian Gulf Region', in George S. Wise and Charles Issawi (eds) *Middle East Perspectives: The Next Twenty Years* (Princeton, NJ, Darwin Press, 1981), pp. 71–9

Kennedy, Edward M. 'The Persian Gulf: Arms Race or Arms Control?', *Foreign Affairs*, vol. 54, no. 1 (October 1975), pp. 14–35

Kennedy, Paul M. *The Rise and Fall of British Naval Mastery* (London, Allen Lane, 1976; London, Macmillan, 1983)

Khalifa, Ali Mohammed *The United Arab Emirates: Unity in Fragmentation* (Boulder, Co, Westview Press; London, Croom Helm, 1979)

Khalilzad, Zalmay 'Soviet Dilemmas in Khomeini's Iran', *Australian Outlook*, vol. 38, no. 1 (April 1984), pp. 1–8

Khuri, Fuad I. *Tribe and State in Bahrain: The Transformation of Social and Political Authority in an Arab State* (Chicago, University of Chicago Press, 1980 (Publications of the Center for Middle Eastern Studies, no. 14))

Kingston, Robert C. 'C^3I and the U.S. Central Command', *Signal*, November 1983, pp. 23–5

—— 'From RDF to CENTCOM: New Challenges?', *RUSI — Journal of the Royal United Service Institute for Defence Studies*, vol. 129 (March 1984)

—— Interview in *Armed Forces Journal International*, vol. 121, no. 12 (July 1984), pp. 67–73. Interview conducted by Benjamin F. Schemmer

—— 'US Central Command: Refocusing the Lens of Stability on a Region in Crisis',

Defence '84, November–December 1984, pp. 29–34

Klare, Michael *Beyond the 'Vietnam Syndrome': U.S. Interventionism in the 1980s* (Washington, Institute for Policy Studies, 1981)

Kostiner, Joseph *The Struggle for South Yemen* (London, Croom Helm; New York, St Martin's Press, 1984)

Koury, Enver M. 'The Impact of the Geopolitical Situation of Iraq Upon the Gulf Cooperation Council', *Middle East Insight*, vol. 2, no. 5 (January–February 1983), pp. 28–35

Koury, Enver M. and Emile A. Nakhleh (eds), with Thomas W. Mullen *The Arabian Peninsula, Red Sea and Gulf: Strategic Considerations* (Hyattsville, MD, Institute of Middle Eastern and North African Affairs, 1979)

Krulak, Victor H. 'The Rapid Deployment Force: Criteria and Imperatives', *Strategic Review*, vol. 8, no. 2 (1980), pp. 39–43

Kuniholm, Bruce R. 'What the Saudis Really Want: A Primer for the Reagan Administration', *Orbis*, vol. 25, no. 1 (1981), pp. 107–21

—— *The Persian Gulf and United States Policy: A Guide to Issues and References* (Claremont, Ca, Regina Books, 1984 (Regina Guides to Contemporary Issues))

El-Kuwaize, Abdullah 'The Gulf Cooperation Council and the Concept of Economic Integration', *American–Arab Affairs*, no. 7 (winter 1983–4), pp. 45–9

Lacey, Robert *The Kingdom: Arabia and the House of Saud* (New York, Harcourt Brace Jovanovich, 1982)

Lawrence, Robert G. 'Arab Perceptions of U.S. Security Policy in Southwest Asia', *American–Arab Affairs*, no. 5 (1983), pp. 27–38

—— *US Policy in Southwest Asia: A Failure in Perspective* (Washington, National Defense University Press, 1984 (National Security Essays, series 84–1))

Ledger, David *Shifting Sands: The British in South Arabia* (London, Peninsular Publishing, 1983)

Lee, David *Flight From the Middle East: A History of the Royal Air Force in the Arabian Peninsula and Adjacent Territories, 1945–1972* (London, HMSO, 1980)

Leffler, Melvyn P. 'From the Truman Doctrine to the Carter Doctrine: Lessons and Dilemmas of the Cold War', *Diplomatic History*, Vol. 7, no. 4 (fall 1983), pp. 245–66

Lenczowski, George 'The Arc of Crisis: Its Central Sector', *Foreign Affairs*, vol. 57, no. 4 (1979), pp. 796–820

—— 'The Soviet Union and the Persian Gulf: An Encircling Strategy', *International Journal*, vol. 37, no. 2 (1982), pp. 307–27

Levy, Walter, J. *Oil Strategy and Politics, 1941–1981*, ed. Melvin A. Conant (Boulder, Co, Westview Press, 1982)

Litwak, Robert *Sources of Inter-State Conflict* (London, Gower, for the International Institute for Strategic Studies, 1981 (Security in the Persian Gulf, no. 2))

Long, David E. *Saudi Arabia* (Beverly Hills, Ca, Sage Publications, for the Georgetown University Center for Strategic and International Studies, 1976 (Washington Papers, no. 39))

—— 'US–Saudi Relations: A Foundation of Mutual Needs', *American–Arab Affairs*, no. 4 (spring 1983), pp. 12–22

—— *The United States and Saudi Arabia: Ambivalent Allies* (Boulder, Co, Westview Press, 1985 (MERI Special Studies, no. 3))

Louis, William Roger *The British Empire in the Middle East, 1945–1951: Arab Nationalism, the United States, and Postwar Imperialism* (Oxford, Clarendon Press, 1984)

Luce, William 'Britain's Withdrawal from the Middle East and Persian Gulf', *Journal of the Royal United Service Institution*. vol. 114, no. 653 (March 1969), pp. 4–10

Luttwak, Edward 'Cubans in Arabia? Or, the Meaning of Strategy', *Commentary*,

vol. 68, no. 6 (December 1979), pp. 62–6
MacDonald, Charles G. 'The United States and the Gulf Conflict Scenarios', *Middle East Insight*, vol. 3, no. 1 (1983), pp. 23–7
McNaugher, Thomas L. 'Balancing Soviet Power in the Persian Gulf', *Brookings Review*, vol. 1, no. 4 (1983), pp. 20–5
—— 'Arms and Allies on the Arabian Peninsula', *Orbis*, vol. 28, no. 3 (fall 1984), pp. 489–526
—— 'Deterring Soviet Forces in Southwest Asia', in Stephen J. Cimbala (ed.) *National Security Strategy: Choices and Limits* (New York, Praeger, 1984 (Foreign Policy Research Institute Series)), pp. 125–54
—— *Arms and Oil: U.S. Military Strategy and the Persian Gulf* (Washington, Brookings Institution, 1985)
—— 'Southwest Asia: The Crises That Never Came', in Barry M. Blechman and Edward N. Luttwak (eds) *International Security Yearbook 1984/85* (Boulder, Co, Westview Press, for Georgetown University Center for Strategic and International Studies), pp. 144–64
McNaugher, Thomas L. and William Quandt *Oil and the Outcome of the Iran–Iraq War* (Cambridge, Ma, Cambridge Energy Research Associates, 1984 (Private Report))
Malik, Hafeez 'Struggle for Power and Oil in the Persian Gulf', *Journal of South Asian and Middle Eastern Studies*, vol. 3, no. 3 (1980), pp. 3–14
—— (ed.) *International Security in Southwest Asia* (New York, Praeger, 1984)
Manning, Robert A. 'America's Newest Tripwire', *Inquiry* (San Francisco), vol. 6 (January 1983), pp. 22–5
Mansur, Abdul Kasim (pseud.) 'The Military Balance in the Persian Gulf: Who Will Guard the Gulf States from Their Guardians?', *Armed Forces Journal International*, vol. 118, no. 3 (November 1980), pp. 44–86
Martin, L. W. *British Defence Policy: The Long Recessional* (London, Institute for Strategic Studies, November 1969 (Adelphi Papers, no. 61))
Martin, Lenore, G. 'Policy Implications of Boundary Disputes in the Persian Gulf', *Middle East Review*, vol. 15, nos 1–2 (1982–3), pp. 25–32
—— *The Unstable Gulf: Threats From Within* (Boston, Lexington Books, 1983)
Meo, Leila (ed.) *U.S. Strategy in the Gulf: Intervention Against Liberation* (Belmont, Ma, Association of Arab–American University Graduates, October 1981 (AAUG Monograph Series, no. 14))
Miller, Aaron David *Search for Security: Saudi Arabian Oil and American Foreign Policy, 1939–1949* (Chapel Hill, University of North Carolina Press, 1980)
Miller, Marshall Lee 'Will Iran or Iraq Close the Strait of Hormuz?', *Armed Forces Journal International*, vol. 121 (December 1983), pp. 24–6
Monroe, Elizabeth 'British Bases in the Middle East: Assets or Liabilities?', *International Affairs* (London), vol. 42. no. 1 (January 1966), pp. 24–34
—— (rapporteuse) *The Changing Balance of Power in the Persian Gulf: The Report of an International Seminar at the International Center for Mediterranean Studies; Rome*, Sir Denis Wright, Chairman (New York, American Universities Field Staff, 1972)
—— *Britain's Moment in the Middle East, 1914–71*, 2nd edn (Baltimore, Johns Hopkins University Press, 1981)
Mossavar-Rahmani, Bijan 'The War and the World Oil Market', *Orbis*, vol. 28, no. 3 (fall 1984), pp. 450–6
Nakhleh, Emile *Arab–American Relations in the Persian Gulf* (Washington, American Enterprise Institute for Public Policy Research, March 1975 (Foreign Affairs Studies, no. 17))
—— *Bahrain: Political Development in a Modernizing Society* (Lexington, Ma, Lexington Books/D. C. Heath, 1976)

—— *The Persian Gulf and American Policy* (New York, Praeger, 1982)
Neumann, Robert G. and Shireen T. Hunter 'Crisis in the Gulf: Reasons for Concern But Not Panic', *American–Arab Affairs*, no. 9 (summer 1984), pp. 16–21
Nevo, Joseph 'The Saudi Royal Family: The Third Generation', *Jerusalem Quarterly*, no. 31 (spring 1984), pp. 79–90
Newsom, David D. 'America EnGulfed', *Foreign Policy*, no. 43 (summer 1981), pp. 17–32
Niblock, Tim (ed.) *Social and Economic Development in the Arab Gulf* (London, Croom Helm, for the University of Exeter Centre for Arab Gulf Studies, 1980)
—— (ed.) *State, Society and Economy in Saudi Arabia* (London, Croom Helm, for the University of Exeter Centre for Arab Gulf Studies, 1982)
Noyes, James H. *The Clouded Lens: Persian Gulf Security and U.S. Policy*, 2nd edn (Stanford, Ca, Hoover Institution Press, 1982 (Hoover International Studies))
Nye, Roger P. 'Political and Economic Integration in the Arab States of the Gulf', *Journal of South Asian and Middle Eastern Studies*, vol. 2, no. 1 (fall 1978), pp. 3–21
Nyrop, Richard F. (ed.) *Area Handbook for the Persian Gulf States* (Washington, USGPO, 1977 (American University, Foreign Area Studies))
—— (ed.) *Saudi Arabia: A Country Study*, 4th edn (Washington, USGPO, 1984 (American University, Foreign Area Studies))
O'Ballance, Edgar 'The Rapid Deployment Force — Another Look', *National Defense*, vol. 66 (February 1982), pp. 34–6, 62
Ochsenwald, William 'Saudi Arabia and the Islamic Revival', *International Journal of Middle East Studies*, vol. 13, no. 3 (August 1981), pp. 271–86
Olayan, Suliman S. 'Saudi Arabia: The Burden of Moderation', *Washington Quarterly*, vol. 6, no. 4 (autumn 1983), pp. 32–41
O'Neill, Bard E. *Petroleum and Security: The Limitations of Military Power in the Persian Gulf* (Washington, National Defense University, October 1977 (Research Directorate Monograph 77-4))
Page, Stephen, *The USSR and Arabia: The Development of Soviet Policies and Attitudes Towards the Countries of the Arabian Peninsula* (London, Central Asian Research Centre; New York, International Publications Service, 1971)
—— 'Moscow and the Arabian Peninsula', *American–Arab Affairs*, no. 8 (spring 1984), pp. 83–91
—— *The Soviet Union and the Yemens: Influence in Asymmetrical Relationships* (New York, Praeger, 1985)
Paget, Julian *Last Post: Aden 1964–67* (London: Faber & Faber, 1969)
Pakravan, Karim, *Oil Supply Disruptions in the 1980s: An Economic Analysis* (Stanford, Ca, Hoover Institution Press, 1984 ((Hoover International Studies))
Parry, R. St P. 'The Navy in the Persian Gulf', *Journal of the Royal United Service Institution*, vol. 75 (May 1930), pp. 314–31
Paul, Jim 'Insurrection at Mecca', *MERIP Reports*, no. 91 (October 1980), pp. 3–4
Perkins, K. 'Oman 1975: The Year of Decision', *Journal of the Royal United Service Institution*, vol. 124, no. 1 (March 1979), pp. 38–45
Peterson, J. E. 'Britain and "the Oman War": An Arabian Entanglement', *Asian Affairs* (London), vol. 63, pt 3 (October 1976), pp. 285–98
—— 'Guerrilla Warfare and Ideological Confrontation: The Rebellion in Dhufar', *World Affairs*, vol. 139, no. 4 (1977), pp. 278–95
—— *Oman in the Twentieth Century: Political Foundations of an Emerging State* (London, Croom Helm; New York, Barnes & Noble, 1978)
—— *Conflict in the Yemens and Superpower Involvement* (Washington, Georgetown University, Center for Contemporary Arab Studies, Occasional Paper, 1981)
—— 'The Yemen Arab Republic and the Politics of Balance', *Asian Affairs*

(London), vol. 68, pt 3 (October 1981), pp. 254–66
—— *Yemen: The Search for a Modern State* (London, Croom Helm; Baltimore, Johns Hopkins University Press, 1982)
—— (ed.) *The Politics of Middle Eastern Oil* (Washington, Middle East Institute, 1983)
—— 'The Arab Response to the Iranian Challenge in the Gulf', in Philip H. Stoddard (ed.) *The Middle East in the 1980s: Problems and Prospects* (Washington, Middle East Institute, 1983), pp. 153–64
—— 'American Policy in the Gulf and the Sultanate of Oman', *American–Arab Affairs*, no. 8 (summer 1984), pp. 117–30
—— 'Defending Arabia: Evolution of Responsibility', *Orbis*, vol. 28, no. 3 (fall 1984), pp. 465–88
—— *Security in the Arabian Peninsula and Gulf States, 1973–1984* (Washington, National Council on US–Arab Relations, 1985)
—— 'Saudi Arabia at the Threshold', in David Partington (ed.) *Middle East Annual — 1984* (Boston, G. K. Hall, 1985)
—— 'The Islands of Arabia: Their Recent History and Strategic Importance', *Arabian Studies*, vol. 7 (1985)
Plascov, Avi *Modernization, Political Development and Stability* (London, Gower, for the International Institute for Strategic Studies, 1982 (Security in the Persian Gulf, no. 3))
Pranger, Robert J. and Dale R. Tahtinen 'American Policy Options in Iran and the Persian Gulf', *AEI Foreign Policy and Defense Review*, vol. 1, no. 2 (1979), pp. 1–29
Price, David Lynn *Oman: Insurgency and Development* (London, Institute for the Study of Conflict, January 1975 (Conflict Studies, no. 53))
—— *Stability in the Gulf: The Oil Revolution* (London, Institute for the Study of Conflict, 1976 (Conflict Studies, no. 71))
—— 'Moscow and the Persian Gulf', *Problems of Communism*, vol. 28, no. 2 (March–April 1979), pp. 1–13
Pridham, B. R. (ed.) *Contemporary Yemen: Politics and Historical Background* (London, Croom Helm; New York, St Martin's Press, for the University of Exeter Centre for Arab Gulf Studies, 1984)
—— (ed.) *The Arab Gulf and the West* (London, Croom Helm, for the University of Exeter Centre for Arab Gulf Studies, 1985)
Quandt, William B. *Saudi Arabia in the 1980s: Foreign Policy, Security, and Oil* (Washington, Brookings Institution, 1981)
—— 'Riyadh Between the Superpowers', *Foreign Policy*, no. 44 (1981), pp. 37–56
—— *Saudi Arabia's Oil Policy* (Washington, Brookings Institution, 1982 (Staff Paper))
—— 'The Gulf War: Policy Options and Regional Implications', *American–Arab Affairs*, no. 9 (summer 1984), pp. 1–7
Quinlan, David A. *The Role of the Marine Corps in Rapid Deployment Forces* (Washington, National Defense University Press, 1983 (National Security Essay Series 82-3))
Ramazani, Rouhollah K. 'Security in the Persian Gulf', *Foreign Affairs*, vol. 57, no. 4 (1979), pp. 821–35
—— 'The Genesis of the Carter Doctrine', in George S. Wise and Charles Issawi (eds) *Middle East Perspectives: The Next Twenty Years* (Princeton, NJ, Darwin Press, 1981), pp. 165–80
—— *The Persian Gulf and the Strait of Hormuz* (Alphen aan den Rijn, Sijthoff & Nordhoff, 1979 (International Straits of the World, vol. 3))
—— 'Iran's Islamic Revolution and the Persian Gulf', *Current History*, vol. 84, no. 498 (January 1985), pp. 5–8, 40–1

Record, Jeffrey *The Rapid Deployment Force and U.S. Military Intervention in the Persian Gulf* (Cambridge, Ma, Institute for Foreign Policy Analysis, 1981 (Special Report))
—— *Revising U.S. Military Strategy: Tailoring Means to Ends* (Washington, Pergamon-Brassey's, 1984; published in co-operation with the Institute for Foreign Policy Analysis). Esp. Ch. 4, 'The Carter Doctrine, Rapid Deployment Force, and Worldwide War Strategy, 1979–Present', pp. 36–48
Ricks, Thomas M. *The Iranian People's Revolution: Its Nature and Implications for the Gulf States* (Washington, Georgetown University Center for Contemporary Arab Studies, April 1979 (CCAS Reports))
Roche, James G. 'Projection of Military Power to Southwest Asia: An Asymmetrical Problem', in Uri Ra'anan, Robert L. Pfaltzgraff, Jr, and Geoffrey Kemp (eds) *Projection of Power: Perspectives, Perceptions and Problems* (Hamden, Ct, Archon Books, 1982), pp. 218–25
Ross, Dennis 'Considering Soviet Threats to the Persian Gulf', *International Security*, vol. 6, no. 2 (1981), pp. 159–80
—— 'Soviet Views Toward the Gulf War', *Orbis*, vol. 28, no. 3 (fall 1984), pp. 437–47
—— 'The Soviet Union and the Persian Gulf', *Political Science Quarterly*, vol. 99, no. 4 (winter 1984–5), pp. 615–35
Rubin, Barry 'The Gulf Arab States and Iran', *Middle East Insight*, vol. 2, no. 5 (January–February 1983), pp. 36–8
Rubinstein, A. Z. 'Soviet Persian Gulf Policy', *Middle East Review*, vol. 10, no. 2 (1977–8), pp. 47–55
—— 'The Soviet Union and the Arabian Peninsula', *The World Today*, vol. 35, no. 11 (November 1979), pp. 442–52
—— (ed.) *The Great Game: Rivalry in the Persian Gulf and South Asia* (New York, Praeger, for the Foreign Policy Research Institute, 1983)
al-Rumaihi, Mohammed 'Kuwaiti–American Relations: A Case of Mismanagement', *American–Arab Affairs*, no. 9 (summer 1984), pp. 77–80
Rustow, Dankwart A. 'U.S.–Saudi Relations and the Oil Crises of the 1980s', *Foreign Affairs*, vol. 55, no. 3 (April 1977), pp. 494–516
Salameh, Ghassane 'Political Power and the Saudi State', trans. from the French by Vivian Steir, *MERIP Reports*, no. 91 (October 1980), pp. 5–22
al-Salem, Faisal 'The U.S. and the Gulf: What Do the Arabs Want?', *Journal of South Asian and Middle Eastern Studies*, vol. 6, no. 1 (1982), pp. 8–32
Samore, Gary 'The Persian Gulf', in David A. Deese and Joseph S. Nye (eds) *Energy and Security* (Cambridge, Ma, Ballinger, for the Harvard Energy and Security Research Project, 1981), pp. 49–110
Saundby, Robert 'Air Power in Limited Wars', *Journal of the Royal United Service Institution*, vol. 103, no. 611 (August 1958), pp. 378–83
Shaw, John A. and David E. Long *Saudi Arabian Modernization: The Impact of Change on Stability* (New York, Praeger, for the Georgetown University Center for Strategic and International Studies, 1982 (Washington Papers, no. 89))
Singer, S. Fred 'Limits to Arab Oil Power', *Foreign Policy*, no. 30 (1978), pp. 53–67
Sirriyeh, Hussein *US Policy in the Gulf, 1968–1977* (London, Ithaca Press, 1984)
—— 'Conflict Over the Gulf Islands of Abu Musa and the Tunbs, 1968–1971', *Journal of South Asian and Middle Eastern Studies*, vol. 7, no. 2 (winter 1984), pp. 73–86
Smiley, David de C. 'Muscat and Oman', *Journal of the Royal United Service Institution*, vol. 105, no. 617 (February 1960), pp. 29–47
Smiley, David de C. with Peter Kemp *Arabian Assignment* (London, Leo Cooper, 1975)

Smith, Malcolm *British Air Strategy Between the Wars* (Oxford, Clarendon Press, 1984)
Smolansky, Oles M. 'Moscow and the Persian Gulf: An Analysis of Soviet Ambitions and Potential', *Orbis*, vol. 14, no. 1 (spring 1970), pp. 92–108
al-Sowayegh, Abdulaziz *Arab Petropolitics* (London, Croom Helm; New York, St Martin's Press, 1984)
Standish, J. F. 'British Maritime Policy in the Persian Gulf', *Middle Eastern Studies*, vol. 3, no. 4 (1967), pp. 324–54
Staudenmaier, William O. 'Military Policy and Strategy in the Gulf War', *Parameters: Journal of the US Army War College*, vol. 12, no. 2 (June 1982), pp. 25–35
Sterner, Michael 'The Iran–Iraq War', *Foreign Affairs* vol. 63, no. 1 (fall 1984), pp. 128–43
Stevens, T. M. P. 'Operations in the Radfan, 1964', *Journal of the Royal United Service Institution*, vol. 110, no. 640 (November 1965), pp. 335–46
Stewart, Richard A. 'Oman: The Next Crisis?', *US Naval Institute Proceedings*, vol. 106, no. 4 (April 1980), pp. 97–102
Stocker, John Joseph 'Rapid Deployment Force', Issue Brief no. IB 80027, Congressional Research Service, Library of Congress. Printed as pp. 327–36 of: US Congress, Committee on Foreign Relations, Subcommittee on Near Eastern and South Asian Affairs, *U.S. Security Interests in Southwest Asia*; Hearings (Washington, USGPO, 1980)
Stoff, Michael B. *Oil, War, and American Security: The Search for a National Policy on Foreign Oil, 1941–1947* (New Haven, Yale University Press, 1980)
Stookey, Robert W. *South Yemen: A Marxist Republic in Arabia* (Boulder, Co, Westview Press; London, Croom Helm, , 1982)
—— (ed.) The Arabian Peninsula: Zone of Ferment (Stanford, Ca, Hoover Institution Press, 1984)
Stork, Joe and Martha Wenger 'US Ready to Intervene in the Gulf War', *MERIP Reports*, no. 125–6 (July–September 1984), pp. 44–8
Sullivan, Robert R. 'The Architecture of Western Security in the Persian Gulf', *Orbis*, vol. 14, no. 1 (spring 1970), pp. 71–91
Szaz, Z. Michael (ed.) *The Impact of the Iranian Events Upon Persian Gulf and U.S. Security* (Washington, American Foreign Policy Institute, 1979)
Tahja, Arooj 'Naval Development in the Persian Gulf', *Naval Forces*, vol. 5, no. 3 (1984), pp. 22–3, 25–9
Tahir-Kheli, Shirin and Shaheen Ayubi (eds) *The Iran–Iraq War: New Weapons, Old Conflicts* (New York, Praeger, 1983 (Foreign Policy Research Institute Series))
Tahir-Kheli, Shirin and William O. Staudenmaier 'The Saudi–Pakistani Military Relationship: Implications for U.S. Policy', *Orbis*, vol. 26, no. 1 (1982), pp. 155–71.
Tahtinen, Dale R. *Arms in the Persian Gulf* (Washington, American Enterprise Institute for Public Policy Research, 1974 (Foreign Affairs Studies, no. 10))
—— *National Security Challenges to Saudi Arabia* (Washington, American Enterprise Institute for Public Policy Research, 1978 (AEI Studies, no. 194))
Templewood, Samuel, Viscount (Sir Samuel Hoare) *Empire of the Air: The Advent of the Air Age, 1922–1929* (London, Collins, 1957)
Thompson, W. Scott 'The Persian Gulf and the Correlation of Forces', *International Security*, vol. 7, no. 1 (1982), pp. 157–80
Townsend, John *Oman: The Making of a Modern State* (London, Croom Helm; New York, St Martin's Press, 1977)
Tucker, Robert W. 'Oil: The Issue of American Intervention', *Commentary*, vol. 59, no. 1 (January 1975), pp. 21–31

—— 'American Power and the Persian Gulf', *Commentary*, vol. 70, no. 5 (November 1980), pp. 25–41
—— 'The Purposes of American Power', *Foreign Affairs*, vol. 59, no. 2 (1980–1), pp. 241–74
—— *The Purposes of American Power: An Essay on National Security* (New York, Praeger, 1981 (A Lehrman Institute Book))
Turner, Louis and James Bedore 'Saudi Arabia: The Power of the Purse-Strings', *International Affairs* (London), vol. 54, no. 3 (July 1978), pp. 405–20
US Congress, Congressional Budget Office *US Projection Forces: Requirements, Scenarios and Options* (Washington, Congressional Budget Office, 1978)
—— *The Marine Corps in the 1980s: Prestocking Proposals, the Rapid Deployment Force, and Other Issues* (Washington, USGPO, 1980)
US Congress, House of Representatives, Committee on Appropriations, Subcommittee on the Department of Defense *Department of Defense Appropriations for 1983; Hearings*, pt. 6: *Readiness Command and Rapid Deployment Force* (Washington, USGPO, 1982)
US Congress, House of Representatives, Committee on Foreign Affairs *The United States and the Persian Gulf;* Report (Washington, USGPO, 1982)
—— *U.S. Security Interests in the Persian Gulf;* Report of a Staff Study Mission to the Persian Gulf, Middle East, and Horn of Africa, October 21–November 13, 1980 (Washington, USGPO, 1981)
US Congress, House of Representatives, Committee on Foreign Affairs, Subcommittee on Europe and the Middle East *Proposed Arms Transfers to the Yemen Arab Republic;* Hearings (Washington, USGPO, 1979)
—— *U.S. Interests in, and Policies Toward, the Persian Gulf, 1980;* Hearings (Washington, USGPO, 1980)
—— *Saudi Arabia and the United States: The New Context in an Evolving 'Special Relationship';* Report (Washington, USGPO, 1981)
—— *Developments in the Persian Gulf, June 1984;* Hearing (Washington, USGPO, 1984)
US Congress, House of Representatives, Committee on Foreign Affairs, Subcommittee on the Near East *US Interests in and Policy Toward the Persian Gulf;* Hearings (Washington, USGPO, 1972)
US Congress, House of Representatives, Committee on Foreign Affairs, Subcommittee on the Near East and South Asia *New erspectives on the Persian Gulf;* Hearings (Washington, USGPO, 1973)
US Congress, House of Representatives, Committee on Foreign Affairs, Subcommittees on International Security and Scientific Affairs, and on Europe and the Middle East *Proposed U.S. Arms Sales to Saudi Arabia:* Hearings (Washington, USGPO, 1980)
US Congress, House of Representatives, Committee on Foreign Affairs and Joint Economic Committee *U.S. Policy Toward the Persian Gulf;* Hearings (Washington, USGPO, 1983)
US Congress, House of Representatives, Committee on International Relations *Oil Fields as Military Objectives: A Feasibility Study*, prepared by the Congressional Research Service, Library of Congress (Washington, USGPO, 1975)
US Congress, House of Representatives, Committee on International Relations, Special Subcommittee on Investigations *The Persian Gulf 1975: The Continuing Debate on Arms Sales;* Hearings (Washington, USGPO, 1976)
—— *United States Arms Policies in the Persian Gulf and Red Sea Areas: Past, Present and Future;* Report of a Staff Survey Mission to Ethiopia, Iran, and the Arabian Peninsula (Washington, USGPO, 1977)
US Congress, House of Representatives, Committee on the Budget *Military Readiness and the Rapid Deployment Joint Task Force;* Hearings, 30 September

and 1 October 1980 (Washington, USGPO, 1980)

US Congress, Senate, Committee on Appropriations, Subcommittee on Foreign Assistance and Related Programs *Sales of Stinger Missiles to Saudi Arabia;* Hearings (Washington, USGPO, 1984)

US Congress, Senate, Committee on Armed Services *Military and Technical Implications of the Proposed Sale to Saudi Arabia of Airborne Warning and Control System (AWACS) and F-15 Enhancements;* Hearings (Washington, USGPO, 1981)

US Congress, Senate, Committee on Foreign Relations *United States Foreign Policy Objectives and Overseas Military Installations,* prepared by the Congressional Research Service, Library of Congress, April 1979 (Washington, USGPO, 1979)

—— *U.S. Security Interests and Policies in Southwest Asia;* Hearings (Washington, USGPO, 1980)

—— *Persian Gulf Situation;* Hearings (Washington, USGPO, 1981)

—— *Arms Sales Package to Saudi Arabia, Parts I and II;* Hearings (Washington, USGPO, 1981)

—— *The Proposed AWACS/F-15 Enhancement Sale to Saudi Arabia:* Staff Report (Washington, USGPO, 1981)

—— *War in the Gulf;* Staff Report, August 1984 (Washington, USGPO, 1984)

US Congress, Senate, Committee on Foreign Relations, Subcommittee on Near Eastern and South Asian Affairs *U.S. Security Interests and Policies in Southwest Asia;* Hearings (Washington, USGPO, 1980)

US General Accounting Office. *Critical Factors Affecting Saudi Arabia's Oil Decisions;* Report by the Comptroller General of the US (Washington, GAO, 12 May 1978)

US Library of Congress, Congressional Research Service *Western Vulnerability to a Disruption of Persian Gulf Oil Supplies: U.S. Interests and Options* (Washington, 24 March 1983)

Van Hollen, Christopher 'Don't Engulf the Gulf', *Foreign Affairs,* vol. 59, no. 5 (1981), pp. 1064–78

Vernant, Jacques 'L'Occident et la sécurité du Golfe', *Defense Nationale,* vol. 37 (May 1981), pp. 135–41

Verrier, Anthony 'Strategically Mobile Forces — U.S. Theory and British Practice', *Journal of the Royal United Service Institution,* vol. 106, no. 624 (November 1961), pp. 479–85

Volman, Daniel 'Commanding the Center', *MERIP Reports,* no. 125–6 (July–September 1984), pp. 49–50, 64

Waltz, Kenneth N. 'A Strategy for the Rapid Deployment Force', *International Security,* vol. 5, no. 4 (1981), pp. 49–73

Warner, Phillip *The Special Air Service* (London, William Kimber, 1971)

Watt, D. C. 'The Decision to Withdraw from the Gulf', *Political Quarterly,* vol. 39, no. 3 (July–September 1968), pp. 310–21

Weeks, Albert L. 'The Risks of Far-Flung Development', *Military Science Technology,* vol. 2, no. 1 (1982), pp. 50–9

Wenger, Martha 'The Central Command: Getting to the War on Time', *MERIP Reports,* no. 128 (November–December 1984), pp. 19–26

West, F. J., Jr 'Limited U.S.–Soviet Conflict and the RDF', *Marine Corps Gazette,* vol. 64 (August 1980), pp. 39–46

Whetten, Lawrence 'Security and South-West Asia: Security Implications of Recent Political Changes', *The Round Table,* no. 273 (January 1979), pp. 31–40

Wiley, Marshall W. 'American Security Concerns in the Gulf', *Orbis,* vol. 28, no. 3 (fall 1984), pp. 456–64

Wilson, A. D. R. G. 'Relevance of Air Mobility to the Middle East', *Army Quarterly,* vol. 69, no. 2 (January 1955), pp. 161–84

Wilson, Desmond P. *The Persian Gulf and the National Interest* (Alexandria, Va, Center for Naval Analyses, 1982)

Wohlstetter, Albert 'Meeting the Threat in the Persian Gulf', *Survey*, vol. 25, no. 2 (spring 1980), pp. 128–88

—— 'Half-Wars and Half-Policies in the Persian Gulf', in W. Scott Thompson (ed.) *National Security in the 1980s: From Weakness to Strength* (San Francisco, Institute for Contemporary Studies, 1980), pp. 123–71

—— 'Les Etats-Unis et la securité du Golfe', *Politique Etrangère*, vol. 46, no. 1 (March 1981), pp. 75–88

Wolfe, Ronald G. (ed.) *The United States, Arabia, and the Gulf* (Washington, Georgetown University Center for Contemporary Arab Studies, 1980 (CCAS Studies in Arab–American Relations))

Yodfat, Aryeh Y. 'The USSR and the Persian Gulf', *Australian Outlook*, vol. 33, no. 1 (April 1979), pp. 60–71

—— *The Soviet Union and the Arabian Peninsula: Soviet Policy Towards the Persian Gulf and Arabia* (London, Croom Helm; New York, St Martin's Press, 1983)

—— *The Soviet Union and Revolutionary Iran* (London, Croom Helm; New York, St Martin's Press, 1984)

Yodfat, Aryeh, Y. and Mordechai Abir *In the Direction of the Persian Gulf: The Soviet Union and the Persian Gulf* (London, Frank Cass, 1977)

Yorke, Valerie 'Security in the Gulf: A Strategy of Pre-emption', *The World Today*, vol. 36, no. 7 (July 1980), pp. 239–50

—— *The Gulf in the 1980s* (London, Royal Institute of International Affairs, 1980 (Chatham House Papers, no. 6))

—— 'Bid for Gulf Unity', *The World Today*, vol. 37, nos. 7–8 (July–August 1981), pp. 246–9

—— 'Oil, the Middle East and Japan's Search for Security', *International Affairs* (London), vol. 57, no. 3 (1981), pp. 428–48

Zabarah, Mohammed Ahmad *Yemen: Traditionalism vs. Modernity* (New York, Praeger, 1982)

Zakheim, Dov S. 'Of Allies and Access', *Washington Quarterly*, vol. 4, no. 1 (1981), pp. 87–96

—— 'Airlifting the Marine Corps: Mismatch or Wave of the Future?', in Uri Ra'anan, Robert L. Pfaltzgraff, Jr, and Geoffrey Kemp (eds) *Projection of Power: Perspectives, Perceptions and Problems* (Hamden, Ct, Archon Books, 1982), pp. 120–37

Zartman, I. William 'The Power of American Purposes', *Middle East Journal*, vol. 35, no. 2 (1981), pp. 163–77

Index

Abadan (Iran) 54, 58, 129–30
'Abd al-'Aziz Al Sa'ud (Ibn Sa'ud, founder of Saudi Arabia) 36–8, 188, 193
'Abd Allah b. 'Abd al-'Aziz (Crown Prince of Saudi Arabia) 193, 198
'Abd al-Nasir, Jamal (President of Egypt) 194
'Abd al-Wahhab, Muhammad 135, 188
Aboukir, Battle of (1798) 10
Abu Dhabi (UAE) 211
   Abu Dhabi Defence Force 211
Aden, British military presence in 51, 56, 80–2, 92–8
   defenses during Second World War 52
   struggle for independence 92–8
Aden Airways 57
Aden Protectorate, air policing in 78–83
Aden Trades Union Congress 94
Afghanistan 125
Ahwar (Aden Protectorate) 25
air facilities in Arabian Peninsula, on eve of Second World War (table) 49
air policing 28–40, 247n2
   in Aden Protectorate 78–83
air routes in Arabian Peninsula 18–28
   political impact of 27–8
Airborne Warning and Control System (AWACS) aircraft 196
airfields in Arabian Peninsula, to end of Second World War (map) 26
airplanes, first use in Arabia 18–20
'Ajman Defence Force 211
Al Bu Sa'id, ruling family of Oman 85
Al Thani, ruling family of Qatar 28
Alford, Jonathan 150
Algiers accord (1975) 128
Amanullah (King of Afghanistan) 33
'Amman (Jordan) 32
Anglo-American rivalry in the Arabian Peninsula, emergence of 58–60
anti-submarine warfare activities in Arabian Peninsula 51
Arab Cold War 214

Arab Nationalists' Movement 94–5, 99
Arabian American Oil Company (ARAMCO) 116–17
Arabian Mission of Reformed Church of America 116
Arabian Peninsula
   post-Second-World-War security assessments 56–63
   role in Second World War 50–6
Arabian Peninsula states, military capabilities of (table) 192
ARAMCO see Arabian American Oil Company
Asad Military City (Saudi Arabia) 198
'Asir (Saudi Arabia) 201
al-Asnaj, 'Abdullah (South Yemeni politician) 94
AWACS see Airborne Warning and Control System aircraft
al-'Ayqa (Oman) 38

BOAC (British Overseas Airways Corporation) 56–7
Baghdad (Iraq) 54, 170
Baghdad Pact 147
Bahrain 25, 27, 115
   Bahrain Defence Force 212–13
   formation of state of 189
   importance during WWII 48
   Italian air raid on (1940) 52
   RAF Air Liaison Officer in 38
   role during Kuwait crisis (1961) 90–1
Balhaf (Aden Protectorate) 25
Bandar Pahlavi (Iran) 55
Bandar Qasim (Somalia) 51, 52
Bani Bu 'Ali (Omani tribe) 11–12, 38–9
Basra (Iraq) 54
Basra-Aden air route 23–7
Batman (Turkey) 163
Bishara, 'Abdullah (GCC Secretary-General) 219
Bismark 16n8
'Blue Line' agreement (1913) 14
Bray, Sir Denys (Foreign Secretary of the Government of India) 42–4
Britain
   administration in Gulf 45–8, 115
   and Aden struggle for independence

267

92–8
and Dhufar rebellion 99–105
and early communications in Gulf 13
and Gulf security, lessons of 229–32
and military deployment to Kuwait (1961) 88–92
and Oman: involvement in Oman War (1950s) 83–8; military assistance to 206
and Persian government (1920s) 21
and Saudi Arabia 60, 112–13
  assistance to early Saudi air force 19
  expatriates in Saudi Arabia 203
and slave trade 13
and United States, rivalry in Arabian Peninsula 58–60
bases in Middle East after Second World War 61
East-of-Suez defence debate 75–105 *passim* 113–14
emerging perceptions of strategic importance of Gulf 40–50
expeditions against 'pirates' in Gulf 10–12
military presence in Arabian Peninsula 98; after Second World War 78–80
official withdrawal from the Gulf 111–15
origins of involvement in Arabia 9–15
post-Second-World-War strategic planning in Middle East 60–3
Residency system in Gulf 12–13
role in Gulf security 150
strategic interests in Arabian Peninsula after Second World War 75–105
British Forces, Arabian Peninsula (BFAP) 80
Brown, Harold (US Secretary of Defense) 152
Brzezinski, Zbigniew (US National Security Adviser) 125, 152
Bubiyan Island (Gulf) 209
al-Buraymi (Oman), Saudi occupation of 85, 113
Busayra (Iraq) 37
Bushire (Iran) 21, 231

C-5A aircraft 164
C-17 aircraft 164
C-141 aircraft 164

Cairo Conference (1921) 20, 30
Cairo West (airfield) 162
CALTEX 116
Canal Zone, British base in 79
Carter, Jimmy 125
Carter Doctrine 126
China, diplomatic relations with Oman 207
Churchill, Winston (British Colonial Secretary and Chancellor of the Exchequer) 20, 30, 32, 34
Collins, John M. 176
Commander British Forces Gulf 98
Committee on Imperial Defence (British)
  Official Sub-committee on the Middle East 46–7
  Persian Gulf Sub-committee 24, 41–5
Congressional Research Service 173
convoy escort activities in Arabian Peninsula 51
Cordesman, Anthony 198
Crater district (Aden) 98
Curzon, Lord (Viceroy of India) 13, 76
Cyprus, British military planning in 79

Da'wa underground movement in Iraq and Kuwait 210
Damavand Line (Dhufar) 102
Dammam (Saudi Arabia) 198, 200
Darby, Phillip 77
Darin (Saudi Arabia) 19
Dawisha, Karen 126
de Gaury, Gerald (RAF Special Services Officer) 37
Defence White Paper (British)
  (1962) 89
  (1966) 97, 114
  (1967) 114
Defense Guidance (US Department of Defense, 1982) 167
Dhahran (Saudi Arabia) 164
  Italian air raid on (1940) 52
  US airfield at 60, 112
Dhofar *see* Dhufar
Dhufar, rebellion in 99–105
  South Yemeni role in 102–3
Dhufar Benevolent Society 99
Dhufar Liberation Front 99, 214
Dhufari Soldiers' Organisation 99
Dickson, H.R.P. (Political Agent, Kuwait) 38
Diego Garcia Island (Indian Ocean)

155, 163
Djibouti 150, 163
Dubai (UAE) 23, 39, 211
　Dubai Defence Force 211
Dunn, Keith A. 168-9

Egypt 239
　and Aden independence struggle 96-7
Epstein, Joshua, M. 169, 170
Erzurum (Turkey) 163
Ethiopia 124
ethnic differences in the Gulf 133-8
Exocet missiles 132

F-15 aircraft 196
Fahud (Oman) 86
Far Eastern reinforcement activities during Second World War 51
Faysal b. 'Abd al-'Aziz (King of Saudi Arabia) 194
　assassination of 144n34
Federation of South Arabia 95-8 *passim*
federation discussions among Gulf states (1968-1971) 114-15, 190
Finkenstein, Treaty of (1807) 10
Fowle, T.C. (Political Resident in the Persian Gulf) 46-8
France
　and Saudi Arabia: expatriates in 203; military assisance to 197, 200
　and the Gulf (nineteenth century) 13-14
　Forces d'Action Rapide 150
　role in Gulf security 149
Front for the Liberation of Occupied South Yemen 95-8 *passim*

GCC *see* Gulf Cooperation Council
Gavin, R.J. 26
Germany, and the Gulf (nineteenth century) 14
al-Ghanam Island (Gulf) 206
Glubb, John Bagot (RAF Special Services Officer) 37
Gulf and surrounding region (map) 156
Gulf Cooperation Council (GCC)
　and Gulf security 185-224
　and primary responsibility for Gulf security 242-6
　arms acquisitions 222-3
　collective air defense system 221
　financial aid to Iraq 246
　formation in 1981 218
　joint military capabilities 223-4
　joint military exercises 221
　Military Committee 221
　organization of 219
　origins of 216-18
　Peninsula Shield exercises 221-2
　political activities of 220
　Rapid Deployment Force 222
　security activities of 220-4
　stated objectives 218
　states of, as mediators 245-6
　Unified Economic Agreement 219
Gulf Foreign Ministers meeting, Muscat (1976) 217
Gulf Investment Corporation 219
Gwadar (Pakistan) 23, 205

Habbaniya (Iraq) 54
Hadramawt air route (proposed) 65n28
Hafr al-Batin (Saudi Arabia) 164
Haig, Alexander (US Secretary of State) 147, 160
Halliday, Fred 124
al-Hamasa (Oman) 85-6, 113
Hammer Line (Dhufar) 102
al-Hasa (Saudi Arabia) 199
al-Hashimi, Faysal (King of Iraq) 30
Hawf (South Yemen) 103
Hijaz, air force 19
al-Hinawi, Ghalib b. 'Ali (Omani rebel and erstwhile imam) 85
al-Hinawi, Talib b. 'Ali (Omani rebel) 85
Hoare, Sir Samuel (British Secretary of State for Air) 42-5
Hormuz, Strait of 173, 207
　US military action and threat to close 173
Husayn, Saddam (President of Iraq) 129, 245

'Ibri (Oman) 86
Ignotus, Miles (pseudonym) 176
ijma', in Saudi Arabia 143n33
Ikhwan movement in Saudi Arabia 32, 36-8, 193
Imperial Airways 20
'Interventionists' 176
Iran
　fall of the Shah (1979) 125
　impact of revolution on Arab littoral of Gulf 213-16

involvement in Dhufar rebellion 104
threat to Kuwait 202
threat to Saudi Arabia 172-3, 202-3
Iran-Iraq war 128-33
  impact on Kuwait 209-10
  lessons for US 172; and Soviet threat 170
Iraq
  Air Officer Commanding, jurisdiction during Second World War 54
  and Kuwait 88-92 *passim*, 202
  and Saudi Arabia 202-3
  British role in 30-2
  Ikhwan attacks on 37-8
  impact of revolution on Arab Gulf states 214-15
  political situation in 137
Iraq Petroleum Company 116
Iraqi Communist Party 137
Islamic Jihad movement 210
Isma'il, 'Abd al-Fattah (President of South Yemen) 142n27
Israel, and Saudi Arabia 202
Italy
  air raid on Bahrain and Dhahran (1940) 52
  and East African campaign (Second World War) 51-3

al-Jabal al-Akhdar (Oman) 87
Jabal Hurriya (South Yemen) 96
Jabal Qamar (Oman) 102
Jabal Samhan (Oman) 100-1
Jabir Al Ahmad Al Sabah (Prime Minister of Kuwait) 218
Jacob, Col. Harold F. (British emissary to Imam of Yemen) 33, 35
al-Janaba (Omani tribe) 38
Japan, role in Gulf security 149
Jask (Iran) 21
Jidda (Saudi Arabia) 198, 200
Jiwani (India), RAF station at 56
joint intervention, as US strategy for Gulf 148-51
Jordan, role in Gulf security 149
Jubayl (Saudi Arabia) 200
Jufair (Bahrain) 113

Kabul 29, 33
Kamaran Island (Red Sea) 52, 66n50
Karaosmanoglu, Ali L. 151
Kavkaz-85, Operation 182n56

Kennedy, Paul M. 75
Kenya 61, 79, 163
Khamis al-Mushayt (Saudi Arabia) 197, 201
Kharg Island (Gulf) 132, 220
Khawr Jarama (Oman) 25
Khomeini, Ayatollah Rouhollah 130
Khormaksar (Aden) 51, 52, 58, 98
Khorramshahr (Iran) 129-30
Khuzestan (Iran) 129-30, 131, 169
  potential Soviet drive on 163-4
King Khalid Military City (Saudi Arabia) 164, 197, 202
Kingston, Lt. Gen., Robert C. (USCENTCOM Commander) 150
Kirkuk (Iraq) 32, 54
Kurds, in Iraq 137
Kuriya Muriya Islands (Arabian Sea) 58
Kuwait 27
  and Ottomans 14
  formation of state of 189
  Ikhwan attacks on 37
  internal security problems in 210
  Iraqi claims on and crisis of 1961 88-92; lessons of 236
  military capabilities of 208-9
  RAF Special Services Officer in 38
  threats to 209-10
Kuwait Oil Company 116

Lahj (South Yemen) 94
Lajes (Azores) 163
Lenczowski, George 123
Leopard Line (Dhufar) 101
Lingeh (Iran) 11
London-India air service 20-2

MacDill Air Force Base (Florida) 153
McNamara, Robert (US Secretary of Defense) 152
McNaugher, Thomas L. 158, 162, 167, 199
Madden, Sir Charles (British Admiral of the Fleet, First Sea Lord, and Chief of the Naval Staff) 43-4
Mahan, Alfred Thayer 16n8
Mahmud, Shaykh (Kurdish governor of Sulaymaniya) 31
Mainbrace Line (Dhufar) 101
majlis, in Saudi Arabia 143n33
Makkawi, 'Abd al-Qawi (Adeni politician) 97

Index 271

Marine Amphibious Brigade 165
Maritime Prepositioned Ship (MPS) flotilla 165
Mark, Clyde R. 176
Masira Island (Arabian Sea) 25, 51
  RAF use of 54, 57, 104
  Sultanate of Oman Air Force use of 205
  US use of 163, 206
Mehrabad (Iran) 54
Mesopotamia, and British interests in 15
Middle East Force (MIDEASTFORCE) see US Navy
military bases, need for 239–40
Military Commander for the Persian Gulf (Government of India) 50
military forces in Arabian Peninsula, emergence of 190–1
Mirbat (Oman) 25, 101
Monroe, Elizabeth 239
Mosul (Iraq) 54
Muhammad bin 'Abdullah ('Mad Mullah' of Somaliland) 29
Muhammad, 'Ali Nasir (President of South Yemen) 202
Muharraq (Bahrain) 58
Mukalla (Aden Protectorate) 25
Mus (Turkey) 163
Muscat (Oman) 27, 206
  government and relations with US (nineteenth century) 59
Muscat and Oman see Oman
Mutla Ridge (Kuwait) 90

al-Nabhani, Sulayman b. Himyar (Omani shaykh) 85
NATO, and Gulf security 150–1
Napoleon 9
Nasser see Jamal 'Abd al-Nasir
National Democratic Front (North Yemen) 136
National Democratic Front for the Liberation of Oman and the Arabian Gulf 100
National Liberation Front (South Yemen) 94–8 passim, 136
Near-Term Prepositioned Ship (NTPS) flotilla 165
Nixon Doctrine 145
Nizwa (Oman) 86
non-intervention, as US strategy for Gulf security 148

North Yemen see Yemen
Noyes, James J. 160, 240

Official Sub-Committee on the Middle East see Committee on Imperial Defence
Ogaden (Ethiopia) 124
oil
  and natural gas reserves (table) 235
  importance of Gulf 232–6
  imports from OPEC producers (table) 234
  world crude production (table) 233
'Oil weapon' 246
Oman
  and province of Dhufar: firqa paramilitary units in 206; Omani military forces in 204; rebellion in 99–105
  control of Sur 38–9
  foreign military assistance to 206
  imamate in 85
  military capabilities 204–7
  Muscat and Oman Field Force 86, 204
  Muscat Levy Corps 204
  political evolution in 187
  rebellion in (1950s) 83–92
  Royal Oman Police 206
  Sultan of Oman's Air Force (SOAF) 205
  Sultan's Armed Forces (SAF) 87, 100–5 passim, 204–7
  Sultanate of Oman Land Forces (SOLF) 206
  Sultanate of Oman Navy (SON) 206
Oman Revolutionary Movement 214
Organisation of Arab Petroleum Exporting Countries (OAPEC) 217
Organisation of Petroleum Exporting Countries (OPEC), US dependence on (table) 234
Organisation for the Liberation of the Occupied South (OLOS) 94–5
Ottoman empire, and the Gulf 14–15

Pakistan
  military personnel in Saudi Arabia 203
  role in Gulf security 151
Palestine
  air control in 40
  British military planning in 79

Index

Pan American Airways 56, 59
Peace Shield system for Saudi Arabia 196
People's Democratic Republic of Yemen, diplomatic relations with Oman 207
People's Socialist Party (Aden) 94
Perim Island (Red Sea) 52
Perpetual Maritime Peace, Treaty of (1853) 12
Persia and Iraq Command (British) 53-5
Persian Gulf Command (US) 55
Persian Gulf Sub-committee *see* Committee of Imperial Defence
Persian Gulf air route 20-3
Peshawar (Pakistan) 33
Petroleum Development (Oman) (PDO) 85, 204
'piracy' in the Gulf 10-12
Popular Front for the Liberation of Oman and the Arabian Gulf (PFLOAG) 100-5, 214

Qabus b. Sa'id (Sultan of Oman) 100
Qasim (Saudi Arabia) 199
Qasr-e Shirin (Iran) 170
Qatar 28
  and the Ottomans 14
  military capabilities 213
al-Qawasim 10-12
Qishm Island (Gulf) 11
Qishn (Aden Protectorate) 25
Qutaybi tribe (Aden Protectorate) 108n17

RAF *see* Royal Air Force
Ra's al-Khayma (UAE) 11, 22-3, 25, 211
  Ra's al-Khayma Mobile Force 211
Ra's al-Hadd (Oman) 54, 56
Ra's Banas (Egypt) 162
Rabizi tribe (Aden Protectorate) 81
Radfan campaign (Aden Protectorate) 95-6
  lessons of 237
Rakhyut (Oman) 102
Rapid Deployment Force *see* US, and Gulf Cooperation Council
Rashid 'Ali (Iraqi politician) 54
Rashid b. Sa'id (Ruler of Dubai) 212
Raysut (Oman) 104, 206
RDF *see* US, Rapid Deployment Force
Record, Jeffrey 157, 162

Red Line agreement (1928) 116
Red Sea, mines in 239
Reunion 150
Reza Khan (later Reza Shah) 21
Riyadh (Saudi Arabia) 199, 200
Riyan (Aden Protectorate) 51, 56, 57
Ross, Dennis 167
Royal Air Force
  Air Liaison Officer in Bahrain 38
  air operations at Aden: 1919-41 (table) 35; 1940-9 (table) 82
  and air control 28-30
  island-staging scheme in Indian Ocean 93
  No. 203 (Flying Boat) Squadron 22
  security responsibilities: in Aden 32-6; in Iraq 30-2; in the Gulf 36-40
  Special Service Officers (SSO) 37-8
Royal Flying Corps 24
Royal Navy, East-of-Suez role 93
Royal Navy Aerial Service 18
Rubinstein, A.Z. 124
al-Rumaytha (Iraq) 32
Russia, and the Gulf (nineteenth century) 14

SL-7 ships 165
Sa'id b. Taymur (Sultan of Oman) 85-8, 99-105 *passim*
Sa'ud b. 'Abd al-'Aziz (King of Saudi Arabia) 188
Salala (Oman) 51, 100-5 *passim*
  RAF use of 56, 57, 104
  Sultanate of Oman Air Force use of 205
Salih, 'Ali 'Abdullah (President of North Yemen) 136, 201
Salmond, Air Vice Marshal Sir John (British Air Officer Commanding Iraq) 31
al-Samawa (Iraq) 32
Sandys White Paper (1957) 83
Sar-e Pol-e Zahab (Iran) 170
Sarfayt (Oman) 101, 102
Saudi Arabia
  and defense of Kuwait (1961) 89
  capabilities to deal with potential threats 201-3
  formation of state of 188
  hegemonic role within GCC 244-5
  High Defence Council 192
  importance during Second World War 50

involvement in Oman rebellion (1950s) 85–6
military capabilities 191–203; Coast Guard 226n18; Frontier Force 226n18; National Guard 193, 198–9; Royal Saudi Air Force 195–7; Royal Saudi Army 194; Royal Saudi Navy 200; Saudi Arabian Land Forces (SALF) 197–8
occupation of Buraimi (1952) 113
politics in 135
revolution in, comparison with Iran 135
security in oilfields 199–200
US role in potential *coup d'état* 174–5
US use of military facilities in 163–4
Sawqara Bay (Oman) 25
Scuiscuiban (Somalia) 51
Second World War
 allied Gulf supply route to Soviet Union during 53–5
 Arabian Peninsula's role in 50–6
 East African campaign of 51–3
 preparations for, in Gulf 48–50
 sectarian differences in the Gulf 133–8
Senior Naval Officer in the Red Sea (British) 52
Shah, Muhammad Reza (Shah of Iran) 135, 245
Sharjah (UAE) 23, 47, 211
 RAF Sepcial Services Officer in 38
 RAF use of 58, 86, 115
 Sharjah National Guard 211
Sharura (Saudi Arabia) 197, 201
Shatt al-'Arab 128
shaykh, traditional political role of 187
al-Shaykh Sa'id (Yemen) 52
al-Shaykh 'Uthman (Aden) 52, 58
Shi'a in Iraq 137
Shi'a population in the Gulf (table) 133
Shinas (Oman) 11
Shultz, George (US Secretary of State) 7
shura, in Saudi Arabia 143n33
Shuwaymiya (Oman) 25
al-Sib (Oman) 205
 agreement of (1920) 85
Sidi Sulaiman (Morocco) 163
Simba, Operation 101
Singapore 33
Socotra Island (Arabian Sea) 51, 52, 57, 124

Somalia 163
South Arabian Army 98
South Arabian League 94
South Arabian air route (Second World War) 55–6
South Yemen *see* People's Democratic Republic of Yemen; Aden Protectorate
Soviet Union
 allied supply route to through Gulf (Second World War) 53–5
 and role of Afghanistan in Gulf attack 169
 as oil importer 141n18
 attack on Gulf, US planning for 166–71
 diplomatic relations in Arabian Peninsula 126–7
 diplomatic relations with Oman 207
 indirect threat to Gulf security 171
 interests and policy in the Gulf 122–7
Southern Theatre of Military Operations 182n53
Special Air Service (SAS; British) 87
 role in Oman 103–4
Standard Oil Company of California (SOCAL) 116
Standard Oil Company of New Jersey 116
state formation in Arabian Peninsula, British role in 189–90
states, emergence of in Arabian Peninsula 186–91
Stirling, Col. David 88
'Strategic consensus' idea 147
'Sudayri Seven' 198
Sudan 239
Sultan b. 'Abd al-'Aziz (Saudi Minister of Defence and Aviation) 192
Sultan's Armed Forces *see* Oman
Super Etendard aircraft 132
Sur (Oman), 1928 rebellion at 38–9, 44

Tabuk (Saudi Arabia) 197
al-Ta'if (Saudi Arabia) 198
Tanker War in Gulf (1984) 132
Taqa (Oman) 101
Templewood, Viscount *see* Hoare, Sir Samuel
Texaco 116
Thamarit (Oman) 100–5 *passim*, 163
Thimble, Operation 102
Thompson, W. Scott 123, 158

Index

threats to Gulf security
  and the Arab-Israeli conflict 138
  and US actions 137–8
  and the 'oil weapon' 138
  external threats 122–7
  internal threats 134–8
  regional threats 127–34
  the paradigm 120–2
  (table) 121
Thumayr (Aden Protectorate) 96
Tornado aircraft 196, 203
Transjordan
  British military planning in 79
  Ikhwan attacks on 36–7
Trenchard, Sir Hugh (British Chief of Air Staff) 29–44 *passim*
Trevaskis, Sir Kennedy (British High Commissioner in Aden) 95
tribe, political role of 187
Trucial Coast 28, 46–7
  see also United Arab Emirates
Trucial Oman Scouts 87, 210–11
Tucker, Robert W. 123, 159, 176
Turkey
  attacks on Iraq (1920s) 31
  role in Gulf security 151
'Twin pillars' policy 145

United States
  activities in Arabian Peninsula (Second World War) 53–60
  and Gulf security, British lessons for 236–8
  and discussion of invasion of Saudi oilfields 176–7
  and Saudi Arabia: military personnel in 203; origins of relations with 114–17; role in development of Saudi military capabilites 195–200
  dependence on OPEC (table) 232
  diplomatic relations in the Gulf 117
  intentions in the Gulf 232–41
  interests in the Gulf in the 1980s (table) 118
  military access agreements in Gulf 152
  military and security coordination with GCC 148
  military assistance to Oman 206
  military options in the Gulf 145–77; and internal threats 174–7; and potential coup in Saudi Arabia 174–5; and regional threats 172–4

  oil companies in Gulf 116
  policy in the Gulf: during Carter administration 146–7; during Reagan administration 147
  policy statement on the Gulf (1985) 7–8
  reaction to 1979 war between the Yemens 125
  relations with Muscat government (nineteenth century) 59
  strategic interests in the Gulf 111–38; in the 1980s 118–19; origins of 111–18
US Army Air Force 59
US Army Corps of Engineers 197
US Army Readiness Command 153
US Central Command (USCENTCOM):
  accomplishments of 239; changing perceptions of role of 238–9; creation of 153; forces assigned to (table) 154
US Geological Survey 247n4
US Navy, Middle East Force (MIDEASTFORCE) 113
US Rapid Deployment Force (RDF): capabilities 155–66; conceptual questions regarding 157–61; exercises 162; facilities in the Gulf region 162–3, (table) 163; operational questions regarding 161–6; origins 151–5; potential performance of 167–77; question of assignment of subordinate units 162; question of command, control and communications 161; question of field hospitals 166; question of force size 162; question of forcible-entry capability 166; question of fuel supplies 166; question of strategic airlift 164; question of strategic sealift 164–5; question of tactical mobility 165; question of water supplies 166; role of Marine Corps in 157; role of US Navy in 160
US Rapid Deployment Joint Task Force (RDJTF) 153
US Transport Command 59
views of Gulf's importance during Reagan administration 241
Umm Qasr (Iraq) 55, 209
United Arab Emirates 244

formation of 139n8, 190
military capabilities 210–12
threats to 212–13
UAE Armed Forces 212
Union Defence Force 211
Yarmuk Brigade 212
'Uqayr agreement (1922) 67n59
urban guerrilla warfare in Gulf, possibility of 237
USCENTCOM *see* US Central Command

Vinnell Corporation 199

Waltz, Kenneth 157, 161
Warba Island (Gulf) 209
Wavell, Lord (Viceroy of India) 18
Western joint role in Gulf security 150
Wilson, A.T. (Civil Commissioner, Iraq) 31
Wilson, Field Marshal Sir Henry (British Chief of Imperial General Staff) 30

Wohlstetter, Albert 123, 158, 160
'Wolfowitz report' 146
Wudam 'Alwa (Oman) 206

Yas Island (Gulf) 64n18
Yemen (North)
  first airplanes in 19
  importance of during Second World War 50
  political evolution in 188
Yemeni Socialist Party 136
Yemens
  crises in (1978 and 1979) 124–5
  political situation in 136–7
  threats to Saudi Arabia from 201–2
  war between (1979), lessons for US 171

'Zagros Mountains' strategy 169–70
Zakheim, Dov S. 150
Zaydis, in North Yemen 136
Zayid b. Sultan (Ruler of Abu Dhabi and President of the UAE) 212